THE METHOD AND CULTURE OF COMPARATIVE LAW

Awareness of the need to deepen the method and methodology of legal research is only recent. The same is true for comparative law, by nature a more adventurous branch of legal research, which is often something researchers simply do whenever they look at foreign legal systems to answer one or more of a range of questions about law, whether these questions are doctrinal, economic, sociological, etc. Given the diversity of comparative research projects, the precise contours of the methods employed, or the epistemological issues raised by them, are to a great extent a function of the nature of the research questions asked. As a result, the search for a unique, one-size-fits-all comparative law methodology is unlikely to be fruitful. That, however, does not make reflection on the method and culture of comparative law meaningless. Mark Van Hoecke has been interested in many topics throughout his career, but legal theory, comparative law and methodology of law stand out. Building upon his work, this book brings together a group of leading authors working at the crossroads of these themes: the method and culture of comparative law.

With contributions by: Maurice Adams, John Bell, Joxerramon Bengoetxea, Roger Brownsword, Seán Patrick Donlan, Rob van Gestel and Hans Micklitz, Patrick Glenn, Jaap Hage, Dirk Heirbaut, Jaakko Husa, Souichirou Kozuka and Luke Nottage, Martin Löhnig, Susan Millns, Toon Moonen, Francois Ost, Heikki Pihlajamäki, Geoffrey Samuel, Mathias Siems, Jørn Øyrehagen Sunde, Catherine Valcke and Matthew Grellette, Alain Wijffels

The Method and Culture of Comparative Law

Essays in Honour of Mark Van Hoecke

Edited by
Maurice Adams
and
Dirk Heirbaut

·HART·
PUBLISHING

OXFORD AND PORTLAND, OREGON
2014

Published in the United Kingdom by Hart Publishing Ltd
16C Worcester Place, Oxford, OX1 2JW
Telephone: +44 (0)1865 517530
Fax: +44 (0)1865 510710
E-mail: mail@hartpub.co.uk
Website: http://www.hartpub.co.uk

Published in North America (US and Canada) by
Hart Publishing
c/o International Specialized Book Services
920 NE 58th Avenue, Suite 300
Portland, OR 97213-3786
USA
Tel: +1 503 287 3093 or toll-free: (1) 800 944 6190
Fax: +1 503 280 8832
E-mail: orders@isbs.com
Website: http://www.isbs.com

Hart Publishing is an imprint of Bloomsbury Publishing plc.

British Library Cataloguing in Publication Data

Data Available

ISBN: 978-1-84946-623-3

Typeset by Forewords Ltd, Oxon
Printed and bound in Great Britain by
CPI Group (UK) Ltd, Croydon CR0 4YY

Preface

Awareness of the need to deepen the method and methodology of legal research is only recent. The same is true for comparative law—by nature a more adventurous branch of legal research—which is often something researchers simply do whenever they look at foreign legal systems to answer one or more of a range of questions about law, whether these questions are doctrinal, economic, sociological, etc. Given the diversity of comparative research projects, the precise contours of the methods employed, or the epistemological issues raised by them, are to a great extent a function of the nature of the research questions asked. As a result, the search for a unique, one-size-fits-all comparative law methodology is unlikely to be fruitful. That, however, does not make reflection on the method and culture of comparative law meaningless. Mark Van Hoecke has been interested in many topics throughout his career, but legal theory, comparative law and methodology of law stand out. Building upon his work, this book brings together a group of leading authors working at the crossroads of these themes: the methodology and culture of comparative law.

We thank Richard Hart, the 'house publisher' of many a book of Mark Van Hoecke, who has been so kind as to also publish this volume.

Maurice Adams, Tilburg
Dirk Heirbaut, Ghent
January 2014

Contents

viii

About the Authors

Maurice Adams is Professor of General Jurisprudence and 'vfund' Professor of Democratic Governance and the Rule of Law at Tilburg University

John Bell is Professor of Law at the University of Cambridge and a Fellow of Pembroke College, Cambridge

Joxerramon Bengoetxea is Professor of Jurisprudence and Sociology of Law at the University of the Basque Country at Gipuzkoa

Roger Brownsword is Professor of Law at King's College London, and Honorary Professor in Law at the University of Sheffield

Seán Patrick Donlan is Lecturer in Law at the University of Limerick

Rob van Gestel is Professor of Theory and Methods of Legislation at Tilburg University

Patrick Glenn is the Peter M Laing Professor of Law at McGill University

Matthew Grellette is Adjunct Professor in Philosophy of Law at both York University and Wilfrid Laurier University

Jaap Hage is Professor of Jurisprudence at the University of Maastricht and Professor of Law at the University of Hasselt

Dirk Heirbaut is Professor of Legal History and Roman Law at Ghent University

Jaakko Husa is Professor of Comparative Law and Constitutional Law at the University of Lapland

Souichirou Kozuka is Professor at Gakushuin University Law Faculty, Tokyo

Martin Löhnig is Professor of Civil Law, of German and European Legal History and of Canon Law at the University of Regensburg

Hans Micklitz is Professor of Economic Law at the European University Institute in Florence

Susan Millns is Professor of Law at the University of Sussex

Toon Moonen is Fellow of the Research Foundation—Flanders (FWO) and doctoral candidate at the University of Hasselt and at Ghent University

Luke Nottage is Professor of Comparative and Transnational Business Law, University of Sydney Law School; Co-Director, Australian Network for Japanese Law (ANJeL)

François Ost is Professor of Law at the Université Saint-Louis (Bruxelles)

Heikki Pihlajamäki is Professor of Comparative Legal History at the University of Helsinki

Geoffrey Samuel is Professor of Law at the University of Kent, at Canterbury

Mathias Siems is Professor of Commercial Law, Durham University, and Research Associate at the Centre for Business Research, University of Cambridge

Jørn Øyrehagen Sunde is Professor of Law at the University of Bergen

Catherine Valcke is Professor of Law at the University of Toronto Faculty of Law

Alain Wijffels is Professor of Legal History and Comparative Law, Universities of Leiden, Leuven and Louvain-la-Neuve; Senior Research Fellow CNRS (CHJ Lille-2)

Table of Cases

Table of Legislation

Netherlands

Norway

South Africa

United Kingdom

United States of America

Table of Conventions, Agreements etc

1

Prolegomena to the Method and Culture of Comparative Law

MAURICE ADAMS AND DIRK HEIRBAUT

I. SETTING THE SCENE

IN MAY 2014, Mark Van Hoecke will retire from his Research Chair of Legal Theory and Comparative Law at Ghent University in Belgium. Those who know him will realise that a purely celebratory Festschrift, followed by the traditional practice of some festivity for handing it over, would be out of the question; for Mark Van Hoecke, legal science is about content, not form. So, to 'mark' the occasion, we have chosen another formula: a publication on a theme that has occupied his thinking over the last two decades or so, and which is of ever growing importance to academic lawyers all over the world.

Throughout his academic career, including the years as a university administrator, Mark Van Hoecke has been interested in many legally relevant topics, but legal theory, comparative law, and method and methodology of law stand out.[1] This volume brings together several authors working at the crossroads of these themes: the method(ology) and culture of comparative law.

From the start of his career in the 1970s, Mark Van Hoecke has been a scholar with a truly international outlook. It is nevertheless fair to say that this volume continues an intellectual voyage that began somewhat later with a publication (with François Ost) that advocated (as early as 1990) a truly European legal education.[2] Comparative law was, of course, part and parcel of

---

[1] As a university administrator he has successively and successfully been Dean and Rector Magnificus of the (then) Catholic University of Brussels, infusing into the curriculum of its law school international and transboundary elements. He has also, significantly, established with François Ost the European Academy of Legal Theory, which offers a Master Degree in Legal Theory (which from 2014/15 onwards will be hosted at the Goethe-University in Frankfurt/Main), and with which Mark is still much involved. See www.legaltheory.net.

[2] F Ost and M Van Hoecke, 'Naar een Europese rechtsopleiding' [1989–90] *Rechtskundig Weekblad* 1001. The article was a real early bird, and has been translated into Danish ('Pa vej mod en faelles euopaeisk jurisdisk uddannelse' [1991] *Ugeskrift for Retsvaesen* 161), German

that. Legal education had to change from a merely local approach to a more integrated one, ie one that could make more sense of legal diversity and that put perspective—possibly subversive perspective[3]—onto national law, or which called this national law into question.[4] This was a plea for a comparative law, broadly defined. Today, we are still struggling to bring such an approach into the regular law school curriculum.

The just mentioned short, but seminal piece was followed up with several articles and books, written or (co)edited, on comparative law and legal research, some of which have become classics in this domain. To mention but a few: 'Hohfeld and Comparative Law';[5] 'Legal Cultures, Legal Paradigms and Legal Doctrine: Towards a New Model for Comparative Law';[6] 'Western and Non-Western Legal Cultures';[7] *The Harmonization of European Private Law*;[8] *Law as Communication*;[9] 'Legal Orders between Autonomy and Intertwinement';[10] *Epistemology and Methodology of Comparative Law*;[11] 'Deep Level Comparative Law';[12] 'European Legal Cultures in a Context of Globalisation';[13] 'Islamic Jurisprudence and Western Legal History';[14] *Methodologies of Legal Research. Which Kind of Research for What Kind of Discipline*;[15] 'Family Law Transfers from Europe to Africa: Lessons for the

('Für eine europäische Juristenausbildung' [1990] *Juristenzeitung* 911), French ('Pour une formation juridique européenne' [1990] *Journal des Tribunaux* 105) and Italian ('Per una formazione giuridica europea' [1990] *Rivista Trimestrale di Diritto Publico* 629).

[3] G Fletcher, 'Comparative Law as a Subversive Discipline' (1998) 46 *The American Journal of Comparative Law* 683; H Muir Watt, 'La fonction subversive du droit comparé' (2000) 52 *Revue internationale de droit comparé* 503.

[4] Interesting later proposals and ideas can be found in C Valcke, 'Global Law Teaching' (2004) 54 *Journal of Legal Education* 160; M Reimann, 'From the Law of Nations to Transnational Law: Why We Need a New Basic Course for the International Curriculum' (2004) 22 *Penn State International Law Review* 397; J Husa, 'Turning the Curriculum Upside Down' (2009) 10 *German Law Journal* 913; and S Chesterman, 'The Evolution of Legal Education: Internationalization, Transnationalization, Globalization' (2009) 10 *German Law Journal* 877-888. See also the Global Law issue of the *Tilburg Law Review* (2012) 17(2), edited by S Musa and E de Volder, with quite some attention for the educational dimension of globalization.

[5] In (1996) 9 *International Journal for the Semiotics of Law* 185.

[6] In (1998) 47 *International and Comparative Law Quarterly* 495 (with M Warrington).

[7] In W Krawietz and C Varga (eds), *On Different Legal Cultures, Premodern and Modern States, and the Transition to the Rule of Law in Western and Eastern Europe* (Berlin, Duncker & Humblot, Sondernheft *Rechtstheorie* 2002) 197.

[8] Oxford, Hart Publishing, 2000 (edited volume, with F Ost).

[9] Oxford, Hart Publishing, 2002.

[10] In KH Ladeur (ed), *Public Governance in the Age of Globalization* (Farnham, Ashgate, 2004) 177.

[11] Oxford, Hart Publishing, 2004 (edited volume).

[12] In M Van Hoecke (ed), *Epistemology and Methodology of Comparative Law* (Oxford, Hart Publishing 2004) 165.

[13] In T Gizbert-Studnicki and J Stelmach (ed), *Law and Legal Cultures in the 21st Century (Plenary Lectures for the 23rd IVR World Congress, Diversity and Unity : Plenary Lectures)* (Warszawa, Wolters Kluwer, 2007) 81.

[14] In JS Nielsen and L Christoffersen (eds), *Shari'a as Discourse: Legal Traditions and the Encounter with Europe* (Farnham, Ashgate, 2010) 45.

[15] Oxford, Hart Publishing, 2011 (edited volume).

Methodology of Comparative Legal Research';[16] 'Do "Legal Systems" Exist? The Concept of Law and Comparative Law';[17] 'Legal Culture and Legal Transplants';[18] and 'Methodology of Comparative Legal Research'.[19]

Many others of Mark's publications could have been listed,[20] but the ones mentioned seem to be the most directly relevant to the theme of this volume. The ability to contribute to this theme lay foremost in our selection of contributors. What counted was not just friendship to the colleague we wanted to honour (albeit that too was certainly applicable to quite a number of the contributors), but especially amity to the academic endeavour Mark stood for and continues to stand for, thus contributing to the further development of the academic debate we all hold dear.

II. METHOD AND CULTURE: APPROACH AND OBJECT

In each of the aforementioned publications, Mark Van Hoecke's professional interest and research focus are combined: he always writes about comparative law from the angle of method and methodology. This observation invites for some elaboration about the title of this volume: *The Method and Culture of Comparative Law*.

The word 'culture' in the title might denote at least two meanings here: it might, on the one hand, refer to one of the natural objects of comparison, ie legal cultures, where the identifying elements of such cultures range from 'facts about institutions' to 'various forms of behaviour', or 'more nebulous aspects of ideas, values, aspirations and mentalities'.[21] On the other hand, it might also refer to what researching this implies or entails in terms of the research approach—ie the method and methodology[22]—when dealing with legal cultures, whether they are national or transnational, which, at least at

---

[16] In J Gillespie and P Nicholson (eds), *Law and Development and the Global Discourses of Legal Transfers* (Cambridge, Cambridge University Press, 2012) 279.

[17] In S Donlan and L Heckendorn (eds), *Concepts of Law: Comparative, Jurisprudential, and Social Science Perspectives* (Farnham, Ashgate, forthcoming).

[18] Forthcoming.

[19] Forthcoming.

[20] To date, his publication list comprises some 170 publications. See the bibliography at the website of Ghent University: https://biblio.ugent.be/person/802000325893.

[21] D Nelken, 'Defining and Using the Concept of Legal Culture' in E Örücü and D Nelken (eds), *Comparative Law. A Handbook* (Oxford, Hart Publishing, 2006) 113 (including an excellent treatment of the methodological problems and questions that come with employing a concept, in the context of comparative legal research, like legal culture). Highly critical about the concept of legal culture is R Cotterrell, 'Comparatists and Sociology' in P Legrand and R Munday (eds), *Comparative Legal Studies: Traditions and Transitions* (Cambridge, Cambridge University Press, 2003) 149; R Cotterrell, 'The Concept of Legal Culture' in D Nelken (ed), *Comparing Legal Cultures* (Aldershot, Dartmouth, 1997) 33; R Cotterrell, *Law, Culture and Society. Legal Ideas in the Mirror of Social Theory* (Aldershot, Ashgate, 2006).

[22] A word of caution is in place here because, as Hage notes in his contribution to this volume, the terms 'method' and 'methodology', although conceptually separable, are many times conflated. On this, see also the next section of this chapter.

first instance, are strange to the researcher. In other words, the title of this volume also refers to the culture of actually doing comparative legal research, something that is also prevalent in most if not all of Van Hoecke's work in comparative law.

These two meanings of the word culture cannot, in this context, be neatly separated. The reason for this is that an 'involved' activity, like doing comparative law, precisely because it deals significantly with legal cultures, does not come naturally to a researcher. Comparative lawyers have to find a way with, and convey information about, legal cultures or traditions whose 'language' (metaphorically understood) they do not necessarily speak; cultures and traditions with specific institutions and unexpressed codes; with their own history, ideology or ideologies and self-image(s); cultures the researcher has not normally been trained, educated or disciplined in and with which he or she is therefore not naturally or intimately connected.[23] The process of trying to understand this 'otherness'[24] (or some of its elements), and the task to convey its intricacies to the reader, demands a particular—'deep level'[25]— research approach that goes far beyond mere fact-finding and the regular (ie purely national) self-evident way of interpreting and understanding the law. Therefore, comparative law explicitly calls for using a research methodology that makes it possible to engage in the cultural context of the topic or issue that is being studied, and in such a way that is comprehensible to the reader.[26] Seen from this point of view, the words 'Method' and 'Culture' in the title of this volume, even in their multiple meanings, refer to each other.

III. THREE MAIN TOPICS

In line with this general theme, the contributions to this volume might be categorised as: (i) method and methodology; (ii) globalisation (or Europeanisation, internationalisation); or (iii) context and interdisciplinarity. However, even if many of the chapters have a focus on one of these topics or categories, most, if not all, also consist of important elements that are evident in the other categories. Therefore, we have chosen not to make this categorisation explicitly visible in the Table of Contents; this could detract the reader from valuable and interesting aspects of chapters that do not at first sight fall into the category that seems most relevant for their purpose. Nonetheless, it makes sense here to dwell a bit on each of these categories and on the chap-

---

[23] In a similar vein, see F Ost, Chapter 5 below.
[24] See too S Millns, Chapter 20 below.
[25] Van Hoecke, 'Deep Level Comparative Law', n 12 above.
[26] On this J Bell, 'Legal Research and the Distinctiveness of Comparative Law' in M Van Hoecke (ed), *Methodologies of Legal Research* 155; M de S-O-l'E Lasser, 'The Question of Understanding' in P Legrand and R Munday (eds), *Comparative Legal Studies: Traditions and Transitions* (Cambridge, Cambridge University Press, 2004) 197.

ters concerned therein, thereby cross-referencing the chapters to the other, less obvious yet still relevant, ones.

A. Method and Methodology

Academic lawyers today face one of the greatest challenges ever. For centuries they have continued to work in the same way. If a medieval law professor were to be revived and teach and do research in a contemporary law school, he would probably not find it that hard to adapt.[27] True, instead of Latin, today's law professors speak in a vernacular; moreover, they use computers and projectors, and more than half of their audiences are young women. However, all of these changes have not affected what is still perceived by many to be the essence of legal education and research, ie to work in line with what Geoffrey Samuel, in his contribution to this volume, calls the authority paradigm. This is the idea that practitioners and academics working within the legal discipline are governed ultimately not by enquiry—the results of which in the end may force those working within the paradigm to abandon their theories in the face of empirical reality—but by textual authority as expressed in statutes and court decisions (rules); texts, moreover, whose authority as such is never put into question. A revived Bartolus would possibly have some catching up to do, but he most probably could function adequately with the method he had already mastered: textual interpretation.

The situation is completely different in other sciences. One cannot imagine a medieval medical doctor being as well prepared for our times—the disciplines that make up the medical and natural sciences have seen too many paradigm shifts for that. This is also true of the much younger social sciences. In any case, this has led to a situation of profound methodological unawareness among academic lawyers (save a few exceptions). As a result, both method and methodology of law are still in their infancy.

Samuel, in his chapter, makes clear that a comparative lawyer may encounter many questions that are at heart epistemological (What is meant by comparison? What is meant by 'law'? What is it to have knowledge of law?), making epistemology and comparative methodology conjoined twins. In exploring their link, Samuel enunciates some ideas that are relevant for any comparatist. Legal epistemology, just like comparative law, is concerned with similarity and difference, and it operates in a context with different 'knowledges' of law, rooted in the work of theorists and in the ideas of practising lawyers. To understand them we have to understand their past, and to really comprehend them we have to learn from the epistemology of other sciences, which can boast a considerable literature. Doing this is quite a challenge, but Samuel also shows a glimpse of what we could achieve, ie an 'escape, from the arid past

---

[27] In a similar vein see G Samuel, Chapter 2 below.

of comparative law, from legal positivism and, above all, from the authority paradigm'. Ultimately, Samuel's contribution might be understood as a plea for interdisciplinarity and external perspectives in legal research. Comparative law, if it is prepared to leave the authority paradigm and its accompanying focus on rules, can indeed be of particular value here, especially if it is to serve as a tool that brings to the fore epistemological issues concerning the technique of comparison, the description of law (ie what is meant by it) and the 'objectivity' of facts.[28]

This invites for an interesting observation, because what is also at play here, so it seems to us, is that the comparatist's understanding of what law is, is not simply one question among others within a comparative method, but relates to a set of background assumptions and conceptions that inform nearly everything comparative lawyers do.[29] If it is indeed true that theories of law play such an important (albeit many times implicit) role in comparative projects—ie that views on what law is, means and does, and on what is interesting about what law is, means and does, inform methodological choices on all levels of the comparative exercise—then it is possible that at least some of the prevalent unease about comparative method may have to be traced back to unease or disagreement about these underlying theories.[30]

Hage makes a sharp distinction between method and methodology of comparative law and legal research. The former refers to the actual way(s) of conducting a more or less specific research project (and also to the standards by which the relevance of arguments found in specific research can be evaluated), whilst the latter is mainly of an epistemological nature. He asks two questions: is comparative law a method for legal research as such, and does it have a proper method of its own? The first can be answered positively, as Hage shows (eg by using examples in the realm of harmonising European private law): comparative law can be of benefit for evaluating potential or actual rules of law, or explaining its content. In answering the second question, Hage formulates what may well be seen as the common creed of the authors in this volume, and which we readily confirm: there is no royal road to comparative law!

Indeed, trying to find a method for comparative law in the abstract, not connected to some kind of concrete question is like chasing a will-o'-the-wisp: trying to find a method for something that is not a question—such as

---

[28] Van Hoecke, 'Deep Level Comparative Law', n 12 above.

[29] This point is made implicitly or explicitly in many chapters in this volume. See, eg R Brownsword, Chapter 14 below; SP Donlan, Chapter 12 below; Samuel, Chapter 2 below. On this, too, see M Adams and JA Bomhoff, 'Comparing Law: Practice and Theory' in M Adams and JA Bomhoff (eds), *Practice and Theory in Comparative Law* (Cambridge, Cambridge University Press, 2012) 8.

[30] A conclusion that should, in turn, temper hopes that the key to sounder comparative law methodology can be found exclusively in developing better understandings of the logical operations involved in the 'act of comparing': cf M Reimann, 'The Progress and Failure of Comparative Law in the Second Half of the Twentieth Century' (2002) 50 *American Journal of Comparative Law* 690.

'comparative law'—is not of any service. Comparative law is a collection of methods that may be helpful in seeking answers to an almost endless variety of questions about law (broadly defined).[31] Thus, diversity in method is not a curse, but a blessing, because it allows a researcher to choose the methods that fit their data, research questions and personal inclinations.

Turning away, for now, from the most fundamental theoretical questions, a second set of questions are in need of answers: what actually is method in comparative law? How to actually conduct comparative legal research? Jaakko Husa makes it clear that, as the goal(s) of the comparative lawyer is (are) mostly different from those of other scientists, so, too, is his method different from the methods of other sciences. Husa identifies a selection of basic research designs for comparison, which have to be made before the research starts or during it. From a methodological point of view, comparative law is mainly heuristic, Husa concludes. However, as a result of the constant and intertwining choices, whether of a technical or a theoretical nature, the specific methods (or combination thereof) a researcher will use can differ. Reading Husa's article will help many fellow travellers to see more clearly the paths opening up for them and the need to enunciate their choices, which constantly evolve and will be revised as the investigation unfolds.[32]

Comparison has many faces, and this book tries to present some of them. In this, comparison is like translation, which is also the subject of François Ost's contribution. The 'penetration of the external by the internal' (European and public international law, private international law, bilingual legal systems) means that no lawyer can escape from comparison and translation. Translation (and comparison) would also occur, and to a certain extent is inevitable, in the situation of a completely isolated, pristine legal system, as jurists would still look to the past, and would also look at one branch of law from the perspective of another. Jurists would therefore benefit from the practice of translation theory, most of all because translation, like comparison, is not limited. It includes more than just words in one language being placed in, or translated into, another;[33] it is also translating different legal cultures. The difficulty that translation thus brings implies ethical responsibility: it is always accompanied by the task of recognition of the difference of the 'other', and of the wish to interact with that other on the basis of the reciprocal admission of the limits of each's own language.

Maurice Adams elaborates on this topic, and also upon a point explicitly made by Valcke and Grellette (see below): attaching labels to unfamiliar notions (including elements of foreign legal cultures) can do as much harm

---

[31] Also M Adams and J Griffiths, 'Against "Comparative Method": Explaining Similarities and Differences' in Adams and Bomhoff, above n 29, 279.

[32] About this last point, see also M Adams, Chapter 6 below; C Valcke and M Grellette, Chapter 7 below.

[33] But see also Millns, Chapter 20 below, who advises that one should avoid literal translation as much as possible in the context of comparative law, because it might result in a poor understanding of the other legal culture.

as good. They may point the researcher in the right direction, but may just as much make him stray from the right path. In any case, the researcher is not neutral when he or she applies a label by which it becomes possible to actually compare at least two legal cultures. Confronted with the challenge of comparing legal cultures, one can decide to come up with a completely independent signifier (a 'language without a national home') or one can apply more broadly known existing labels (such as ones from Roman or English law). A pragmatist would possibly plead for the latter alternative, as it would make his or her work more accessible than using a narrative that is neutral to any legal system or culture.

Whatever the choice may be, any translation involves a kind of treason towards the original concept. At worst, it leads to deception of the reader and even a displacement of the original concept that one wants to compare, especially if its legal culture does not have a strong enough voice of its own. Adams proposes a way out of this dilemma. Admitting that complete neutrality is a holy grail, which one can quest for but never find, he defends controlled comparison: one can use the terminology of an existing system, but a comparatist should constantly work in a 'spirit of conceptual tentativeness'. The researcher can start with familiar existing terms, but should be aware of their limitations and constantly revise them in light of the evolving research and growing insight.[34] As the researcher grows into the subject, the terms of comparison should be changed for ones that better fit the research project at hand.[35]

Ideas of functionality and of functional equivalence (still) play a prominent role in contemporary comparative scholarship. This may come as something of a surprise, given that critical scholarship has long taken issue with views of comparative law as the comparison of 'solutions' to 'problems' that are supposedly clearly identifiable and more or less identical across systems.[36] But it seems that, to some degree at least, while critical theoretical writing on comparative law often consists of broad-based attacks on functionalist premises—especially in the form voiced by Zweigert and Kötz[37]—many practical

[34] A similar conclusion (ie comparison is never neutral, but the tendency to measure jurisdictions by one's own familiar standards can be somewhat mitigated) is reached by Millns, ibid.

[35] According to K Popper, *The Logic of Scientific Discovery* (London, Hutchison, 1972) 31–32, the scientific process is such that the starting point may be constantly revisited as the investigation unfolds. See also Valcke and Grellette, Chapter 7 below.

[36] In the social sciences, 'functionalism' generally refers (whether or not explicitly and consciously) to the idea that 'the *consequences* of some behavior or social arrangement are essential elements of the *causes* of that behavior' (original emphasis; see AL Stinchcombe, *Constructing Social Theories* (New York, Harcourt, Brace & World, 1968) 80 for a still careful analysis and discussion of the circumstances in which a functional explanation may be appropriate).

[37] K Zweigert and H Kötz, *An Introduction to Comparative Law* (Oxford, Oxford University Press, 1998) 34ff. Glendon et al not only state that the principle of functionality in comparative law is now recognised to have wide applicability, but also that it is 'probably comparative law's principal gift to twentieth century legal science'. MA Glendon, MW Gordon and PG Carozza, *Comparative Legal Traditions (in a Nutshell)* (St Paul, West Group, 1999) 9. The first full-scale criticism of this sort of functionalism in comparative law is G Frankenberg, 'Critical Compari-

efforts at comparison are instead concerned with incrementally refining and supplementing functionalist ideas, and with navigating creatively functionalism's acknowledged limitations.

Given the central place functionalism occupies in comparative law, Catherine Valcke and Matthew Grellette have put it under their microscope. Their analysis of the propositions behind the functionalism of Zweigert and Kötz should be obligatory literature for any functionalist researcher. The same holds for their analysis of the critics of Zweigert and Kötz's functionalism. Valcke and Grellette are also critics, though of the best kind. They show the weak points, but not to demolish the comparative legal building. Instead, they propose an amended model, a kind of functionality 2.0, as it were, thus bringing the work of both Zweigert and Kötz and the latter's critics to a synthesis. First of all, for identifying materials for a comparison, legal labels can be misleading in the extreme. Using legal functions for identification ensures that the researcher does not compare quite different phenomena. According to Valcke and Grellette, function is also useful for analysing the materials selected, as a functionalist comparison aiming at the actual operation of the law would give more visibility to legal formants, which have hitherto been less visible. Putting two systems side by side would inevitably lead to some previously obscured formants coming out of the woodwork.

Like thinking about the method and methodology of comparative law, thinking about the method and methodology of comparative legal history is still in its infancy.[38] Some comparative legal historians, such as Matt Dyson, have focused on what they can learn from comparative law.[39] Martin Löhnig goes the other way in his contribution, since he moves beyond historical comparative law that compares legal concepts. Instead, he argues for attention to the social processes of transformation behind these concepts. Even traditional national legal history is now no longer possible without comparison. Comparison can help to fill in gaps if not enough historical sources are available. It can help to go from an isolated empirical result to a more general theory,

---

sons: Re-thinking Comparative Law' (1985) 26 *Harvard International Law Journal* 411. See too P Legrand, *Fragments on Law-as-Culture* (Deventer, Tjeenk Willink, 1999); R Hyland, 'Comparative Law' in D Patterson (ed), *A Companion to the Philosophy of Law and Legal Theory* (Cambridge, Blackwell, 1996) 184. For critical overview articles see M Graziadei, 'The Functionalist Heritage' in P Legrand and R Munday (eds), *Comparative Legal Studies: Traditions and Transitions* (Cambridge, Cambridge University Press, 2004) 100; R Michaels, 'The Functional Method of Comparative Law' in M Reimann and R Zimmermann (eds), *The Oxford Handbook of Comparative Law* (Oxford, Oxford University Press, 2006), 381. For important qualifications see J Husa, 'Farewell to Functionalism or Methodological Tolerance?' (2003) 67 *Rabels Zeitschrift für ausländisches und internationales Privatrecht* 419; J De Coninck, 'The Functional Method of Comparative Law: Quo Vadis?' (2010) 74 *Rabels Zeitschrift für ausländisches und internationales Privatrecht* 318.

[38] See, eg the special 2013 issue of *Rechtskultur* on methodology, or A Musson and C Stebbings, *Making Legal History: Approaches and Methodologies* (Cambridge, Cambridge University Press, 2012).

[39] See, eg M Dyson, 'Divide and Conquer: Using Legal Domains in Comparative Legal Studies' in G Helleringer and K Purnhagen, *Towards a European Legal Culture* (forthcoming).

or to test a theory based on limited research, eg for one country. In short, the methodology of comparative legal history can learn from comparative law, but it also has something to offer in return, which might well explain the relatively high number of contributions from comparative law's sister discipline in this book.

B. Globalisation

H Patrick Glenn has aptly and repeatedly observed that, for a long time, comparative law and comparative legal scholarship have generally been marked by constructivist purposes: as a means for state building and local law reform.[40] In this sense, comparative law has lent support to the idea of law being an exclusively national phenomenon: an instrument in the nationalisation of the law. Looking at the region where the editors of this volume come from, ie continental Europe, up until the nineteenth century, when the nation state had already been in formation for some time,[41] there were quite a number of legal sources available which interacted or competed with each other for prominence: eg canon law, local statutes, custom, case law, Roman law (the overarching and unifying source) and the Bible (the latter being the most 'binding' of all). It was more specifically the ideal of codification—prominently entering the legal scene in the wake of the French revolution[42]—which demanded to put an end to this situation: law was identified exclusively with written and national

[40] See, albeit in passing, HP Glenn, Chapter 13 below. See also HP Glenn, 'The Nationalist Heritage' in P Legrand and R Munday (eds), *Comparative Legal Studies Traditions and Transitions* (Cambridge, Cambridge University Press, 2003) 76–99; HP Glenn, 'A Transnational Concept of Law' in P Cane and M Tushnet (eds), *The Oxford Handbook of Legal Studies* (Oxford, Oxford University Press, 2003) 839–862. This constructivist approach is very much promoted in what has arguably been the most influential handbook of the discipline for a long time: K Zweigert and H Kötz, *Introduction to Comparative Law* (Oxford, Oxford University Press, 1998): 'In its *applied* version, comparative law suggests how a specific problem can most appropriately be solved under the given social and economic circumstances' (11, original emphasis; similar statements can be found throughout the introductory and methodological chapters of the book). See also M Adams, 'Comparative Law in a Globalizing World: Three Challenges' (2013) 17 *Tilburg Law Review* 263 (on which this section is partly based).

[41] The rise of the nation state is, of course, a complex, dialectic development. Usually one is referred to the Peace of Westphalia (1648) as the starting point, although the concept of the state as such has developed from the thirteenth century onwards. For nuance and details see M van Creveld, *The Rise and Decline of the State* (Cambridge, Cambridge University Press, 1999); H Spruyt, *The Sovereign State and its Competitors: An Analysis of Systems Change* (Princeton, Princeton University Press, 1994). On the term state and its use, see A Guéry, 'The State. The Tool of Common Good' in P Nora (ed), *Rethinking France. Les lieux de mémoire*, I (Chicago, University of Chicago Press, 2001) 1.

[42] Just as the concept of the nation state, the concept of codification has older roots than the French Revolution and Napoleon (with whom it is generally associated). For nuance and details see, inter alia, J Vanderlinden, *Le concept de code en Europe occidental* (Brussels, ULB Editions de l'Institut de sociologie 1967); F Wieacker, *A History of Private Law in Europe with Particular Reference to Germany* (Oxford, Clarendon Press, 1995); P van den Berg, *The Politics of European Codification. A History of the Unification of Law in France, Prussia, the Austrian Monarchy and the Netherlands* (Groningen, Europa Law Publishing) 2006.

law.[43] National codified law was on the one hand to be the exclusive source of law, identifiable through a local *Grundnorm*, or rule of recognition,[44] and on the other hand was to contain the solution for just about every situation conceivable (law's adequacy).[45] As a result, legislative positivism became the ideal, and systemic closeness the result. So, although, paradoxically, the content of national law was the result of the mining of comparative sources,[46] extranational inspiration was not really a necessity anymore once the funnel of codification had been applied to it. National law was thought to be self-supporting, and the legal system was predominantly understood as an entity in which *demos*, law creation and a specifically delineated area were intimately bound.[47] Since the nineteenth century it was: *La Nation, la loi,* (and possibly) *le roi*—in that order. As a result, comparative law withered in the margin, both in terms of the law school's curriculum and in terms of research;[48] an intellectual pastime if ever there was one.

In recent years, comparative law has witnessed a revival, especially as a result of globalisation, which Twining loosely describes as the developments and interactions which are making the world more interdependent with respect to ecology, economy, communications, language, politics, etc.[49] Comparative lawyers now also have to adapt their analytical and educational toolkits to other than constructivist purposes, and also to the realities of a largely fragmented and fluid regulatory landscape.[50] A number of challenges stand out, especially because a lot, if not most, of comparative law is still typically concerned with

---

[43] It even suffered, as Gény said, from a 'fétichisme de la loi écrite codifiée'. F Gény, *Méthode d'interprétation et sources en droit privé positif: essai critique*, I (Paris, Librairie Générale de Droit et de Jurisprudence, 1919) 70.

[44] These terms come from H Kelsen and HLA Hart, respectively. On the neglect of Hart of comparative legal scholarship see the (posthumously published) monograph by AWB Simpson, *Reflections on 'The Concept of Law'* (Oxford, Oxford University Press, 2011) 157ff. The universalistic aspirations of his concept of law did not seem to really invite Hart for comparative observations. It could and should have, though.

[45] However, the reality fell far from the ideal of a code without gaps excluding all other legal sources (see, eg G Weiss, 'The Enchantment of Codification in the Common Law World' (2000) 25 *Yale Journal of International Law* 11), as codifiers could not foresee everything and in some cases did not even want to try to do so.

[46] See Glenn, 'The Nationalist Heritage', above n 40, 84.

[47] Rousseau's thinking has been of great influence here. See J Miller, *Rousseau. Dreamer of Democracy* (New Haven, Yale University Press, 1984). A development similar to the one just described with regard to the process of codification in continental Europe could be witnessed in the common law through the evolution of the doctrine of *stare decisis*, which was only firmly rooted in the English legal system by the end of the nineteenth century. On this see J Evans, 'Change in the Doctrine of Precedent during the Nineteenth Century' in L Goldstein (ed), *Precedent in Law* (Oxford, Oxford University Press, 1987) 35–72.

[48] A comparative approach in any case sometimes seems to be more a matter of being *en vogue*, instead of really bringing useful insights to the issue being researched. MC Ponthoreau, 'Le droit comparé en question(s). Entre pragmatisme et outil épistémologique' (2005) 57 *Revue internationale de droit comparé* 9.

[49] W Twining, *Globalisation and Legal Theory* (Cambridge, Cambridge University Press, 2000) 4.

[50] P Zumbansen, 'Transnational Comparisons: Theory and Practice of Comparative Law as a Critique of Global Governance' in Adams and Bomhoff, above n 29, 189–90.

traditional legal questions: what is the law in at least two national jurisdictions, and how do they compare in terms of similarities and differences?

To avoid misunderstandings: the issue for comparative law is not so much whether or not the nation state will sooner or later fade away. We do not think it will, at least not in the foreseeable future. Let it also be clear that, depending on the topic to be dealt with, it is to a greater or lesser extent still possible and sensible to engage in traditional multi-jurisdictional state-centred comparative law. So, too, will the long established purposes and aims of comparative law continue to be relevant for many years to come (including its constructivist purposes).[51] Globalisation is nevertheless challenging state-centred approaches to comparative law; globalisation is a very complex and hybrid phenomenon, and law is no longer fully parochial, though also usually not fully cosmopolitan.[52] But whatever it may be, in a globalising world, comparative law, in order to avoid becoming too restricted in scope and insufficient to meet new challenges,[53] should also self-consciously and explicitly encompass a dynamic approach to supplement its customary and more static perspective, to be able to answer questions such as: how do the societal changes that occur as a result of globalisation impact on the configuration of legal traditions or culture; how do these adapt or maintain their distinctiveness; how is law used in relation to other legal cultures and traditions; and how do new legal configurations become assimilated, rejected or refashioned in a host legal system?[54]

[51] The European unification process is, for example, very much built on the traditional constructivist ambitions of comparative law. For a concise overview of the aims of comparative law see G Dannemann, 'Comparative Law: Study of Similarities or Differences?' in Reimann and Zimmermann, above n 37, 416.

[52] As Twining puts it: 'it includes empires, spheres of influence, alliances, coalitions, religious diasporas, networks, trade routes, migration flows, and social movements. It also includes subworlds such as the common law world, the Arab world, the Islamic world and Christendom, as well as special groupings of power such as the G7, the G8, NATO, OPEC, the European Union, the Commonwealth, multi-national corporations, crime syndicates, cartels, social movements, and non-governmental organisations and networks. All of these cut across any simple vertical hierarchy and overlap and interact with each other in complex ways. These complexities are reflected in the diversity of forms of normative and legal ordering.' W Twining, 'Globalisation and Comparative Law' in Örücü and Nelken, above n 21, 70.

[53] See also NHD Foster, 'The Journal of Comparative Law: A New Scholarly Resource' (2006) 1 *Journal of Comparative Law* 4.

[54] H Muir Watt, 'Globalization and Comparative Law' in Reimann and Zimmermann, above n 37, 589 (with further references). See, too, Demleitner, who states that in its 'classic' form comparative law is restricted in scope and insufficient for the needs of the present situation, consisting mainly of an introduction to legal systems focusing on the common law/civil law divide and the domestic systems of a few Western jurisdictions, such as France and Germany, together with comparisons between certain areas of private law (particularly obligations) in those systems. N Demleitner, 'Combating Legal Ethnocentrism: Comparative Law Sets Boundaries' (1999) 31 *Arizona State Law Journal* 737. This is what Twining calls the 'Country and Western' tradition of comparative law, contrasting especially between the 'parent' civil and common law systems, and mostly dealing with private law. Twining, above n 49, 185ff. Similarly, Pihlajamäki, Chapter 9 below, argues for less focus by legal historians on the standard stories of European legal history (especially with a focus on Germany). An excellent and full-scale analysis of the relation between globalisation and (national) law has recently been published by H Lindahl, *Fault Lines of Globalization. Legal Order and the Politics of A-Legality* (Oxford, Oxford University Press, 2013).

These questions are prominently present in this volume—for example, in the chapter by comparative legal historian Heikki Pihlajamäki.[55] Comparison of law can be synchronic, but it can indeed just as well be diachronic. The latter is traditionally the hunting ground of the legal historian. Legal historians used to be national legal historians, but they are increasingly becoming comparative legal historians.[56] Quite a few problems that confront comparative law also impact comparative legal history. In the latter's case, an additional dimension can make the comparison more complicated. A legal historian can compare past legal cultures in the context of a common era, or he or she can work completely diachronically with a comparison of legal cultures in different eras. Paradoxically enough, this may actually make the comparison less complex if the situation at one place at one time corresponds better with that at another place at another time than with a contemporary. This lesson is one which many comparative lawyers have already taken to heart, albeit unconsciously, as they delve into the goldmine of legal history.

Pihlajamäki argues that national legal history is out. Leading legal historians see their discipline as European, and the next enlargement is already visible with pleas for a global legal history.[57] No one can deny the attraction of a global legal history, but one may wonder whether the time has yet come for it. Legal historians are still trying to get a grip on regional and national legal histories,[58] and European legal history is still quite young as a discipline. Pihlajamäki pleads for a European legal history, but does not want to get rid of national (or regional) legal history. The latter is still valuable, but the researcher should be aware of the international context, since legal institutions move over borders. Moreover, even if no interaction with the outside world were to exist, identifying similarities and differences between legal systems would still be helpful in finding explanations. In short, a national framework is not anathema, as long as the researcher places it within a European context. Pihlajamäki strongly suggests that we should not stop there and that we should also try to look for an even broader context, the global setting of European legal history, ie one that is not confined to nineteenth-century nationalism and positivism, but one that compares larger units to other larger units. Pihlajamäki stresses that comparative consciousness is necessary for a legal historian, because it helps the researcher to test hypotheses and prove

---

[55] See also the chapter by M Löhnig, Chapter 8 below.

[56] Pihlajamäki being a case in point, as he is the articles editor of a new review *Comparative Legal History* (the name says it all), published by Hart.

[57] See T Duve, 'Von der Europäischen Rechtsgeschichte zu einer Rechtsgeschichte Europas in globalhistorischer Perspektive' (2012) 20 Rechtsgeschichte, 17. See also T Duve, 'European Legal History—Global Perspectives. Working Paper for the Colloquium European Normativity—Global Historical Perspectives', Max Planck Institute for European Legal History Research Paper Series, 2013-6, available at http://papers.ssrn.com/sol3/papers.cfm?abstract_id=2292666.

[58] See, eg the *Oxford History of the Laws of England*. The majority of its volumes are still awaiting publication. General surveys of regional legal history, like K Kroeschell, *Recht unde Unrecht der Sassen. Rechtsgeschichte Niedersachsens* (Göttingen, Vandenhoeck & Ruprecht, 2005), are still rare.

or falsify them. He or she also needs to think comparatively at least insofar as to find out how legal influences, transfer, translations or transplants move from one legal order to another. Without a consciousness of legal transfers, one is, according to Pihlajamäki, completely at a loss in attempting to explain changes in a particular legal system. This is true not only for peripheral legal systems, but for larger ones as well.

In his chapter, Matthias Siems is picking up this precise challenge, and builds on the legal transplants debate in order to revive it in a new direction. To date, this debate has been framed, on the one hand, in the language of the pessimists, who claim that legal transplants are at least disruptive to the incoming legal and socio-cultural system, and may even be impossible. On the other hand, optimists acknowledge and support lawmakers in copying foreign rules, often admitting that legal transplants do not work as smoothly in all instances as in the country of origin. Siems analyses a third type of reaction, namely, that legal transplants work even better in the transplant country than in the original one. Borrowing from statistics, he calls these 'overfitting legal transplants'. The success depends on the specifics of the case, and Siems can be credited for identifying some of these specifics (illustrated by examples). Let it be clear, though, that the quest for overfitting legal transplants is not about finding quick 'silver bullets', but about carefully understanding why domestic and foreign laws differ, and how a subsequent legal transplant may affect an existing legal system.

In his chapter, Alain Wijffels, like Pihlajamäki a legal historian and comparative lawyer, addresses comparative lawyers by making clear in a few pages what *ius commune* is and what it is not. We refer the reader to his article for clarification on that issue, but would like to emphasise here that the *ius commune* existed in a context of pluralism and, thus, of some comparison. In his chapter, he emphasises that the Roman–canonistic *ius commune* tradition provided a theoretical and methodological pre-requirement for handling legal complexity, which included a diversity of both particular and common laws, including creating a comparative basis for those different systems; and also that, as a matrix and practical instrument of public governance developed in the Middle Ages, it retained a degree of the common foundations of public law and especially fair governance in diverging political systems during early modern times. These are some lessons for the contemporary comparative lawyer, for example those who are working in the context (or at the service) of European unification: the history of *ius commune* indeed shows that basic values of a legal culture can be transmitted to an era when that legal culture has undergone a wholesale metamorphosis, under the condition that they are carried and defended by jurists who remain at the centre of public governance: in the courts, but also at the heart of government.

Seán Donlan, in his chapter, battles the use of concepts that fail to catch the normative reality within which legal norms function, and which has always been much broader than law proper. Thus, the Western idea of law as 'state law' is itself such a concept. By turning it into the standard, the researcher relegates non-Western or non-standard forms of normativity to a place in the shadows. However well intended his intentions may be, the researcher thus becomes guilty of conceptual colonisation. Donlan stresses that state legality is actually just one type of legality, and legality itself is only one form of normativity. There are no great Chinese walls between them, and 'there is no single legal norm', Donlan states, that can be encapsulated 'in a coherent and neatly hierarchical system'; the reality is too complex for that. Therefore, we need the language of hybridity to catch it. The comparative lawyer should not stick to a shallow concept of law, but try to capture 'a thicker image of normative legal hybridity'. To better illustrate this, Donlan delves into his own research on Louisiana and the complex hybrid there. Adding William Ewald's 'law in minds' to the traditional distinction of law in the books and law in action,[59] he also emphasises the importance of research into the normative and legal hybridity of the practice and the consciousness of norms. Ultimately, normative and legal hybridity is part of a wider context, as the generation, application and interpretation of norms also receives external influences of politics, economics and ideologies.

C. Context and Interdisciplinarity

In line with all of this, comparative law requires a renewed research agenda, fitting, among other things, the type of questions identified in the previous section (B). According to Örücü, the community of comparative lawyers has responded to the criticisms of the 'old order', which focused heavily on legal doctrine and black letter law, in four strands of research: comparative law and legal philosophy (comparative jurisprudence); comparative law and legal history (comparative legal history); comparative law and culture (comparative legal cultures); and comparative law and economics.[60]

In this volume, the second and third strands Örücü identifies are prominent. Indeed, it is these approaches that might be able to signal the deeper cultural context of law and legal—or legally relevant—institutions. As Donlan writes in his chapter, 'the insistence on context significantly problematizes the concept of closed and discrete systems of rules'. A contextual approach, however, calls for resort to other disciplines than the law. The question then arises as to how much context is needed for answering the type of questions that were identified in the previous paragraph (B). Or, to put it differently:

---

[59] W Ewald, 'Comparative Jurisprudence (I): What Was It Like to Try a Rat?' (1994–95) 143 *University of Pennsylvania Law Review* 1889.

[60] E Örücü, 'Critical Comparative Law: Considering Paradoxes for Legal Systems in Transition' (June) *Electronic Journal of Comparative Law* section 1.2, available at http://www.ejcl.org/41/art41-1.html. See too Foster, above n 53, 5.

are we looking for 'law in context' or for 'context in law'?[61] Is it about using context to explain the form or content of law, or is it about revealing what the context itself is?

The answer depends, we would say, on what one wants to know, on the aim(s) of the comparative research project in other words. In this sense, context as such can refer to many different things: how a legal rule relates to other legal rules, or to its social, political, economic, religious etc environment. But however vague it is or can be, there is nonetheless something more to say about this: it is possible to make a general and broad division between projects that implement a turn towards jurisprudence and those that look rather towards the social sciences or the study of culture. The first cherishes the merits of an internal perspective for comparison, designed to develop an understanding of foreign legal systems 'on their own terms'.[62] In many of its manifestations, this turn towards jurisprudence, or the elaboration of an internal perspective on foreign law, relies heavily on insights drawn from hermeneutics and the humanities more generally.[63]

However, it is when a shift is made, from efforts at understanding foreign law and legal institutions to attempts at measuring or explaining the emergence, development or effect of foreign law (an external perspective), that an even greater engagement with other disciplines becomes necessary. What is at stake here, as David Nelken has pointed out, is the possible replacement or supplementation of legal, historical and philosophical scholarship with concepts and more empirical methods taken from the social sciences.[64] And, although contributions that clearly fall into this last category are not available in this volume, it is worthwhile to make the reader aware of what challenges this poses. To be sure, each of the aforementioned approaches has

---

[61] D Nelken, 'Comparative Law and Comparative Legal Studies' in Örücü and Nelken, above n 21, 21.

[62] An approach used in the work of Mitchell Lasser and Catherine Valcke. See especially M de S-O-l'E Lasser, *Judicial Deliberations. A Comparative Analysis of Judicial Transparency and Legitimacy* (Oxford, Oxford University Press, 2004). See also C Valcke, 'The Different Rhetorics of the French and English Law of Contractual Interpretation' in JW Neyers, R Bronaugh and SGA Pitel (eds), *Exploring Contract Law* (Oxford, Hart Publishing, 2008), 77ff; C Valcke, 'Convergence and Divergence among English, French, and German Conceptions of Contract' (2008) 16 *European Review of Private Law* 29; C Valcke, 'Comparative History and the Internal View of French, German, and English Private Law' (2006) 19 *Canadian Journal of Law & Jurisprudence* 133. See further JC Reitz, 'How to Do Comparative Law' (1998) 46 *American Journal of Comparative Law*, who somewhat exaggeratingly states that 'the primary task for which comparative lawyers are prepared by their training and experience is to compare law from the interior point of view.' (628). See too M Adams and JA Bomhoff, 'Comparing Law: Practice and Theory', above n 29, 9ff.

[63] In making clear what this amounts to, the work of HLA Hart is still of prime inspiration (which itself builds on P Winch, *The Idea of a Social Science* (1958)). See especially HLA Hart, *The Concept of Law* (Oxford, Oxford University Press, 1961) 97ff. One of the more constructive interpretations of this perspective is to be found in DN MacCormick's *Legal Reasoning and Legal Theory* (Oxford, Oxford University Press, 1978) 275ff and his *HLA Hart* (London, Edward Arnold, 1980) 36ff. In the context of comparative law see also V Grosswald Curran, 'Cultural Immersion. Differences and Categories in US Comparative Law' (1998) 46 *American Journal of Comparative Law* 43.

[64] Nelken, above n 61, 16.

its challenges, opportunities and limitations. But the more extensive the input from the non-legal discipline (or the non-hermeneutic disciplines), the more potential problems there will be for the legal scholar not just in integrating the different disciplines (the problems will be multiplied), but also in terms of ability: the researcher has to be knowledgeable in more than one discipline (being able to build on it), and possibly even able and versatile in doing non-legal research himself.[65]

H Patrick Glenn, in his chapter, indeed analyses the phenomenon and development of comparative law as joint efforts with other sciences (philosophy of law, sociology and anthropology of law, law and economics). The recurrent theme is that comparison is always present, though its level and intensity may vary. The variation is itself actually a manifestation of a notion underlying all these comparisons: the objective pursued invariably determines the method and depth of the comparison. Consequently, there is, as Glenn also noters, no 'one-size-fits-all method' of comparative law. This does not mean that anything goes, only that researchers can choose and tailor their methods of research to fit very different objectives. In fact, this has also allowed comparative law itself to constantly evolve with the times. In the early modern era, before the term comparative law even existed, it served to construct national legal systems.[66] That task achieved, comparative law set itself to the taxonomy of new national legal systems. Once again, this was only a transient stage, as national legal systems moved from autonomy to interdependence. Glenn's overview illustrates Samuel's thesis that in order to know (comparative) law we have to know what it has been. To understand the changes of comparative law today, we must also look at the changes comparative law underwent in the past.

As context is a crucial element of any meaningful comparative exercise, Roger Brownsword analyses it from the angle of what he calls the regulatory environment. In a way, he is following up on Donlan's plea for normative and legal hybridity. Brownsword makes us aware that, just as is the case with those who contest a state-centric concept of law, there is a debate going on amongst those specialised in regulation about how to understand 'law'. A regulator can use a normative register, eg by forbidding something, but he also has a non-normative register at his disposal. Using technological instruments, a regulator can ensure that the 'regulatees' no longer have the possibility of acting in an undesired way (think, for example, of an alcohol ignition interlock in a car; it eliminates the problem of drunk driving because the drunk can no longer drive). The wider moral issues this confronts us with are worthy of more

---

[65] Realistically that might well require group work. See also Pihlajamäki, Chapter 9 below; D Heirbaut, 'A Tale of Two Legal Histories' in D Michalsen (ed), *Reading Past Legal Texts* (Oslo, Unipax, 2006) 91. For a helpful overview of dimensions of interdisciplinary legal research see BMJ van Klink and HS Taekema, 'On the Border. Limits and Possibilities of Interdisciplinary Research' in BMJ van Klink and HS Taekema (eds), *Law and Method. Interdisciplinary Research into Law* (Tübingen, Mohr Siebeck, 2011) 7.

[66] A theme that is also prevalent in A Wijffels, Chapter 11 below.

research. For the comparative lawyer, the main lesson is that he should look at the regulatory environment in all its normative and non-normative manifestations and the place of a particular law within it.

As we have noted, 'the' context does not exist—or, rather, it is impossible for the researcher to completely grasp the context in all its riches and complexity. He can only try to get a handle on one or more of its aspects from the angle he chooses. Brownsword's perspective promises to be highly rewarding for today's societies. Others are valuable too. There is no single exclusive method for comparative law and neither is there a single, exclusive angle for grasping the complex realities of a legal system for the purposes of comparison, as the latter varies itself all the time. For John Bell, the institutional context is the soil in which legal rules are rooted, and which can particularly explain differences between legal systems. A researcher wanting to understand and not just describe legal rules has to study the institutions that formulate, interpret and apply them. Bell pays particular attention to the organisations, procedures, personnel and ethos that play a part in the operation of the law. As legal institutions are not free from the influence and pressure of non-legal (eg political) institutions, the latter also belong to the institutional context. Bell broadens the context to be studied considerably. However, he also offers a way to narrow it down again. Institutions, their actors and their relationships change over time. Consequently, the institutional context is one of evolution. This means that the professions behind them, in particular the legal professions, have to be a prime subject of research.

Context and institutions are also central to Jørn Øyrehagen Sunde's ideas on legal culture. Legal culture has an intellectual element, ie ideas and expectations shaping law, which is made operational by its institutional element (institutions for conflict settlement and norm production). Making a legal-cultural analysis is no longer obligatory only for scholars, as the internationalisation that law brings has given law a new dimension and every practising lawyer has to cope with it. Øyrehagen Sunde illustrates this with examples from his homeland, Norway. If Norwegian lawyers have to deal with law produced outside their borders, they need a knowledge not just of the outside legal cultural context, but also of their own, because sometimes different countries have to apply law in the same way. This means that every country has to de- and recode it so that this will happen. Thus, paradoxically, even when the goal is the element of the inside legal cultural context, a thorough understanding of the latter in comparison to the outside element is still necessary. Norway is not a member of the European Union, yet the EU is the dominating outsider in many cases. To Øyrehagen Sunde, its influence is even more pervasive than that of the European Court on Human Rights.

If, in Norwegian law, the EU has already become a major player, it is hard to overestimate its impact on the legal systems of the EU Member States. Currency crises, austerity measures and a political backlash against the EU, as described by Joxerramon Bengoetxea, have led to some soul searching. In

Europe, the time of the old nation-state as the great forum has passed. Europeans need to find a new identity, and the challenge is to accommodate the pluralism of regional identities within Europe and remain open to the cosmopolitan legal order. Bengoetxea does not yet present us with an answer as to what exactly the comparative lawyer may contribute. Nevertheless, it should be clear that the old way of just working on unifying the legal systems of Europe is not enough.

If European lawyers are willing to accept a global framework, this will also make it possible for others to help them. Luke Nottage and Souichirou Kozuka, scholars from Australia and Japan, respectively, have analysed the politics of recent contract law reform in Japan. As they have indicated, there are parallels with contract law reforms in France and Germany, or the Common European Sales Law in the EU. Going global may mean a heavier burden for the European comparatist, but also more hands to reduce that workload. The specific micropolitics of contract law reform in Japan are fascinating in themselves. Building on Sacco's legal formants, Nottage and Kozuka analyse the power play amongst various interest groups and individuals within them, which ultimately determines the success of the reform and its content. Their analysis is not just a variant of Sacco's analysis, but also an application of Bell's institutional approach, as propagated in this volume. The dominating players in the Japanese legal world are the judges of the Supreme Court and the Ministry of Justice. The law professors are only the sidekicks of this bureaucratic coalition, if only because professors are bound to disagree somewhat amongst themselves. On the other hand, if law professors can present a 'global standard' this is not without some influence. In this sense, the human fallacy of a thirst for recognition also haunts Japanese law scholars. Some foreign and international rules did make it into the reform, even though their practical application in Japan remains doubtful. Nonetheless, at least the academics championing them scored.[67]

Toon Moonen reminds us that, at least in the Western world, the context of comparative law is democracy and the rule of law. If, however, majority view (and accompanying decision-making) and fundamental human rights protection clash, constitutional courts face the challenge of legitimating their constitutional review. Methodology in this case is not just a scholar's tool; it is also useful for convincing legal professionals, and society at large, of the reasonableness of their decisions. Given the important role of supranational courts, comparative law has a prominent role to play. On the one hand, these courts have to keep in mind a diversity of national audiences, but on the other hand national constitutional courts have to strive for acceptance of their

---

[67] Like Nottage and Kozuka, Alain Wijffels wants scholars to appraise conflicting interests in an analysis of legal formants. He also reminds us that an analytical framework is already available, the *Interessenjurisprudenz*. In applying it, the scholar should distinguish between the comparisons applied by the scholars and practitioners which one studies and one's own methods to assess their achievements.

decisions at both a national and a transnational level. Due to the international dimension, the deliberative approach Moonen pleads for confronts the judges with an enormous challenge. After all,

> the responsibility of the judge goes so far that it is her duty to consider if all democratically rational approaches and solutions are on the court's discussion table, especially if for some reason they were not (adequately) represented in court, and even if she feels not particularly attracted to it.

Consequently, the judge has to be a comparatist, who does not just look at the debates inside his or her own country, but also those outside it. He or she has to be capable of decoding their legal-cultural context, but also of encoding his own decisions for an optimal communication to national and foreign audiences.

Finally, Susan Millns, in her chapter, notices a lack of consensus as to the aims and methods for effective comparative law. But whatever aim is pursued by it, she firmly concludes that, without any consideration for the contexts in which the law is applied (with particular attention to legal cultures and traditions, and to charting differences), comparison cannot sensibly be carried out. Just like many others in this volume, she thinks that textual analysis of legal norms is insufficient to explain the differences between legal cultures. After identifying some difficulties that the European public lawyer might face, she proceeds by making a case for more comparative law in the realm of public law, thus setting out a research agenda. One of the key questions for research in European comparative public law is the extent to which fundamental rights, in the light of technological and scientific progress, and of potential assaults upon both physical and mental integrity, are protected in equal measure across Europe; and what can explain differences between jurisdictions as far as this is concerned.

IV. ROUNDING UP

If comparative law does not want to fade away into oblivion, we have to rethink its role as a scholarly discipline. In an increasingly interdependent era that makes ever-greater demands on our ability to understand the (legal) world with which we are confronted, comparative law can be of tangible benefit and a centrepiece of legal education and research. All this, of course, makes the task of comparative law even more complex than it already was: integrating new challenges into the comparative discipline raises questions of feasibility and practicality, of what still should/can be national in legal education, of how much non-law should be part of the curriculum, of making lawyers sensitive of the non-orderly world of borders and non-borders, etc. The challenges are formidable indeed, but they cannot be ignored. The chapters in this volume are witness to this challenge.

Having said all this, the many contributions to this volume, and especially the sheer diversity they collectively represent, also reveal a feature of comparative law that we believe we have to continue to cherish: comparative law is about much more than generating truth claims, about suggesting solutions to specific problems, about the efficiency of norms, about practical applications, etc. It is all these things, but it is ultimately also about bringing 'something to light' (as Heidegger would have it): an activity that is specialised in imagination, because in all its diversity it reveals many different valuable ways of looking at the law and its role in society; a way of possibly understanding at least a little bit of the multiple reality the law represents.

In line with this, one final question may be on the lips of many readers of this book: is all this attention for methodological issues, especially in the context of comparative law, really necessary? Can a comparatist not just go ahead without letting these issues drag him or her down? Is comparative law, at least from a quotidian perspective, not something researchers simply do whenever they look at foreign legal systems to answer one or more of a range of questions about law, whether these questions are doctrinal, economic, sociological, etc? And, in the race for EU funding, is comparative law's place not after all quite humble?

As far as the last question is concerned, according to Rob van Gestel and Hans Micklitz, in their chapter, comparative law increasingly serves to legitimise preordained reform plans. Scholarly research is then an instrument that should be concerned with serving its economic and political masters, and it should be acknowledged that this does not always allow for a well-elaborated methodology. Both authors are not *in se* against 'bridging the gap between research and the market'. They do, however, deplore that in many cases this degrades into 'advocacy scholarship', which first and foremost aims to defend the contractor's interest and entails only the thinnest veneer of methodology.

As gatekeepers of our profession, this should concern us all. Eventually 'an ongoing instrumentalisation of comparative legal research can easily undermine the public trust in legal scholars in general and comparative lawyers in particular', Van Gestel and Micklitz write. Therefore, it is our duty to instil in aspiring lawyers a sense of the authentic imagination comparative law can stimulate. But for that we more or less need a sense of what we are doing when we 'do' comparative law, and this is first and foremost an epistemological and methodological endeavour. This book is essentially about this endeavour and we hope that it contributes a small part to that, thus honouring a scholar who has inspired us all to put comparative law at the heart of our research.

2

What is Legal Epistemology?

GEOFFREY SAMUEL

PROFESSOR MARK VAN Hoecke, to whom this essay is dedicated, has long recognised that comparative law as a subject raises questions of an epistemological nature. What kind of knowledge, he asks, do we need for carrying out comparative research?[1] Van Hoecke has also argued that in order to develop a suitable methodology of comparative law one needs a better understanding of methodology in domestic legal systems.[2] In his own survey of methodology he shows how the fundamental relationship between the methods employed by lawyers and jurists and the construction of legal theories have passed through different meanings of the term 'science' with the result that legal doctrine today finds itself in a 'schizophrenic situation'. It is caught in a 'hermeneutical–empirical' dichotomy where one school sees it applying a methodology similar to disciplines like theology and literature whilst another school considers that law is no different from other social science disciplines such as sociology and should, as a result, be applying social science empirical methods.[3] This kind of dichotomy, as Professor Muir Watt notes, raises questions about the 'epistemological functions' of academic writing and, indeed, about 'access to knowledge' in general.[4]

Taking its cue from this reference to epistemology, the purpose of this contribution is to look at the notion as applied to law and to investigate exactly what is meant by the expression 'legal epistemology'. Can it provide insights that take one beyond the insights already provided by the many works on legal theory and legal philosophy?

Legal epistemology as an identified and defined zone within what a common lawyer would call 'jurisprudence' emerged in France definitively in 1985 with

---

[1] M Van Hoecke, 'Deep Level Comparative Law' in M Van Hoecke (ed), *Epistemology and Methodology of Comparative Law* (Oxford, Hart Publishing, 2004) 165.

[2] M Van Hoecke, 'Preface' in M Van Hoecke (ed), *Methodologies of Legal Research: Which Kind of Method for Which Kind of Discipline?* (Oxford, Hart Publishing, 2011) v.

[3] M Van Hoecke, 'Legal Doctrine: Which Method(s) for What Kind of Discipline?' in Van Hoecke, *Methodologies of Legal Research*, ibid, 2–3.

[4] H Muir Watt, 'The Epistemological Function of "la doctrine"' in Van Hoecke, ibid, 123.

the publication of a book on the topic by the law professor Christian Atias.[5] This was followed by further publications on the same topic by the same author, perhaps (from a student's point of view) one of the most useful being a small introductory work published in 1994.[6] That the topic should emerge so clearly in France rather than in a country within the common law tradition ought not to surprise because France has never had a category equivalent to 'jurisprudence'. That is to say, it does not have a single category that basically embraces all aspects of legal theory and abstract reflection on law. French jurists have tended, instead, to distinguish between legal philosophy, general theory of law, legal sociology, and, now, legal epistemology. General theory, one leading work explains, is distinguished from legal philosophy in that general theory is a question of observing the permanent elements of a legal system so as to determine its concepts, techniques, principal intellectual constructions and so on.[7] Legal philosophy, in contrast, is more interested in extracting law from this technical context with the aim of discovering its meta-juridical signification, that is to say, the values that it pursues and the relation between law and what might be termed a total vision of mankind and the world.[8] These two domains in turn are to be distinguished from legal epistemology, which is 'a critical study of the principles, postulates, methods and results of knowing the law'.[9] Legal epistemology is the study of the modes of legal knowledge (*modes de connaissance du droit*); it is the critical study of legal knowledge itself.[10]

Accordingly, while legal theory and legal philosophy are concerned with the question of what law is, legal epistemology poses a rather different question. What is it to have knowledge of the law? These distinctions between the domains may at first sight seem simple enough, yet a moment's reflection will surely result in a series of sceptical queries. Does not the legal philosophy question about what law is contain by implication the legal knowledge issue? Does not the general theory question—a question about the concepts, intellectual constructions and techniques of law—overlap considerably with legal epistemology? Perhaps, after all, the Anglo-American approach of placing all three domains within a general category of 'jurisprudence' makes sense.

There is no doubt that the subject category of jurisprudence has as one of its aims to provide epistemological insights into law. Where, however, the category has proved less helpful is in respect of comparative law and comparative

---

[5] C Atias, *Épistémologie juridique* (Paris, Presses Universitaires de France, 1985). This is not to suggest that the idea of legal epistemology was unknown before 1985.

[6] C Atias, *Épistémologie du droit* (Paris, Presses Universitaires de France, 1994). A subsequent, more substantial book on legal epistemology by this author is *Épistémologie juridique* (Paris, Dalloz, 2002). This 2002 book is not an updated version of the 1985 book, despite having the same title.

[7] J-L Bergel, *Théorie générale du droit*, 5th edn (Paris, Dalloz, 2012) 5.

[8] Ibid.

[9] Ibid.

[10] Ibid.

legal studies. The problem that arises here is that the emphasis in jurisprudence has tended to be on the fashioning of universal legal theories whereas the preoccupation in comparative law has been the reverse. When comparatists ask the question of what is 'law' they are doing so in the context of a particular legal culture or tradition, and the presumption is that each culture or tradition has its own epistemological paradigm. In comparative law the emphasis is not on a universalist definition of law because such definitions run the risk not only of masking the particularities of individual legal cultures but also of imposing themselves on a tradition which is actually very different from the ones from which the universal definitions have been fashioned. In other words, there is the danger of legal imperialism. Even within Europe this is a problem. Can, or should, the institutional categories of the civil law be imposed on the common law? Some writers seem to regard such an institutional system as a form of transnational science and thus of as much relevance to English law as to the German or French systems.[11] Other writers are far more sceptical: the common law has a completely different epistemological mentality.[12] Or take norm theory. Can all legal systems be reduced to a pyramid of descending norms or do some traditions, like the common law, simply not think in these terms?

These kinds of question have given rise over the last couple of decades to a body of literature that is generally regarded as falling not within jurisprudence, but within the category of general theory of comparative law. When these problems are combined with others faced by comparatists—in particular, problems of methodology—one soon finds that the legal theory and philosophy (jurisprudence) literature is not that helpful. As Mark Van Hoecke indicates, many of the methodological difficulties encountered in comparative law are essentially linked to a number of epistemological problems concerning the technique of comparison, the description of law and the 'objectivity' of facts.[13] Thus comparative law might be said to focus on two questions: what is meant by 'comparison' and what is meant by 'law'?[14] The first question is concerned, broadly speaking, with how comparison can generate its own particular knowledge; that is to say, how the comparison of several objects can produce knowledge that could not be produced from the analysis of each of them independently.[15] This investigation involves a number of methodological dichotomies, such as the ones between macro- and microcomparison, between universalist and differential approaches, and between genealogical and ana-

[11] See, eg P Birks, 'Definition and Division: A Meditation on *Institutes* 3.13' in P Birks (ed), *The Classification of Obligations* (Oxford, Oxford University Press, 1997) 1.
[12] See, eg J Hackney, 'More than a Trace of the Old Philosophy' in Birks, *Classification of Obligations*, ibid, 123.
[13] M Van Hoecke, 'Deep Level Comparative Law' in Van Hoecke, *Epistemology and Methodology of Comparative Law*, above n 1, 165.
[14] See generally G Samuel, 'Droit comparé et théorie du droit' (2006) *Revue Interdisciplinaire d'Études Juridiques* (no 57) 1.
[15] Y Chevrel, *La littérature comparée*, 5th edn (Paris, Presses Universitaires de France, 2006) 3.

logical comparisons. This first question equally embraces the various schemes of intelligibility that underpin the differing methods used by comparatists. In particular, there are important debates between functionalist, hermeneutical and structuralist approaches.[16] As for the law question, which of course cannot really be divorced from the comparison question, there is the issue of what actually forms the object of comparison. Is it a question of comparing rules, norms, concepts, institutions, categories, systems, factual situations, reasoning techniques or what? The dominance of the rule model of law in legal theory and philosophy means that the traditional jurisprudential literature is often unhelpful. Consequently the gap is being filled by a literature that can be described as epistemological in its orientation.

However, this is not to suggest that legal epistemology is confined to comparative legal studies. In fact, the focus on epistemology in law has been equally stimulated by research into legal artificial intelligence (AI) systems, which also raises the question of what it is to have legal knowledge.[17] Other questions that fall within the domain of legal epistemology are these. What gives legal knowledge its validity as legal knowledge? What is the nature of a discipline?[18] Is the knowledge within a discipline cumulative?[19] Have there been scientific revolutions within this or that discipline?[20] How should assertions in law be validated?[21] These questions are not exhaustive, but they represent some of the more important issues that have been posed within the social and human sciences more generally. It should be evident, then, that legal epistemology is by its very nature interdisciplinary. This is not to assert, it must be said at once, that there are not epistemological theories that are, for want of a better term, internal to law. Hans Kelsen's pure theory was an attempt to provide such an epistemological model; its purity is to be found in its effort to separate law from all other social science knowledge and social norms.[22] However, in asserting such a singular universalist theory of law and legal knowledge, it is arguable that Kelsen was more of a legal theorist and philosopher than an epistemologist.[23] He was not studying the various principles, concepts, notions and methods used by jurists in any critical and descriptive sense.[24] He was more of an idealist. For example, there is no place in his pyramid of norms

[16] See further G Samuel, 'Dépasser le fonctionnalisme' in P Legrand (ed), *Comparer les droits, résolument* (Paris, Presses Universitaires de France, 2009) 405.

[17] R Susskind, *Expert Systems in Law* (Oxford, Oxford University Press, 1987).

[18] J Boutier, J-C Passeron and J Revel (eds), *Qu'est-ce qu'une discipline?* (Paris, Éditions de l'École des Hautes Études en Sciences Sociales, 2006).

[19] B Walliser (ed), *La cumulativité du savoir en sciences sociales* (Paris, Éditions de l'École des Hautes Études en Sciences Sociales, 2009); G Samuel, 'Is Legal Knowledge Cumulative?' (2012) 32 *Legal Studies* 448.

[20] Atias (1994), above n 6, 93–103.

[21] L Soler, *Introduction à l'épistémologie* (Paris, Ellipses, 2000) 43–45.

[22] D Lloyd and M Freeman, *Lloyd's Introduction to Jurisprudence*, 8th edn (London, Sweet & Maxwell, 2008) 307–08.

[23] M Troper, *La philosophie du droit* (Paris, Presses Universitaires de France, 2003) 38.

[24] cf Atias (1994), above n 6.

for the dichotomy between public and private law, yet these two categories have been, and remain, fundamental to legal thought.[25] A descriptive episte-mology of law cannot, in other words, ignore notions that have been and are used by lawyers in such a conceptual and instrumental way.

Nevertheless, this reference to Kelsen's theory indicates how difficult it is to separate on occasions epistemology from philosophy. One reason for this dif-ficulty is the flexibility of this latter category, which can easily be expanded to embrace questions about the nature and validity of knowledge. Consequently, as a French epistemologist noted, it has not been easy to distinguish between epistemology and the philosophy of science.[26] The difference, according to this author, seems to be found in the idea of a linear progress as opposed to a circular one, this latter being a progress *réflexif* on the part of those actu-ally involved with the practice of science.[27] In other words, epistemology is a reflection on the part of practitioners rather than pure theorists, and this in turn is a useful reminder that all metascience is not necessarily philosophical.[28] Within the discipline of law there has been a marked shift in the content of the common law jurisprudence course during the twentieth century, which perhaps indicates a rethinking of the scope of what amounts to legal philosophy. In the earlier part of the century there was considerable emphasis on legal concepts, such as ownership, possession, contract and personality, but this gradually disappeared from the syllabus during the second half.[29] The emphasis today is on philosophical theories, with considerable space being devoted, first, to particular individual philosophers, like Kelsen, Hart and Dworkin, and, sec-ondly, to certain Anglo-American schools, like realism, critical legal studies and feminist jurisprudence. This reorientation was no doubt partly caused by a lack of space, given the enormous expansion of schools of thought during the last century; but it is still legitimate to ask if this practical reason has not provoked in its wake a rethinking of what amounts to legal philosophy. Reflections upon legal concepts such as ownership and contract have generated their own categories, such as the philosophy or theory of property, contract, tort and equity. Perhaps, then, one can reach an analogous conclusion to the one suggested by Robert Blanché: epistemology inhabits an intermediate zone between the practice of science and philosophy.[30]

If legal epistemology is to be considered as inhabiting the zone between pro-fessional positive law and legal philosophy—by no means a non-contentious view, it must be said—the next question is whether the approach is scientific

---

[25] JW Jones, *Historical Introduction to the Theory of Law* (Oxford, Oxford University Press, 1940) 139–63. See also B Bonnet and P Deunier (eds), *De l'intérêt de la summa divisio droit public-droit privé* (Paris, Dalloz, 2010).

[26] R Blanché, *L'épistémologie*, 3rd edn (Paris, Presses Universitaires de France, 1983) 16–20.

[27] Ibid 17.

[28] Ibid, 19, 120.

[29] One of the last jurisprudence textbooks in England reflecting the older syllabus was RM Dias, *Jurisprudence*, 5th edn (London, Butterworths, 1985).

[30] Blanché, above n 26, 20.

(black letter) or philosophical. Blanché has noted how epistemology has slowly detached itself from philosophy but, equally, how it cannot completely ignore the teachings of the old philosophers.[31] Indeed, certain scientists have become philosophers, yet the reverse is far more difficult since one needs to be versed in scientific culture before one can risk saying anything useful on epistemology.[32] Is the same true of law? It is difficult to imagine any serious analysis of notions such as ownership or possession without a deep knowledge of the practical examples in Justinian's *Digest* and in the huge mass of common law cases and legislative provisions. A good knowledge of the positive law of property would appear to be a necessity.[33] Even the more abstract notions, such as rights and duties, if they are to have relevance for epistemology, surely need to be anchored as much in positive case law as in theoretical speculation? Certainly one of the leading theories on the notion of a right gains its epistemological credibility in the deep positive law learning of its author.[34]

Perhaps one should distinguish, accordingly, between a philosophical and a scientific (positivist approach) epistemology? However, Robert Blanché, in respect of the sciences, preferred the distinction between an internal and external epistemology,[35] one which, by way of analogy, would surely find favour with some legal philosophers who talk of an internal and external point of view with regard to law.[36] The practitioner or the law teacher working primarily on practical problems and who fashions or adapts concepts is perhaps generating epistemological notions without really knowing it. Indeed, these notions become absorbed within the positive law itself.[37] Those working externally are more detached from this black letter problem solving and deliberately adopt something of a philosophical approach even if their object remains, say, legal cases and legislative texts. These 'external' epistemologists might be searching for, say, a theory of the law of contract or the law of property. This said, one must add to this dichotomy the point, underlined by Christian Atias, that different categories of jurist do not use exactly the same knowledge.[38] The legislator, the judge and the professor all have rather different knowledge models. John Bell, similarly, has talked of different legal cultures within the same system.[39]

Another complicating factor is paradigm orientations. If one thinks in terms of a dichotomy between jurists working within an authority paradigm and jurists working outside such a paradigm, one has perhaps arrived at a new

---

[31] Ibid, 29–30.

[32] Ibid, 31.

[33] See, eg DR Harris, 'The Concept of Possession in English Law' in A Guest (ed), *Oxford Essays in Jurisprudence* (Oxford, Oxford University Press, 1961) 69.

[34] W Hohfeld, *Fundamental Legal Conceptions* (New Haven, Yale University Press, 1919; reprint, 1966).

[35] Blanché, above n 26, 33.

[36] Atias, 37–39.

[37] *Cf* Blanché, above n 26, 33.

[38] Atias, 21.

[39] J Bell, *French Legal Cultures* (Cambridge, Cambridge University Press, 2001).

means of distinguishing between an internal and an external epistemology.[40] This notion of an authority paradigm is founded on the idea that practitioners and academics working within certain disciplines, such as theology and law, are governed ultimately not by enquiry—the results of which in the end may force those working within the enquiry paradigm to abandon their theories in the face of empirical reality—but by textual authority. The foundational texts in theology and in law can never be questioned in terms of their authority and this limits quite severely not just the scope for scientific enquiry, but also even the scope of hermeneutical investigation.[41] Yet the authority paradigm does not accord with the 'scientific' and philosophical approach dichotomy; many legal philosophers, especially those who have sought to identify the source of legal rules and to separate them from other norms, could be said to be working within the authority paradigm. Consequently, it is necessary to distinguish between different categories of legal philosophers and theorists. There are those working within the authority paradigm and there are those working outside of it; equally, there is a third category of theorist who is working partly within and partly without such a paradigm. Those theorists working outside of the paradigm are unlikely to be quoted in textbooks on positive law or in judgments—one thinks, for example, of John Griffith's book on the politics of the judiciary[42]—while those within the paradigm, such as Herbert Hart, are likely to be treated as authoritative.[43] A theorist working in the area of, say, law and economics might be seen as operating partly within and partly without the paradigm and, in consequence, might or might not find themselves being quoted by judges.

Another issue of approach identified by Robert Blanché in respect of the sciences is the dichotomy between the diachronic and the synchronic, the latter being described as a direct approach while the former is regarded as an *ana-lyse historico-critique*.[44] As this epistemologist noted, the normal approach adopted by scientists is one that sees science in its actuality and this is, in some ways, hardly surprising.[45] Scientific research and application is about the here and now. The same can be said about law; thus, if one looks both at legal education and at legal theory, the emphasis is almost exclusively on law that is currently in force and on theories that are fashioned to comprehend this actuality. As Ronald Dworkin implied, one does not need to know the history of mathematics to be a good mathematician.[46] Of course, the notion

---

[40] G Samuel, 'Interdisciplinarity and the Authority Paradigm: Should Law Be Taken Seriously by Scientists and Social Scientists?' (2009) 36 *Journal of Law and Society* 431.

[41] Ibid. See also G Samuel, 'Is Law Really a Social Science? A View from Comparative Law' [2008] *Cambridge Law Journal* 288.

[42] J Griffith, *The Politics of the Judiciary*, 5th edn (London, Fontana, 1997).

[43] This is not to suggest that those working outside of the authority paradigm will have no influence on those working within the paradigm, and indeed on judges themselves. However, these works are unlikely to form part of 'positive' legal knowledge.

[44] Blanché, above n 26, 33–39.

[45] Ibid, 34.

[46] R Dworkin, *Law's Empire* (London, Fontana, 1986) 14.

of precedent, relevant to the common law systems, implies a certain historical
dimension to legal knowledge, but past cases are normally to be understood in
terms of their present relevance rather than as historical documents in themselves. It is perfectly possible, therefore, for law graduates never to have studied
legal history. As for historical jurisprudence, it has remained both discred-
ited and largely ignored since the nineteenth century,[47] although by definition
natural law theory tends to have something of a historical dimension, given
its association with the expression *ius naturale* and with the jurisprudential
schools of the past. Legal positivism, in contrast, is (or was) regarded as scientific and thus ahistorical. Indeed, why should the positivist study old law?

However, the twentieth century saw a major resurgence of the diachronic
approach in the natural sciences thanks to historians of science such as Gaston
Bachelard and Thomas Kuhn.[48] The importance of these two scholars was
that they presented a historical vision that was very much at odds with the
traditional linear and progressive view of the development of scientific knowledge. Bachelard saw this development in terms of inertia and epistemological
obstacles, and thus invited the scientific community to see scientific knowledge
more as a matter of rupture than continuity. Kuhn presented a similar picture,
arguing that science went through paradigm changes that were so radical that
they amounted to scientific revolutions.[49] The importance of the historical
approach is clearly evident in these writings in that, as Blanché says, it 'offers
a good means of analysis in separating, by the date and by the circumstances
of their appearance, the various elements which have contributed to form little
by little the notions and principles of . . . science'.[50]

Do these diachronic insights into the sciences hold any epistemological lessons for jurists? Certainly Blanché's observation about history permitting one
to appreciate the step-by-step formation of science would appear most relevant to legal knowledge. There is a long history of legal thought, from early
Roman law to modern legal thought, and this history is fundamental to legal
epistemology in several respects. First, the institutions, concepts and categories that are in use today have, for the most part, come originally from the
Roman law sources. The history of law in continental Europe is, then, in
one respect simply a history of Roman law.[51] Secondly, the methods used by
jurists have themselves been fashioned by history. Indeed, the whole formation of the civil law tradition is in some ways a history of differing methods;
so Christian Atias talks not of a progression in method, but a sedimentation.

---

[47] *Cf* P Stein, 'The Tasks of Historical Jurisprudence' in N MacCormick and P Birks, *The Legal Mind: Essays for Tony Honoré* (Oxford, Oxford University Press, 1986) 293.

[48] See in particular T Kuhn, *The Structure of Scientific Revolutions*, 2nd edn (Chicago, University of Chicago Press, 1970).

[49] J-P Astolfi and M Develay, *La didactique des sciences*, 4th edn (Paris, Presses Universitaires de France, 1996) 26–27.

[50] Blanché, above n 26, 36.

[51] See generally Stein, *Roman Law in European History* (Cambridge, Cambridge University Press, 1999).

Different methods have built up one upon another.[52] Thirdly, many of today's legal theories have their roots in notions that can be traced back to Roman sources. For example, the seeds of natural law, positivism, social contract and even the great nominalism versus universalism debate are to be found in the *Digest*. In fact, the philosophical thesis asserted by Ronald Dworkin, despite his disavowal of history, belongs within a tradition that can be traced back to the seventeenth-century French jurist Jean Domat.[53] Anyone interested in the formation of the principles, concepts, methods and theories associated with legal knowledge would therefore seem almost obliged to adopt at some point a diachronic approach.[54] Even the development of the common law cannot escape from this civilian historical development since, as Peter Stein has pointed out, while 'English law has remained relatively free of Roman influences, English jurisprudence has traditionally turned for inspiration to the current continental theories, necessarily based on Roman law'.[55]

Less easy is the identification, within the history of legal thought, of the kind of epistemological obstacles, ruptures and scientific revolutions that were identified in the sciences by Bachelard and Kuhn. Have there been scientific revolutions? There have certainly been important changes of method over the centuries, but none of these changes amounted, arguably, to a revolutionary paradigm change in that there is no period in which a jurist from one century would not be able to understand a jurist from another century.[56] As Peter Birks once said, the Roman jurist Ulpian could probably participate in the UK Supreme Court today 'without a moment's preparation'.[57] Much more relevant is another diachronic model identified by Robert Blanché with respect to the sciences. Discussing the dichotomies between concrete and abstract science and between inductive and deductive reasoning, he makes the point that these two forms of reasoning mark just two stages in the development of science, the stages themselves being framed within an initial stage and a final stage. 'In fact,' he continued, 'it appears that all the sciences follow, in distinguishing themselves only by their degree of advancement, a similar course, passing or being called to pass, successively through the descriptive, inductive, deductive and axiomatic stages.'[58]

If one applies this four-stage diachronic framework to the development of the civil law tradition, it certainly seems to have relevance. It could be said that the period of the XII Tables was one where Roman law was at its descriptive

---

[52] Atias, 66–77.

[53] M-F Renoux-Zagamé, 'Domat Jean' in P Arabeyre, J-L Halpérin and J Krynen (eds), *Dictionnaire historique des juristes français XIIe-XXe siècle* (Paris, Presses Universitaires de France, 2007) 254.

[54] On which see generally Jones, above n 25.

[55] P Stein, *Legal Evolution: The Story of an Idea* (Cambridge University Press, 1980) 123.

[56] Samuel, 'Is Legal Knowledge Cumulative?', above n 19.

[57] P Birks, 'Roman Law in Twentieth-Century Britain' in J Beatson and R Zimmermann (eds), *Jurists Uprooted: German-Speaking Émigré Lawyers in Twentieth-Century Britain* (Oxford, Oxford University Press, 2004) 249, 267.

[58] Blanché, above n 26, 65.

stage passing into the inductive stage towards the end of the Republican era.[59] This inductive stage continued throughout the medieval period of Roman law (glossators and post-glossators)[60] until the humanist revolution of the six-teenth century, when jurists like Doneau and, a century later, Domat took methodology into its deductive period.[61] The nineteenth-century German pan-dectist jurists then attempted to go further and to axiomatise legal thought.[62] Two difficulties, however, emerge from this attempt at diachronic rationalisa-tion. The first is that it does not seem to apply to the common law, which appears never to have advanced beyond the inductive stage. This, no doubt, can be explained by the lack of any (or much) humanist influence on legal thought, which, in turn, may be the result of an absence of any university tradition before the nineteenth century.[63] Secondly, the twentieth century saw something of an abandonment of the idea that law as an axiomatic science; the influence of writers like Perelman might be said to have returned civil law thinking back on itself, if not back into an inductive stage, at least to a stage that is pluralist in its approach.[64] Rather than an axiomatic or 'scientific' approach, this Belgian jurist emphasised the importance of argumentation in which the syllogism is just one argument amongst many. Arguments based on analogy, induction, pragmatism (functionalism) and the like are the essence of legal reasoning, since law itself is founded less in rules and texts and more in the conflict of interests and values.[65]

The importance of Perelman's reflections is that they indicate that the four-stage diachronic progression is limited in its explanatory value. While it does seem to provide a general picture of methodological development from early Roman times to the German Civil Code, it does little more than this since method itself is more complex and cannot be fully analysed and explained by such broad categories. While not abandoning a diachronic orientation, one needs therefore to return to a synchronic approach and to ask serious ques-tions about the methods employed by jurists.

Yet when methods are studied synchronically, Mark Van Hoecke argues that

> there is a somewhat schizophrenic situation in which one discipline, legal doctrine, is basically studying law as a normative system, limiting its 'empirical data' to legal texts and court decisions, whereas other disciplines study legal reality, law as it is.[66]

---

[59] Jones, above n 25, 3–9.
[60] Ibid 13–21, 23.
[61] Ibid 38–39. See also Renoux-Zagamé, above n 53.
[62] Ibid 65; Van Hoecke, *Methodologies of Legal Research*, above n 2, 9.
[63] JH Baker, *The Oxford History of the Laws of England: Volume VI 1483–1558* (Oxford, Oxford University Press, 2003) 12.
[64] S Goltzberg, *Chaïm Perelman: L'argumentation juridique* (Paris, Michalon, 2013).
[65] Ibid 110–111.
[66] Van Hoecke, *Methodologies of Legal Research*, above n 2, 2.

He does not advocate abandoning the legal doctrine approach, but he does go on to say that all too often 'it lacks a clear methodology and the methods of legal doctrine seem to be identical to those of legal practice; it is too parochial', and thus 'there is not much difference between publications of legal practitioners and of legal scholars'.[67] Can a focus on legal epistemology overcome the problem identified by Professor Van Hoecke? It would, of course, be idle to assert that legal theorists and legal philosophers have ignored legal reasoning.[68] However, it is arguable that this literature has tended to remain within the authority paradigm—or is too parochial, as Mark Van Hoecke puts it—with the result that there has been little interdisciplinary research with regard to the way jurists analyse and view, for want of a better term, social reality. Some may dispute this, but if one turns to comparative law this want of interdisciplinary research becomes particularly evident. There has been much attention focused on the functional method[69] and, more recently, hermeneutics;[70] yet there is little scholarship placing these methodological schemes in some kind of epistemological context. What are the alternatives to functionalism and to hermeneutics?[71] In social science epistemology, there are bodies of literature on schemes of intelligibility and on paradigm orientations; indeed, there is considerable work on epistemology in the social and human sciences.[72] However, not only is much of the work ignored by jurists, but social science theorists themselves think that jurists have little to offer social scientists.[73] This of itself suggests that there is a job for legal epistemology.

So what is legal epistemology? The work of Van Hoecke has done much to permit both legal theorists and comparative lawyers to build upon the pioneering books of professor Atias with the result that it is now possible to provide some clear distinctions between legal theory and philosophy on the one hand and legal epistemology on the other.

The first of such distinctions is that legal epistemology is necessarily situated at a different level from theory and philosophy because it takes as its object legal knowledge. What is it to have knowledge of law? Such a question involves an object domain that embraces at one pole the detailed rules and regulations to be found in texts and cases and at the other pole the theories that have tried both to explain law and to understand the philosophies that have underpinned it. In between these poles there are other knowledge points, ranging from institutions, concepts, notions and categories (together with their

---

[67] Ibid 3.

[68] For a survey of some of the Anglo-American literature see Lloyd and Freeman, above n 22, 1550–63.

[69] See, eg R Michaels, 'The Functional Method of Comparative Law' in M Reimann and R Zimmermann (eds), *The Oxford Handbook of Comparative Law* (Oxford, Oxford University Press, 2006) 339.

[70] See P Legrand, *Le droit comparé* (Paris, Presses Universitaires de France, 3rd ed, 2009).

[71] See further Samuel, 'Dépasser le fonctionnalisme', above n 16.

[72] See in particular J-M Berthelot (ed), *Épistémologie des sciences sociales* (Paris, Presses Universitaires de France, 2001).

[73] Ibid 12–13.

histories) to the reasoning methods employed by lawyers. Of course, a complete separation between theory, philosophy and epistemology is impossible, as has been seen. Yet one important distinction is to be found in the concerns of each domain. Legal theory and philosophy is universalist in its aims; the purpose of such theories and philosophies is to reduce and unify. Legal epistemology does not have this aim as such. It is as much concerned with difference as with similarity, and thus operates within a context in which there are different knowledges of law rather than a single idea of legal knowledge.[74] Epistemology does not seek to evaluate, say, Kelsen's theory in relation to Dworkin's or Hart's.[75] Instead, it is orientated towards understanding these theorists within their historical and methodological (using the term to embrace schemes of intelligibility and paradigms) settings.

A second distinction is epistemology's more practical character, inasmuch as it has a clear and direct role in understanding legal knowledge for the purpose of, for example, research into AI and law. It also underpins comparison in law in the way that it forms the basis of the two guiding questions. What is meant by comparison and what is meant by law? This practical characteristic also results from the requirement that epistemological reflection is rooted as much in the concepts, notions, categories and reasoning methods of practising lawyers as in the theories fashioned by legal philosophers. In the natural sciences, as has been mentioned, philosophers with no practical experience are unlikely to make good epistemologists; the same can probably be said of jurists. The epistemologist will, in short, be as much concerned with legal textbook writers, professional opinion and judgments as with the literature produced by theorists and philosophers. Again, one must not over-exaggerate the distinctions, since many of the American realists were practical lawyers working, for example, in the field of commercial law. Yet this may be one reason why such theorists have made important contributions to aspects of epistemology (the categorisation of facts for instance).

A third distinction is that it is probably impossible to comprehend law as a body of knowledge without a comprehension of the history of legal thought and reasoning, including, of course, the language through which the discipline has expressed itself. One reason for this can be found within the discipline of history itself. 'In order to understand what history is,' wrote Donald Kelley, 'we must first ask: What has history been?'[76] Similarly, one might say that in order to understand what law is we must first ask what law has been. As a discipline, law is both old and, seemingly, remarkably stable, given the arguable absence of any scientific revolutions.[77] Yet a history of legal thought reveals both continuity and change, and it is these changes that allow one to see the

---

[74] *cf* Van Hoecke, 'Legal Doctrine', above n 3, 4–11.
[75] Atias, above n 6, 140.
[76] D Kelley, *Foundations of Modern Historical Scholarship* (New York, Columbia University Press, 1970) 2.
[77] See further Samuel, 'Is Legal Knowledge Cumulative?', above n 19.

various forms of methodological sedimentation that underpin contemporary legal thinking.[78] Much of the language and many of the fundamental categories used by Western lawyers were developed by the Romans; the reasoning and interpretation issues also have equally long histories.[79] Legal epistemology cannot escape from an investigation of how this language has evolved over the centuries and how it has reflected and interacted with perceived social, political and economic reality. Moreover, this understanding of Western legal thought ought to permit the epistemologist to appreciate law as local knowledge; that is to say, to appreciate difference between what constitutes legal knowledge within differing traditions.

Finally, comprehending the way in which law interrelates with social, political and economic reality means that the legal epistemologist must be located, by necessity, within an interdisciplinary context. How does legal knowledge relate to knowledge from other disciplines? To what extent has legal knowledge imported knowledge from other disciplines? Have other disciplines imported legal knowledge? In addition, the legal epistemologist must have an understanding of epistemology of the natural and the social sciences. What is the relevance of writers like Thomas Kuhn, Gilles-Gaston Granger, Robert Blanché and Jean-Michel Berthelot to legal knowledge? As Christian Atias has suggested, legal epistemology can learn from the theories and histories of other bodies of knowledge; it can learn from their errors, their deficiencies and their changes.[80] Moreover, many of the postulates, methods and paradigms employed by lawyers have their roots beyond law as a discipline or as an object of science. Even positivism results not from law itself as a body of rules or norms but from the postulate that there is a 'science' of law, for if law is a science it must have an object, namely rules or norms.[81] Behind the various authoritative methods of law—for example, the literal rule in statutory interpretation or the 'reasonable bystander' test employed in contract—some kind of more general social science scheme of intelligibility is at work. Describing facts is equally a problem that transcends the boundary of law as a discipline; 'in the positive sciences too it is now generally accepted that an informative, scientific description of reality is only possible when embedded in, and guided by, theoretical constructs'.[82] Such interdisciplinarity might seem daunting to some lawyers, but Mark Van Hoecke is optimistic. Positive law might be trapped within its own history and culture, yet other disciplines, such as sociology, politics and economics, usually offer a means of escape from the constrictions of one's own

---

[78] Atias, above n 6, 184–90.

[79] See, eg I Maclean, *Interpretation and Meaning in the Renaissance* (Cambridge, Cambridge University Press, 1992).

[80] Atias, above n 6, 29.

[81] Ibid 141–42.

[82] M Van Hoecke, 'Deep Level Comparative Law' in Van Hoecke, *Epistemology and Methodology of Comparative Law*, above n 1, 170.

legal mentality.[83] What is legal epistemology? If nothing else, it is a means of escape from the arid past of comparative law, from legal positivism and, above all, from the authority paradigm.

---

[83] Ibid, 191.

3

Comparative Law as Method and the Method of Comparative Law

JAAP HAGE[1]

I. INTRODUCTION

COMPARATIVE LAW IS a discipline within legal research that has gained considerable popularity during the last decades, a popularity that has no doubt profited from the efforts to harmonise the law of the Member States of the EU.[2] This growing popularity has spawned an increase in attention both for the justificatory role of comparative law within legal research (comparative law as method) and for the method of comparative law itself. In this contribution these two issues will both be addressed, in an attempt to answer two questions:

1. Is comparative law a method, or a set of methods, for legal research?
2. Does comparative law have a proper method of its own?

These two questions will be answered in Sections III and IV, respectively, of this chapter. As a foundation for the arguments of these two sections, Section II will address the nature of a scientific method. In a sense, this foundational section contains the core of this chapter's argument.

Before continuing the argument, however, I will first make the notion of comparative law more precise, and adopt a broad notion in order not to prejudice the results of my argument. For the purpose of the present chapter, 'comparative law' is assumed to mean the comparison of the law of differ-

[1] The author thanks Jaakko Husa and Maurice Adams for valuable comments on a draft version of this chapter, which allowed him to formulate the main message better.
[2] See M Van Hoecke, 'Legal Cultures, Legal Traditions and Comparative Law' [2006] *Nederlands Tijdschrift voor Rechtsfilosofie en Rechtstheorie* 331; JM Smits, *The Making of European Private Law* (Antwerp, Intersentia, 2002).

ent jurisdictions, legal families or legal traditions, with a special eye on the similarities and the differences.

To avoid a possible misunderstanding, it may be useful to point out first that the two questions only deal with the narrow issue of comparative law in connection with legal method, and not primarily with questions of whether comparative law is valuable or useful in some function other than as legal method.

II. WHAT IS A SCIENTIFIC METHOD?

A. Method and Methodology

Before addressing the nature of a scientific[3] method in some detail, it may be useful to point out a possible terminological confusion between a method and methodology. As will be argued below, a method is basically a set of standards by means of which the relevance of arguments can be evaluated. These standards have implications for the way in which scientific research is to be conducted. The term 'method' is consequently sometimes also used for the way in which a particular investigation is carried out.

Methodology is the study of the proper standards for scientific arguments. It is not a standard itself, but rather a discipline that belongs to, or borders on, the philosophy of science, and—as we will soon see—on ontology. This chapter contains a study in methodology.

If method and methodology are confused, and in particular if a method is denoted as a methodology, it is easy to overlook that a method needs to be justified.[4] One sometimes encounters legal research which pays attention to the method that was employed but devotes little or no attention to the question why this method is suitable for the kind of research that was performed. Awareness that every method requires an underlying methodology may lead to an increased attention for the choice of a method (or methods), and in this way to better legal research.

---

[3] The notion of 'science' adopted here is that of the tradition in which there can be sciences in the humanities, not only physical sciences.

[4] The work of JM Smits, *The Mind and Method of the Legal Academic* (Cheltenham, Edward Elgar, 2012), illustrates that confusing method and methodology does not necessarily lead to such an oversight. On p 109 Smits writes about the unclear *methodology* used by lawyers, but in the subsequent sections Smits shows an acute awareness of the relevancy of a domain theory for a research *method*.

B. Method in Two Senses

When considering the nature of scientific method, the first thing that springs to one's mind is a particular way of doing research.[5] A method may contain guidelines on how to conduct an interview, on the statistical techniques that must be used to extract information from a data set, on the tests that need to be performed to diagnose a disease, on the circumstances under which an experiment may be conducted, on the sources and interpretation maxims that must be used to establish a claim in law, and so on.

All of these guidelines indeed belong to a scientific method, but I will argue that they only do so in a derived sense. Underneath the guidelines lies a theory about good reasons in scientific discussions. The guidelines are meant to ensure that research in which the guidelines are respected will lead to relevant information concerning the question that the research aims to answer. If an interview is conducted wrongly, the interviewer may influence the answers that she will receive in an improper way and the answers cannot provide relevant information. If the wrong statistical techniques are used, the results will not be relevant for the question the researcher wants to answer. If an experiment is conducted under wrong circumstances, the outcome of the experiment will be unreliable and therefore irrelevant. If a lawyer bases his research on the wrong sources (or no sources at all) he cannot be sure to arrive at a right answer to his question, and so on.

The claim concerning scientific method that is put forward here is that a method consists first and foremost of one or more standards by means of which the relevance of information as support for a particular conclusion can be evaluated. In a derived sense, a method is a set of guidelines on how research is to be conducted in order to obtain this relevant information.

C. The Toulmin Scheme

In a critical discussion of the traditional syllogistic model of arguments, Toulmin developed a scheme that represents the layout of arguments as he saw it.[6] This 'Toulmin scheme' has become quite influential in argumentation theory,[7]

---

[5] The Encyclopedia Britannica defines scientific method as 'mathematical and experimental techniques employed in the natural sciences; more specifically, techniques used in the construction and testing of scientific hypotheses', available at http://www.britannica.com/EBchecked/topic/528929/scientific-method (last accessed on 25 March 2013). Kuno Lorenz defines a 'Methode' as 'in nach Mittel und Zweck planmässiges (= methodisches) Verfahren, das zu technischer Fertigkeit bei der Lösung theoretischer und praktischer Aufgaben führt', Lemma 'Methode' in J Mittelstrass (ed), *Enzyklopädie Philosophie und Wissenschaftstheorie* (Stuttgart, JB Metzler, 1995) Teil 2, 876.

[6] S Toulmin, 'The Layout of Arguments' in S Toulmin, *The Uses of Argument* (Cambridge, Cambridge University Press, 1958) 94–145.

[7] See D Hitchcock and B Verheij (eds), *Arguing on the Toulmin Model. New Essays in Argument Analysis and Evaluation* (Dordrecht, Springer, 2006).

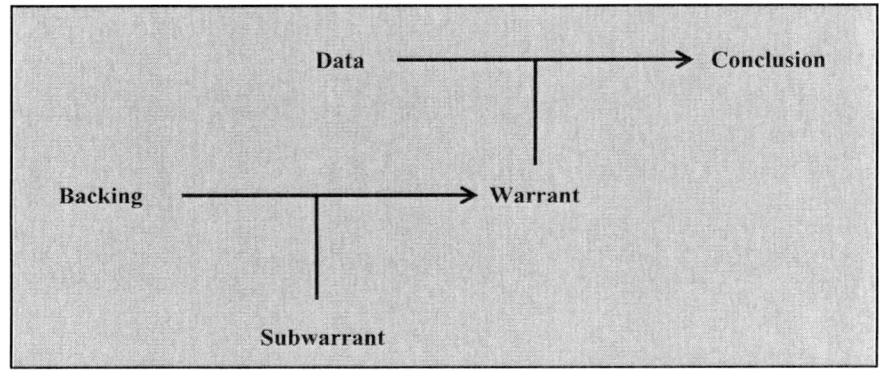

Figure 1

and it can also be used to provide more insight in the nature of a scientific method. A slightly adapted version of the scheme is presented in Figure 1.

The main idea behind this schema is that the two 'premises' in a syllogistic argument fulfil different roles. One premise, represented as 'data', contains factual information. The other premise, represented as 'warrant', indicates that the data are relevant for the conclusion. A legal example would be that the data contain the information that Harold is a shoplifter, and that the warrant informs us that shoplifters are punishable. Together, the data and the warrant allow us to derive, provisionally, that Harold is punishable. Notice that in Toulmin's interpretation the warrant is not a statement. It does not, for instance, tell us that all shoplifters are punishable. It indicates that the fact that somebody is a shoplifter warrants us to conclude that this person is punishable.

The warrant indicates which data are relevant for the conclusion. The set of all warrants for the conclusion that somebody is punishable determines the set of facts from which punishability can be concluded. This makes it possible to formulate guidelines for collecting data that support a particular conclusion. Such a guideline might, for instance, be: collect data that show that somebody did something that was declared punishable in the penal code.

Warrants are a kind of inference rules. They inform us what can be concluded from particular data, or—conversely—what kind of data is required in order to support a particular conclusion. Warrants are not descriptive sentences that can be true or false. It is therefore not possible to establish the 'truth' of a warrant by means of sensory perception or any other technique to acquire factual information. However, the use of a warrant can be justified by adducing information which links the data to the conclusion of the warrant. Such information might, for instance, be that the penal code contains a provision that makes shoplifters punishable. This information consists of data, but Toulmin uses a special name ('backing') for the data that support the use of a warrant. Since a backing also consists of data, its relevance must be supported by another warrant. In the scheme above, this is indicated as 'subwarrant'.[8]

D. Method and Domain

The backing of a warrant must make it plausible that the facts that are identified by the warrant as relevant for the conclusion are indeed relevant. As Toulmin pointed out, this makes backings domain dependent.[9] An inference rule (warrant) in the field of logic needs a different kind of support than one in the field of history, and an inference rule in physics requires another justification than one in law. It may also be the case that rules from different jurisdictions or different legal traditions need different justifications. This is an important observation, and to make its implications explicit we will take a closer look at some examples.

(i) Logic

In deductive logic, an argument is valid if it is (logically) impossible that all the premises of the argument are true while the conclusion is false. A system of deductive logic is usually characterised in two ways. One way (the semantics) focuses on the truth values of the premises and the conclusion of arguments. Semantics makes it possible to determine whether a particular sentence (the intended conclusion of an argument) must be true if a set of other sentences (the intended premises of the argument) are true.

The other way (the inference system) contains one or more inference rules. These inference rules specify which sentences may be derived from one or more (other) sentences. An important demand on logical systems is that the inference rules only allow the derivation of conclusions which must be true if the premises from which they were derived are true. The inference system must 'match' with the semantics. Logical systems which satisfy this demand are called 'sound'.[10] Soundness is a crucial characteristic for systems of deductive logic and therefore the justification of an inference rule consists in pointing out that the rule only allows one to derive true conclusions from true prem-

---

[8] Toulmin himself does not discuss the notion of a subwarrant, but the account of it given here sits well in his model of argumentation. Obviously, the subwarrant can also be supported by a backing and a subsubwarrant, and so on. Toulmin's model of argumentation is hierarchical and suffers from the drawback that it may lead to an infinite regress. This problem can be solved by replacing the hierarchical model by a coherentist one, but a discussion of this possibility is beyond the scope of this chapter. Interested readers are referred to JC Hage, 'The Method of a Truly Normative Legal Science' in M Van Hoecke (ed), *Methodologies of Legal Research. What Kind of Method for What Kind of Discipline?* (Oxford, Hart Publishing, 2011) 19–44 and to J Hage, 'Three Kinds of Coherentism' in M Araszkiewicz and J Šavelka (eds), *Coherence: Insights from Philosophy, Jurisprudence and Artificial Intelligence* (Dordrecht, Springer, 2013) 1–32.

[9] *The Uses of Argument*, above n 6, 104.

[10] NJJ Smith, *Logic. The Laws of Truth* (Princeton, Princeton University Press, 2012) 358.

ises. The backing for a logical inference rule (warrant) should therefore contain that information.

(ii) Physics

The warrants in physics are the physical laws which physical research aims to discover. There are several ways in which the adoption of such laws can be justified. One is that a law is derived from other laws. A famous example is that Kepler's laws about the movement of planets around the sun are justified by deriving them from Newtonian mechanics.[11] A second way is to argue that empirical data inductively support the adoption of a law.[12] And a third way is to argue that a hypothetical law has been tested thoroughly by deriving observable consequences from it, but was nevertheless not falsified.[13]

In particular, the second and third ways of justifying the adoption of a physical law are based on the assumption that the laws themselves may not be amenable to perception, but that their effects are. The question is then how to 'derive' the law from its observable effects. The inductive/support approach and the deductive/falsification approach differ fundamentally in their answers to this question, but they share the presupposition that the justification of physical laws lies in an argument based on the observable effects of the presumed laws.

(iii) Social Sciences

One of the aims of social sciences is to make human behaviour understandable.[14] These sciences may, for example, be used to explain why people in a cemetery are dressed in black. A possible explanation would be based on the warrant that people who attend funerals are often dressed in black, and this warrant can be supported by the data that people who attend funerals tend to be mourning and that black is the conventional colour to show mourning. These data show that wearing black is a rational thing to do under the circumstances. In general, data which show that a warrant is in conformity with the demands of rationality are suitable to justify the use of this warrant.

---

[11] See http://en.wikipedia.org/wiki/Kepler's_laws_of_planetary_motion#Relation_to_Newton.27s_laws (last accessed on 14 July 2013).

[12] G Haas, 'Induktion' in *Enzyklopädie Philosophie und Wissenschaftstheorie* 2, 232–34; AF Chalmers, *What Is This Thing Called Science?*, 3rd edn (Indianapolis, Hacket, 1999) 41–58.

[13] Chalmers, ibid, 59–73.

[14] More ambitious accounts of social science aim to find laws that govern social reality, just like the laws in physical reality. See H Kincaid, 'Defending Laws in the Social Sciences' in M Martin and LC McIntyre (eds), *Readings in the Philosophy of Social Science* (Cambridge, MA, MIT Press, 1994) 111–30.

(iv) Law

In law, warrants are often legal rules. The adoption of a rule as a valid legal one can, according to legal positivists, be justified by pointing out that the rule can be found in a recognised source of law, such as a judicial decision, legislation or a treaty.[15] There are also other legal warrants, such as legal principles, which are identified on the basis of their content, not their origin.[16]

(v) In General

As the above examples illustrate, different knowledge domains require different kinds of data to support warrants that allow inferences in these domains. The reason is that the relevancy of data as support for a warrant depends on the nature of the domain. The use of a warrant should lead to true, or at least reliable, conclusions, and warrants should therefore only be accepted if their use leads to such conclusions. The nature of a knowledge domain determines what kind of warrants satisfy this condition and therefore also which facts must be present if a warrant is to be acceptable. Let me illustrate this using the above examples.

In deductive logic, the domain is completely determined by the semantics which determine the truth values of sentences. Therefore the inference rules must be adapted to the semantics.

In physics, the warrants (the laws) must match the facts, or—better—our observational knowledge about them. That is why physics is considered to be an empirical science and why the facts which match the conditions and the conclusions of physical warrants count as evidence for the acceptability of these warrants.

In social sciences, at least where they are concerned with the understanding of human behaviour, it is presupposed that humans mostly act rationally. Therefore, data which show some behaviour to be rational support warrants that connect factual situations with human behaviour.

In law, finally, the fashionable presupposition is that those rules are valid legal rules which stem from an official source of law. For that reason, data about what these sources are and about the origin of rules (the warrants) in these sources (for example, this rule can be found in the Code Civil, Article such and such) are relevant to support a rule as warrant in legal arguments.

The four knowledge domains—logic, physics, social sciences and law—have been selected as examples because they are quite different in nature. These differences between the domains are reflected in the kinds of warrants (laws, rules) that can be used to obtain knowledge in these domains. Or, to say the

---

[15] J Raz, 'Legal Positivism and the Sources of Law' in J Raz, *The Authority of Law* (Oxford, Clarendon Press, 1979) 37–52.

[16] R Dworkin, 'The Model of Rules I' in R Dworkin, *Taking Rights Seriously* (London, Duckworth, 1978) 14–45.

same thing in method-related terminology, the nature of knowledge domains is an important determinant for the methods to be used in obtaining knowledge about these domains.

(vi) Method and Research Questions

It is not only the knowledge domain that determines the proper method to use in answering research questions; the questions themselves are important, too. The point can be illustrated by means of a legal example. Even if one assumes that the content of the law is determined by the sources that underlie a legal system, it still makes a difference for the method that is to be used whether the research question is descriptive, explanatory or evaluative. The method to look up the law in handbooks, in case law or in legislation is better suited to answer the question what the content of the law is than to explain or evaluate that content. The law may be explained by means of historical data (which problem led to the legislation in question?), by political developments (eg the conquest of Europe by Napoleon) or by (legal-)economic considerations (which rules serve the interests of the land-owning nobility? Which rule is the most efficient one?). And law may be evaluated by predicting the consequences of rules and measuring them against some standard (which rules will promote transnational trade within Europe?).

III. COMPARATIVE LAW AS METHOD

After the lengthy introduction about the nature of scientific method, it is time to address the first question which this chapter aims to answer, namely, whether comparative law is itself a method. Does comparative law research provide us with, in Toulmin's terminology, data that support a conclusion about some other topic? The main alternative for the view that comparative law is a method is that it is a research topic itself. In that case, the question that needs to be addressed is which data are relevant to answer comparative law questions—the question after the method of comparative law. That will be the topic for the next section.[17]

A. Heuristics and Justification

If a method is primarily an indication of which data are relevant to support conclusions in a knowledge domain, then method belongs to the field of justification, as opposed to that of heuristics. The distinction between heuristics and justification (or legitimation, for that matter) has sometimes been depicted

---

[17] The theoretical possibility that comparative law neither is, nor has, a method will be ignored here.

as that between two phases in a research project, and has on that interpretation rightly been criticised for separating two processes which coincide in time. But it is also possible—and, in my eyes, better—to interpret the distinction as being between a process of hypothesis formulation and the 'logic' of justification. Justification in this interpretation is not a process but an argument, and as such can be sharply distinguished from the process of hypothesis formulation.

So, if comparative law is seen as a method, it has nothing to do with the process of doing comparative research. On this view, comparative law is seen as an amount of data which is typically collected by doing comparative legal research and is relevant for some conclusion. If one sees comparative law as a process of doing research, then, on this view, comparative law is not a method.

If comparative law is considered to be a method, the next question is which conclusions can be supported or justified by data obtained from comparative law research.[18]

B. Which Conclusions are Supported by the Results of Comparative Law?

Obviously many kinds of conclusions can be supported by the results of comparative law. To mention just one example, one might draw conclusions about the desirability to educate more lawyers in one country than in another, based on an investigation about the relative complexity of the countries' legal systems. Rather than trying to list all of the possible conclusions for which comparative law research might provide relevant data—an impossible task—it seems more useful to characterise in general some issues for which comparative law may, or may not, provide supportive information. The more interesting questions for our present purposes are legal ones. The question is then narrowed down to whether comparative law is a legal method.

Let me start by excluding an important field. It is obvious that comparative law research provides interesting results for comparative law questions. For instance, one should conduct comparative research if one wants to know whether and how the 'defects of will' (eg fraud and mistake) are regulated differently in Germany and in the UK.[19] However, comparative law does not then function as a method for some particular domain, but rather as the object of research.[20]

---

[18] Note the difference between this method-related question and the wider question addressed by K Zweigert and H Kötz, *An Introduction to Comparative Law*, 3rd edn (Oxford, Clarendon Press, 1998) 13–14 (after the functions of comparative law).

[19] See R Sefton-Green (ed), *Mistake, Fraud and Duties to Inform in European Contract Law* (Cambridge, Cambridge University Press, 2005).

[20] I mention this seemingly obvious point since I discovered that some PhD students in Maastricht considered the results of comparative law relevant for their research, because the topics of their PhD theses were comparative by nature.

That comparative law is a legal method is not obvious.[21] Most legal questions deal with the content of a particular legal system, whether it be national, subnational, supranational or international. Why would comparative information be relevant for the answers to these questions? One would expect that answers on questions about the positive law of a particular legal system can be answered on the basis of information about this legal system alone, and that comparative information does not have much to offer in this connection.[22]

(i) McEvoy's List

Illustrative in this connection is the list of purposes to which comparative law can be put, drawn up by McEvoy.[23] McEvoy lists (and discusses) the following purposes: to find out whether

- European law can be harmonised or unified;
- a particular body of laws (eg the laws of the EU Member States) can become a system;
- the human mind is universal within the broader context of cultural groups and academic disciplines;
- law should be harmonised.

One may agree or disagree with this list of purposes, but none of these questions is a typical legal one. With the exception of the third question, they all have law as their topic, but not one of them deals with the content of law.

(ii) Von Bar's Discussion

In a paper about the comparative law of obligations,[24] Von Bar directly addresses the question to what extent comparative law is used in typical legal contexts. His observations are that 'courts rarely make use of comparative law based arguments', and that legislators sometimes use comparative law:

1. where this can add to the support for a political decision that has already been taken;

---

[21] Here my view seems to diverge from that of M Adams, 'Doing What Doesn't Come Naturally. On the Distinctiveness of Comparative Law' in Van Hoecke, *Methodologies of Legal Research*, above n 8, 229–40. However, Adams informed me in comments on a draft version of this chapter that he hardly considers comparative law worthy of the classification 'method'.

[22] But *cf* JM Smits, 'Comparative Law and its Influence on National Legal Systems' in M Reimann and R Zimmerman (eds), *The Oxford Handbook of Comparative Law* (Oxford, Oxford University Press, 2006) 513–38.

[23] S McEvoy, 'Descriptive and Purposive Categories of Comparative Law' in PG Monateri (ed), *Methods of Comparative Law* (Elgar, Cheltenham, 2012) 144–62.

[24] C von Bar, 'Comparative Law of Obligations: Methodology and Epistemology' in M Van Hoecke (ed), *Epistemology and Methodology of Comparative Law* (Oxford, Hart Publishing, 2004) 123–36.

2. in cases where the national law must harmonise with foreign law because of coordination issues; and

3. to draw inspiration from to solve rather narrow, but socially pressing, problems.

Of these three ways in which a legislator can use comparative law, only the second one (harmonisation) is a case where comparative law data provide a reason why legislation should be made and for its content. We will return to the inspiration issue later. But the main 'legal' use of comparative law, according to Von Bar, is made in academic writings. Von Bar does not indicate, however, whether this use is to justify scientific conclusions or, if so, which kinds of conclusions. He does, however, mention the use of comparative law as a research object.

(iii) In Search for Better Law

A major motivation for conducting comparative law research is to find good, if not the best possible, law.[25] The idea is that information about rules in foreign systems tells us something about the quality of those rules, and about the possibility and the desirability of adopting them in one's own legal system. Indeed, information about how a rule, or—more probable—a set of rules, works, and under which boundary conditions, can be very helpful in evaluating such rules as possible candidates for the own legal system. It should not be forgotten that, for this purpose, the comparative law data should be complemented by one or more standards at the hand of which the evaluation takes place (one cannot just 'see' whether a rule functions well), but this does not detract from the relevancy of comparative law data and therefore of the fruitfulness of comparative law as a method.

Note, however, that this function of comparative law does not lie in describing the law or in justifying legal solutions for particular kinds of cases, but in evaluating rules as possible candidates for some legal system. Only if one treats legal science as a truly normative science, as a science that aims at answering questions such as 'What is the right thing to do?', does this function of comparative law also support the description of law.[26]

(iv) Explaining the Content of Law

There is one branch of comparative law research which clearly contributes to the explanation of the content of law, and that is research on legal

---

[25] Zweigert and Kötz, above n 18, 15.
[26] See J Hage, 'The Method of a Truly Normative Legal Science' in Van Hoecke, *Methodologies of Legal Research*, above n 8, 19–44.

transplants.[27] Another type of explanatory research for which comparative law may be useful is the attempt to explain developments in law from factors, legal or non-legal. If particular factors go hand in hand with particular developments in law in a similar way in different jurisdictions, this provides support for the conclusion that these factors caused the developments.

(v) Harmonisation of Law in Europe

A particularly important source of inspiration for comparative law research has been the attempts to harmonise law—in particular, private law—in Europe. Yet it is not clear beforehand how comparative law data would be relevant for conclusions about harmonisation. McEvoy writes that such data would be relevant for deciding whether European law can be harmonised, but if that is true, it is only so under particular assumptions.

European private law can 'easily' be harmonised by introducing a single civil code that is declared binding for all EU Member States. The content of that code could, within certain boundaries of what is reasonable, be arbitrary. Most likely, there would be much resistance against such a move, and there is much to be said against introducing a civil code in this way. But if one wants information that is relevant for answering the question how a uniform European civil code can successfully be introduced, the required information would be of the prediction type. It should answer the question under what circumstances, including the content of the code, could a uniform private law code be introduced in Europe without causing too much resistance. It seems doubtful whether comparative law research would provide the most relevant information in this connection.

Things would, of course, be different if Europe were to strive for a common private law, which is by and large the greatest common factor of the private law systems of the Member States. Some proposals, such as the Draft Common Frame of Reference,[28] may create this impression. Whether such compromises would lead to good law remains to be seen, though.[29]

Much more likely is that comparative research inspires the design of suitable European private law. But providing inspiration belongs to the field of heuristics, rather than to the field of legitimation and method.

---

[27] J Fedtke, 'Legal Transplants' in JM Smits (ed), *Elgar Encyclopedia of Comparative Law*, 2nd edn (Northampton, Edward Elgar, 2012) 550–54; M Graziadei, 'Comparative Law as the Study of transplants and Receptions' in M Reimann and R Zimmerman (eds), *The Oxford Handbook of Comparative Law* (Oxford University Press, Oxford, 2006) 441–76.

[28] C von Bar, E Clive and H Schulte-Nölke (eds), *Principles, Definitions and Model Rules of European Private Law. Draft Common Frame of Reference (DCFR)* (München, Sellier European Law Publishers, outline edition, 2009).

[29] See R Rijgersberg and H van der Kaaij, 'A Plea for Rigorous Conceptual Analysis as a Central Method in Transnational Law Design' (2013) 1 *Recht en Methode in onderzoek en onderwijs* 48.

C. Comparative Law as a Heuristic Tool[30]

Scientific method has to do with the testing and selection of hypotheses, and requires a set of pre-existing hypotheses as the fuel on which to run. Scientific method does not generate the hypotheses itself; there is no method for framing correct hypotheses. Nevertheless, the availability of good hypotheses is crucial for science, because scientific method consists of selecting the best hypothesis from the ones available. Without good 'fuel', the process of generating good scientific knowledge cannot fly. Although there is no method which can guarantee the production of good hypotheses, there are techniques to increase the chance that good hypotheses are generated. Such techniques are called 'heuristics'.[31] Heuristics can take many forms, varying from having a good night's sleep, via taking some alcoholic drinks to increase inspiration, to studying the already available hypotheses and their shortcomings.

This last heuristic in particular is often very fruitful. Indeed, it is seldom possible to devise fruitful hypotheses as potential answers to research questions if one is not familiar with the problem field and the theories (that is, as yet non-refuted hypotheses) circulating in it. Here lies an important role for comparative law, because it is highly possible to view the law of different jurisdictions as so many hypotheses about the most viable solution for some societal problem.[32] The experiences with these regulations provide indications about the quality of the solutions, and suggest what should be maintained and where improvement is desirable. In other words, the study of comparative law can be a valuable heuristic tool. That has nothing to do, however, with comparative law as a method.

IV. THE METHOD OF COMPARATIVE LAW

A. The Need for 'Deep Level' Comparison

The literature of comparative law contains many contributions which claim to deal with the method(s) of comparative law. A large part of the discussion deals with the issue how 'deep' the comparison between different systems

---

[30] This subsection was taken from J Hage, 'Comparative Law and Legal Science' in AW Heringa and B Akkermans (eds), *Educating European Lawyers* (Cambridge, Intersentia, 2011) 65–77.

[31] The idea of heuristics was elaborated in I Lakatos, 'Falsification and the Methodology of Scientific Research Programs' in I Lakatos and A Musgrave (eds), *Criticism and the Growth of Knowledge* (Cambridge, Cambridge University Press, 1970) 91–196. More recently it has gained widespread popularity in artificial intelligence, in connection with intelligent search. *Cf* J Haugeland, *Artificial Intelligence. The Very Idea* (Cambridge, MA, MIT Press, 1989) 176–79.

[32] This is also stressed in Smits, 'Comparative Law and its Influence', above n 22.

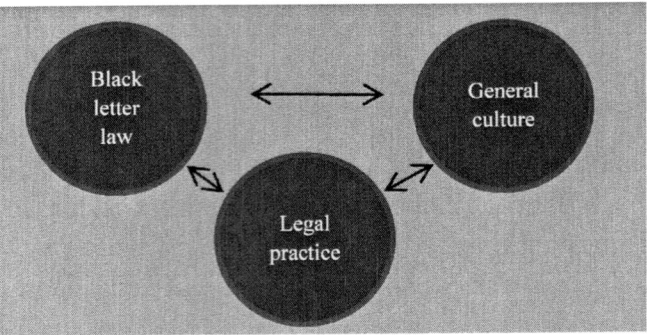

Figure 2

should go.[33] The nature of the issue is perhaps most easily illustrated by means of a small schema (Figure 2).

Part of the law of a jurisdiction is black letter law (treaties, legislation, case law). The operation of this black letter law depends on how legal agents (judges, barristers, legislators, etc) use it in their work. And this, in turn, depends on the general culture of the country or region within which the law and the legal agents must function. Moreover, the law and the behaviour of legal agents are themselves determinants of the general culture. So what we in fact have is a complex interrelation between—at least[34]—general culture, black letter law and the work of legal agents. The discussion on how comparative law research should be conducted deals to a large extent with the question of what should be taken into consideration in the research. Is it possible—or desirable—to compare only individual rules or doctrines of black letter law, or should one also take into account how these rules are used in legal practice, or even look at the background general culture too ('deep level' comparison)? A related question is whether it is really possible for a comparativist to understand a foreign culture and therefore—assuming the relevance of this culture to the investigation—to understand foreign law. As we will see, these questions, formulated in a general way, make little sense.

B. If Comparative Law is a Method

If comparative law is used as a method—that is, if comparative data are used as reasons to support a particular conclusion—the precise comparative data

---

[33] *Cf* the title of Van Hoecke's insightful paper 'Deep Level Comparative Law' in M Van Hoecke (ed), *Epistemology and Methodology of Comparative Law* (Oxford, Hart Publishing 2004) 165–96.

[34] No doubt it can be argued that even more factors are at work in this interaction, but the three mentioned figure most prominently in the comparatist literature.

that are required will depend on the conclusion that is supported. For example, if the research question is whether the legislation of a particular country has been influenced by the legislation of another country, it does not make sense to look at the way in which legal agents deal with this legislation, or even at the different cultures in which the legislation must function. This may be different, though, if one also wants to explain why such influence is present. And if the question is whether it makes sense to transplant insolvency law or marital law from, say, Germany to China, which have widely different cultures, it is almost certain that the general culture must be taken into account too. If comparative law functions as a method, the reason why comparative law was adopted will also indicate what kind of comparative law should be used.

C. If Comparison is the Research Question

It is very possible that comparative research is not done in order to answer non-comparative questions, but that comparison itself constitutes the purpose of an investigation. This is the case, for instance, if one wants to know whether the definitions of crimes are more concrete in one country than in another country, what the role of good faith is in the contract law of different jurisdictions,[35] what the relation is between intention and negligence (culpa) in criminal law,[36] or how the laws of different jurisdictions deal with divorce.

If an investigation is aimed at answering such comparative research questions, it depends one one's view of the research domain and on the research question which data are relevant for answering the question. For instance, if one wants to compare the definitions of crimes in the UK with those of Polynesia, one must first decide how to deal with crime definitions in the common law—a decision which must be rely on a view about the principle of legality in criminal law and its relation to judge-defined crimes. This is part of a theory about the nature of criminal law. And if one wants to investigate how different jurisdictions deal with divorce, one must decide—and make one's research question accordingly more specific—whether the question only concerns the law, or whether it takes in the law as part of the different cultures in general. Depending on how the law is defined and on the research question that must be answered, different sets of data may be relevant and different ways of conducting research may be appropriate. But there is no generally applicable method for conducting research that aims at answering comparative law questions.[37]

---

[35] R Zimmerman and S Whittaker (eds), *Good Faith in European Contract Law* (Cambridge, Cambridge University Press, 2000).

[36] GP Fletcher, *Basic Concepts of Criminal Law* (New York, Oxford University Press, 1998).

[37] A similar view seems to transpire from the title of Van Hoecke's *Methodologies of Legal Research. What Kind of Method for What Kind of Discipline?*, above n 8.

V. CONCLUSIONS

Two questions were central in this chapter:

1. Is comparative law a method for legal research?
2. Does comparative law have a proper method of its own?

By way of an extensive preliminary, the second section of this chapter addressed the nature of a scientific method. The first step in this connection was to distinguish between method in the primary sense and method in a derived sense.

Method in the primary sense is a set of standards that determine what are relevant data on the basis of which research question is to be answered. This characterisation of scientific method was elaborated using the Toulmin scheme—in particular, the distinction between data and warrant.

Method in the derived sense consists of a number of concrete guidelines on how to conduct research, and more specifically on which data to collect and how to collect them.

Based on the Toulmin scheme, it was argued that the appropriate method depends on the knowledge domain, and on the research question that is to be answered.

The first of the two research questions of this chapter was answered cautiously in the affirmative. Comparative law can play some role in evaluating actual or potential rules of law, for instance by showing what the effects of these rules are in different jurisdictions. Although the attempts to harmonise European private law have no doubt boosted comparative law research, it is not very clear how this kind of research would contribute to this harmonisation, unless as a source of inspiration.

Finally, there is a clear role for comparative law data in explaining the content of law, especially where legal transplants are at stake.

There are thus some legal research questions for which data resulting from comparative law research are relevant in the sense that they can be used to justify the answers. But comparative law can play a more important role as a source of inspiration to formulate hypotheses that must derive their justification from other kinds of research.

The second of the questions has no general answer. There are many ways of conducting proper comparative law research, but the method for doing so depends strongly on the purpose for which comparative law research is performed (whether it is used as method itself or as a heuristic tool), on the view one has of the particular domain on which the comparative research is performed and on the research question one aims to answer. The conclusion must be that there is no such thing as the single proper way of conducting comparative law research.

4

Research Designs of Comparative Law— Methodology or Heuristics?

JAAKKO HUSA

I. INTRODUCTION

COMPARATIVE LAW IS practised in many branches of law, and for many different aims and purposes. Due to this variety, it is impossible to make a definition that would be universal and appropriate in every situation. Despite the variety, a reasonably universal definition can be made. It corresponds sufficiently well with the view that the great majority of comparatists hold about comparative law. However, such perception is inevitably a kind of mainstream average that is necessary for getting an insight into the nature of the methodology in the field. Here, the mainstream of comparative law roughly refers to such comparative law that had its origin in the early nineteenth century, when extensive national codifications in civil law were undertaken in mainland Europe, specifically in Germany and France. Modern academic comparative law as we know it today is largely the offspring of legal thinking born in the nineteenth century. Before that time, the systematic and scientific nature of comparing laws had not been a cognisant goal. When the continental legal doctrine was transformed, comparative law also changed: it became more scientific. We can thus speak about the scientification or academisation of comparative law as a discipline.[1]

In spite of the above-mentioned scientification, the basic idea of legal comparison appears rather uncomplicated. Schlesinger has summed it up well: 'To compare means to observe and to explain similarities as well as differ-

---

[1] Paradigmatic representative of this line of thinking is most likely: K Zweigert's and H Kötz's *Introduction to Comparative Law*, 2nd edn (Oxford University Press, Oxford, 1998). Its original version was published in German at the beginning of the 1970s and since then it has been translated into numerous other languages.

ences'.[2] In other words, it is a question of similarities and differences found in comparison, and attempts to explain the reasons for the differences and similarities. The basic idea itself is plain, but the practical realisation is not always so simple. This is due, to a great extent, to the nature of comparison, which consists of several different phases that are not always logically related or follow each other in a consistent manner.

Comparison contains several phases, so the study of comparative law has to be conceived of as a research process.[3] Comparative study is a creative chain of research processes where progressive understanding of the research objects is typical. The comparison process can be seen as a series of steps that are carried out by the comparatist and result in a conclusion, ie a rational reconstruction of the systems under comparison.[4]

In general, the scientific research process follows a certain predetermined procedure whereby the study of the research subject is followed, after intermediate phases (data collection, analysis, etc), by reporting of the results.[5] In the case of comparative law, there are no straightforward processes. There are bound to be setbacks, and the researcher inevitably has to back off and reinterpret or dismiss conclusions made earlier. It is also noteworthy that process phases are interdependent. This means that the next phase of the process can have a complementary effect on the previous phase or can even change it completely. Comparative study is in a continuous epistemological stir. Reading and interpreting source literature, acquiring additional information and comparing the legal information from different sources aim at contributing to progress made in charting the differences and similarities, as well as in the attempt to give them rational explanations. Different phases take their turn, and every now and then it is necessary to return to the original assumptions—this is, in fact, a hermeneutical spiral.[6]

Yet the spiral nature of the research process is not that uncommon. All research processes contain phases where it is necessary to impose limitations, and make choices and specifications that have an effect on the progression of the process. Van Hoecke points out that, in principle, legal research does not differ from other disciplines as far as the main methodological aspects go.[7]

---

[2] RB Schlesinger, 'The Past and Future of Comparative Law' (1995) 43 *American Journal of Comparative Law* 477.

[3] *Cf* M Adams, 'Wat de rechtsvergelijking vermag—Over onderzoeksdesign' (2011) 60 *Aers Aequi* 192 (distinguishing different phases of research).

[4] *Cf* J Bell, 'Legal Research and Comparative Law' in M Van Hoecke (ed), *Methodologies of Legal Research* (Oxford, Hart Publishing, 2011) 167–71.

[5] According to this line of thinking, theories must be tested by observation and only empirical testing offers (inductive) confirmation of a theory: see I Niiniluoto and R Tuomela (eds), *The Logic of Epistemology of Scientific Change* (Helsinki, Acta Philosophica Fennica, 1973).

[6] On the hermeneutical spiral see GR Osborne, *The Hermeneutical Spiral: A Comprehensive Introduction to Biblical Interpretation* (InterVarsity, Downers Grove, IL, 1991) appendices 1 and 2.

[7] M Van Hoecke, 'Legal Doctrine: Which Method(s) for What Legal Discipline' in Van Hoecke, *Methodologies of Legal Research*, above n 4, 11 (ascertaining and discovery of facts, construction of hypotheses/theories).

The comparatist also has to make choices, which determine how the research proceeds. A decision has to be made on which legal systems are compared and which elements are selected for the comparison. What is the material like (extent/depth) and which factors determine its acquisition? How is the material acquired? How far does the researcher's knowledge of languages carry? Is empirical field research needed or is it possible to manage the project by using only documental materials that already exist? The choices that are made depend on the aims set for the comparison, as well as on the comparatist's own research interests (knowledge interest, ie *Erkenntnisinteresse*). The availability of source material—not only understanding it—is also of importance in this respect.

II. METHOD—METHODOLOGY

Comparative law as a target-oriented action aimed at new knowledge cannot commence from completely haphazard starting points. Accordingly, both before the research and also during it, methodological choices that are related to the manner the topic will be studied have to be made concerning the acquisition and utilisation of the research material. One of the basic characteristics of scientific research is the systematical nature in which the problem is approached and maximal justifiability of methods is sought. It is essential that the selected approaches to the problem are justified openly and rationally. The role of advance planning cannot be exaggerated. The comparatist also needs a predetermined basic strategy by means of which the research design of comparison, as well as the viability of the research results that comparison possibly brings about, is strengthened.

But what do we mean when we speak of method? The method can refer to a scientific research method with a very specific scientific definition, in which case methodology refers to a study of such scientific methods. A method according to this view is a special way by means of which a chain of study functions that take specified steps towards a predetermined goal are made. In natural sciences, exactness, accurate measurements and prediction of phenomena are emphasised. This model is followed in many disciplines. For example, economics is strongly based on scientific modelling and statistical methods. However, in legal research, the concepts of method and methodology are inevitably broader, just like in other cultural studies. The versatility of method as a concept has its origin in the word method itself: the word is a combination of Greek words *metá* (μετά) and *odós* (οδός), which refer to walking along a path or following a certain route. Together, these words form *méthodos* (μέθοδος), or method. Method in connection to comparative law means all the practices and operations by means of which pieces of information about the phenomena are collected, and the justifiable principles with which interpretations of research objectives are made and on which argumentation is based. Due to the plurality of law, it is also a question of a plural matter, or method<u>s</u>.

Because of the ultimate research objective of comparative law, ie legal culture, the method cannot be explained by emphasising only its accuracy, which is done in natural sciences. It really is a path to be followed. Therefore, methodological hints and instructions have to be understood as hints on how to follow the path. Simply because the study topics and study interests differ from one researcher to another, it is not possible to present a normative accurate methodology in comparative law.

Örücü has made an appropriate comment on the methodology of comparative law: 'how this comparison is to be carried out has no standard answer'. According to her, speaking of methodology of comparative law cannot be accurate; instead, we should speak about 'methods employed in comparative law research'.[8] Yet, regardless of the limitations, it is possible to propose methodological guidelines of some kind. It is obviously true that points of view vary between research topics. According to Bradley, for example, the comparative family can be related to social sciences: 'Comparative legal studies in this area involve applied political analysis: as such comparative family law qualifies as social science'.[9]

In spite of the above, the crude starting point for comparative law is possibly not so obscure. Comparative law can in principle make use of any method that can be used to find answers to questions that interest comparatists. In general, the research process of comparative law is hermeneutic, ie understanding, in nature. The hermeneutic approach is used because the aim is to understand and interpret a person's or institution's legally relevant behaviour, legal culture or legal text, and to understand the meanings conveyed by legal language. This kind of approach is also typical to research in qualitative social science and humanities.[10]

The fact that in comparative law the ultimate aim is to explain differences and similarities does not make it any the less hermeneutic; the question is what kind of research process is needed for legal cultural explanation.[11] Explanation becomes possible through understanding, since statistics does not replace the creative research process of the comparatist. Even though statistical information is useful, and in most cases is underused in comparative law, the comparatist must remember that there are no statistics that could

---

[8] E Örücü, 'Methodology of Comparative Law' in JM Smits (ed), *Elgar Encyclopedia of Comparative Law* (Cheltenham, Edward Elgar, 2006) 446.

[9] D Bradley, 'Family Law' in Smits, ibid, 333.

[10] See, eg EA Kinsella, 'Hermeneutics and Critical Hermeneutics' (2006) 7 *Forum Qualitative Sozialforschung/Forum: Qualitative Social Research* 19, available at http://nbn-resolving.de/urn:nbn:de:0114-fqs0603190.

[11] *Cf* Bell, above n 4, 167–69.

explain, for example, why judges feel bound to the doctrine of legal sources of their country.[12]

Now, we can at least distinguish different broad research strategies or research designs. The basic strategies of comparative research can be divided into two categories according to qualitative criteria. Strategy here means simply a plan by means of which attempts are made to reach the goals set for comparison. On the one hand, methodological choices of a technical nature have to be made, while, on the other hand, strategic choices of a theoretical nature must be carried out.[13] They do not necessarily follow each other in strict chronological order but, rather, take turns throughout the research process. Keeping them separate is not unproblematic either, because the theoretical approach and technical dimension are often interrelated, as pointed out above.

III. TECHNICAL METHODOLOGICAL DESIGN

The technical nature of methodological choices in comparative law refers to the close connection that the choices have to the research material (data). The research material in this connection can be enacted law, data about the application practices of law and traditional/customary law or (empirical) attitudes and beliefs of those who operate in the legal professions. In making strategic choices of a technical nature, the researcher makes decisions that to a great extent determine what will be the nature, extent and method of acquisition of the research material. These questions are of such a nature that they have to be considered before the actual collection of material and data begins.

On the basic level, there are at least five different technical choices (listed below). These phases can alternate during the research process, and the comparatist can end up changing the basic solution made at the start. The list is not exhaustive, but it probably covers the most common research design choices that have to be made in practical methodology.

A) Micro/macro
B) Longitudinal/traverse
C) Multilateral/bilateral
D) Vertical/horizontal
E) Monocultural/multicultural

The micro/macro dimension is related to the extent to which different judicial systems are compared; in other words, it is fundamentally a question of scale, or micro/macro dimension. On the micro level, it is possible to compare certain institutions (eg marriage, contracts) or special issues, while on the macro

---

[12] For a more detailed account see R Michaels, 'Comparative Law by Numbers?' (2009) 57 *American Journal of Comparative Law* 765.

[13] These distinctions and the following text are based on J Husa, *Oikeusvertailu—teoria ja metodologia* (Helsinki, Lakimiesliiton kustannus, 2013) [*Comparative Law—Theory and Method*].

level it is the function of legal systems and their fundamental characteristics that are compared.[14] In a standard comparative law setting, the comparison is between modern systems, where the main interest is not in the legal system of the past. When comparative law is of practical nature, it is often also traverse, because the court or legislator pursuing a legal solution is usually not *ex officio* interested in the rules and regulations or legal history of the past. On the other hand, longitudinal comparison takes its point of comparison from legal history, and therefore it is often more theoretical of nature and aims at general knowledge. In longitudinal comparative law (comparative legal history), the research compares one or more judicial systems in different periods of time.[15]

The basic strategic solution of comparative law is of a technical nature and can be related to the sources of research material (the number of legal systems), in addition to the time or depth dimension. In bilateral comparative law, the comparison is carried out between (at the most) two legal judicial systems. The advantage of bilateral comparison is concentration on a very limited amount of material, which means that only two cases are studied, but they are studied thoroughly. The aim in such cases is to get as deep as possible into the legal systems under study by getting acquainted with their predominant doctrines, the interpretations generally made and the historical development.[16] In multilateral comparative law, the comparison takes place between more than two legal systems. Such an approach can be called variable-oriented research, the main advantage of which is the great number of research objectives compared. This means that the generalisability level of the information improves, but the weakness of the depth level is a problem. In the variable-oriented study it is not easy to get below the surface, and the research can easily become just an organised description of statute law.

Verticality and horizontalism are connected to the question concerning the diversity of judicial systems. National legal systems are not the only legal systems, but legal systems can also be on other levels. Legal systems can be classified on the national–international axis, although this classification is rough and losing significance. An increasing number of national norms are indebted to international law in terms of content, or arise from it in some other way. Also, the supranational law that EU law represents when it forms its own legal order that is independent of national and international law has to be added to the axis, whereas the competence of international organisations

[14] See, eg G Cuniberti, *Grand systémes de droit contemporains* (Paris, LGDJ, 2011) 13 ('À un niveau micro-juridique, il est tout d'abord possible de comparer des institutions particuliéres, ou des questions particuliéres . . . À ce niveau macro-juridique la comparaison a alors pour objet le fonctionnement des systémes juridiques, et leurs caractéristiques fondamentales').

[15] See D Ibbetson, 'The Challenges of Comparative Legal History' (2013) 1 *Comparative Legal History* 1.

[16] M de SO-L Lasser's *Judicial Deliberations—A Comparative Analysis of Judicial Transparency and Legitimacy* (Oxford, Oxford University Press, 2004) is an example of a case study concentrating on a small number of cases. Lasser studies comparatively the French Cour de cassation, the US Supreme Court and the European Court of Justice.

is usually limited by the national sovereignty of the Member States. There are also, for example, the Hindu, Islamic and Jewish customs of family law that are applied in cultural subcommunities, as well as the customary rules of indigenous peoples, which lack official recognition in spite of their empirical efficiency.

Horizontal comparison deals with comparison of legal systems (eg on the national level USA–Finland–France) that are on the same level with regard to quality. It is a question of comparison between the legal systems of states. Vertical comparison, on the other hand, takes place between legal systems that are on qualitatively different levels, so that comparison can concern, say, the guarantee of impartial legal proceedings offered by, for example, international law, EU law or the legal system of the UK. The starting points for vertical comparison are (i) the existence of different legal systems and (ii) the parallelism and entrenched nature of different legal systems. The more pluralism there is, the more there are polycentric levels of entrenched normative orders, the interrelations of which are not to be organised by means of simple hierarchy.[17] It must also be understood that different norms adapt to each other and change somewhat in their interaction with each other. For example, with their decisions, common law courts can change customary law or business practices into precedents.[18] On the other hand, in a civil law country the legislator can codify precedents.

Culture can have a different role as part of a research process of comparative law. One of the basic choices for comparison can be the decision of what cultural grounds are used when legal systems are selected for comparison. When, for example, Western and non-Western legal systems are compared, it is a case of intercultural comparative law. Whether, in other aspects, the systems belong to the same, more general cultural sphere does not have a decisive impact because the decisive factor is the nature of the legal system (or, more restrictedly, the nature of some limited field of law). Comparison is internal when it takes place between two or more legal systems belonging to the same legal culture. The choice between these two basic methods depends—in the same way as with the previous choices—on the aims and purposes of the comparison and the comparatist's own aspirations and preferences. Language skills

---

[17] See J Husa, 'The Method is Dead, Long Live the Methods—European Polynomia and Pluralist Methodology' (2011) 5 *Legisprudence* 249.

[18] In recent years, research and discussion on comparative law have brought about several themes and fields of study that differ from the vertical or traditional comparison between states, which earlier was mainstream. This is partly due to globalisation of law and to some extent to legal integration in Europe. We are now talking about comparative law that is different from the old one but has several characteristics that are typical of the earlier comparative law: desire to cross national borders in search of information, a pluralistic view on sources of law and multiculturalism, as well as methodological openness in comparison to national legal doctrinal study of law. The most interesting and challenging of these new horizons is the so-called transnational or global law. It is not just a new area of judicial regulation but also a new way to perceive law unrestricted by vertical levels. See R Michaels, 'The True Lex Mercatoria: Law Beyond the State' (2007) 14 *Indiana Journal of Global Legal Studies* 447.

(the capacity to make use of legal information material in foreign languages) are also of importance. Furthermore, the availability and comprehensibility of the material can influence the choice.[19]

IV. THEORETICAL METHODOLOGICAL DESIGN

The theoretical methodological choices usually have to be made when the research material has been collected and some idea of it has been ascertained. The comparatist has gathered legal cultural 'biopsies' of the judicial system that he/she examines. Naturally it is impossible to have an entire legal system or legal systems under study simultaneously; therefore the material gathered (eg provisions, court decisions, information on judicial procedures and legal history) is a kind of reconstruction of the actual topic to be researched. Such a fictive 'biopsy' is also a sample of the legal culture and language from which the comparatist has to form a reconstruction and the source material that he/she would have to be able to deal with when performing research operations.

The first-stage contact with the material takes place before the basic choices of its acquisition are made, but also during its acquisition, systematisation and organisation. Once the comparatist has become familiarised with the first-stage contact material, he/she must form a preliminary idea about how to proceed in the research. The comparatist has to decide on the precise research topic, ie what is compared, how the actual comparison can take place (the *tertium comparationis*, or comparative framework) and what the basic theoretical strategy by means of which the comparison proceeds is. This is the second-stage contact with the material. Basic theoretical-methodological choices have to be made, a more general theoretical frame of reference (common point of comparison) must be constructed and the research topic has to be outlined in greater detail. Obviously, more specific choices cannot be made without a reasonable amount of information to start with. There are at least four such basic choices:

A) Functional comparison
B) Structural comparison
C) Systemic comparison
D) Critical comparison

In functional comparison, the formulation of the problem usually considers the following question: which legal institutions and practices have a similar problem-solving function in the legal systems under study? In functional comparison, the aim is to locate how the same (or almost the same) socio-legal problem X is solved in different legal systems. The provisions and practices

---

[19] See M Van Hoecke and M Warrington, 'Legal Cultures, Legal Paradigms and Legal Doctrine: A New Model for Comparative Law' (1998) 47 *International and Comparative Law Quarterly* 495, 508–13.

compared are selected because it is considered that, by their means, an attempt can be made to solve the same socio-legal problem.[20] In other words, the research design in functional comparative law is based on the (from the comparatist's point of view) factual—not conceptual or terminological—analogy of the institutions, rules and principles.

In the literature, functional comparative law has long held the position of the basic model or paradigm among the theoretical frames of reference, while other models have mainly complemented it. The idea of functional comparison is based on the fact that different provisions, institutions and practices can have similar functions in different legal systems. Provisions and practices that on the face appear to be similar (eg terminological similarities) can have different functions in different legal systems despite their apparent similarity. Curiously, though, comparative law's functionalism has fairly little to do with the forms and applications of functionalism that are recognised in other fields of science.[21]

Functional comparison has been mainstream for a long time, although it has also been heavily criticised.[22] For decades, mainstream comparative law has been based on the recognition of corresponding socio-legal concerns. The standard approach is the comparative research method, which belongs to the sphere of mainstream comparative law research and mainstream theory and is commonly called functional comparative law. This crude method has not developed in a vacuum; it was influenced by practitioners of private international law, and private-law comparatists have polished it into its present form. The approach is still at the centre of mainstream research, although critical comparatists have increasingly criticised it since the late 1990s. However, the problem with this criticism is that the critics have not been able to offer an alternative heuristic rule-of-thumb method that would be at least reasonably clear.[23]

In structural comparison, similar structural elements are searched for (or occasionally an attempt is made to explain their lack).[24] When structurally similar elements are found, they are studied in order to be able to explain what

---

[20] See Zweigert and Kötz, above n 1, 34–47.

[21] For more detailed analysis see J Husa, 'Functional Method of Comparative Law—Much Ado about Nothing?' (2013) 2 *European Property Law Journal* 4 (arguing basically that functionalism in comparative law has little to do with scientific versions of functionalism and that it is a crude rule-of-thumb approach).

[22] Classical attack on comparative functionalism, G Frankenberg, 'Critical Comparisons: Rethinking Comparative Law' (1985) 26 *Harvard International Law Journal* 411.

[23] See J Husa, 'Methodology of Comparative Law Today: From Paradoxes to Flexibility?' (2006) 58 *Revue internationale de droit comparé* 1095.

[24] It is important to state that research of legal structures is not connected to the structuralism known in anthropology and sociology. Behind that kind of structuralism (eg Claude Lévi-Strauss), the idea that society consists of different symbolic systems is common. In social-scientific structuralism, the idea is to study the effect of structures on the behaviour of people as members of their communities. Such structuralist analysis is also based on the study of relations formed by symbols. In this kind of structuralism, elements of human culture are conceived in terms of their relationship to an overarching structure (eg language as a system of signs). See M Lane, *Introduction*

kind of functions they have in the legal system that is being examined, or how they were born and how they acquired their present forms (eg the institution of trust in common law). It is a question of the study of legal architecture, which the legal historian Stolte sketches as follows: 'the modern codes of private law have been built with the same bricks, although, of course, under different architecture'.[25] Stolte speaks about Central European codifications and of how the end results differed in spite of the same Roman components (norms, institutions, doctrines). Different codifications were built of the same legal bricks in the context of a different architectural idea and legal cultural context.

Structural comparison can be seen as a specialised application of functional comparison. In structural comparison, it is possible to examine, for example, the division of legal systems into different branches of law, the similarity or differences of which are the study topic. On the microlevel, the structural comparatist could, for example, try to explain why and how in England trust makes a kind of double ownership possible, unlike in Central European and Nordic law, where the same functions are handled differently. However, research on comparative law quite rarely identifies itself with specific focus on structures of legal order.[26] Structural research is often close to comparative legal theory, from which it is sometimes difficult to distinguish.[27]

The best-known research approach used in present-day comparisons, which is somewhere between functional and structural comparison, has its origin in Italy.[28] The so-called dynamic approach is connected to functional structural comparative law. Sacco, the main developer of the approach, observed that attention should be paid to sources of several kinds when the similarity or difference of law in different systems is studied. It is a question of legal cultural rules that determine how law is established, administered and researched in the system in question. It is a question of legal cultural justification and theoretical developments that concern the establishment and administration of law. Sacco and his followers use the term *formanti giuridici* for this concept. The English language translation for the term is legal formant. Basically, it is a question of a legal culturally extended interpretation of the source of law as wider and more contextual than a rule or institution.[29]

---

to Structuralism (New York, Basic Books, 1970). It is also possible to practice comparative law with a structuralist emphasis, but most cases involve research on less colourful legal structures.

[25] B Stolte, 'Is Byzantine Law Roman Law?' (2003) 2 *Acta Byzantina Fennica* 111, 122.

[26] However, see B Häcker, *Consequences of Impaired Consent Transfers—A Structural Comparison of English and German Law* (Tübingen, Mohr Siebeck, 2009).

[27] Eg N MacCormick and RS Summers (eds), *Interpreting Precedents—A Comparative Study* (Dartmouth, Ashgate, 1997).

[28] Though there are few examples, eg J Sandstedt, *Förarbeten till en komparativ sakrättsdialog* (Bergen, Universitet i Bergen, 2012).

[29] See, eg R Sacco, 'Legal Formants: A Dynamic Approach to Comparative Law' (1991) 39 *American Journal of Comparative Law* 1.

In system comparison, a particular legal institution or constituent part that belongs to a legal system is detached from its national context and is compared to overall solutions concerning similar legal cases in other systems. The objects compared are selected from different systems and set in the theoretical context constructed by the comparatist.

If the object selected for comparison is included in the researcher's own system, it becomes possible, by means of system comparison, to observe one's own national solution as if from outside: how do the arrangements in one's own law relate to the corresponding laws of other systems? In macrocomparative law, this has been one of the most popular research methods used when common law and civil law have been compared in countless books and articles.[30]

The Achilles heel of system comparison is its tendency to epistemically break loose from the legal systems from which the legal solution models under comparison come. On the one hand, this approach enables the accumulation of knowledge that is separate from national legal systems and therefore provides for theoretical comparative law. On the other hand, problems are readily found when withdrawing from concrete legal systems and studying solutions that have been abstracted from them. The most central of these problems concerns the fact that comparatists can misunderstand a solution model unless they decide to investigate the whole body of foreign legal systems (which is simply not possible). The problem can be partly avoided if functional equivalents are looked for when objects for comparison are chosen. This highlights that system comparison is very often a constituent part of functional comparison. Sometimes it is very difficult to distinguish system comparison from structural comparison, part of which it can also be. A system can be considered functional, while structures are not necessarily so.

The critical approach is even more unclear than the previous ones, and defining it with the accuracy that was possible for the previous three basic dimensions of comparative research is not possible. Criticalness is usually of two types: (i) a critical attitude to earlier comparative law and its tendency to concentrate excessively on similarities and practical objectives; or (ii) in the research approach, an attempt is made to include dimensions that are not descriptive to the same extent as has been the case in traditional comparative law.[31] These approaches can be called method criticism and content criticism.

One of the most vigorous critics of comparative law is Legrand, whose comparison theory is paradoxically also one of the most criticised of the past few years. Some comparatists more or less swear by him while others—the

---

[30] Quite recently, mixed jurisdictions (eg South Africa, Scotland, Malta, Israel) have risen to form a third major legal family: see VV Palmer (ed), *Mixed Jurisdictions Worldwide—The Third Legal Family* (Cambridge, Cambridge University Press, 2012).

[31] Critical approaches have certain connections to post-modern comparative law, which views law as an organic creature and entertains certain amounts of epistemological scepticism and moral relativism. For more detailed analysis see D Richers, 'Postmoderne Theorie in der Rechtsvergleichung?' (2007) 67 *Zeitschrift für ausländisches öffentliches Recht und Völkerrecht* 509.

majority—maintain that Legrand exaggerates, to say the least. Legrand has been known in European legal academia since the 1990s mainly because he sharply opposed the idea of European law becoming legal culturally uniform. Another central characteristic is his emphasis on diversity—Legrand's central idea is to emphasise the differences in comparative study, while it has been traditional in the field to emphasise similarities. According to Legrand, comparative law is research on the fundamental differences and legal mentalities of different systems, and in this research the methodological guideline is precisely their dissimilarity and the legal cultural originality of law.[32]

Another example of the critical research approach that is important from the point of view of comparative law is the critical and conscious research that has been built around legal orientalism. With the international importance of China growing, Chinese law has become an increasingly popular sector in the research of foreign law and comparative law. Legal orientalism and the discussion related to it reflect well the kind of methodical and theoretical problems that are involved. Orientalism as a concept and the related postcolonial discussion were extensively introduced into the theoretical and methodological discussion of comparative law relatively recently. Comparative law was not in the frontline of oriental studies, but followed behind legal anthropology, ethnology and history.[33]

The postcolonial theory is a rough way to perceive a more extensive research tradition. In short, postcolonial theory refers to decolonisation and postcolonialism: it deals with the tradition of critical emancipatory theory that followed the dismantling of colonial power. Postcolonialism is quite closely related to the study of ethnicity and racism, as well as to feminist research and literature. From the perspective of comparative law, the crux of the matter is that Western ideas of law are no longer automatically accepted as the primary yardstick for legal cultures. Accordingly, attempts are made to give the constitutive other in law a voice of its own.[34]

V. METHODOLOGY OR HEURISTICS?

Presented above is a selection of basic research designs for comparison that have to be made either before research is undertaken or during it. At the same time, it has become obvious that the methodological toolbox does not consti-

---

[32] See P Legrand, 'European Legal Systems are not Converging' (1996) 45 *International and Comparative Law Quarterly* 52; *Le droit comparé*, 4th edn (Paris, Presses Universitaires de France, 2011); 'Foreign Law: Understanding Understanding' (2011) 6 *Journal of Comparative law* 67; 'Siting Foreign Law: How Derrida Can Help' (2011) 21 *Duke Journal of Comparative and International Law* 595.

[33] See T Ruskola, 'Legal Orientalism' (2002) 101 *Michigan Law Review* 179; 'Law Without Law, or Is "Chinese Law" an Oxymoron?' (2003) 11 *William and Mary Bill of Rights Journal* 1.

[34] This has to do more generally with the new trends in comparative law and the movement against epistemological ethnocentrism. See, eg D Kennedy, 'New Approaches to Comparative Law: Comparativism and International Governance' (1997) 2 *Utah Law Review* 545.

tute an exact methodology but instead contains a number of useful rules of thumb. Due to the variety of legal cultures and the interests of the comparatists, the methodology of comparative law is mainly of a heuristic nature. The exactness of natural sciences is only partly realised in legal comparison. Because each individual case is different in comparative study, reasoning of a general nature on common comparative methodology and its relation to the methodology of comparative law is not very meaningful.[35] This does not, however, mean that there could not be justifiable and rational approaches in comparative law.[36]

Altogether, there is no reason to sink into methodological anarchy or deep relativism; rather, we should look in the direction of heuristics. Heuristics is related to the research process because it is an approximation method by which it is usually possible to get a satisfactory end result.[37] Crucially, due to its fundamental nature, the heuristic method is not exact.[38] Typical heuristic methods are rules of thumb or educated academic guesses, both of which are based on limited but sufficiently large amounts of information. In the context of the research process, this means that the comparatist need not consider the approach methods in a vacuum. Heuristics offers pre-considered solution approaches to how comparative research can be carried out. It is a question of a kind of art of discovery, which is based on the Greek word for 'I found' or 'I exposed', *hevrísko* (εὑρίσκω). Functionalism is a typical example of a heuristic approach of this kind.[39]

The methodology of comparative law can be defined as a heuristic compilation of rules of thumb on exposure and discovery in the field of comparative law. In other words, the comparatist should have some kind of conscious guidelines for what he/she is doing and why he/she is doing it. An overall idea about the comparison process helps in the research process, and this offers a natural place and function for non-normative comparison methodology. Naturally, this way of outlining the methodology of comparative law does not agree with the strict way of distinguishing the exact methodology from heuristics. This ambiguous state of affairs is also reflected in the writing in the field.[40]

---

[35] *Cf* B Jaluzot, 'Méthodologie du droit comparé—bilan et perspective' (2005) 57 *Revue internationale de droit comparé* 29, 48.

[36] Notwithstanding, there are scholars who seem to have somewhat stronger belief in 'the comparative method'. See, eg JC Reitz, 'How to Do Comparative Law' (1998) 46 *American Journal of Comparative Law* 617 ('comparative method is simple to describe, it is difficult to apply').

[37] Heuristics does not refer here to methodological premises (see Bell, above n 4, 174) but to the nature of comparative law methodology in general.

[38] See O Kiss, 'Heuristic, Methodology or Logic of Discovery? Lakatos on Patterns of Thinking' (2006) 14 *Perspectives on Science* 302. 'Heuristic contains "sign-posts", while methodology tells us, even if provisionally, whether we are going in the right direction. One step in a research program can be treated as progressive or degenerating only in hindsight, when we see future developments. Appraisal of research programs is as fallible as the theories themselves' (317).

[39] See Husa, 'Functional Method of Comparative Law—Much Ado about Nothing?', above n 21.

[40] See M Van Hoecke (ed), *Epistemology and Methodology of Comparative Law* (Oxford, Hart Publishing, 2004).

Most textbooks give methodological advice and offer hints, but there is no intimate link to the research process. This is partly due to the heuristic nature of comparative law, which means that getting acquainted with exemplary research (ie good books and articles) and learning from them is of great importance. However, something changed as the twentieth century moved into the twenty-first: the idea of a single correct method was rejected.[41] It should be said, however, that the idea of methodological pluralism does not necessarily mean that comparative law as an independent field of research has come to the end.[42]

At the beginning of this article, a presentation was made of Schlesinger's way to perceive comparative law as a field of legal studies that studies differences and similarities and attempts to explain the reasons for them. One of the recent ambitious aims of comparative law is to intelligibly explain the relationship between humankind and their law in different contexts. Understanding is necessary for the comparatists to be able to explain the reasons for the differences and similarities they have found: why in system A the prerequisite for liability for damages is clear causation (causal connection) between the act and the damage caused, but in system B an assumption of causal connection combined with the intentionality or negligence of the damaging party is sufficient. Circular reasoning cannot be a sensible way: in system A the matter is caused by provision X and in system B the matter is caused by provision Z. Such an explanation is adequate because it does not explain why in systems A and B different models have been adopted to solve the same socio-legal problem (defining the party liable for compensation in case of accident). From there, it follows that there has to be a wider perspective, but, while seeing things in a wider perspective, the view of the methodology of comparative law must also be taken into consideration.

It is especially difficult for comparatists to break loose from the influence of their own legal culture and to look at their own and foreign law fairly without any unintentional bias. In this respect, the comparatist's work comes close to (but does not identify with) anthropology and ethnography: for lack of direct scientific evidence, statistical conclusions and conclusive evidence, text material has to be interpreted, and different hints and clues have to be looked for. In short, the power of deduction and legal cultural literacy are more essential than statistics and information of national doctrinal study of law.[43]

---

[41] See VV Palmer, 'From Lerotholi to Lando: Some Examples of Comparative Law Methodology' (2005) 53 *American Journal of Comparative Law* 261; see also Husa, 'From Paradoxes to Flexibility' above n 23.

[42] This has been proposed by M Reimann, 'The End of Comparative Law as an Autonomous Subject' (1996) 11 *Tulane European and Civil Law Forum* 46.

[43] Difference with any other form of 'scientific' research is not necessarily significant: cf Van Hoecke, 'Legal Doctrine', above n 7, 13 ('scientific "observation" is not neutral perception of facts that would present themselves spontaneously. We are always faced with a specific reading of selected facts, steered by the research question'). With comparison, the problem also concerns the research language that is used to describe the different systems in a manner that is not neutral in a strict scientific sense. Adams points out that the comparatist (*rechtsvergelijker*)

The comparatist's job becomes all the more challenging when he/she begins to look for clues needed for explanation. The task is comparable to detective work, where the criminal is uncovered by means of small details or clues that do not reveal anything to someone who is uninformed on the matter. In the same way, the hunter or tracker is capable of reading seemingly unimportant traces (footprints, broken branchs, fallen leaves etc) to formulate a picture that is not concrete as such. It is a question of observations forming a narrative continuum where it is possible to understand the plot and its development. On the basis of the material that the comparatist has gone through and analysed, it is possible to proceed towards explanations up to the point where the interpreted and organised pieces of evidence fit together.[44] In the same way, the comparative research report should have a plot and be a comprehensible entity for its readers, not a list of facts like a telephone book (moving from one country to another).

Methodologically looking for clues—in the case of comparative law, particularly in the explanatory phase—is compatible with ethnographer Geertz's methodological concept 'thick description'.[45] In this case, it means a thick description of the legal cultures under study. Legal cultures here are systems that are constructed of an established legal 'system of meanings': these systems are the epistemological frame of legal culture (written, unwritten) where various actors (legislator, judge and researcher) are in interaction with legal norms. While the comparatist attempts to explain differences and similarities, he/she simultaneously conceptualises and theorises the research objects; it is a question of reconstruction of law, where the comparatist, from the viewpoint of an outsider, simulates the action of lawyers in different systems. Thickness offers some kind of methodological backing: the thinner the description, the more unconvincing the credibility. On the other hand, the idea of a 'thick description' in comparative law has been criticised as being overly demanding.[46]

VI. CONCLUSION

The above-described comparative law research does not fulfil the requirements for research design in natural sciences, neither does it contain exact

must realise that descriptive terms are never entirely neutral and that they may lead to bias: M Adams, Chapter 6 below.

[44] This approach has been labelled 'micro-historical' by C Ginzburg, 'Microhistory: Two or Three Things That I Know about It' (1993) 20 *Critical Inquiry* 10.

[45] For more on this approach see C Geertz, *The Interpretation of Cultures: Selected Essays* (New York, Basic Books, 1973) 28 ('The aim is to draw large conclusions from small, but very densely textured facts; to support broad assertions about the role of culture in the construction of collective life by engaging them exactly with complex specifics').

[46] For example, according to Michaels, 'This kind of description that is not possible through abstraction and generalization, is often what we most need in comparative law': R Michaels, 'Explanation and Interpretation in Functionalist Comparative Law—a Response to Julie de Coninck' (2010) 74 *Rabels Zeitschrift für ausländisches und internationales Privatrecht* 351, 356.

methodology; however, it still attempts to avoid open bias and prejudice. Comparative law tries to get rid of ethnocentrism, though it is probably impossible to completely break loose from the influence of one's own cultural sphere. Neither can a comparatist become fully detached from his/her own conception of the world and his/her own deeply rooted basic ideas.[47] Notwithstanding, it is still possible to attempt to decrease adverse effects, and the legal theoretic discourse that is known as 'methodology of comparative law' can be of great help here. Nevertheless, heuristic methodology differs from classical scientific exact methodology, which tends to be of a normative nature.[48]

Due to factors that delimit cultural vision, comparatist naturally mostly looks for such explanatory factors as he/she finds possible and sensible on the basis of his/her experience of the world. Therefore, he/she also unconsciously refrains from many such potential explanatory models as another comparatist might perhaps find significant. That is why literature on the history of law and sociology of law, as well as other multidisciplinary literature (offering non-legal contexts for law), is important: because, by means of it, the comparatist can expand the horizon of their understanding. The expansion of the horizon is the key factor, and the methodology being heuristic does not affect that at all, just like heuristics has nothing to do with the idea that comparative methodology should not be taken seriously.[49] To describe the research designs in comparative law as heuristic methodology is not a belittling epithet; quite the contrary, for it is an outcome of epistemological realism.

---

[47] Yet this does not mean that we should choose between ethnocentrism and cultural relativism because these are but extreme ends. See J Schacherreiter, 'Das Verhängnis von Ethnozentrismus und Kulturrelativismus in der Rechtsvergleichung—Ursachen, Ausprägungsformen und Strategien zur Überwindung' (2013) 77 *Rabels Zeitschrift für ausländisches und internationales Privatrecht* 272.

[48] Typically scientific methodological rules are empirically as follows. 'If one's goal is y, then one ought to do x': L Laudan, 'Progress or Rationality? The Prospects of Normative Naturalism' [1987] *American Philosophical Quarterly* 19, 24.

[49] Cf G Samuel, 'Taking Methods Seriously (Part One)' (2007) 2 *Journal of Comparative Law* 94.

5

Law as Translation

FRANÇOIS OST

I F IT BE relevant and desirable to suggest translation as a paradigm for
thinking about the grammar of our plural world—a world which can
never again close up on its idiolects, and which strives to escape just as
much from oneness of language as from oneness of thought: a post-Babel
world, in other words, wise to the inanity of the tall tower of monism and
yet eager to transcend its own pluralism of mere juxtaposition—then we may
suppose that the domain of law represents a privileged field of application
for this paradigm of translation. This is what the present brief study aims to
demonstrate. I will content myself with staking out the field of the enquiry[1]—
a field well known to Mark Van Hoecke, that indefatigable mediator of ideas
and cultures.

The task is thus to take the measure of the translation phenomena that
appear in the juridical field. No doubt the first thought that springs to mind
in this regard is the zone of contact where national law encounters foreign
law, resulting more often than not in a difficult confrontation between different languages: public international law (see Section I), private international
law (Section II) and comparative law (Section III) are the required approaches
for this study. But the whole problematic soon broadens and grows singularly
complex, bringing into its purview, step by step, the law in its entirety (as
a function of that central insight of translation theory according to which
translation is by no means limited to interlinguistic exchanges but extends to
include the communication occurring within the same linguistic community).[2]
This is because, on the one hand, juridical multilingualism can also be a
description of the national legal systems—in countries like Belgium and
Canada, for example. On the other hand, it is because the difficulties of terminology translation which we encounter in private international law and in
European law are merely the signs of problems in describing institutions that

---

[1] For more details, cf F Ost, *Le droit comme traduction* (Québec, Presses de l'université de
Laval, 2009); F Ost, *Traduire. Défense et illustration du multilinguisme et de la traduction* (Paris,
Fayard, 2009).
[2] P Ricoeur 'Le paradigme de la traduction' in *Le juste* (Paris, Éditions Esprit, 2001) 125.

are deeply rooted in different traditions of justice—which unfailingly leads the lawyer-translator into the very depths of the respective juridical orders that thus confront each other; and this is something which thereby frequently stimulates him to undertake some very beneficial critical querying of his own categories and taxonomies. Moreover, the emergence of regional European law and of what we call 'globalised law' (Section IV) is a further factor bringing the translation paradigm into the heart of national juridical orders. Sometimes this is a supranational system moulded by comparative law that is imposed upon national systems as a fully fledged component with superior authority, and sometimes, as in the case of globalised law, it is in a variety of forms of borrowing of foreign juridical solutions, with contagion from models of importation which are assumed to be effective, and under more or less spontaneous bombardment by principles that are judged to be legitimate.

One must go further: even assuming that a juridical order could develop in a closed vessel, shielded from foreign traditions and contained within an absolute monolingualism, the phenomena of translation (from *de facto* to *de jure*, from the speech of one branch of law to another's, from one juridical epoch to another, from the speech of an expert to that of a lawyer, etc) would still nonetheless be characteristic of the whole of juridical discourse (see Section V), thus raising not only methodological questions of great interest, but also ethical issues to which we must also pay attention (see Section VI).

But it is not enough to establish the importance of the translation operation for understanding the logic of juridical discourse; one must also show precisely what translation theory contributes to the task of clarifying not only the essential juridical operations of translation in the strict sense (ie translation between languages), but also those of comparison and qualification. Within the limits of the present study, however, it is not possible to develop this analysis. I will content myself, therefore, with recalling briefly, at the end of this study, some of the lessons to be drawn from the very rich general theory of translation (Section VII), leaving the reader to make the necessary transpositions, and especially so in view of the experience of the man whom these lines are intended to honour. In the various domains to which I have alluded, a methodology is needed—something like the grammar of 'networked law'; and, although the general theory of translation is well qualified to do this job, it also has much to learn from being informed about the experience accumulated in the field by juridical practice and doctrine. I will, of course, undertake only 'soundings' of such an immense and turbulent ocean; but in each of these soundings, nonetheless, a structure will clearly emerge—a structure in which I will recognise the characteristic marker of translation—being as far removed from any timid reliance on what is proper to it (its idiolect, its national juridical system) as it is from the dangerous and illusory fascination with the idea of having one single unitary system (a universal language, an imperial model of law). Networked law searches for its grammar, in the space between monolingualism and esperanto (to which we must add pidgin and sabir languages, these being made up of unreflective borrowings), ie in the translational model.

I. PUBLIC INTERNATIONAL LAW AND MULTILINGUAL NATIONAL LAWS

Public international law in its classical form (both public and private) believed it could repress the other, the foreign, the foreign language, and force it out beyond its borders. Based on a philosophy of 'everyone in his own place', expressed in the Westphalian dogmas (arising from the Treaty of Westphalia in 1648) of the internal supremacy of the state and of equality and of external sovereignty, this international law needed to go no further than managing the multilingual diplomatic contacts necessitated by their unavoidable dealings with each other in the context of the family of nations (despite the fact that, as we must remind ourselves, French served until recently as the international language of diplomacy). We find a typical illustration of this in Article 33 of the Vienna Convention on the law of treaties, the aim of which is to rule on the specific question of the interpretation of multilingual treaties. Three rules result from this provision. The first of them establishes a general principle: 'When a treaty has been authenticated in two or more languages, its text is valid and has force of law in each of these languages' (Article 33-1). This principle is then supplemented by paragraph 3 of Article 33: 'The terms of a treaty are presumed to have the same meaning in the various authenticated texts'. In spite of this assumption of the oneness of the treaty and the presumption that accompanies it, Article 33 nevertheless establishes two rules capable of resolving the divergences of meaning which are likely to arise between one version and another. The second part of paragraph 1 sets out a formal rule of preference: '[the text of the treaty is valid and has force of law in each of the languages in which it has been authenticated] unless the treaty states, or the parties agree, that in case of a divergence of meaning, one definite text will decide the issue' (and, as we know, for a long time it was the French-language version which played the role of this overriding third language). Moreover, paragraph 4 for its part proposes a substantial rule of conciliation:

> except where one particular text has force over others in accordance with paragraph 1, when the comparison between authentic texts manifests a difference of meaning which cannot be resolved by applying Articles 31 and 32 [which define the normal rules for interpreting treaties], the meaning to be adopted is the one which, having regard to the object and the aim of the treaty, best reconciles the texts.[3]

---

[3] On this question, *cf* AP Papaux, 'Commentaire ad article 33. Interprétation de traités authentifiés en deux ou plusieurs langues' in P Klein and O Carter (eds), *Commentaire des Conventions de Vienne de 1965 et 1986 sur le droit fes traités* (Brussels, Bruylent, 2006) 1373–402.

Without developing any further this complex system which simultaneously asserts the uniqueness of meaning of the treaty and acknowledges the possible diversity amongst its versions—requiring that either a choice between them or a 'best possible' reconciliation of them be made—let me here note merely that, on a more practical level, since international law remains, like international society, a major contributor to the relations of force, the 'egalitarian' translation system put in place by Article 33 is heavily biased by national interests and by the self-interpretation made by states of the treaties which bind them. Let me also note that international commitments are full of intentional ambiguities—these being the only thing that can allow compromises to be worked out; so here the linguistic diversity is only the reflection of a disagreement whose resolution is deferred. In this regard, I recall the radical ambiguity which affects Resolution 242 of the UN Security Council relating to the withdrawal of Israel from 'the' Palestinian territories occupied by her: 'from territories' according to the English version, 'from the territories' according to the French version (but let it be noted that the French delegate stated an explicit reservation in favour of the French version only).

It is clear also that in European law the principle of equal dignity of the different languages of the Community is in force; from the very beginning, a political choice was made in favour of multilingualism, to such an extent that it could be claimed that 'the language of Europe is translation'. Regulation No 1 of the EEC, dated 15 April 1958, recognised the official nature of each of the national languages of the Community, and the need to write the Community's directives and regulations in each of these languages. Thus, following the latest enlargements, Europe has no fewer than 23 official languages, giving rise to no fewer than 506 language combinations for translation purposes.[4]

However, the situation of multilingual states shows that it is not enough to externalise the questions of translation. Here again, we encounter at times a rule of preference and at other times a rule of conciliation.[5] Of preference, see, for example, Article 40 of Quebec's law on interpreting, which stipulates that 'in cases where the French text diverges from the English text, the French text shall prevail'. In a comparable sense, we have also the example of Article 8 of Canada's law on the official languages of the country, which gives 'preference to the version which assures the best achievement of its objects according to the spirit, the intention, and the true sense of the text'. Of conciliation, as in Article 7 of the Belgian law dated 31 May 1961 concerning the use of languages in matters of legislation: 'divergences shall be resolved in accordance with the will of the legislator as determined by the normal rules of interpretation giving no pre-eminence to one of the texts over the other'.

---

[4] JC Piris, 'Union européenne: comment rédiger une législation de qualité dans 20 langues et pour 25 États membres' (2005) 121–22 *Revue de droit public* 475.

[5] F Ost, and M van de Kerkchove, *Entre la lettre et l'esprit. Les directives d'interprétation en droit* (Brussels, Bruylant, 1989) 72.

The case of Canada turns out to be one of the most interesting ones for the problematic of translation, adding to the bilingualism of terminology the duality of the juridical traditions—the common law and the *droit civil* having mutually cross-fertilised each other in the course of several centuries during which both were applied, while the whole picture was accompanied by various phenomena of reciprocal contamination or, indeed, of retrotransfer of juridical terms. Indeed, it has been noted that, even though certain terms from the common law are today 'contaminating' juridical French, a good number of its expressions nonetheless have an origin in . . . French, since in England, up until the eighteenth century, a juridical jargon of Franco-Norman origin was prevalent, having crossed the Channel with William the Conqueror in 1066 (this was the French law which three different measures adopted by the English Parliament, in 1362, 1650 and 1731, struggled hard to repress).[6]

This hybridisation has been pushed so far in Canada that some writers, who have observed the prevailing practices of mixed teaching and research, for example at McGill University Faculty of Law, and also the juridical practices which such teaching and research are based on, have no hesitation in announcing the emergence of a synthetic 'bijuridism' which is able to derive the most appropriate solutions 'beyond' or 'between' the two versions, French and English, of the texts. This is not so much a case of a hegemonic choice of one language to the detriment of the other or of an egalitarian juxtaposition of the two, nor is it even a case of a wise conciliation between the two texts in question; it is more a case of a new thing arising by way of and thanks to the terms provided by the one language and the other.[7] Thus I have already identified, at the end of this opening discussion, no fewer than four different solutions to the Babelian dilemma.

II. PRIVATE INTERNATIONAL LAW

With the science of the conflicts between laws, 'foreignness' is no longer camping at the borders: private situations are configured which, on account of certain of their elements, trigger the application of more than one set of national laws simultaneously. The tribunals of the local area are called upon to carry out any desirable connections, with the result that in the end it is inevitable that the foreign law will be taken into consideration (and therefore qualified and translated). Though it is impossible in such cases to apply the national law unilaterally, it is still necessary to know from which juridical system the rule to resolve conflicts of laws comes, on the basis of which the connections, qualifications and translations will function. Rationally, it is

---

[6] A Bulier, 'De la "commune ley" à la Common Law' [2006] *Revue de droit international et de droit comparé* 44.

[7] D Jutras, 'Énoncer l'indicible: le droit entre langues et traditions' (2000) 4 *Revue internationale de droit comparé* 781.

tempting to imagine a single unified, universal and integrated system of private international law, but this universalist option has never been successfully imposed, with the result that, if we exclude the hypothesis of international agreements, each juridical order regulates and decides, on its own behalf and according to its own logic, its relations with the whole set of other juridical orders.[8] Were we, for that matter, going to be locked inside a purely particularist system which would be no more than the extension of internal private law to situations containing an element of foreignness (and this in deliberate ignorance of what's involved in the foreign solutions)? Not at all: the entire effort of the discipline of the conflicts of laws consisted in bringing about a functional articulation of the normative orders in question,[9] notably on the basis of comparative jurisprudence, and starting out from the categories and methods of the local juridical instance—hence, an operation which in its every aspect is like a translation.

No doubt we will only rarely find the exact equivalent of a national juridical concept in a foreign system, just as the 'word for word' approach is scarcely imaginable or desirable in matters of translation. The result would be that the solution will be holistic and global—resulting from the taking into consideration of the sentence and the text on the one hand, and on the other hand the institution and the economy of the law. François Rigaux, who makes this observation, adds that the comparability thus established rests on a postulate of the 'communicability of juridical systems', which is itself linked to an intuitive view of the 'unity of humanity', that is: as long as we accept to focus on the functional core whose effect is that human beings each in their own way have tried to deal with problems that are fundamentally similar.[10] What remains to be determined, of course, is the syntax of this metalanguage of the conflicts of laws, accepting in advance the limits of the exercise, which arise both from the national (and therefore multiple) origin of this grammar (just as, in matters of language, translation is always carried out on the basis of a definite language and not from a superordinate language presumed to be perfect) and from the often approximate nature of its analogical judgements of equivalence, and sometimes from the recognition of its limits: in other words, the untranslatable cases, represented here by the public-order exception invoked to block a foreign solution even when the latter has been designated by the rule of national conflict, when the content of that solution turns out to be decidedly not assimilable into the host system of law.

---

[8] F Rigaux, *La loi des juges* (Paris, Éditions Odile Jacob, 1997) 151.
[9] H Batiffol, *Aspects philosophiques du droit international privé* (Paris, Dalloz, 1956) 27.
[10] F Rigaux, above n 8, 152–56.

III. COMPARATIVE LAW

For a long time, comparative law was practised in the same way as a philatelist collects stamps or an entomologist collects insects: you lined up juridical concepts and solutions by assigning them a place and a rank, statically and without concern for the living relationships which could be established between the entities thus juxtaposed. Comparative law remained a marginal academic specialty and one which was fairly esoteric. Here again, anything foreign was still relegated to the frontiers, frozen in the exoticism of its juridical otherness, or else hastily assimilated into vast universalist systems: these projective and hegemonic comparisons opened out on to the 'great systems' (René David), just like those planispheres which reconstructed the map of the world centred on the continent that the author was from (and this was without even mentioning the notorious distinction between the 'civilised nations' and the others who were relegated to the darkness of the time before there was law).

Admittedly, there were times when the national legislator 'looked over the hedge' when there were parliamentary debates about such-and-such a bill to reform the legislation; there was no incongruity in invoking a foreign legislation that had achieved success, in order to inspire or legitimise an internal reform. Jean Carbonnier himself, the great artisan of the reform of family law in France in the 1970s, makes a malicious reference to this method: 'travellers from afar can lie with impunity'.[11]

But juridical comparatism did not affect the language and the substance of internal law in any other way. Besides, many held forth eloquently, as Pierre Legrand is still doing today,[12] on the possibility of comparing, exactly as some people proclaim the impossibility of translation as a matter of principle. That the convergences which would arise through this exercise would necessarily be superficial and deceptive was the claim, as long as they failed to carry out the transfer of the meaning inherent in the rules and the concepts—a meaning immersed in a culture and a tradition which, according to this hypothesis, are not exportable. Hence the only legitimate comparatism should take the form of a differential analysis of juridical cultures, insisting on the differences much more than on the pseudo-convergences.

The result was that ultimately the main benefit of juridical comparatism would be for internal use only, as if Janus's gaze directed at the institutions of other countries could do no more than produce by reflex action a new look at our own solutions. Horatia Muir Watt expects from this confrontation with alternative models the benefits of a 'subversive function' comparable to that which is exercised in the US by the multiple currents of critical legal studies. In the absence of any similar perspective in European law, compara-

---

[11] J Carbonnier, *Essais sur les lois* (Evreux, Répertoire du notariat defrénois, 1979) 191.
[12] P Legrand, 'Sur l'analyse différentielle des juriscultures' (1999) 4 *Revue internationale de droit comparé* 1053.

tive law could at least play some part in dragging our juridical orders out of their dogmatic slumber.[13]

It is clear that, whether it is hegemonic-assimilative or critical-differentiating (a division which is also found, term for term, in the field of translation), comparison was always directed to an object that remained external to it, as if the different juridical orders remained mutually impermeable to one another.

This is the very situation that is changing radically today: the juridical orders are on the move, they are communicating with one another, they are copying each other, they are swapping solutions, they are hybridising themselves in a thousand and one ways (though we must not ignore the phenomena of dominance which inevitably twist and slant such exchanges), with the result that comparative law has ceased to be the study of the platonic relationships between juridical systems viewing each other from the outside and is becoming, to use the expression of H Patrick Glenn, the study of an 'integrated law'[14]—a law which introduces into the heart of the internal juridical mechanisms other, composite matter, hybrid concepts (some would call them bastard concepts), imported solutions that are only 'more or less' under control. Often, on the initiative of legal practice, which is the real motor of this integration, and is a factor which is not constraining but which indeed has real power, cross-border solutions are being elaborated (contract templates, standard models of governance, financing arrangements, etc) which circulate all the more freely because the professional mobility of lawyers is increasing and because information can be stored and communicated universally through the internet. 'Integration' will soon affect all juridical activities: the making of laws, at the crossroads of diverse influences; the dialogue which judges must engage in across frontiers; the teaching of law, which is transnational too (thanks especially to the Erasmus exchange programme), which means that comparatism is being integrated into every branch of legal practice rather than being isolated in a marginal and specialised option.

To these manifestations of 'globalised law' (see below) is added, within the European regional space, the decisive impact of community law: to say that it is riddled with juridical comparatism is a major understatement.[15] Concerning the European Court of Justice, judge Lenaerts wrote that it is 'a laboratory of comparative law', since its constant concern is to ensure the best possible effectiveness (in terms of acceptability and legitimacy) of the solutions which it adopts, by forging them in the crucible of the main national traditions.[16] As

---

[13] H Muir Watt, 'La fonction subversive du droit comparé' (2000) 3 *Revue internationale de droit comparé* 503; in the same sense, *cf* G Monateri, 'Critique et différence: le droit comparé en Italie' (1999) 4 *Revue internationale de droit comparé* 989.

[14] HP Glenn, 'Vers un droit comparé intégré' (1999) 4 *Revue internationale de droit comparé* 84.

[15] F van der Mensbrugghe (ed), *L'utilisation de la méthode comparative en droit européen* (Namur, Presses Universitaires de Namur, 2003).

[16] K Lenaerts, 'Le droit comparé dans le travail du juge communautaire' in Van der Mensbrugghe, ibid, 123. The author talks about a principle of 'loyal cooperation' (126), which leads

for the 'legislative' process of elaborating directives and regulations, we know how extensively it is informed by comparative law (in the law of the environment especially, but also in the domain of consumer protection or competition law),[17] even if the exercise sometimes remains by implication confined to the preparatory stages or if, in certain cases, comparison is only used as an *ex post facto* alibi intended to legitimise a community decision that has already been adopted.[18]

We can see that comparison/translation has once and for all gained permanent and essential currency, no longer merely at the margins of juridical systems, in the limbo of the space between laws, but in the very heart of the national systems—affecting, by that very fact, the canonical distinction between the same and the other. Obviously what remains to be done is to think through the methods of comparative law which has moved into our house at its own invitation: this is the delicate question of the construction of equivalents—likewise a central problem in the methodology of translation.

IV. GLOBALISED LAW

Globalised law must be distinguished from the law of globalisation; the latter is still derived from the classical perspective of the international, given that it proceeds to put in place structures of world governance starting out from states (this is the United Nations perspective); globalised law, on the other hand, results from a much more radical perspective of transnational penetration, the result of a more-or-less spontaneous convergence of national laws seeking to align themselves with standards and models that are dominant or seductive.

We are witnessing, then, an astonishing spread, and at times a very rapid one, of concepts ('universal service'), of values ('transparency', 'good governance'), of models and practices, founded on efficacity and economic rationality or, in other domains, democratic legitimacy, bringing in its wake forms of hybridisation and acculturation of the national systems and their specific vocabulary. This 'soft globalisation' explains, for example, why 'the Swiss legislator, without being obliged to, is transforming into national law the norms of the WTO or the *soft law* of the OECD'.[19] This 'modelling' of juridical instruments, which tends to select the most powerful instruments

---

judges to 'seek resources' in a permanent way in the common juridical conceptions of the Member States in order to arrive at 'the best solution in the middle line' (167).

[17] P Lannoye, 'L'approche comparatiste au Parlement européen' in Van der Mensbrugghe, ibid, 27ff.

[18] F van der Mensbrugghe, 'Comparative Methodology as a Means of Dissipating Tension' in Van der Mensbrugghe, ibid, 41ff.

[19] C-A Morand, 'Le droit saisi par la mondialisation. En guise de prélude' in C-A Morand (ed), *Le droit saisi par la mondialisation* (Brussels, Bruylant, 2001) 10.

imposed by practice, is related to a form of 'natural selection'[20] and leads to a specialisation in the language of the law and a series of differentiated languages, conferring upon each sector of economic life its transnational regulation: thus, in the margins of the *lex mercatoria* (which is already very old), we have witnessed the development of a *lex petrolae*, a *lex bursarum*, a *lex informatica*, a *lex bioethica*, etc.[21]

This phenomenon, which has been called 'de facto internormativity'[22] (insofar as it proceeds from voluntary adjustments and not from a legal obligation), presents multiple facets: sometimes it proceeds from economic constraint (think, for example, of the nations of the former Soviet bloc or the emerging countries rising up out of underdevelopment and obliged to align themselves promptly with the standards of the globalised liberal economy) and sometimes from intellectual fascination (such as the phenomena of borrowing, sometimes unconscious, of practices, arguments and forms of motivation studied by Monateri in the case of Italy),[23] but in all cases it leads to forms of hybridisation, if these borrowings are selective and partial (it is rare for a juridical system to be adopted in its entirety), which certainly increases the debate about the legitimacy of these 'legal transplants':[24] is it ultimately a matter of a unique language, of translation that respects differences, or is it rather a case of a heteroclite *sabir* language, of the poorly mastered pidgin of an over-hasty globalisation?

In order to inject a bit of order into this normative proliferation, Mireille Delmas-Marty introduced, some years ago, a welcome distinction between two forms of globalisation: globalisation proper, which arises out of market forces, and universalisation, which takes its inspiration from the ethical ideals of fundamental rights.[25] Thus we are apparently witnessing the joint action, at times convergent and at times conflictual, of these two sorts of globalised law: the former tends to impose everywhere the dogmas of free competition and to dissolve those national policies which cannot be subsumed under a liberal perspective; and the latter speaks the language of human rights and tends to universalise the principle of the irreducible dignity of the human being, in the name of which it is legitimate for collectivities to organise themselves to preserve their rights, sometimes against the demands of free competition. However opposed to each other these two forms of globalised law may be in

---

[20] A Martin-Serf, 'La modélisation des instruments juridiques' in E Loquin and C Kassedjan (eds), *La mondialisation du droit* (Dijon, Litec, 2000) 180.

[21] E Loquin and L Ravillon, 'La volonté des opérateurs, vecteurs d'un droit mondialisé' in Loquin and Kassedjan, ibid, 123.

[22] M Delmas-Marty, *Les forces imaginantes du droit. II. Le pluralisme ordonné* (Paris, Seuil, 2006) 41ff.

[23] Monateri, above n 13, 97.

[24] On this question, *cf* A Watson, *Legal Transplants* (Edinburgh, Edinburgh University Press, 1974); see also the criticisms of R Sacco, *La comparaison juridique au service de la connaissance du droit* (Paris, Economica, 1991) 115ff; W Ewald, 'Comparative Jurisprudence: the Logic of legal Transplants' (1995) 43 *American Journal of Comparative Law* 489.

[25] M Delmas-Marty, *Trois défis pour un droit mondial* (Paris, Seuil, 1998).

their ideological goals, they nonetheless present astonishing formal similarities as regards their 'subversive' action upon the coherence of national juridical systems. In both cases, what is at stake is a language of principles, largely liberated from state juridical sources, something like a new natural law creeping in to the tissue of internal orders and profoundly modifying their economy. Consider in this regard the example of the irresistible penetration of the language of human rights into all of the branches of law, spilling over from their branch of origin, constitutional law, to take the form today of a transnational benchmark of legitimacy for all juridical mechanisms.

What is at stake in the planetary game that is being played out today consists of the balancing out of these two forces of globalisation. Will it be possible to harmonise their respective powers and to ensure something like a translation from one language into the other? This is the perilous and often disappointing exercise to which, for example, the Disputes Settlement Body, which is the body within the WTO that has jurisdiction in the resolution of trade disputes is devoted when it deals with questions related to the protection of the environment, for example, whilst its dominant logic is obviously the promotion of free competition. It is the same exercise, but with more felicitous outcomes, when fundamental human rights are today invoked before the Court of Justice of the European Union, since this latter body is not yet a party to the European Convention on Human Rights, yet has nevertheless decided to recognise the main ones among these fundamental rights as 'general principles of community law'.

Let us acknowledge, however, that the universalist method—the one which aims to universalise human rights by means of major planetwide agreements— is often still stuck in the mud and marking time, for want of a body having jurisdiction over these fundamental rights on a worldwide scale, and also on account of the 'imperial' policy of the US, since it is now the only global superpower. With the 'Americanisation of law',[26] we are witnessing an alternative strategy of an entirely Babelian kind: the imposition of a single language and a single juridical model on the scale of the one power which is capable of dictating its law everywhere. It must be noted that the US has not ratified the major universal treaties (the Kyoto Protocol, the Rome Convention on the International Court of Justice, and so on), or has ratified them only belatedly and with many reservations (as in the case of the UN Pacts on civil and political rights), so it is clear that the US really intends to universalise its own law. Indeed, in numerous domains (the fight against corruption, money laundering and drug trafficking, the fight against terrorism using the Patriot Act of 2001, rules of accounting for companies quoted on the US stock markets, regulating the internet, etc) the US has almost completely succeeded in imposing its model on the entire world, just as, in the case of the trial of Saddam Hussein, the option of Americanising the tribunal was preferred

---

[26] 'L'américanisation du droit', 45 *Archives de philosophie du droit*, 2001.

over the setting up of a supranational jurisdiction. The conclusion, drawn by Mireille Delmas-Marty, is that:

> this attitude, accompanied by a tendency to favour private-sector players, encourages the promotion of the market as the only model capable of universal application, whereas the majority of real instruments having universal significance (human rights, crimes against humanity, the common good) derive very much from the sweet will of the US.[27]

Faced with this Babelian ambition, how will the universalism of human rights be able to make its voice heard, a plural voice which, since it is well able to manage differences, especially thanks to the technique of the domestic margin of appreciation, is related to the procedures of translation? This is what must be studied in the coming years. However, let me note here again that the 'dialogue of the judges', which is so much talked about today—this informal judicial forum which reaches beyond borders and orders of juris-diction—(according to Julie Allard and Antoine Garapon)—manifests the same tension between the market and fundamental rights that we have just alluded to. Consequently, these authors are using the term 'judges' business' in a very opportune way to express the ambivalence of this dialogue which can be interpreted sometimes as a form of diplomacy that is more or less aiming to conquer and impose, quietly, a given juridical model (the common law versus Roman/Germanic law, adversarial model versus investigative model, etc) and sometimes, on the contrary, as the construction of a supranational juridical argumentation in the context of a globalised public space which there-after concretises the 'universal hearing' which Chaïm Perelman talks about.[28] Between collaboration and competition, 'judges' benevolence'[29] or continua-tion of (economic or political) war by judicial means, cooperative dialogue or language of force, the judges too are mobilised in the great Babelian game of globalised law.

V. LAW IN DAY-TO-DAY PRACTICE

The foregoing brief survey of the domains reserved for international law (public and private), for comparative law and for globalised law should already have convinced the reader (at least, I hope so) of the pertinence and importance of the problematic of translation for an understanding of law today, even to the point where the notion of 'domain reserved' for these branches, supposedly distinct from 'law in day-to-day practice', loses most of its legitimacy. What I have tried to suggest is precisely the penetration of

---

[27] M Delmas-Marty, *Les forces imaginantes du droit. I. Le relatif et l'universel* (Paris, Seuil, 2004) 404.

[28] J Allard and A Garapon, *Les juges dans la mondialisation* (Paris, Seuil, 2005).

[29] G Canivet, 'Les influences croisées entre juridictions nationales et internationales. Éloge de la bénévolance des juges' (2005) 4 *Revue des sciences criminelles* 799.

the external by the internal or of the other into the same. Nonetheless—and this justifies the present continuation of this study—if it were possible to radically isolate a juridical order of world trade and to study it therefore in the 'purity' of its tradition, the coherence of its internal ordering and the uniqueness of its language, it would still be a question, decisively, of the logic of translation.

Every time a jurist puts a norm or an institution or a procedure into a historical perspective, it is already a question of translation: by doing so, he is bringing two historical periods closer to each other, sometimes going beyond the linguistic obstacles inherent in temporal distance—this diachronic depth (which was practised systematically by a civil law specialist like De Page) being often of a nature to shed light on the nature and function of the institution in question.

It is also a question of translation when one situation (concubinage, for example) is successively viewed from the angle of the different branches—civil law, social law, tax law—which is what leads Xavier Thunis to write that 'in the broad sense, all jurists are comparatists without knowing it'.[30] Whether it concerns the needs of teaching (what could be more pedagogical than a comparison?), of law practice (the obligations of the attorney are not the same as those of the business manager, those of the tenant are different from those of the usufructuary) or the commentary in jurisprudence (we know the delights of bringing out the divergences in jurisprudence between this or that chamber of a high jurisdiction), comparison is inherent to the profession of jurist, and hence so also is translation between the respective spheres of meaning both close and distant.

Translation yet again: when it comes to 'translating' the technical language of the court-appointed expert, when the legal adviser transposes into a juridical convention the arrangements desired by his clients, or when the parliamentary draftsman transposes into an acceptable juridical form the political will of a party or a government.

Another example of translation: when fact and law are brought together—and here we are at the heart of the juridical procedure—at the end of the double operation of checking/qualifying the fact and applying/interpreting the law.

Far from being reserved to only the specialists in private international law, the qualification or orientation of the litigious situation towards this or that juridical institution (and, more precisely, the choice of the qualifying concept inscribed in the hypothesis of such-and-such a norm) is the most normal and common operation carried out by jurists—to be convinced of this, one need only look at the qualification checking exercised by the Appeals Court. But if the complex of the facts requires to be configured around the rule, the rule, in turn, must be remodelled towards its own satisfactory application to the

---

[30] X Thunis, 'L'empire de la comparaison' in Van der Mensbrugghe, above n 15, 11.

dossier. Who would still maintain that this step is like a simple syllogism, as if it were enough to deduce in an a priori way and *ne variatur* the solution of which legal category applies? Here again, it is a matter of weighing it up, negotiating, adjusting it by means of trial and error, which is exactly what happens in the work of the translator: these are two worlds, both close to and distant from each other, foreign and yet familiar, which must be brought together and brought into dialogue with each other. In this operation, the judge 'translates' the discourse of the author (who is sometimes at a distance of several centuries, as in the case of the Code Napoléon) into that of the contemporary reader; he translates the letter of the text into the language of the spirit which must be given to it in view of the legitimacy and efficacity which we have a right to expect from a juridical text; he brings the part (this or that clause of a contract, this or that article of law) together with the whole (the juridical system seen in its entirety).

The Italian constitutional judge Gustavo Zagrebelsky is right to emphasise that the judge must serve two masters (exactly as the translator must): he seeks the norm which fits the special case just as well as it fits the juridical order. In so doing, he 'is in the service of neither the one nor the other, but of the one and the other'.[31]

It may perhaps be contended that today the classical method of interpretation of texts is a step backwards, since the judge is often required, due to the complexity and novelty of the questions before him, to work without or almost without a safety-net, using only a simple toolkit of very general principles, which obliges him to undertake a weighing up of the interests which confront him more directly with the weight of the forces and interests in conflict—think, for example, of the delicate question of the acceptability of aircraft noise in the vicinity of airports. But these forces, these interests, these values in conflict, have to be weighed up, ie have to be brought down to a common measure in spite of their heterogeneity. Despite their apparent incommensurability (here one may think of the American Supreme Court judge Scalia, who mocked this method by saying that it consisted of wondering whether 'this stone is heavier than that line is long'[32]), the judge must shoulder the task of 'constructing equivalents': he must translate a moral harm into a financial compensation, he must translate the language of health or of safety or of quality of life into the language of employment, of economic prosperity, of national imperatives—and the other way around, with the same feeling of approximation and sometimes of failure that every translator feels when his task is completed.

---

[31] G Zagrebelsky (M Leroy trans), *Le droit en douceur* (Paris, Economica, 2000) 131.
[32] Dissenting opinion of Judge Scalia in *Bendix Autolite v Miswesco Enters*, 486 US 888, 897 (1988).

VI. A QUESTION OF ETHICS LIKEWISE

Thomas Kuhn, the author of the theory of paradigms, had the merit of emphasising that a paradigm was not only the bearer of a hypothesis and of a method (resting upon a world-view and translated into 'well-chosen examples'), but that it was also accompanied by a set of values.[33] This applies especially well to the question of the translational paradigm with which this chapter concerned, and which, no doubt more explicitly than is the case for other intellectual operations, turns out to carry an ethical exigency. Translation is straight away accompanied by a recognition of the difference of the other and of the wish to undertake with that other an interaction on the basis of the reciprocal admission of the limits of each other's own language: in the activity of translation, what Antoine Berman nicely termed 'the test of the foreign' is being tried out.[34]

Seen from this angle, the bringing together of the fact and the law can be analysed also and above all as the coming into contact (often a traumatising contact, at least in its premises) of the discourse of the individual with that of the man of laws. Here we are, of course, not limited to envisaging the translator to whom every accused person who does not speak the language of the court has a right; generally speaking, every citizen subject to law requires the intervention of a lawyer or juridical counsel, or some other person initiated into the language of the law, for the purpose of bringing about the coming together of two language-universes (which are also 'forms of life', as Wittgenstein reminds us) which are a priori very far from each other.

The exigency of 'accessibility' to the tribunal (Article 6 of the European Convention on Human Rights) here takes on an ethical profundity which passes via the medium of language; in order that justice should be done, what is at stake is to give a hearing to the parties first of all, without reducing the content of their discourse to what is a priori 'encodable', assimilable into the legal hypothesis. Beyond the traditional calling into question of juridical jargon, this is an ethical exigency of humanity that makes its voice heard here: to do justice to the words of the individual subject to the law, in its specificity and sometimes in its strangeness, before dispensing justice. This is a question of recognition, of listening, of equality in principle of all those who are subject to the law, and it is a question of a cooperative dialogue.

As is emphasised by James Boyd White, what is asked of the judge is this rare quality of being able to place himself successively in the place of each of the parties, which implies that he must recognise both the pertinence and the legitimacy of the discourses that confront each other at the same time as he perceives their respective limits—including perceiving the pertinence and limits of the juridical language.[35] Only on this condition will the judgment be

---

[33] T Kuhn, *La structure des révolutions scientifiques* (Paris, Flammarion, 1972) 216ff.
[34] A Berman, *L'épreuve de l'étranger* (Paris, Gallimard, 1984).
[35] JB White, *Justice as Translation* (Chicago, University of Chicago Press, 1990) 262.

audible to both parties. In the best case, he will do more and go further than merely 'deciding between' the appellants by allotting to each his share (to do only that, all you need is a sword); instead, he will bring the protagonists to the beginnings of a reciprocal recognition, an indispensable prerequisite for each of them to resume their participation in the social bond that had been compromised.[36]

On the ethical terrain likewise, it turns out that law is a privileged laboratory for the translational paradigm.

VII. SOME GAINS FROM TRANSLATION THEORY

The foregoing elaborations have permitted me, at the end of my rapid staking-out of the juridical field, to take the measure of numerous important applications of the translational paradigm in the field of law. But then, you will ask, what use can this approach be in terms of translation? Rather than go back now over the various questions raised in the preceding paragraphs, in order to shine upon them the light of the translational paradigm, I propose in conclusion to run through some of the essential gains arising from this problematic of translation.

The first point consists in recalling that translation is not limited to the mere transfer of a verbal message from one language to another (translation in the strict sense); it is also understood in the broader sense, of the interpretation of any signifying ensemble within one and the same linguistic community. This is because difference passes through the heart of every natural language and not just along its frontiers: difference, and hence strangeness, opacity, the non-coinciding of the self with itself—this is the post-Babel dispersion and confusion. How could it be otherwise, since there does not exist anywhere a lexis which would coincide, term for term, without loss and without excess, in a perfect transparency, with the things that its words aim to name? Rather than dictionaries with univocal definitions, we have encyclopedias which are a summation of usage, of conventions, of traditions relative to these words and which express our more or less successfuls efforts at naming these things. But this weakness of natural languages is also their strength: their semantic plasticity and their floating usages reveal astonishing possibilities of meaning, and permit us precisely to carry out translational adjustments and creativity in language. Because they are at the same time both less and more than a lexis, these languages are condemned to be constantly (re)translated, condemned to be susceptible to infinite signifying virtualities.

The second of the chief gains acquired from translation theory consists in the identification of translation's two limit points, which are like its Scylla

---

and Charybdis. On the one hand, there is the hasty and often arrogant statement of omnitranslatability, according to which translation comes down to a simple decoding of a more-or-less encrypted message, whose code one only needs to master in order to solve its difficulties. On the other hand, there is the denial of translation, anchored in the conviction that the deep structures of languages and cultures are incommensurable with one another and therefore in reality no transposition between them is possible. In the first case, we think we can get to the common basis of all the languages, which would make translation between them possible, so we make great efforts to detect, beneath the apparent buzzing confusion of languages, these hidden structures which would either take us back to an originary matrix whose traces have been lost in the darkness of time or forward to an absolutely rational language which remains to be constructed, but whose lines of force we are already in a position to discern. Placed in the service of political/cultural ambitions, these postulates increase, as one might suspect, the danger of a hegemonic translation policy, one that enslaves, a policy of the sort that imperial Rome practised towards the Greek heritage which she appropriated. In the other case, the postulate of untranslatability—despite the existence of massive and ancient translations which are not all 'unfaithful beauties', and although it can claim its authority from a certain degree of incommensurability of natural languages—could also feed into some regrettable political/cultural attitudes inspired by the fear or the rejection of the other, the refusal of all forms of cross-breeding, and the timid falling back onto one's own idiolect. Since its beginnings, the history and theory of translation has never ceased to oscillate between these two extremes, succumbing at times to its traps, and at times succeeding in coming up with a third way, which makes translation into an exercise which is just as necessary as it is approximate, and which must therefore always be started anew.

The methodological version of the dilemma, which is of more direct interest to us here and which constitutes the third gain of translation theory, consists in emphasising the eternal tension between the vow of fidelity and the suspicion of betrayal which runs through this whole problematic. The translator, as has been written, is that servant forced to serve two masters at the same time and who cannot but betray both the one and the other. But this excess of unworthiness (*traduttore, traditore*), just like this over-rigorous insistence (fidelity to what—to the word, to the letter, to the spirit, to the source language, to the target language?) proceeds from a common misconception: the belief, even now, that it is possible to say the same thing in different words, as if there existed some universal super-lexis—a supranatural and immutable language—which could guarantee the change, without loss or distortion, from one language to another, because it would be able to tell the truth of things 'as they are in themselves'. However, we must get away from this illusory belief (which reproduces at the inter-linguistic level the fantasy of a pure lexis which we have already denounced at the intra-linguistic level); we must mourn the sad passing of the idea of a perfect language and come to terms with the fact that there does not exist any criterion of good translation. Thus, we will make do with 'an equivalence that is not identical' (Paul Ricoeur) and, when we translate, we will content ourselves with saying 'practically the same thing' (Umberto Eco). Along this path, a very rich set of methodologies has developed, seeking to bring the (national) reader closer to the (foreign) author. A study of these methodologies reveals an astounding degree of convergence with our analysis of the work of the judge: Valery Larbaud refers to the 'weighing of words' practised by the translator;[37] Umberto Eco, for his part, speaks of the quest for the most advantageous compromise, but remains conscious of the sacrifices that you must know how to make; as for Paul Ricoeur, he alludes to the 'construction of comparables' with a view to establishing this 'equivalence without being identical', which is, as regards translation, the sole form of higher 'justness' (justice?) that one can lay claim to.[38] In the best case, the balance that is negotiated between the other and the same, the old and the current, the letter and the spirit, can take the form—beyond the problematic of the more-or-less great 'fidelity'—of what Jacques Derrida calls *une traduction relevante*, a 'relevant translation';[39] that is to say, a translation which is not only pertinent or well adapted, but which 'raises' the translated work, in the triple meaning of what, first of all, 'raises' a culinary preparation and gives it taste; secondly, of what elevates the translated work, hoisting it up to the heights and making it equal to the strongest of its potentials; and thirdly, in the Hegelian sense of sublation, that which transcends and preserves at the same time. A translation, indeed, brings about the putting-to-death of the translated text and yet at the same guarantees it a form of survival. In this way we will have accomplished the essential function of what Walter Benjamin called 'the task of the translator': to take responsibility for and germinate in one's own language the seed of meaning which dwells in the source language without truly coming to be heard therein.[40]

---

[37] V Larbaud, *Sous l'invocation de Saint Jérôme* (Paris, Gallimard, 1997) 76.

[38] P Ricoeur, 'Un "passage": traduire l'intraduisible' in P Ricoeur, *Sur la traduction* (Paris, Bayard, 2004) 62ff.

[39] J Derrida, *Qu'est-ce qu'une traduction relevante?* (Paris, L'Herne (carnets), 2005).

[40] W Benjamin, *La tâche du traducteur* (1923) in M de Gandillac, R Rochlitz and P Rusch (eds), *Œuvres*, vol I (Paris, Galimard (Folio), 2000) 244ff.

6

Controlled Comparison and Language of Description

MAURICE ADAMS[1]

E VERY NOW AND then, I enjoy watching nature documentaries, and in particular those by Jacques Cousteau, the famous French oceanologist. There is an episode where—if I remember correctly—part of the coast of Somalia is explored. Cousteau's divers are at the beach, fully equipped and ready to explore the waters. This to the great amusement of the local population; to the locals, the creatures on the beach must be an unfamiliar species of dolphins: they have the same smooth skin and general appearance, despite the fact that they have limbs and are able to walk. Nonetheless, dolphins they must be!

We all experience the desire to characterise unfamiliar phenomena in terms or categories we think we understand or recognise; this makes the unexpected manageable. As the example above shows, this desire can be so seductive that it can lead to deception. As far as comparative law is concerned, this can be quite a problem. Is there a way to overcome this seduction? This is a question I want to deal with in this chapter, and I will build on a debate that took place in the 1960s in order to do so. But to be able to do this, I will first need to start with a discussion on the specific characteristics of comparative law.

I

What is it that justifies comparative law as an independent discipline?[2] This question is relevant, since comparison is inseparably connected with doing research in the humanities and social sciences—either of which the legal

---

[1] A previous version of this chapter was published in Dutch as 'Eenvoud en verleidelijkheid: Rechtsvergelijkende analyse en taal van descriptie' (2011) 60 *Ars Aequi Maandblad* 796.

[2] See also M Adams, 'Doing What Doesn't Come Naturally. On the Distinctiveness of Comparative Law' in M Van Hoecke (ed), *Methodologies of Legal Research* (Oxford, Hart Publishing, 2011) 229–40.

domain is a part.[3] Nearly any claim we make as lawyers, as well as every distinction we draw, will implicitly or explicitly be set against something else. A legal arrangement can only be qualified as satisfactory or good because there is another arrangement by which it can be measured; such an arrangement is never good just in and of itself. When judges are looking for principles to help decide on an unprecedented or unregulated situation, they tend to rely on ana-logical reasoning, ie they apply a rule for a comparable situation, be it a real or hypothetical one, to the situation at hand. Also, ordering and classifying cases in a specific field or domain—call it the pursuit for consistency—is very much a comparative activity; it is an exercise which can only be done because there are a number of cases that can be situated against each other. Comparing, in other words, is a fundamental principle of legal research.[4] It even provides the inevitable and inescapable frame of reference for scientific activity in the humanities and social sciences.[5] More generally and even stronger: '[t]hinking without comparison is unthinkable. And, in the absence of comparison, so is all scientific thought and scientific research.'[6] Therefore, it could be argued that there really is nothing very special about doing comparative law. To be sure, legal research has some distinctive features, but comparativeness is not one of them; that quality is part and parcel of all (legal) research.

> [I]n major respects, comparative law is an instance of the more general form of legal research [which is hermeneutic, interpretative and institutional]. The way in which it attempts to reconstruct both the foreign and the researcher's own legal systems is similar to general legal research on either of those systems.[7]

If all this is true, what then could possibly justify, or be the point of, dis-tinguishing comparative law from other kinds of legal research? Why not simply refer to what doing legal research amounts to, then add a few words of warning on the choice of countries and so on? There must be more to be

---

[3] On this see, eg B Bix, 'Law as an Autonomous Discipline' in P Cane and M Tushnet (eds), *The Oxford Handbook of Legal Studies* (Oxford, Oxford University Press, 2003) 975–87; C McCrudden, 'Legal Research and the Social Sciences' (2006) 122 *Law Quarterly Review* 623.

[4] Also in this vein, VV Palmer, 'From Lerotholi to Lando: Some Examples of Comparative Law Methodology' (2005) 53 *American Journal of Comparative Law* 262.

[5] Knowing what I do not know, I do not wish to make any statement in this chapter about what are called the positive or natural sciences.

[6] GE Swanson, 'Frameworks for Comparative Research' in I Vallier (ed), *Comparative Methods in Sociology* (Berkeley, University of California Press, 1971) 141. Also quoted by Palmer, above n 4, 261. The anthropologist Clifford Geertz formulated the same view somewhat more subtly: 'Santayana's famous dictum that one compares only when one is unable to get to the heart of the matter seems to me . . . the precise reverse of the truth; it is through comparison, and of incom-parables, that whatever heart we can actually get to is to be reached': C Geertz, *Local Knowledge* (New York, Basic Books, 1983) 233. More direct is J Hall, *Comparative Law and Social Theory* (Baton Rouge, Louisiana State University Press, 1963) 9: 'to be sapiens is to be a comparatist'.

[7] J Bell, 'Legal Research and the Distinctiveness of Comparative Law' in Van Hoecke, above n 2, 175 (Bell qualifies this statement to the extent that he clearly recognises that there are pecu-liar challenges to comparative law, especially in terms of having to make explicit, to a foreign audience, the broader social and cultural context and assumptions of a foreign legal systems or legal concepts).

said on this, for why else would the phrase 'comparative law' proudly carry the term 'comparative' in its banner? If, indeed, it does not want to be dismissed as a pleonasm—'Thinking about the law is by definition comparative, Silly!'—comparative law should at the very least pose some specific challenges other than the problems lawyers and legal researchers routinely face.[8]

One of the main reasons there is something special or distinctive about doing comparative legal research, something that calls for a specific approach and specific methods, is that legal comparatists must, among other things, immerse themselves in a foreign and therefore strange legal culture. Such an 'involved' activity does not come naturally because legal comparatists have to deal with one or more legal cultures whose 'language' (metaphorically understood) they do not speak, ie cultures with different institutions and unexpressed codes; their own histories, ideologies and self-images; systems they have not normally been trained, educated or disciplined in, and with which they are therefore not naturally or intimately connected to. This process of trying to understand foreign or strange legal cultures (or some of their elements) with an eye for subsequent comparison manifests particular problems because it goes far beyond mere fact-finding and the regular (ie national) way of legal interpretation, where one almost self-evidently engages the social context when determining the meaning of the law. The problems that the law addresses and the solutions that it intends to provide are very much connected to the socio-cultural environment from which these problems and solutions arise, and the comparatist should engage with this environment. This specific problem justifies the existence of the research discipline known as comparative law. Furthermore, the repeated assertion that comparative law is not an area of law seems to support this point.[9] In any case, thorough understanding and comprehensive description of foreign legal cultures—in the manner described above—indeed raises mainly methodological questions.

II

In the 1960s, a debate took place that was related to the issue described in the previous section: which conceptual framework ought to be used to describe

---

[8] Palmer, above n 4, 262–63; *cf* HP Glenn, 'Aims of Comparative Law' in JM Smits (ed), *Elgar Encyclopedia of Comparative Law* (Cheltenham, Edward Elgar, 2006) 59.

[9] Palmer, above n 4, 262–63. See also WJ Kamba, 'Comparative Law: a Theoretical Framework' (1974) 23 *International and Comparative Law Quarterly* 486. All this led Kahn-Freud to quip that there is no such thing as comparative law: 'The trouble is that the subject . . . has by common consent the somewhat unusual characteristic that it does not exist': O Kahn-Freud, 'Comparative Law as an Academic Subject' (1966) 81 *Law Quarterly Review* 41. Part of Kahn-Freud's observation is due to the somewhat established and misleading English terminology—'comparative *law*'. This suggests that there is in fact a separate *legal* domain. This problem does not exist in Dutch (rechts*vergelijking*), or in German (Rechts*vergleichung*). In both languages, the term refers to an activity: *comparing* law. French has the same 'problem' as English: '*droit* comparé'.

a foreign legal culture (or legal system[10])? How are the characteristics of the foreign system represented most efficiently? The initiation for the debate was a study by Max Gluckman, a South African legal anthropologist, about the process of dispute resolution in the Barotse tribe in former Northern Rhodesia (today known as Zambia).[11] Gluckman opted for a conceptual framework, based first and foremost on English law, and secondly on Roman–Dutch law. 'I consider that very many of [the Barotse legal] concepts can, without distortion after careful and perhaps lengthy description and discussion, be given English equivalents . . .'[12]

As was to be expected, Gluckman's methods received criticism, most notably from fellow anthropologist Paul Bohannan: the terminology of English law and Roman–Dutch law might well be suited to the description of the English and South African legal systems, but certainly not for the description of the 'folk law' of an African tribe.[13] According to Bohannan, these legal systems were to be described in the native terms and categories that evoked their individuality. In other words, they should not be forced onto the Procrustean bed of the principles and concepts of a different legal culture. This would only lead to tunnel vision and confusion because the foreign legal culture would then be viewed and understood as a function of this different legal culture. '[I]t simulates understanding through the use of a familiar word. Such simulation leads—almost inevitably, I think—to an assumption of comparability of everything called by the same word—and this is a difficulty that is almost impossible to correct.'[14]

Gluckman appeared to only agree in part with this criticism.[15] Indeed, he too believed that a legal anthropologist should strive to describe the legal system at issue in a way that would reflect its individual character. And where there would be no reasonable equivalent of the original (ie African) terminology available, then the original terminology would prevail. However, in cases where there was an equivalent, he did not consider it a problem to use—in his

---

[10] In this text, I will treat terms such as legal culture, system, etc, as synonymous, referring to these norm constellations that are foreign to that of a comparatist. This applies to systems that are physically or culturally close to ours (within Europe, for example) or far away. For the problems concerning the term legal culture see D Nelken, 'Defining and Using the Concept of Legal Culture' in E Örücü and D Nelken (eds), *Comparative Law. A Handbook* (Oxford, Hart Publishing, 2007) 109–32.

[11] M Gluckman, *The Ideas in Barotse Jurisprudence*, 2nd edn (Manchester, Manchester University Press, 1967; originally published in 1965 as *Storrs Lectures on Jurisprudence at Yale Law School*); M Gluckman, 'Reappraisal' in M Gluckman, *The Judicial Process among the Barotse of Northern Rhodesia (Zambia)* (Manchester, Manchester University Press, 1967); M Gluckman, 'Concepts in the Comparative Study of Tribal Law' in L Nader (ed), *Law in Culture and Society* (Berkeley, University of California Press, 1997) 349–73. See also SF Moore, 'Comparative Studies' in L Nader (ed), *Law in Culture and Society* 341–46.

[12] Gluckman, *The Judicial Process*, ibid, 380–81.

[13] P Bohannan, 'Review of *The Ideas in Barotse Jurisprudence*' (1967) 36 *Kroeber Anthropological Society Papers* 94; P Bohannan, 'Ethnography and Comparison in Legal Anthropology' in Nader, ibid, 401–18.

[14] Bohannan, 'Ethnography', ibid, 403.

[15] M Gluckman, 'Concepts in the Comparative Study of Tribal Law', above n 11, 349–73.

case—English or Roman law terminology, though, if necessary, with a comprehensive description of the original Barotse concept. In fact, he preferred such an approach. '[I]t seems to me that the refinements of English, and in general European, jurisprudence provide us with a more suitable vocabulary than do the languages of tribal law.'[16] As a result, and with regard to the concept of 'ownership', he was prepared to state that

> I consider that when writing in English, the use of the English equivalent term, general and multiferential in its common-sense meaning, brings out implications in the English meaning of 'owner' as well as perhaps a significant core of similarity in the Barotse meaning of *mung'a*. The alternative in the extreme is to make communication impossible.[17]

Gluckman argued that it would not only be possible to communicate more effectively about a foreign system using this familiar—ie English and Roman–Dutch—terminology, but that this would be even more effective in revealing the similarities and differences between the legal systems researched.

In this respect, the difference in opinion between Gluckman and Bohannan seemed to be a matter of nuance and taste. It is even possible to argue that they were both partially right, but that Gluckman was the more pragmatic of the two: in practice, it is impossible to objectively describe a foreign system, and a language of communication is indispensable. Gluckman therefore believed that one should be able to use a language that is recognisable for the stranger, especially a language that allowed the making of subtle distinctions. Bohannan argued that such a research strategy would inevitably lead to confusion and tunnel vision (bias), and that this should be avoided at all costs. It seemed as though both Gluckman and Bohannan only focused on the negative aspects of the other's approach.

III

There is, however, I think, more to the story, and this is set against a background of differing views concerning the goals of legal anthropology and comparative law, respectively. Gluckman was mainly interested in reaching a higher level of abstraction; he wanted to investigate whether some of the fundamentals of a specific legal system, in his case of the Barotse tribe, also had a further-reaching and broader meaning. For Gluckman, these fundamentals were potentially more than just incidental legal concepts; he viewed them as part of a larger question: what is the relation between the local legal concepts and the socio-economic context of these concepts? He also wanted to be able to explore and explain that relation:

[16] Ibid, 367.
[17] Ibid, 357.

I am interested, like most social anthropologists, in specifying the folk conceptions of particular people as clearly as I can and then trying to explain why they are as they are, and how they differ from folk conceptions of others, in terms of social and economic background.[18]

He was concerned with description as well as comparative analysis, no doubt taking to heart the statement that 'he who knows one society, knows no society'.[19] Bohannan, on the other hand, was primarily interested in describing and understanding the foreign legal system in and on its own terms, rather than comparing it. As Clifford Geertz had it: '"law," here, there, or anywhere, is part of a distinctive manner of imagining the real'.[20] Therefore, since each legal construct must and can be seen as a discrete epistemological construct, the differences between legal cultures is irreducible.[21] As a result, it is, for example, 'not possible for a civilian to think like a common-law lawyer'.[22] Bohannan, indeed, believed that in the microworld of the legal conceptual framework of the Tiv, a Nigerian tribe he had investigated himself,[23] the whole organisation of the legal system could be found. Gluckman, on the other hand, looked at the concepts and principles of Barotse law as part of a larger (comparative) objective, whereas Bohannan was mostly interested in studying the (Tiv) concepts themselves because he considered them a reflection of the whole organisation of the legal system.[24] Speaking about a foreign legal culture in terminology taken from a legal language unknown to that culture 'gives the *illusion* of getting somewhere'.[25] The discussion between Gluckman

---

[18] Ibid, 354.

[19] Attributed to Fahrenfort. Cited by A Köbben, 'De vergelijkend-functionele methode in de volkenkunde' [The comparative-functional method in anthropology] in A Köbben, *Van primitieven tot medeburgers* [From Primitives to Fellow Citizens] (Van Gorcum, 1964) 24.

[20] C Geertz, *Local Knowledge: Further Essays in Interpretative Anthropology* (New York, Basic Books, 1983) 184 (I will not go into Geertz's nuanced argumentation). Bohannan's approach is in tune (though not identical) with what later came to prominence as 'difference theory'. Specifically, in comparative law it gained prominence after Frankenberg published his critique of functionalism *à la* Zweigert and Kotz: G Frankenberg, 'Critical Comparisons: Re-thinking Comparative Law' (1985) 26 *Harvard International Law Journal* 411. For important nuances of functionalism see J Husa, 'Farewell to Functionalism or Methodological Tolerance?' (2003) 67 *Rabels Zeitschrift für ausländisches und internationales Privatrecht* 419.

[21] On all this see R Caterina, 'Comparative Law and the Cognitive Revolution' (2003–04) 78 *Tulane Law Review* 1506 (and surrounding pages). Caterina calls for a more empirical approach towards questions of difference and similarity between legal systems (in his case because cognitive sciences might cast doubt on a presumption of difference in comparative law: 'Of course cultural diversity cannot be denied, and one merit of comparison is that it challenges old certitudes. But must comparative lawyers (or anthropologists) deliberately seek "astonishment"? Must they "purposefully privilege the identification of differences?"' (1546, quoting Clifford Geertz and Pierre Legrand, respectively). See also G Dannemann, 'Comparative Law: Study of Similarities or Differences?' in M Reimann and R Zimmermann (eds), *The Oxford Handbook of Comparative Law* (Oxford, Oxford University Press, 2006) 416.

[22] P Legrand, *Fragments on Law-as-Culture* (Zwolle, Tjeenk Willink, 1999) 64.

[23] See P Bohannan, *Justice and Judgment Among the Tiv* (Prospect Heights, IL, Waveland Press, 1957).

[24] Moore, above n 11, 343.

[25] Bohannan, 'Ethnography', above n 13, 402 (my italics).

and Bohannan appeared to be at cross-purposes because they both had a different research focus and research objective.

In any case, and as far as I am concerned, comparative law should not only focus on understanding and describing the foreign legal system, but should also strive to obtain more general ideas that follow from the identified differences and similarities between the legal systems. As just mentioned, this was Gluckman's objective more than it was Bohannan's. However, it is striking that comparative law often limits itself to only describing a foreign legal system (and often does so in a rather sophisticated manner). If, however, we want to give the term 'compare' an independent meaning, by explicitly bringing information from the different legal systems together, by comparing them to each other and by discussing the relation between the systems at hand, more should be done. The question then becomes: what can we learn about the legal systems vis-à-vis each other, and do the reported differences and similarities fit in comparative and explanatory frameworks?

For the purposes of description, Bohannan argued in favour of a completely neutral language, an 'independent language without national home',[26] because he felt that Gluckman's conceptual framework was too closely connected to an existing system. A computer language like Fortan was an example of such an independent language. Bohannan realised that such an approach would be biased as well, but the bias would be more noticeable. 'Obviously we cannot become biasless—rather, we must investigate our biases and institute controls for them. Obviously human beings cannot compare (or do anything else) without culture; rather we must control the logic of the culture of comparison.'[27] Such a controlled comparison was to start from the inside and work towards the outside (not the other way around), according to Bohannan. The systems should be allowed to speak for themselves and they should be researched separately, based on their own terms and categories, and ultimately there should be an analytical framework—the aforementioned 'independent language without national home'—as the basis for the actual comparison. 'This new language . . . is a logical structure of interrelated propositions about the working of society and culture.'[28] For Bohannan, comparability and comparison were first and foremost a result of research, a conclusion, something that could only be found or postulated after the systems or cultures at issue had been fully explored, based on their individual characteristics. Comparability could certainly not be advanced by using a language of description that was intimately linked to a specific legal system.

[26] Ibid, 416.
[27] Ibid, 416.
[28] Ibid, 416–17.

> Comparison must be done in a *controlled way*, with great awareness and sensitivity to the original meaning, and with a set of methods that allow us to utilize what we are doing toward some specific ends beyond merely buttressing a position.[29]

Nevertheless, Bohannan would not dare to claim that Gluckman's conclusions about the system of dispute settlement with the Barotse were wrong; he just believed that Gluckman's method did not allow us to verify it.

> Please note that I did *not* say that the [Barotse] and the English do not have fundamentally similar ideas, but only that by [Gluckmans] method of exposition there is no possible way for a reader to discover whether they have or not.[30]

Avoiding research bias is, of course, an important objective of any type of research, but Gluckman stated that we nevertheless should also consider the practical dimensions of comparative legal research:

> It must be a very blinkered mind that, when an anthropologist speaks of contract in an African tribe, immediately thinks of the English or French or Roman–Dutch or Roman contract. 'Contract' has a general meaning of enforceable agreement; and one can use it—and must use it—to discuss the different conditions, forms, incidents, and remedies for breach of contract in various social conditions.[31]

This is why he argued that

> In a study of government one may use the word 'legislature' to cover British Parliament, American Congress, German Bundestag and Reichstag, French Chambre des Députés, Japanese Diet, all for purposes of general discussion in order to draw attention to similarity while insisting on difference. Some word is necessary for purposes of general discussion. In discussing several systems of law, therefore, one may speak of ownership, contract, property, succession, marriage, betrothal, judge, decision, all to draw attention to a core of similitude while defining differences.[32]

Open communication about new insights should indeed realistically be possible. Bohannan also appeared to acknowledge this when he wrote that the dispute with Gluckman 'boils down to this question: is it more difficult for a reader to keep in mind a set of narrative terms or a set of glosses on English words . . . ?'[33] He nevertheless maintained that the second approach was too misleading. The fact of the matter, according to him, was that 'good ethnography is hard to read . . . [E]very ethnographer owes it to himself, the people the studies, and his colleagues not to blunt the edge of his material.'[34]

---

[29] Ibid, 410 (my italics).
[30] Ibid, 411.
[31] M Gluckman, 'Concepts in the Comparative Study of Tribal Law', above n 11, 364.
[32] Ibid.
[33] Bohannan, 'Ethnography', above n 13, 402.
[34] Ibid 403.

IV

It seems clear to me that the anthropologist-ethnographer, as well as the legal comparatist, need to interpret foreign legal data as much as possible in their unique social context. The description of foreign legal systems or cultures should in other words do justice to its unique characteristics. Bohannan seemed very much aware of this and accepted its consequences without compromise. But, since common sense is a virtue for the legal comparatist (as is sympathy for the reader![35]), to me the real question is whether using an existing language is as disruptive as Bohannan took it to be. Is there indeed bias if familiar terminology—terminology stemming from one specific system—is used in comparative law? And does it really prohibit controlled comparison?

As far as the last question is concerned, I do not think it does—or, at least, not necessarily. This appreciation is confirmed by the fact that Bohannan, as an anthropologist and ethnographer, does not seem to fully realise that, in order to compare something, there needs to be similarity—to a certain degree—between the different jurisdictions regarding the matter at hand; a similarity that is represented in the research question and in the comparative conceptual framework which initiates the research. In any case, comparison is useless if there is no similarity between the systems or cultures. In this regard, the legal comparatist needs more specifically to postulate comparability and similarity at the start of the research. Comparability and similarity are not only possible results of the research, as Bohannan seems to suggest, but are especially the necessary and presupposed starting points. Such a presumption of comparability is, of course, not completely unfounded, but based on prior knowledge and/or preliminary investigation. At the very least, it is an educated guess, and this guess shows itself in the terminology on which the research question is framed and on which the research project builds. But, of course, one has to realise that the true nature of the comparability/similarity of legal systems, including its conceptual framework and accompanying vocabulary, is only revealed by the research itself. It is important to note here that this implies that the focus of a research project needs to be adjusted repeatedly—stepping back and making a landscape picture (distance and similarity), and coming near and making close ups (difference). There is, however, no other way than to start with a broad conceptual framework and research question, based on a general view of the situation at issue and a presumption or appearance of similarity.[36] In due course, more and more details will emerge as a result of an accurate description of the uniqueness of a system, including a willingness

---

[35] For a more extensive discussion see also K Lemmens, 'Comparative Law as an Act of Modesty: A Pragmatic and Realistic Approach to Comparative Legal Scholarship' in M Adams and JA Bomhoff (eds), *Practice and Theory in Comparative Law* (Cambridge, Cambridge University Press, 2012).

[36] Even Pierre Legrand, the difference thinker *par excellence*, admits this. See P Legrand, 'The Same and the Different' in P Legrand and R Munday (eds), *Comparative Legal Studies: Traditions and Transitions* (Cambridge, Cambridge University Press, 2003) 283: 'I accept that no compari-

to recharacterise the original framework and vocabulary, the research question and the general situation.

In my opinion, controlled comparison is a function of this permanent change in perspective; a continuous process and also part of the research procedure. Controlled comparison refines the research process permanently, even if you start with using a familiar conceptual framework.[37] Since Bohannan was so focused on describing a foreign legal system from an almost exclusively micro- or internal perspective, he did not seem to realise that it is in fact this permanent change in perspective that is essential to doing comparative law. This might well cater for the troubles he identifies on Gluckman's approach.

Bohannan's view may ultimately result in the description of a legal system being reduced to merely background information and deep context. By following his methodology, you will run the risk of losing the notion that the principles of a legal system might transcend their local origin and have a further-reaching meaning than just their specific embeddedness.[38] Bohannan's view may thus give rise to a solipsism that will in the end make comparison very difficult.[39] The building of a conceptual framework, and theory building based on comparison, will as a result become almost impossible. Bohannan did not seem to be fully aware of the 'comparative' consequences of his research strategy. In the end, this is the result of the fact that, in his capacity as a legal anthropologist and ethnographer, he might never have been really focused on comparison as such.

V

In one of his articles, Mark Van Hoecke writes that

the ambition of comparative law has always been to develop some neutral framework, some common language with which several legal systems could be described in a way accessible to and completely understandable by lawyers belonging to any one of those legal systems. *We are not discussing here the problems it entails.* We wish merely to emphasise that some (relatively) neutral, objective, accessible description is a key ambition of comparative law.[40]

---

son can be initiated without a comparatist taking the view that there is an apparent sameness between the objects of comparison, that they seem alike in at least one respect'.

[37] However, attention to case selection is a prerequisite, but this is something few lawyers pay attention to. See R Hirschl, 'The Question of Case Selection in Comparative Constitutional Law' (2005) 53 *The American Journal of Constitutional Law* 125.

[38] *Cf* JM Donovan, *Legal Anthropology* (Lanham, AltaMira Press, 2008) 166.

[39] He does appear to be aware of this (although not taking consequences): 'It seems to me that I did not say anything so absurd': Bohannan, 'Ethnography', above n 13, 405.

[40] M Van Hoecke and M Warrington, 'Legal Cultures, Legal Paradigms and Legal Doctrine: Towards a New Model for Comparative Law' (1998) 47 *International and Comparative Law Quarterly* 530 (italics added).

In this chapter I discuss part of the challenge Mark Van Hoecke did not wish to touch upon in that 1998 article, by discussing the implications of the debate between Gluckman and Bohannan. Regardless of whether we embrace Gluckman's or Bohannan's view, the comparative lawyer has to realise—and this is a fundamental restriction of every form of comparative research—that there are no descriptive terms that are entirely neutral or unbiased. So let us now return to the question I posed at the beginning of this chapter: is it possible for the legal comparatist to escape the temptation of describing a foreign system in terms or categories he thinks he knows or recognises? The answer is undoubtedly no. However, by now the issue (and the accompanying question) has gained a different identity, and is more about whether using legal terminology that is linked to a specific legal system is too detrimental to effective or useful legal comparison. I do not think this is necessarily so. But doing this necessitates that the researcher should permanently work in a 'spirit of conceptual tentativeness': the researcher needs to avoid normative preconditions and be willing to replace the original conceptual and terminological framework with a better-suited one,[41] realising that whatever terms one uses will inevitably carry traces of the normative preoccupations of those who use the natural language from which the terms used derive. As with all other classifications, a comparative framework was (and is) always subject to correction in the light of better insight. A continuous process of 'perspective change'— ie 'controlled' comparison—can ensure that this correction will actually take place. Neutrality in comparative law can then at least be a worthwhile aspiration, even if existing and familiar terms are chosen as a means of description.

---

[41] M Adams and J Griffiths, 'Against "Comparative Method": Explaining Similarities and Differences' in Adams and Bomhoff, above n 35, 2012.

7

Three Functions of Function in Comparative Legal Studies

CATHERINE VALCKE AND MATHEW GRELLETTE

I. INTRODUCTION

COMPARATIVE LAW FUNCTIONALISM is widely associated with Konrad Zweigert and Hein Kötz's view that '[t]he basic methodological principle of all comparative law is that of functionality'.[1] In their seminal *An Introduction to Comparative Law*, the two authors develop that general statement into an elaborate model structured around four basic propositions. The first is a conception of law that can be described as 'thickly functionalistic': law as conceptually distinct from, yet causally connected to, real human problems, with the causal connection being quite substantial. Whereas most people would agree that law is *to some extent* aimed at solving problems, Zweigert and Kötz insist that that is its *main* (perhaps *only*) purpose, with the result that it is in fact best explained in terms of functionality.[2] The second proposition in Zweigert and Kötz's model is sociological: the problems that law aims to solve, they posit, are roughly the same everywhere. The third proposition is their notorious *praesumptio similitudinis*, which logically follows from the preceding two: if law is mainly about solving problems and problems are roughly the same everywhere, it follows that law too is, or in any event should be, roughly the same everywhere.[3] The fourth and final proposition is their 'convergence' thesis about comparative law: insofar as the world may not in fact be as described under the third proposition, it falls to

---

[1] K Zweigert and H Kötz, *An Introduction to Comparative Law*, 3rd edn (Oxford, Oxford University Press, 1998) 31. See also AE Platsas, 'The Functional and the Dysfunctional in the Comparative Method of Law: Some Critical Remarks' (2008) 12.3 *Electronic Journal of Comparative Law* (www.ejcl.org): 'functionality remains the epicenter of the comparative method of law and . . . its drawbacks [stand only to] remind us that the principle is susceptible to further refinement'.
[2] Zweigert and Kötz, ibid, 30.
[3] Ibid, 31.

comparative law to make it so.[4] Indeed, Zweigert and Kötz's overall convergence agenda can be coherently explained in terms of these four propositions: if law across the world can be tied through a central function that is external to it, namely, that of attending to a same set of social problems, it makes sense to think of that law as ultimately forming just one world legal system, containing all and only the rules that best answer to that task.

It does not, however, follow from Zweigert and Kötz's account being fully coherent that it cannot be impugned on other grounds. In fact, critiques have been mounting which typically aim to topple the edifice by undermining one or several of the foundational propositions just listed.[5] Mark Van Hoecke, for one, has forcefully argued that the problems targeted by the law are themselves largely a matter of social construction, with the result that (i) any line between them and their legal solutions is bound to remain elusive and (ii) the problems, like the solutions, most likely vary from society to society.[6] Others have decried all functionalist accounts as inherently defective for presumably blind to a central dimension of law, namely, its symbolic/expressive value.[7] Yet others have expressed strong views against the *praesumptio similitudinis*: that two purported legal 'scientists'[8] would just presuppose *ex ante* what they mean to find *ex post* has struck many as rather unscientific, to say the least.[9] Finally, the convergence thesis has likewise had its fair share of detractors. In particular, it has been claimed that the disaggregated, rule-based method

---

[4] Ibid, 30.

[5] See generally LJ Constantinesco, *Traité de droit comparé* (Paris, LGDJ, 1983) vol III, 63–71; G Frankenberg, 'Critical Comparisons: Re-thinking Comparative Law' (1985) 26 *Harvard International Law Journal* 411; A Watson, *Legal Transplants: An Approach to Comparative Law*, 2nd edn (Athens, GA, University of Georgia Press, 1993); W Ewald, 'Comparative Jurisprudence (I): What Was It Like to Try a Rat?' (1994–95) 143 *University of Pennsylvania Law Review* 1898; D Kennedy, 'New Approaches to Comparative Law: Comparativism and International Governance' (1997) 545 *Utah Law Review* 588; M Van Hoecke and M Warrington, 'Legal Cultures, Legal Paradigms and Legal Doctrine: Towards a New Model for Comparative Law' (1998) 47 *International Comparative Law Quarterly* 495; M Graziadei, 'The Functionalist Heritage' in P Legrand and R Munday (eds), *Comparative Legal Studies: Traditions and Transitions* (Cambridge, Cambridge University Press, 2003); G Samuel, 'Epistemology and Comparative Law: Contributions from the Sciences and Social Sciences' in M Van Hoecke (ed), *Epistemology and Methodology of Comparative Law* (Oxford, Hart Publishing, 2004); R Michaels, 'The Functional Method of Comparative Law' in M Reimann and R Zimmermann (eds), *The Oxford Handbook of Comparative Law* (Oxford, Oxford University Press, 2006); R Hyland, *Gifts: A Study in Comparative Law* (Oxford, Oxford University Press, 2009); J Husa, 'Functional Method in Comparative Law: Much Ado About Nothing?' (2013) 2 *European Property Law Journal* 4–21; O Brand, 'Conceptual Comparisons: Towards a Coherent Methodology of Comparative Legal Studies' (2007) 32 *Brooklyn Journal of International Law* 419; M Tushnet, 'Some Reflections on Method in Comparative Constitutional Law' in S Choudhry (ed), *The Migration of Constitutional Ideas* (Cambridge, Cambridge University Press, 2011).

[6] M Van Hoecke, 'Deep Level Comparative Law' in M Van Hoecke (ed), *Epistemology and Methodology of Comparative Law* (Oxford, Hart Publishing 2004) 38–43. See also, Hyland, ibid, 69–78.

[7] Brand, above n 5, 415; Hyland, ibid, 107.

[8] Zweigert and Kötz, above n 1, 29–30.

[9] As per Michaels, above n 5, 369: 'Perhaps no statement in the history of comparative law has been criticized more'. See also: Samuel, above n 5; Graziadei, above n 5; Husa, above n 5.

deployed by Zweigert and Kötz (and the 'common core' scholars more generally[10]) is inappropriate even by its own functionalistic standards, as it yields a distorted picture of how law actually operates.[11]

The effectiveness of these critiques, and what their success would entail for comparative law functionalism as a whole, however, remain to be fully determined. With a view to contributing to that inquiry, we here propose to describe two uses of functionality in comparative legal studies that arguably stand up to them. First, admitting to just a minimal means–end connection between law and social problems makes it possible for comparative lawyers to use functionality for the preliminary purpose of identifying the legal data to be compared—'functionalistic identification'. Second, those willing to suppose a somewhat thicker such connection would be in a position, in addition, to analyse said data from a functional perspective—'functionalistic analysis'. Each of these uses, we argue below, offers a coherent stripped down version of Zweigert and Kötz's model that is largely immune to the critiques just described.

II. 'FUNCTIONALISTIC IDENTIFICATION'

For any comparison to be meaningful, it must be impartial as between the various objects being compared. That is, it must proceed so as to avoid skewing the analysis in favour of one (or some) of them. In twosome comparisons, this means using a comparative criterion that is applicable to both objects yet privileges neither—an 'invariant point of reference', or *tertium comparationis*.[12] But it also entails first delineating the objects in a neutral way, for the identity and scope of each will inevitably affect the final conclusions, quite apart from the criterion used to compare them.

This delineating act is particularly delicate when it comes to law, as legal objects come in a variety of shapes and forms, some of which are quite elu-

---

[10] Eg J Gordley (ed), *The Enforceability of Promises in European Contract Law* (New York, Cambridge University Press, 2001); R Schlesinger (ed), *Formation of Contracts: A Study of the Common Core of Legal Systems* (New York, Dobbs Ferry, 1968) vol I, 30–41; M Bussani, 'Current Trends in European Comparative Law: The Common Core Approach' (1998) 21 *Hastings Comparative & International Law Review* 785.

[11] Tushnet, above n 5; C Valcke, 'The French Response to the World Bank's *Doing Business* Reports' (2010) 60 *University of Toronto Law Journal* 197; R Michaels 'Explanation and Interpretation in Functionalist Comparative Law—A Response to Julie de Coninck' (2010) 74 *Rabels Zeitschrift für ausländisches und internationales Privatrecht* 351, 356; Frankenberg, above n 5, 436; Constantinesco, above n 5; LM Friedman 'Some Thoughts on Comparative Legal Culture' in DS Clark (ed), *Comparative and Private International Law: Essays in Honor of John Henry Merryman on His Seventieth Birthday* (Berlin, Duncker & Humbolt, 1990).

[12] The issue, first raised by G Radbruch (*Über die Methode der Rechtsvergleichung* (Heidelberg, 1905)), has been the object of a voluminous literature in comparative law (eg H Kötz, 'Comparative Law in Germany Today' (1999) *Revue internationale de droit comparé* 753, 758–61) and beyond (G Sjoberg, 'The Comparative Method in the Social Sciences' (1955) *Philosophy of Science* 106).

sive. Different yet equally appropriate legal comparisons can (and do) pertain to legal concepts, legal rules, sets of legal rules, legal domains, forms of legal reasoning or entire legal systems. Whichever unit is chosen, however, must be the same on both sides: rules can only be properly compared to rules, legal domains to legal domains, and so on. Moreover, this balance must also be respected within categories: the particular rule or set of rules chosen on one side must be compared to the corresponding rule or set of rules on the other. The trouble is that concepts, rules and domains are, like all intellectual constructs, delineated only vaguely at best, with the result that it is not always clear where each begins and ends. The risk is high, therefore, that what may look like counterpart legal objects in fact are not, and that the whole comparative process accordingly is rigged from the outset.[13]

So how are comparative lawyers to check on their comparisons being evenly balanced? What kind of criteria should they use to delineate the counterpart rules or domains in each jurisdiction? One thing seems clear: legal labels are particularly unreliable in this respect. Few matters have been more firmly established by comparative law than that the labels attached to concepts, rules or entire areas of law are not standardised across jurisdictions but, rather, are determined locally, with the result that the same label may capture different realities (and a different label, similar realities) in different jurisdictions.[14] One intending to compare, for example, the law governing 'freedom of expression' in two jurisdictions would indeed be ill-advised to rely on that label alone for the purpose of identifying the relevant body of law in each, for it could be that some situations captured by that label in one jurisdiction are designated through a different label ('defamation'?) in the other. Focusing on area labels would do no better, moreover, as the freedom of expression cases treated as 'constitutional' matters in one system might span a number of legal domains ('delictual law', 'criminal law', 'administrative law'?) in the other, some of which might not even exist in the first.[15] As a result, the comparative lawyer confining her investigation to the 'constitutional law' of each system would end up missing out on a whole pool of second-jurisdiction cases speaking directly to her issue. She would, in short, be comparing apples and oranges.

But what else is there, besides labels? Function arguably offers a promising alternative. As Ernst Rabel and others have explained, the functions discharged

---

[13] M Van Hoecke, 'Deep Level Comparative Law' in M Van Hoecke (ed), *Epistemology and Methodology of Comparative Law* (Oxford, Hart Publishing 2004) 170.

[14] Ibid, 174–75; AT Von Mehren, 'Civil-Law Analogues to Consideration: An Exercise in Comparative Analysis' (1959) 72 *Harvard Law Review* 1009, 1010; Zweigert and Kötz, above n 1, 28–45; R Sacco, 'Legal Formants: A Dynamic Approach to Comparative Law (Installment II of II)' (1991) 39 *American Journal of Comparative Law* 343; Michaels, 'The Functional Method of Comparative Law', above n 5; Graziadei, above n 5.

[15] Van Hoecke, 'Deep Level Comparative Law', above n 13, 178.

by legal rules, unlike their labels, do tend to cut across jurisdictions.[16] Indeed, it seems reasonable to think that a core of same social problems—individuals killing one another, not doing what they promised to do, trespassing on one another's property, etc—are attended to in most, if not all, jurisdictions. If so, such problems might well provide the jurisdiction-neutral point of entry we are looking for.

Consider once again our comparative lawyer interested in freedom of expression. Rather than searching for relevant materials through such key words as 'freedom of expression' or 'constitutional law', she could ask herself how each jurisdiction typically handles 'citizens bad-mouthing one another in public'. Such problem-based formulation would naturally take her across labels and categories, to all the materials bearing on the issue in each jurisdiction. That these materials might be labelled or classified differently in the two jurisdictions would no longer matter, in other words. That particular formulation admittedly may not eliminate all risks of bias as it too includes some labels—'citizens', 'public'—which likewise might designate different realities in the two systems. Should she discover that this is in fact the case, she could try yet another formulation, something along the lines of 'passport-carrying individuals bad-mouthing one another in newspapers'.[17] (But what of 'bad-mouthing' and 'newspapers'?) The basic point remains, however, that the risk of bias would decrease as she would move away from legally heavy formulations towards more strictly factual ones. In all cases, of course, she might still miss some relevant materials here and there, but that is a different problem from such problems as those that may impugn her searching process from the outset, and one that in any event besets all (even exclusively domestic) legal research.

If anything, that process might yield too much material. It may prove over-inclusive, since the fact that law is systematically connected downwards to social problems does not entail that social facts are, in turn, upwardly connected to nothing but law. Social problems naturally call into play a number of different responses, not all of which are properly 'legal'. Our comparative lawyer indeed might discover that, in at least some of her targeted jurisdictions, the means deployed to address 'citizens bad-mouthing one another in public' are primarily social (or economic or religious) in nature. Some of these jurisdictions, that is, might have no formal law bearing on the matter simply because, say, the local lawmakers consider that public bad-mouthing

---

[16] E Rabel, *The Conflict of Laws: A Comparative Study*, 2nd edn (Ann Arbor, MI, University of Michigan Press, 1945) vol 1; M Schmitthoff, 'The Science of Comparative Law' (1939–41) 7 *Cambridge Law Journal* 96; Zweigert and Kötz, above n 1, 31 ('Incomparables cannot usefully be compared, and in law the only things which are comparable are those which fulfil the same function.').

[17] According to K Popper, *The Logic of Scientific Discovery* (London, Hutchison, 1972) 31–32, the scientific process is such that the starting point may be constantly revisited as the investigation unfolds.

is properly controlled through social stigma alone.[18] Problem-based research simply does not discriminate between legal and non-legal solutions. This is not to suggest that functionalistic identification is ineffective as such, however; only that the materials thus identified may need to be sorted at a later stage.

It accordingly seems that, insofar as it can be assumed that law is at least minimally causally connected to social problems, legal function offers a promising alternative to legal labels as a standard for identifying the requisite counterpart materials in the various systems under comparison. The more so, in fact, were such functionalistic identification shown to stand up to the five critiques listed above—which we endeavour to do next.

Critiques

The last two of the above critiques, respectively relating to the *praesumptio similitudinis* and the convergence thesis/common core approach, can be summarily dismissed, as they have no present application. Functionalistic identification, as we saw (and as its designation confirms), only speaks to the first stage of the comparative process; it says nothing as to what is to happen to the data once collected. It accordingly is free of any kind of presuppositions concerning the nature and content of that data (it being similar or different, independently meaningful or not, etc), or the state and ideal direction (convergence or divergence) of world law more generally. As such, it is naturally immune to critiques that target such presuppositions.

The first three critiques call for careful consideration, however. With respect to the first, we need do no more than emphasise that an elusive law/fact dichotomy is all that functionalistic identification requires. Our freedom of expression enthusiast need not settle on a starting formulation that is entirely law-free; she only needs to make sure that whatever law may be included in it *is not the law she is about to investigate*—in other words, that the same notion not serve as constant and variable within the same analysis.[19] Recall that the aim at this identification stage is quite modest: it is not to find a *tertium comparationis* valid across jurisdictions, only one suitable between her target jurisdictions. And, whereas the formulation 'citizens bad-mouthing one another in public' would clearly be an inappropriate starting point where the conceptions of 'citizens' and 'public' are themselves a part of what is to be investigated, that same formulation might be acceptable with respect to jurisdictions whose respective conceptions of 'citizens' and 'public' would have,

---

[18] See Zweigert and Kötz's 'Title Insurance Companies' example, wherein land title reliability is secured through official registration in Germany but through private insurance companies in the US, above n 1, 35. See also Michaels, 'The Functional Method of Comparative Law', above n 5, 20; Husa, above n 5.

[19] G Sjoberg, 'The Comparative Method in the Social Sciences' (1955) 22 *Philosophy of Science* 106–117.

say, already been independently determined. All that our comparativist really needs, then, is the possibility to adjust her formulation to the degree of legal/ factualness required for her particular purpose: she needs different degrees of legal/factualness, not a categorical law/fact dichotomy.

Likewise with respect to the objection concerning the variability of social problems across jurisdictions: functionalistic identification does not require that all social problems be the same across all jurisdictions, only that the problems used in the context of particular studies be common *across the jurisdictions involved in those studies.* So, whereas our comparatist does need 'citizens bad-mouthing one another in public' to be considered a problem worthy of legal solution in all the jurisdictions she is about to investigate, it matters not that the same situation may be considered unproblematic else-where. Of course, the same reasoning that leads us to think that she can identify all the law bearing on her problem via that problem (viz law being at least minimally connected to social problems) also suggests that a jurisdiction not beset by that problem will likely have no law on it. But this would only mean that her purported target jurisdictions could not be impartially com-pared on that basis, as they simply lack the requisite counterparts for being so. Whatever issue she undertakes to investigate in a number of jurisdictions must have attracted legal responses in all of them.

The third of the above critiques deserves the most attention, as it could potentially undercut even the thin version of functionalism at play here. Should functionalistic identification prove inadequate for hermeneutic/expressivist comparative law projects, which tend to law's symbolic rather than functional dimension, its value would be much reduced indeed. But such worries can be readily assuaged.[20] The only materials likely to be missed through function-alistic identification are those that would escape our central assumption of a minimal law/fact connection to begin with, ie materials not in fact used in legal practice. And the projects for which that method would be inadequate would correspondingly be those whose scope needs to be so large as to capture even such practically inert materials. This is unlikely to include hermeneutic investigations, however. While hermeneutics attends to the meaning (rather than the function) of human institutions, it also insists that meaning is to be primarily derived from actions rather than words. Max Weber himself con-sidered that words are 'meaningful' only insofar as they are actually acted on, insofar as they have crystallised into 'meaningful acts' proper.[21] Likewise, it seems that very few, if any, comparative lawyers still hold on to the view that legal texts can have meaning outside particular contexts of application. While some 'legal transplant' scholars may be taken to suggest as much, their work

---

[20] See generally Michaels, 'Explanation and Interpretation in Functionalist Comparative Law', above n 11, 356–58.

[21] M Weber, *Economy and State* (New York, Bedminster Press, 1968) vol 1, 4. See also C Geertz, *Local Knowledge*, 3rd edn (New York, Basic Books, 2000).

ultimately shows otherwise.[22] Even the 'common core' scholars—perhaps the most 'bare rule'-prone of all comparative lawyers—take care to supplement their rule surveys with summary descriptions of the contexts from which these rules were drawn.[23] Lastly, even if (hermeneutical or other) comparative projects encompassing materials not acted on could in fact be found, there would be room to query whether these even qualify as 'comparative *law*' projects to begin with. Seeing that most definitions of law in circulation make reference to some notion of effectiveness (or enforcement or potential enforcement),[24] such projects might arguably be better slotted under the likes of 'comparative linguistics', 'comparative literary criticism' or 'comparative philology'. In the end, though, the most potent argument in favour of using problem-based research across comparative law projects quite simply is that that is how domestic lawyers do it: if that method is good enough for domestic lawyers across jurisdictions, surely it is so for the purpose of comparing the law of these jurisdictions![25]

In sum, the fact that domestic legal research always begins from real-life situations appears to confirm that law is at least minimally connected to social problems. If so, there is good reason to think that functionalistic identification could profitably be extended to most, if not all, comparative law projects, hermeneutic ones included.

III. 'FUNCTIONALISTIC ANALYSIS'

Functionality can also be useful to comparative lawyers for tasks other than just identifying the materials for comparison; in particular, it can be used for analysing those materials. Yet it may be that these first need to be sorted: while it was just argued that problem-based research is unlikely to under-include, we also saw that it may prove over-inclusive. Indeed, that problem-based research does not discriminate between legal and non-legal solutions to social problems constitutes a benefit for some comparative law projects,[26] but amounts to unhelpful over-inclusiveness for others.[27]

This suggests that, whereas comparative lawyers might indeed all proceed the same way at the identification stage, their paths will likely diverge immediately thereafter, for they will then need to extract, from the initial pool of

---

[22] Watson, above n 5.

[23] Eg Gordley, above n 10.

[24] Eg HLA Hart, *The Concept of Law* (Oxford, Oxford University Press, 2012) 116; H Kelsen, *Pure Theory of Law* (Cambridge, Cambridge University Press, 1967) 54; A Ross, *On Law and Justice* (Berkeley, University of California Press, 1959) 34.

[25] Admittedly, all law may not involve documentary research. In oral, documentless traditions, for example, it may be that justice is administered with no (or little) reference to the past. But any comparison involving such systems would then most likely have to likewise be observational rather than documentary.

[26] Eg Zweigert and Kötz, above n 1, 34–5.

[27] Brand, above n 5, 419.

materials, those materials that speak to their particular project. Whereas legal and non-legal materials alike might speak to sociologically inclined projects (perhaps better regarded as projects in 'comparative sociology'?[28]), the large majority of extant comparative law studies take little or no account of non-legal materials.[29] Moreover, these 'strictly legal' comparative studies further fragment into a number of different approaches. One of these is the sort of hermeneutic approach just discussed, which involves privileging legal materials heavily laden with symbolic value (perhaps some ubiquitous phraseology, or an argument structure prominent in decisions from certain courts), but another, perhaps more common, approach is functionalistic insofar as it aims to analyse how law actually operates to resolve the problems it targets.

Representatives of this latter approach include Rodolfo Sacco, and perhaps even Rabel. To Rabel, law essentially is a 'science' like any other, one that ultimately aims to uncover causes and effects in much the same way that the natural sciences do.[30] Students of law accordingly should, in his view, turn their minds to:

> everything that affects the law, such as geography, climate and race, developments and events shaping the course of a country's history—war, revolution, colonization, subjugation—religion and ethics, the ambition and creativity of individuals, the needs of production and consumption, the interests of groups, parties and classes. Ideas of every kind have their effect, for it is not just feudalism, liberalism and socialism which produce different types of law; legal institutions once adopted may have logical consequences, and not least important is the striving for a political or legal ideal. Everything in the social, economic and legal fields interacts.[31]

Sacco's writings are more formalised and more pointedly focused on judicial decisions, but their ultimate point is much the same. A proper study of law, on his account, looks to investigate all 'legal formants', by which he means all 'factors present today which determine how cases will be resolved in the near future'.[32] Some such formants are fully explicit (eg statutory rules, judicial decisions, scholarly interpretations), but others much less so. Among the more cryptic formants—Sacco calls them 'cryptotypes'[33]—one finds judges' educational backgrounds and cultural biases, religious affiliations and personal dispositions—in fact, anything that may surreptitiously or even unconsciously impact their decisions. Finally, in between the fully explicit and most cryp-

---

[28] Watson, above n 5, 5.

[29] Which is not to say that they take little account of non-legal factors operating on legal materials, as we see next in the text.

[30] DJ Gerber, 'Sculpting the Agenda of Comparative Law: Ernst Rabel and the Façade of Language' in A Riles (ed), *Rethinking the Masters of Comparative Law* (Oxford, Hart Publishing, 2001) 200.

[31] E Rabel, 'Aufgabe und Notwendigkeit der Rechtsvergleichung' in *Recueil des travaux suisses présentés au Congrès international de droit comparé*, cited in Zweigert and Kötz, above n 1, 32.

[32] R Sacco, 'Legal Formants: A Dynamic Approach to Comparative Law (Installment I of II)' (1991) 39 *American Journal of Comparative Law* 23.

[33] Sacco, 'Legal Formants (Installment II of II)', above n 14, 384.

tic formants lay the 'synecdoches', which aim to convey entire phenomena through just partial representations.[34] But all legal formants, however explicit or not they may be, are ultimately determined through their being to some extent causally related to the outcome of judicial decisions. In sum, whereas standard legal dogmatics analyse law from the standpoint of intellectual relevance, Rabel and Sacco alike worry, more broadly, about all that is causally relevant to it.[35]

Admittedly, nothing said so far much departs from the standard realist fare, and Rabel and Sacco are indeed card-carrying legal realists. They are *comparative* legal realists,[36] however, for comparison plays a central role in their account. Legal comparison is crucial, they contend, for the purpose of unearthing non-explicit legal formants. Explicit formants are, of course, readily identifiable, but non-explicit ones tend to remain elusive even, and in particular, to those primarily affected by them. Indeed, cultural and other societal influences are such that people are only dimly aware of them, if at all.[37] Because they come to people naturally, 'as a function of belonging to the community',[38] they are never openly questioned or even discussed. They are just taken for granted, thus largely hidden from sight.

Yet they can become visible through comparison. When two different cultural frameworks are set side by side, the peculiarity of each cannot but emerge from the contrast with the other. Nothing can simply be 'taken for granted' once an alternative has been shown to exist: each of the two options *ipso facto* becomes relative, contingent, one of many. Accordingly, it is the confrontation inherent in comparison that, on Sacco's account, causes even the most obscure legal formants to come to light and, in time, be articulated. As Sacco describes it:

---

[34] Ibid, 386.

[35] 'The comparative method is founded upon the actual observation of the elements at work in a given legal system. The dogmatic method is founded on analytical reasoning. The comparative method examines the way in which . . . jurists work with specific rules and general categories. The dogmatic method offers abstract definitions.' Sacco, 'Legal Formants (Installment I of II)', above n 32, 25.

[36] See generally Frankenberg, above n 5; MA Glendon, 'Comparative Law as Shock Treatment: A Tribute to Jacob WF Sundberg' in E Nerep and W Warnling-Nerep (eds), *Sartryck ur: Festskrift till Jacob WF Sundberg* (Stockholm, Juristförlaget, 1993); V Grosswald Curran, 'Cultural Immersion, Difference and Categories in US Comparative Law' (1998) 46 *American Journal of Comparative Law* 43; N Demleitner, 'Challenge, Opportunity and Risk: An Era of Change in Comparative Law' (1998) 46 *American Journal of Comparative Law* 647.

[37] 'Man continually follows rules of which he is not aware or which he would not be able to formulate well. Few would be able to formulate the linguistic rule we follow when we say "three dark suits" and not "three suits dark" whereas in special context we might speak of "the meadows green" . . . Our visible, superficial language [reflects] latent linguistic patterns that are more permanent than the visible ones.' Sacco, 'Legal Formants (Installment II of II)', above n 14, 384–85.

[38] P Legrand, 'European Legal Systems Are Not Converging' (1996) 45 *International and Comparative Law Quarterly* 56 (here clearly motioning to Savigny's *Volksgeist* and Herder's *Zeitgeist*). Likewise P Legrand, *Fragments on Law-as-Culture* (Deventer, Tjeenk Willink, 1999) ('the framework of intangibles within which an interpretive community operates, which has normative force for this community . . . and which, over the *longue durée*, determines the identity of a community as community').

The jurist who deals with a single system always runs into certain features that he takes to be 'obvious' and hence that he does not perceive, identify, or report. These features remain as cryptotypes until the comparativist is struck by the differences in mentality that he observes among different legal environments. When he undertakes the work necessary to describe such differences, he describes the systems themselves.[39]

Comparison ultimately is what makes it possible 'to describe empirically how the law of a country actually functions'.[40]

Functionality hence can be useful to analyse as well as identify the materials of legal comparison. What is more, the kind of functionalistic analysis just described arguably withstands, as we will now see, the same five critiques that were discussed with respect to functionalistic identification.

Critiques

The analytic use of functionality proposed by Rabel and Sacco clearly presupposes a law–social problem connection thicker than the minimal one at play where only identification is at stake, for functionality can contribute to 'explaining' law only to the extent that causal factors actually contribute to making it the way it is: the greater that contribution, the greater will be functionality's explanatory power. Still, there is no need to go quite as far as to assume, with Zweigert and Kötz, that such factors are singularly determinative (their 'thickly functionalistic' conception of law). Indeed, none of the other axioms associated with Zweigert and Kötz's extreme position, which axioms were the targets of our five critiques, are present here.

Certainly, there is little room for any kind of presumption concerning the similarity of social problems or their legal solutions across jurisdictions (the sociological or legal *praesumptio similitudinis*). If anything, the above account shows the legal formant approach to be premised on difference, not similarity. Indeed, the local actors' awareness is raised thanks to their peculiar cryptotypes *clashing* against the different ones at play in the next jurisdiction. The greater the sociological and legal differences between any two jurisdictions, then, the more likely it is that local cultural frameworks will come to rise from obscurity.

But that reasoning also suggests that functionalistic legal analysis may be consistent with a narrower version of the *praesumptio similitudinis*.[41] Under

---

[39] Sacco, 'Legal Formants (Installment II of II)', above n 14, 388. Likewise M Lasser, *Judicial Deliberations: A Comparative Analysis of Judicial Transparency and Legitimacy* (Oxford, Oxford University Press, 2004) 19; J Bell, *French Legal Cultures* (London, Butterworths, 2001) 21; JQ Whitman, "The Neo-Romantic Turn" in P Legrand and R Munday (eds), *Comparative Legal Studies: Traditions and Transitions* (Cambridge, Cambridge University Press, 2003) 340.

[40] Sacco, ibid, 388.

[41] J Husa, 'Farewell to Functionalism or Methodological Tolerance?' (2003) 67 *Rabels Zeitschrift für ausländisches und internationales Privatrecht* 424–32.

the ontological version discussed so far, the presumption purports to represent an actual state of affairs, viz world law as in fact roughly the same across territories. Yet Zweigert and Kötz's own language at times suggests that it can also be viewed as a mere heuristic, ie as just a tool for facilitating the analytic process.[42] As such, the presumption would merely posit a hypothetical state of affairs against which to better grasp the actual state of world law, which might conceivably prove useful to even such sanguine difference theorists as Sacco and Rabel. Indeed, if Karl Popper is right when he describes science as necessarily proceeding from the falsification of antecedent theories,[43] legal difference can be expected to be most obvious where it emerges from the falsification of legal similarity, which consequently would be best posited at the outset. And Popper's falsification theory, it is worth noting, if anything, aligns quite well with the realist awareness-via-confrontation credo. At the same time, a heuristic *praesumptio similitudinis* would necessarily be transient, and thus possibly appropriate in some, though not in other, circumstances. Seeing that contrast is the ultimate objective, a presumption of similarity would be appropriate where one anticipates findings of difference. However, where one sees, as Zweigert and Kötz do, world law as instead tilting towards greater convergence, the opposite—*praesumptio* dis*similitudinis*—would in fact be preferable, for any increasing similarity in world law presumably should be more glaring as against a hypothetical state of legal difference.[44] For this reason and the others recounted in Section I, an ontological *praesumptio similitudinis* is actually far more consistent with Zweigert and Kötz's overall account than a heuristic one, despite their occasional words to the contrary. This reasoning, of course, also serves to confirm that the heuristic presumption, unlike the ontological one, coheres with the difference theorists' own functionalistic analysis. Most importantly for present purposes, however, the critiques traditionally levelled at the *praesumptio similitudinis* (viz that it misrepresents social problems and world law) have no traction against its heuristic version.

This obviously also takes care of Zweigert and Kötz's 'convergence thesis', which is absent here for the same reason that an ontological *praesumptio similitudinis* is: any movement towards harmonisation would serve to reduce legal differences and, thus, also the overall contrasting potential which the legal formant theorists so desperately seek. After all, comparative legal realists are generally quite clear about their seeking to enlighten domestic lawyers

---

[42] Zweigert and Kötz, above n 1, 36: 'As a working rule this presumption is very useful'; 'At the outset of a comparative study it serves as a heuristic principle'; 'a useful working hypothesis'.

[43] Popper, above n 17.

[44] Hence Pierre Legrand's proposed *praesumptio dissimilitudinis* in 'The Return of the Repressed: Moving Comparative Legal Studies beyond Pleasure' (2001) 75 *Tulane Law Review* 1048. See also Frankenberg, above n 5 453; Hyland, above n 5, 194. By the same reasoning, however, the latter theorists would do best to adopt a heuristic presumption of similarity, as their preferred different outcomes presumably would be most obvious as against hypothetically similar ones.

wherever they may be, with the aim of ultimately fostering, not eradicating, legal difference.[45] As for the 'common core approach', finally, it too is clearly not logically entailed by the comparative legal realist project, as confirmed by the fact that legal realists typically are heavily committed to contextualising, as both an analytic tool and a normative agenda.[46]

IV. CONCLUSION

Functionality can be useful to comparative lawyers in two ways, neither of which is vulnerable to the critiques traditionally levelled against comparative law functionalism. Function offers an impartial criterion for identifying cross-jurisdictional legal materials that are amenable to mutual comparison. It also provides an interesting angle from which to analyse these materials. As such, functionalistic identification and analysis presuppose a somewhat thinner law/fact connection than is posited by Zweigert and Kötz, and are largely immune to the standard objections against these scholars' own functionalist account. While functionalistic identification is likely to be appropriate for all 'comparative law' projects proper, it makes no claim about law being categorically distinct from facts, or about law (or facts) being somehow similar across jurisdictions. As for functionalistic analysis, whereas it (by definition) is appropriate only where there is an interest for law's functional dimension, it too is entirely agnostic as to world law being in fact (or ideally) similar or different, convergent or divergent, or whatever else.

---

[45] See Sacco's discussion on the importance of ridding domestic lawyers from their 'fetish' views ('Legal Formants (Installment I of II)', above n 32, 24) and 'great optical illusion' ('Legal Formants (Installment II of II)', above n 14, 385).

[46] However, it does not follow from the common core approach not being logically entailed by legal formant analysis that, conversely, this analysis cannot be used by common core scholars. See Bussani, above n 10.

8

Comparative Law and Legal History: A Few Words about Comparative Legal History

MARTIN LÖHNIG

I. TWO WAYS—TWO GOALS?

SEEN FROM THE perspective of legal history, comparative law can indicate two different approaches, because legal history itself has no genuine comparative method. Instead, a legal historian may either use the toolkit of comparative law and practise 'historical comparison of laws' or help himself to the instruments of comparative law and practise 'comparative legal history'. The decision of which route to take is not determined by specific preconceptions, but depends on one's research interest.

A. Historical Comparison of Laws

Historical comparison of laws is a doctrinally centred method that focuses on the intellectual history of legal concepts, which first describes several legal systems and then compares with each other. The objects of comparison are, therefore, different doctrinal concepts and developments from different periods and jurisdictions. The findings can be used to evaluate and, if necessary, amend one's own doctrinal 'equipment'. They can also serve to explore the possibilities of or even consciously work towards legal unification at the supranational level. Historical comparison of laws can thus be used to create a foundation for a European law, particularly a European private law, for it is in the field of private law that historical comparison of laws is typically engaged in. Historical comparison of laws strives to develop a common European jurisprudence based on Roman law studies in the Middle Ages and in modern times. Roman law in this context appears as a methodological and substantive element in a European codification of private law.

However, comparison that is focused on legal harmonisation involves the risk that some of the differences as well as the peculiarities of smaller jurisdictions will get lost. Moreover, only comparing doctrinal structures does not meet the demands of functional comparative law. Such an approach is necessarily blind to possible explanations for differences, which are not rooted in doctrinal thinking. However, these shortcomings can be avoided if the historical comparison of laws frees itself from the one-sided goal of legal harmonisation and does not neglect the functional aspect. Additionally, it should use the toolkit of comparative legal history to explain possible differences.

B. Comparative Legal History

Comparative legal history, on the other hand, does not focus mainly on doctrinal aspects. In fact, its danger, as long as it claims a place in legal science, lies in its comparative neglect of doctrinal matters. To anticipate somewhat, comparative legal history can only succeed if it makes use of the tools of historical comparative law. Because jurisprudence has always formulated doctrines, comparative legal history has to take doctrinal developments into account.

Comparative legal history's starting point is in historical scholarship: over the past three or four decades, historical scholarship has come to recognise that comparison can be a useful method for analysing historical causes, assessing developments, and understanding one's own and other cultures (including legal cultures) better. Comparative historical scholarship has been praised as the 'epitome of innovative research in history and a great hope for qualitative advances in knowledge'.[1]

The young discipline of comparative legal history can try to obtain these advances in knowledge for legal history (a field, incidentally, which has been said to be in crisis for several decades now). It thereby moves closer—in methodological terms—to other areas of historical scholarship. However, comparing specific phenomena—and legal norms, too, are specific phenomena—is not enough to find explanations, much less to categorise developments. Rather, one has to compare possible relationships between specific phenomena in their historical context. Usually, a comparison of individual aspects of different legal cultures will be designed synchronically. However, diachronic comparison is another possibility, as societies and legal cultures can be in comparable situations at different times, as in processes of reception, nation building and industrialisation. Admittedly, diachronic comparison loses the common era context,[2] but this, in turn, may be helpful for typification. Therefore, comparative legal history can adopt a functional approach, too. It is important,

---

[1] F Jaeger, 'Der Vergleich in der Ideengeschichte der Gesellschaft' in H Kaeble and J Schriewer (eds), *Diskurse und Entwicklungspfade: Der Gesellschaftsvergleich in den Geschichts- und Sozialwissenschaften* (Frankfurt am Main, Campus Verlage, 1999) 401.

[2] H Kaelble, *Der historische Vergleich* (Frankfurt am Main, Campus Verlage, 1999) 15.

however, that it is not facts but relations which are being related to each other, and that this happens in their socio-historical context, which alone can explain these relations.[3]

Using reception processes as an example, one can demonstrate the difference between possible research goals and the historical comparative or, conversely, the comparative historical methods necessary to satisfy them.

For instance, one could be interested in how a specific body of legal rules— eg Roman civil law or French jurisdictional and procedural law—was received in different legal systems. Were similar doctrinal and institutional structures created? What differences have emerged, and by what thought processes? A historical comparative approach could satisfy this research interest and compare several jurisdictions that have received specific bodies of law. It would be necessary to contrast the various doctrinal pathways as well as the legal rules that the jurisdictions compared enacted. This could help one to find better legal solutions, along with the intellectual and historical causes of differences in the current law. It could also help us to perceive that different legal systems might operate on different underlying value systems. Moreover, it could help us to assess the chances for legal harmonisation on a national or supranational level.

Of course, one's research interest might also be the reception process itself as a cultural act. Comparing different reception processes might show up typologies as well as national peculiarities. It might also reveal what conditions have to be met for reception to succeed. What different forms of reception are there? Can identical solutions and regulatory approaches work in different social and political contexts? If one was researching the reception of Napoleonic law in early nineteenth-century Europe, for instance, a comparative legal history approach would focus not on doctrinal aspects, but on the comparison of different social processes, differences in political decision-making and differences in legal adaptation processes. Thus, comparative legal history would not choose for its reference point a social reality that it posits as pre-legal, identify the legal norms that regulate this reality and then compare these norms with each other. Instead, the *tertium comparationis* would be the legal norms of different legal systems, which are similar or even identical because they were transferred from the same source even though the social context, broadly defined, varied. One would compare the social and political processes which led to the transfer of foreign law, the reception process itself and the consequences of that reception.

---

[3] J Schriewer, 'Problemdimensionen sozialwissenschaftlicher Komparatistik' in H Kaelble and J Schriewer (eds), *Vergleich und Transfer—Komparatistik in den Sozial-, Geschichts- und Kulturwissenschaften* (Frankfurt am Main, Campus Verlage, 2003) 24.

II. THE 'ACID BATH OF COMPARISON' (WEHLER)

A. Preface

Comparative legal history is a very young discipline. This is because historical scholarship generally—in whose methodological footsteps comparative legal history is following—was pressed into the service of building national consciousness until well into the twentieth century.[4] If at all, comparison only served as a kind of auxiliary argument to emphasise the strong points of one's own nation. It was only in the 1970s that comparison was finally put forward as the best way to go for historical scholarship. And even today, this 'best way' is only rarely embarked upon, for it is a thorny and arduous path. The range of larger legal historical narratives was similarly constricted and impoverished, as fact, which can still be seen today in the structure of low-quality dissertations in legal history: '1.) The Roman Law, 2.) The Prussian Land Law 3.) The German Civil Code'.

Even today, studies in comparative legal history are rare commodities. That is because in a comparative study, as trivial as this may seem, several objects of enquiry are at first on an equal footing and have to be examined separately. Comparing them and putting them into relation to each other is the real goal, which might lead to certain conclusions. This kind of work is very hard, especially because the systems one is comparing might have influenced each other. One cannot simply posit that they did not. Discovering common ground is of no value if one does not inquire whether there were cross-influences or not.[5]

What, then, is the epistemic interest? Comparison should—and, once again, this may seem trivial—reveal the similarities and the differences and, if possible, explain them.[6] In short, comparison is either about gaining insight into similarities and knowledge of general correlations or about contrasting and understanding differences in order to highlight the unique quality of what has been compared.

B. Objects of Comparison

What to compare if not legal norms and their evolution in the strict sense? As already said, it is not facts, but relations, which are being related to each other. Since law is always a part of the wider culture and helps to organise and legitimate social, economic and political institutions, comparative legal history cannot ignore the cultural context. Topics that recommend

---

[4] Kaelble, above n 2, 9.
[5] Cf Kaelble, above n 2, 21.
[6] M Bloch, 'Pour une histoire comparée des sociétés européennes (1928)' in M Bloch, *Mélanges historiques I* (Paris, EHESS, 1983) 17.

themselves to the comparative legal historian are therefore institutions and institutionalisation processes, as well as interdependencies between social, economic and legal history. Suitable topics are, for example, processes of democratisation, reception and industrialisation; the effects of a totalitarian past; and the effects of value changes (which are especially noticeable in family law, for example); in short, they are historical processes of transformation with a bearing on the legal system in its widest sense.[7] These topics, in turn, are documented in legal sources, which form the basis of any research project in comparative legal history: legal norms, records of legislative debates and procedures (including failed ones), court decisions, administrative decisions with specific commands or prohibitions, contracts, wills and contemporary works of legal scholarship.

Comparison in this sense, however, is not the mere charting of developments by comparing 'before' and 'after' (for instance, German family law in the 1950s and in the 1970s); such a study would only describe a development or relationship, not compare it. It would be quite otherwise, however, if the family law systems of Germany, France and the US were compared and related to each other. This is exactly what Jens Beckert,[8] a sociologist, did several years ago for the law of inheritance. His book *Unverdientes Vermögen [Inherited Wealth]* set standards for comparative legal history as well. Beckert did not content himself with mere description, but asked: 'Why similarities and differences at the same time? Different economic conditions, interest groups, national peculiarities?'.[9] Through asking these questions, he turned comparative legal history into a resource for current debates on inheritance law and policy.

C. Describe—Explain—Generalise

Comparison can be merely descriptive at first, and can thus highlight the distinctiveness of certain developments. It is only when looking at several German states in the nineteenth century, for instance, that one can tell whether a liberal judiciary developed sooner rather than later in any particular one of them. And one can only begin to appreciate the strong liberal current in Baden when comparing the Badisch development in civil procedure or in the field that has become known as commercial law with the development in other states. Good

---

[7] *Cf* Kaelble, above n 2, 9.

[8] J Beckert, *Unverdientes Vermögen—Soziologie des Erbrechts* (Frankfurt am Main, Campus Verlag, 2004).

[9] T Duve,' Review of J Beckert, "Unverdientes Vermögen—Soziologie des Erbrechts"' (2005) 7 *Rechtsgeschichte—Legal History* 199.

work on criminal procedure has been done by Nobili[10] (on how judges form their opinions) and by Müßig[11] (on the legally competent judge).

Descriptive comparison brings out the peculiarities of the object compared, and frequently this will be the legal system with which the person doing the comparison is the most familiar. Conversely, it might show that the object of comparison is not so special after all. Moreover, comparison can call into question previous supposed certainties by broadening one's own parochial view. Even if the primary goal is to understand one's own (legal) history better, comparative work cannot be denigrated as purely national provided it treats its several objects of comparison equally and does not reduce 'foreign' legal histories to mere foils for its own.

The path of comparison leads from the descriptive level to possible explanations, and to their verification or falsification. There is hardly any other method that is as good as historical comparison at distinguishing good explanations from bad.[12] Comparison helps develop hypotheses and, as Hans Ulrich Wehler has put it, it is the 'optimal test' for 'the cogency of hypotheses'.[13] For example, Hannes Siegrist's study *Advokat, Bürger und Staat* [*Lawyers, Citizens, and State*][14] on the professionalisation of attorneys in Germany, Switzerland and Italy allows one to test the hypothesis that massive differences in the autonomy of lawyers' associations stem from the different role the state has played in the histories of these countries.

Comparative analysis of historical processes can help reject as incorrect causal explanations that were based on purely national research. For example, social security laws cropped up in industrialised Germany at about the same time as in pre-industrial Hungary, but they arrived on the scene much later in early industrialised England. This finding may lead one to doubt whether the degree of industrialisation and the power of the labour movement (and fear of it) were crucial factors.[15] Comparison thus draws attention to causes that one might otherwise have missed; or it makes clear that dominant explanatory models—while by and large correct—do not capture the full extent of the complexity. Additionally, comparison can help with formulating hypotheses. If certain characteristics can be found in objects A and

---

[10] M Nobili, *Die freie richterliche Überzeugungsbildung: Reformdiskussion und Gesetzgebung in Italien, Frankreich und Deutschland seit dem Ausgang des 18. Jahrhunderts* (1974) (Baden-Baden, Nomos Verlagegesellschaft, 2001).

[11] U Seif (Müßig), *Recht und Justizhoheit. Historische Grundlagen des gesetzlichen Richters in Deutschland, England und Frankreich* (Berlin, Duncker & Humblot, 2003).

[12] Kaelble, above n 2, 41.

[13] H-U Wehler, 'Einleitung' in H-U Wehler (ed), *Geschichte und Soziologie* (Köln, Kiepenheuer & Witsch, 1972) 24.

[14] H Siegrist, *Advokat, Bürger und Staat. Sozialgeschichte der Rechtsanwälte in Deutschland, Italien und der Schweiz* (Frankfurt, Klostermann, 1996).

[15] Cf Kaelble, above n 2, 51.

B, for instance, it stands to reason that these characteristics will be present in object C as well.[16]

Comparative research can also bridge the gap between isolated empirical results and the more general assertions of theory.[17] If one accepts the transfer of the comparative method from the natural sciences to history, then one has to transfer the basic assumptions of natural scientific comparison along with it—at least in part. Thus, one has to assume that this method may produce theorems or explanatory models, and that it may allow for the identification of patterns and ideal types. It is about the 'internal logic of the same phenomena in different societies'.[18] However, if one abstracts in this manner in the human sciences, one cannot ignore—as one can in the natural sciences— that there is a tension between (assumed) natural regularities and chains of causation, on the one hand, and human freedom, the open-ended history that does not repeat itself, on the other.[19] Still, legal historical comparison beyond the descriptive and explanatory levels makes sense only if one accepts the former category, too, ie if one assumes that certain basic forms of social and symbolic acts exist, even if these are modified by different cultures and their differing development paths, which lend to life in any particular legal community its distinctive time- and place-specific cast.[20] For example, developments in modern family law in different European states follow certain patterns, although the basic patterns are pulled into slightly different shapes by different social and political circumstances.

III. CONCLUSION

Jumping into the 'acid bath' of comparative legal history—ie going beyond mere description—is not easy, and it probably comes as no surprise that comparative legal history is still in its infancy.

What one needs is a sufficiently large number of objects of comparison, each of which can form the topic of a sophisticated study. Relations and processes cannot be compared cursorily. Rather, one has to take account of both the potential for success and the reach of resistance against certain processes. The same goes for alternative patterns of development. These alternative possibilities cannot be ignored or denigrated simply because they did not prevail or do not fit the model. The risk of failing to capture the true complexity of one's research topic is arguably the biggest challenge facing comparative work

---

[16] H-G Haupt and J Kocka (eds), *Geschichte und Vergleich—Ansätze international vergleichender Geschichtsschreibung* (Frankfurt am Main, Campus Verlag 1996) 12.

[17] *Cf* K Popper, *Logik der Forschung* (1934) (Tübingen, JCB Mohr (Paul Siebeck), 1973).

[18] Kaelble, above n 2, 13.

[19] *Cf* J Schriewer, 'Problemdimensionen sozialwissenschaftlicher Komparatistik' in Kaelble and Schriewer, above n 3, 20.

[20] H Siegrist, 'Perspektiven der vergleichenden Geschichtswissenschaft. Gesellschaft, Kultur und Raum' in Kaelble and Schriewer, ibid, 305.

in legal history today. In addition, there are the intricacies of transfer analysis, which I referred to above. Last but not least, comparison frequently has to contend with wide-ranging questions and necessitates the use of sources in many different languages.

As a result, research in comparative legal history is possible only after one has conducted several individual studies first. These studies are still missing for many areas as the state of research continues to vary considerably from country to country and from region to region. It is only after careful and well-planned preparation that one can move on to comparison in a second step. As a result, comparative legal history of necessity frequently requires an international team of scholars who collaborate according to precise terms of agreement over a protracted period.

9

Comparative Contexts in Legal History: Are We All Comparatists Now?

HEIKKI PIHLAJAMÄKI

I. INTRODUCTION

COMPARATIVE LEGAL HISTORY sounds fashionable, at least in some circles. But what does it mean when we say we write legal history comparatively? It is easiest to take a liberal standpoint and refuse to define the method, approach or whatever we prefer to call it in any way. The 'let all the flowers bloom' approach is nice and sympathetic: why bother about methodological barriers and definitions, when all we actually want to have is relevant research?

So far, so good. We should not become obsessive about defining disciplinary boundaries now that we have finally managed to start removing them. However, we cannot avoid defining our work methodologically for at least two reasons. For one thing, in order to transgress disciplinary boundaries we had better be aware of just what we are crossing. It is good for a legal historian to possess a command of the sociological, economic or philosophical method, but he or she ought perhaps to be aware when boundaries are crossed. I thus agree with Heirbaut when he says that legal historians ought to stick 'to the legal context [, leaving] the rest . . . to specialists of other aspects of history, ideally in a team in which the legal historian is a cherished member'.[1] Heirbaut is correct in highlighting the importance of being aware of one's key competences.

The second reason for which I think defining methods has some significance is a much more mundane one, which has to do with a phenomenon called gatekeeping, which practically all law professors take part in, whether they like

---

[1] D Heirbaut, 'Exploring the Law in Medieval Minds' in A Musson and C Stebbings (eds), *Making Legal History: Approaches and Methodologies* (Cambridge, Cambridge University Press, 2012) 130.

it or not. Gatekeeping takes place every time we choose new colleagues for faculties or assess research proposals, for instance. We define not only what is good and not so good, but at times also what 'international private law', 'labour law' or 'procedural law' is. And yes, the concept of 'comparative legal history' increasingly often begs for a definition as well.

I have a gatekeeping position of my own as the Articles Editor of *Comparative Legal History*, which Hart Publishing established in 2013.[2] Our 'statement of purpose' reads:[3]

> Articles will explore both 'internal' legal history (doctrinal and disciplinary developments in the law) and 'external' legal history (legal ideas and institutions in wider contexts). Rooted in the complexity of the various Western legal traditions worldwide, the journal will also investigate other laws and customs from around the globe. Comparisons may be either temporal or geographical and both legal and other law-like normative traditions will be considered. Scholarship on comparative and trans-national historiography, including trans-disciplinary approaches, is particularly welcome.

The statement of purpose is precise in defining almost everything acceptable geographically, substantially and temporally: all regions of the globe, both 'internal' and 'external' approaches, all fields of law and all time periods can basically be considered. Comparisons may be temporal or geographical, and can deal not only with law, but with other normative traditions as well. Rather tolerant, one might conclude. However, in our everyday work as editors of the journal, my colleagues and I, if not constantly, at least every once in a while run into the very heart of the methodological problem: what is a comparison? In this chapter, I will clarify how I understand the term, and hopefully not only that. My purpose is also no less than to say something of the future of legal history—although necessarily from one limited angle.

I will start with a short historiography of legal history (II), then shift to what I call a traditional understanding of comparative legal history as geographical and temporal comparisons (III). The fourth section will attempt to define my own understanding of comparative legal history in the light of three examples. The last section (IV) will summarise and conclude the article.

II. A SHORT HISTORIOGRAPHY OF LEGAL HISTORY: THE DISCIPLINE AS A BY-PRODUCT OF NINETEENTH-CENTURY NATIONALISTIC *RECHTSWISSENSCHAFT*

To understand contemporary discussions on comparative legal history—or comparative law, for that matter—it is indispensable to see them against the backdrop of the nineteenth century and the birth of the 'legal science' of

---

[2] The first issue came out in May 2013. The journal is the flag-bearer of European Society of Comparative Legal History. The Chief Editor of the journal is Dr Seán Donlan.

[3] http://www.hartjournals.co.uk/clh/index.html (accessed on 1 October 2013).

Rechtswissenschaft. Historical issues became an integral element of legal studies in the works of Friedrich Carl von Savigny and his followers. What was new in their works was not only the fact that they integrated history with contemporary law, at least in their programmatic writings,[4] history being a central avenue to the correct understanding of the law in force; the Historical School also emphasised the importance of the national characteristics of law, in much the same way as other followers of early nineteenth-century Romanticism did with poetry, languages and other cultural phenomena.

The teachings of the Historical School soon started to concentrate their efforts on arranging the normative material 'scientifically' as a system, while the historical inquiries became increasingly detached from legal dogmatics. Both served the nineteenth-century national legal development in an important, albeit distinct, way. National legal dogmatics arranged the normative material inherited as part of the Roman law tradition or pouring out from national legislative bodies and administrative agencies. Legal historians, in turn, provided an important slice of the nationalistic narrative, explaining how history had led national states to the particular situations in law they found themselves in. Because of the legitimising tendency, much of the legal history became *dogmengeschichtlich*, explaining legal developments predominantly from the point of view of legislative development.

While positive law and legal scholarship became overwhelmingly nationally oriented in the nineteenth century, counter-movements arose as well. Modern international law is largely a product of the late nineteenth and early twentieth centuries,[5] although it might be artificial to credit national positive law for its inception in any direct way. Perhaps more importantly, comparative law emerged almost simultaneously with the Historical School, turning legal scholarship inwards from the age-old *ius commune* tradition. Starting in the nineteenth century as a response to practical legislative needs, comparative legal scholarship acquired more academic overtones as the century wore on. The Conferences of the Société International de Droit Comparé in Paris (1900) and The Hague (1936) are often seen as turning points in the history of modern comparative law.[6]

Despite these two clearly cosmopolitan features of the nineteenth and most of the twentieth century, legal history remained steadfastly on national tracks. This holds true for every country. Thus, for instance, classics such as Heinrich Mitteis's *Deutsche Rechtsgeschichte* (1949), Frederick Pollock and Frederic Maitland's *History of English Law before the Time of Edward I*, vols I–II

---

[4] See FC von Savigny, *System des heutigen römischen Rechts I-VIII* (Berlin, Veit, 1840–49).

[5] On the birth of international law as a modern legal discipline see M Koskenniemi, *The Gentle Civilizer of Nations* (Cambridge, Cambridge University Press, 2002).

[6] See C Petit, 'From Paris to the Hague: Edouard Lambert and *Droit Commun Législatif*' in C Peterson (ed), *History and European Private Law: Development of Common Methods and Principles* (Stockholm, Institutet för rättshistorisk forskning, 1997) 137–50.

(1898) and Adhémar Esmein's *Cours élémentaire d'histoire du droit français* (1898) all operate in an overwhelmingly national framework.

Interesting deviations from the pattern are the early nineteenth-century attempts at a universal legal history. The most important example of this is Eduard Gans's work on the law of inheritance (*Erbrecht in weltgeschichtlicher Entwicklung*, 1824). Perhaps universal legal history can best be seen as the last vestige of ius commune type of universal legal thinking rather than modern cosmopolitanism. The all-encompassing approach was doomed to disappear as legal positivism gained ground.[7]

III. COMPARATIVE LEGAL HISTORY EMERGES

The nationalistic legal histories have served their purpose for as long as national positivism in legal positivist has maintained its position as the dominant paradigm. Cracks in the edifice of the legal positivist paradigm have, however, been apparent during the last few decades, and this is the case for legal history as well.

New cosmopolitan strands of legal history appeared even before comparative legal history—in the narrow sense of the term. The Argentine historian Ricardo Levene founded probably the first clearly non-national school of legal history in the 1920s. The field that Levene, together with his Spanish colleague Alfonso García-Gallo, defined as their object of study was *Derecho indiano*, best translated as Spanish colonial law. We should, however, not miss the fact that, even though Levene's legal history broke the boundaries of national states, he was inspired by a sort of Latin American nationalism. It was the 'common' early modern legal history of Latin America that came to be created through *Derecho indiano*.[8] The pan-American background of Spanish colonial legal history is indeed interesting when we turn to the next major cosmopolitan school of legal history in the Western world, initiated by Francesco Calasso and Helmut Coing in the decades following the Second World War.

Much has been written about Francesco Calasso[9] and Paul Koschaker,[10] who were deliberately turning from their national legal history (Italian and German, respectively) to what came to be known as European legal history. Another major name that ought to be mentioned in this context is Franz Wieacker, whose classic *Privatrechtsgeschichte der Neuzeit* (1967) made a lasting impact on legal history. The work of the founding fathers of European legal history and the success of their paradigm has often been associated with the need of Italian and German scholars to contribute to the rebuilding of

---

[7] I am deliberately excluding Roman law and canon law from the scope of this chapter. Neither field of study by nature ever has a national focus.

[8] See H Pihlajamäki, 'La invención del derecho indiano: las raíces cosmopolitanas de la disciplina' (2010) 22 *Revista Chilena de Historia del Derecho* 583.

[9] See F Calasso, *Introduzione al diritto commune* (Milano, Giuffré, 1951).

[10] See P Koschaker, *Europa und das Römische Recht* (München, Beck, 1947).

Europe after the catastrophes that the early nineteenth-century nationalism had brought on Europe. Another important socio-political context for the rise of European legal history was the founding of the European Coal and Steel Community in 1956 as an economic federation, first uniting Belgium, Italy, West Germany, France, the Netherlands and Luxembourg, then extending in the subsequent decades to more and more countries, thus forming the European Economic Community and then the European Union. As the national legal positivist paradigm no longer dominated completely, giving space to the new European law, so in legal history a demand for wider views also arose. Institutionally, this led to the founding of Max-Planck-Institute for European Legal History in Frankfurt in 1964, with Helmut Coing as its first director.

The paradigms of neither *Derecho indiano* nor European legal history were comparative in the strict sense, replacing the former national framework with a larger framework. In *Derecho indiano*, this was the Spanish colonial law in its many different forms, and in European law it was *ius commune*, 'the common European law'. Neither of these approaches ever became dominant. That they would have even intended to completely replace national legal history would have indeed seemed a strange idea to the founding fathers of these schools. *Derecho indiano* and European legal history were wider platforms from which common features of law could be observed, but they never questioned the need for purely national legal histories.

Both of these schools of legal history have also been criticised, and for similar reasons. The original idea of *Derecho indiano* as a 'common law' for all Spanish colonies has long since given way to an understanding of Spanish colonial law as a body of law with many different local variations. The hold of the Spanish lawgiver was never intended to lead to complete uniformity. Local circumstances were taken into consideration from on the outset, and local norm-givers (for instance the *audiencias*) were also given powers of their own. Furthermore, local variations in customary law developed even when statutory law might have looked the same.[11]

European legal history, developed after the works of Calasso, Coing, Koschaker and Franz Wieacker by such giants of legal history as Manlio Bellomo and Reinhard Zimmermann, has also attracted its share of criticism. Douglas Osler published his by now almost classic article on the 'myth of European legal history' in 1997. Osler claimed that the standard versions of European legal history had been written from the German point of view, beginning at Bologna and culminating in the glorious *Begriffsjurisprudenz* of the nineteenth century. In this story, countries such as Spain and the Netherlands and even Italy are left with a minor role to play. Italy is certainly the cradle of jurisprudence, but disappears from the story after the middle ages.

---

[11] On local variation in practice see CR Cutter, *The Legal Culture of Northern New Spain, 1700–1810* (Albuquerque, University of New Mexico Press, 1995).

Spain only appears when the School of Salamanca is discussed, the Netherlands when elegant jurisprudence is considered. And so forth.[12]

The omissions of the standard European legal history, repeated in so many textbooks, could be multiplied. The standard story tends to say little about the British Isles, except perhaps in order to contrast continental law with English common law. Scandinavia does not exist and neither does Eastern Europe. It is no wonder that legal historians from these peripheries of Europe generally do not feel at home with textbooks on European legal history emanating from the pens of their German colleagues. I suspect that my Belgian, Dutch. French, Italian and Spanish colleagues do not feel completely at ease with most of the textbooks either, which explains the abundance of national legal histories all over Europe.

What is the problem with the traditional German- and Italian-oriented legal histories? The problem is that in these histories it is always the European heartland that sets the standard. You follow the standard more or less in time, and you follow the development in the heartlands more or less completely. Thus, the reception of *ius commune* takes place in Spain 'early' and 'thoroughly', and in Sweden 'late' and 'only partially'. There is little to be said about Russia, because there is no learned law. The standard of European legal history is, in other words, learned law, the *ius commune*, Roman law and canon law.

Being 'standard' means that the legal history of the peripheries is constantly measured against the centre. In international conferences and scholarly works, for instance, the question is how the learned law of proof developed in Sweden, to what extent Russian judges received legal education in the nineteenth century and how notarial functions were handled in early modern England. This is all fine in that it forces us 'peripherals' to look at our legal past with comparative glasses on. We cannot write national legal histories once we put ourselves in contact with the centre, but we must tell them how our legal history differs from that of the centre and to what extent it is similar to it.

Then what is the problem? Surely the way the influences go makes a difference. Since legal transplants, transfers or whatever they are called seldom travel from the periphery to the centre, it might make sense to see how the periphery adopts legal influences. The problem is that we legal historians active in the peripheries perhaps depart too rarely, when working comparatively, from those features that are essential in our histories. The legal historical agenda, or menu, is set by the centre, which can sometimes be irritating to colleagues working outside the core countries. Hurt feelings aside, however, this is only a minor problem, and not even always the case. A much more serious problem is that the heavily centralised agenda of comparative legal history works, despite what I just said, for the benefit of the periphery—and for its benefit

---

[12] DJ Osler, 'The Myth of European Legal History' (1997) 16 *Rechtshistorisches Journal* 393.

only. The agenda forces the peripheral legal historians to consider how their legal past differs from the centre's legal past, but it rarely forces the centre to rethink their own legal histories from a larger perspective.

We legal historians are trying to get a grip of our discipline as a global phenomenon,[13] when in fact a truly European legal history remains to be written. Could comparative legal history solve the problem? I think it could. A truly European legal history would need to be comparative in both the strict and broad senses of the term. I will now try to elaborate the way I see comparative legal history.

IV. CAN COMPARATIVE LEGAL HISTORY REPLACE THE NATIONALISTIC PARADIGM?

I will approach my definition of comparative legal history with the help of three examples. The first one is a comparative study by Richard Ross on early modern legal communication. The second is a hypothesis for a study not realised (at least, not yet) on plea bargaining and jury trials. The last example comes from an article I have written on the institution of the notary public.

As mentioned above, comparative legal history in its paradigmatic format follows that of comparative law. To take an example, Richard Ross's excellent article on early modern legal communication compares the way the British and Spanish empires built the communication channels from their respective American colonies to the European metropolises. Ross works systematically, comparing the way the British and the Spaniards employed legal professionals, the extent to which they allowed appeals from the American courts to the appeals instances in London and Madrid, and how each colonial power organised its control over the colonial administration.[14] No doubt this is comparative legal history, and excellent as such.

It may sound obvious, but not every research problem calls for a classic comparative set-up. Sometimes, indeed often, problems emanate from more parochial concerns. Take, for instance, the question of why plea bargaining has gained such tremendous importance in the US during the past few decades.[15] If we are interested in solving this legal historical problem, we do not need to solve the corresponding problem in all the countries to which

---

[13] I have, needless to say, nothing against global legal histories. See, eg T Duve, 'Von der Europäischen Rechtsgeschichte zu einer Rechtsgeschichte Europas in globalhistorischer Perspektive' in Social Science Research Network, *Max Planck Institute for European Legal History Research Paper Series* (2012–01).

[14] See R Ross, 'Legal Communications and Imperial Governance: British North America and Spanish America Compared' in CL Tomlins and M Grossberg (eds), *Cambridge History of Law in America, Vol. 1, Early America (1580–1815)* (Cambridge, Cambridge University Press, 2008) 104–43.

[15] See, eg M Langer, 'From Legal Transplants to Legal Translations: The Globalization of Plea Bargaining and the Americanization Thesis in Criminal Procedure' (2004) 45 *Harvard International Law Journal* 1.

the institution has spread recently; instead, we need to understand what is so specific about the US to enable such a curious institution to emerge—and do so well. To find out what is specific about it, we would probably need to place the plea bargaining institution in its procedural context. Plea bargaining cannot be understood in isolation from the jury trial, because it is the jury trial that plea bargaining replaces. Bringing the jury into the discussion would lead one to ask whether the decline of the jury trial is a consequence of the availability of plea bargaining, or whether other reasons could explain the demise of the jury trial. To develop the hypothesis a little further, one would do well to consider the decline of the jury trial in its international context. An international comparison would immediately show that the jury and similar institutions of lay representation (such as the *nämnd* in Finland and Sweden, or the *Schöffen* in Germany) have been slowly but surely on the decline in recent decades. The reasons for the decline of the jury in other countries, whatever they might be, would then quite possibly help us to understand why the jury trial has undergone a well-nigh extinction in the US.

Although the case of plea bargaining and jury trial was made up as an exercise for the purposes of this article only and has not been developed into an actual research project yet, it could well be. I will now take an example of a study that I have actually carried out and in which I utilised a comparative context in a rather similar way. This has to do with the institution of the *notarius publicus*, the notary public. At the same time, it is an example of a study in legal history emanating from the concerns of the centre, as defined above. This, however, is not our main concern now. The notary public is a figure known practically everywhere in continental European law, excluding the Nordic countries (Denmark, Finland, Iceland, Norway and Sweden). The question that naturally arises is why these countries did not adopt the institution of the notary.

To find the answer, the comparativist needs to know why the institution arose in the jurisdictions where it exists. Notaries existed in ancient Rome. The origins of the modern notary public are in late-Carolingian Italy, where the notary public evolved into an institution responsible for the keeping of public documents (*instrumenta publica*). Drawing up and attesting the credibility of all kinds of legal documents thus became the main task of the notaries.[16] The figure of the notary public is thus inseparable from a written legal culture that pays increasing attention to written documents. Contracts, wills and other instruments shaping the legal position of the individual were, from the High Middle Ages onwards, increasingly often in writing. Towards the end of the

---

[16] See O Condorelli, 'Profili del notariato in Italia Meridionale, Sicilia e Sardegna (secolli XII–XIX)' in M Schmoeckel and W Schubert (eds), *Handbuch zur Geschichte des Notariats der europäischen Tradition* (Baden-Baden, Nomos, 2009) 65–124.

Middle Ages, these instruments also started to enjoy high priority as pieces of evidence—hence the maxim *lettres passent témoins*.[17]

The emergence of the notary public is, furthermore, part and parcel of the rise of the *ius commune*. The learned bodies of law, Roman and Canon, are connected to the professionalisation of law. Notaries came to form one such profession, which spread everywhere where the *ius commune* did. This is where we find the clue to understanding the Nordic situation and the lack of the notaries in these countries.

The training of legal professionals began late in the Nordic countries: the University of Copenhagen was founded in 1479, and the first Swedish law faculties started functioning only in the seventeenth century. Although training abroad was not uncommon, the legal professionals trained abroad were mainly recruited by the Catholic church, until the Reformation, and after that by the central governmental institutions of the crown. The judiciary remained very much reliant on laymen for a long time. Local variation exists within the Nordic countries, but in many regions of Finland and Sweden, for instance, lower courts in the countryside remained virtually lawyer-free far into the twentieth century. The high courts, the first of which date to the seventeenth century (the High Court of Svea, founded in 1614), were staffed partly by noblemen and partly by learned lawyers, although it should be noted that learnedness did not require full doctoral degrees.

Although considerable amounts of learned law percolated through into Swedish legal life, the *Rezeption* never penetrated as thoroughly as in the European heartlands. Why this was so cannot be treated here in detail. Suffice it to say that the economic resources were long insufficient for a corps of lawyers to emerge and subsist. Since the crown relied largely on the peasant estate as far as running the judiciary was concerned, learned law was not much in demand. The demand for a legal profession consequently remained limited as well. It is not difficult to understand that, if even advocates were few, no room was left for a separate notarial branch to develop. Furthermore, the lay-dominated legal cultures of Northern Europe were practically oriented, and the use of the written document was certainly less prevalent there than elsewhere. Insofar as written documents were used, much less attention was attached to their accuracy than in the legal cultures in other parts of Europe.

It is now time to extract some lessons of the three examples above, attempting to define comparative legal history in some useful way. I would advocate a rather liberal way of defining the comparative approach to legal history. First, comparative legal history can use a systematic method of comparison in much the same way comparative law can. The comparative legal historian can thus (as in the first example, drawing on Ross's article) choose a certain number of essential features that the objects of comparison have in common and then

---

[17] See, eg the recent chapter by M Schmoeckel, 'Convaincre par l'écrit: La force des documents' in B Durand (ed), *Ars Persuasionis: Entre doute et certitude* (Berlin, Duncker & Humblot, 2012) 165–78.

analyse their functioning. This is how Ross proceeded in surveying the workings of judicial appeals in the colonial judiciaries of England and Spain, and the organisation of legal control mechanisms in the colonies.

But comparative legal history can also be less systematic. The comparative legal historian can take a national or regional legal institution as his concern, exactly as a traditional legal historian working within the boundaries of a national legal system would. However, and this is a major difference to the traditional method, the comparative legal historian would always position the research object in an international context. Without this context, the comparative legal historian would feel at risk of losing something essential in trying to answer his or her research questions. The reason why the comparative legal historian would feel this way is that law is an international phenomenon. Not only do legal institutions transfer from one country to another, but the mechanisms through which they change or remain the same are often similar in different countries. Comparative contexts, therefore, can turn out to be true treasure-houses of explanations.

Does this leave any room for purely national legal history? I do not think so—at least, not for national legal history, which is completely detached from anything else. Legal history, which orients itself according to the boundaries of national states only, was a product of nineteenth-century nationalism and national legal positivism. Since that kind of law has become a thing of the past, the legal history that emerged as its by-product has become equally antiquated. Such legal history tends to stress the specificity of national legal history, even when the features that are considered specific are not so for that particular country at all.

This does not, however, mean that the national state might no longer serve as one possible framework of research. Of course it can, taking into consideration the fact that national states were important law-producing entities long before they became primary motors of legal change. The point of comparative legal history is, however, that one should always be aware of the international context of any legal phenomenon occurring even within a national framework. Sometimes, perhaps, the comparative context will show less in the final research report than in some other cases, but the context should always be there.

Comparative consciousness is not necessary simply because it helps the researcher to test hypotheses and prove or falsify them. A legal historian needs to think comparatively at least as much in order to find out how legal influences, transfers, translations or transplants move from one legal order to another. Without a consciousness of legal transfers, one is completely at a loss in attempting to explain changes in a particular legal system. This is true not only for peripheral legal systems, but for larger ones as well.

A telling example of the lack of comparative legal history in larger countries is the way the history of American legal formalism and realism has traditionally been written. So much has been written about both strands of thought that one might be tempted to doubt whether anything essential could still be missing—and yet there is. None of the major contributions to the history of legal formalism have paid attention to the corresponding phenomenon on the European continent, and especially in Germany. That corresponding phenomenon is *Begriffsjurisprudenz*, conceptual jurisprudence.

Legal formalism and conceptual jurisprudence have so much in common that it is indeed hard to understand why so little comparative work has been written on them.[18] Both schools of thought replaced natural law on their respective home turfs (although in Germany this occurred with the Historical School in between). Both conceptual jurisprudence and legal formalism wished to bring order to what they felt was a messy state of legal sources. For formalists like Christopher Columbus Langdell, this meant reducing the huge number of precedents to a manageable number of cases, and for the Historical School, the predecessor of the *Begriffsjurisprudenz*, using the historical method to sieve out the most important sources from the jungle of cases, customary law rules, Roman law and statute law. Both schools brought order to law through ordering their sources into a system. Bringing in both the social and political context can at last be partially explained by the needs of the rising capitalism of the late nineteenth century. Whether these similarities can all be agreed upon is not the point here. Be it this way or that in the detail, these two schools clearly would merit a comparative study, or indeed several.

Exactly the same must be said of American legal realism and its European counterpart, Scandinavian legal realism. Both developed, one could well assume, as responses to the needs of the emerging welfare state in the US on the one hand and in Sweden and Denmark on the other. Both schools of legal thought were willing to open legal reasoning to arguments other than purely legal, American legal realists usually emphasising the importance of the social sciences and Scandinavians the so-called 'real arguments' (*reella övervägan-den*). As an overwhelming proportion of the realism studies have concentrated on the differences between the different strands of thought within American realism, it is actually not surprising that comparisons with the Scandinavian variant have been rare.[19]

V. CONCLUSIONS

American legal realism, prevalent in the academic circles of the US in the inter-war period, managed to become so influential that it practically disappeared

---

[18] See, however, D Rabban, 'American Responses to German Legal Scholarship: From the Civil War to World War I' (2012) 1 *Comparative Legal history* 13.

[19] See, however, G Alexander, 'Comparing the Two Legal Realisms—American and Scandinavian' (2002) 50 *American Journal of Comparative Law* 133; H Pihlajamäki, 'Against Metaphysics in Law: American and Scandinavian Realism Compared' (2004) 52 *American Journal of Comparative Law* 469. Toni Malminen (University of Helsinki) is currently preparing a dissertation comparing American and Scandinavian realism.

soon after the Second World War. 'We're all realists now', it has often been said.[20] Should all of us legal historians become comparatists now? Perhaps not in the strict sense of the term, although comparing A and B systematically is a great asset in one's methodological toolbox. But my answer would definitely be yes if we mean comparative legal history in the broader sense. Legal historians, even if using the national state as their basic unit, should always be able to place their object of research in a broader context, be it European or global.

The need to locate a research unit within a broader context concerns not only a national framework vis-à-vis Europe and the globe, but larger units in relation to others larger units as well. Understanding the specificity of European law requires an understanding of the specificity of other major legal systems, such as Islamic law or Chinese law. A truly modern European legal history would, I believe, do just this. A European legal history, while extracting and defining the particular features of the continent's legal history, would also draw not only on the experiences of the centre but also those of the various peripheries. Perhaps—just perhaps—our understanding of which regions in different epochs and regarding different subjects and areas of law have been centres and which peripheries might change. A European legal history of the modern kind would then also have a lot to say about the way legal influences have travelled, and still do, from one normative order to another. Perhaps a global legal history could use a similar blueprint?

---

[20] The phrase was coined by G Peller, 'The Metaphysics of American Law' (1985) 73 *California Law Review* 1151, 1152.

10

The Curious Case of Overfitting Legal Transplants

MATHIAS M SIEMS[1]

I. INTRODUCTION

ACCORDING TO MARK Van Hoecke and Mark Warrington, it has been 'a constant element in legal history' that legal systems influence each other.[2] Understanding such legal influence should not be limited to the positive law. Rather, the trend in contemporary comparative law is to consider the 'attitudes towards law and the degree to which it is embedded in society and its general culture'.[3] But this leads to the question on which scholars of 'legal transplants'[4] often disagree. On the one hand, pessimists claim that legal transplants are at least disruptive to the incoming legal and socio-cultural system, and maybe even impossible. On the other hand, optimists acknowledge and support lawmakers in copying foreign rules, though they often admit that in not all instances do legal transplants work as smoothly as in the origin country.[5]

It is no surprise that this debate about legal transplants is one of the main topics of comparative law, since it is closely related to one of the core questions about our understanding of the relationship between law and society.

[1] I thank the participants of the workshops of the North East Regional Obligations Group (NEROG) in Sheffield (July 2012) and the British Association of Comparative Law (BACL) in Cambridge (September 2011) for helpful comments.
[2] M Van Hoecke and M Warrington, 'Legal Cultures, Legal Paradigms and Legal Doctrine: Towards a New Model for Comparative Law' (1998) 47 *International and Comparative Law Quarterly* 495, 533.
[3] Ibid, 502. See also M Van Hoecke, 'Deep Level Comparative Law' in M Van Hoecke (ed), *Epistemology and Methodology of Comparative Law* (Oxford, Hart Publishing, 2004) 165.
[4] Some prefer other terms such as 'legal circulation', 'cross-fertilisation', 'diffusion' or 'migration'. See, eg V Perju, 'Constitutional Transplants, Borrowing, and Migrations' in M Rosenfeld and A Sajo (eds), *The Oxford Handbook of Comparative Constitutional Law* (Oxford, Oxford University Press, 2012) 1306–308; D Nelken, 'Legal Transplants and Beyond: Of Disciplines and Metaphors' in A Harding and E Örücü (eds), *Comparative Law in the 21st Century* (New York, Kluwer, 2002) 30–31.
[5] For references see Section III below.

Here, on the one hand, the 'mirror view of law and society' assumes that law reflects the society in question; for instance, that there is an organic connection between a particular people—its beliefs, culture and morals, as well as its social, political and economic forces—and its legal system. On the other hand is the view that law is largely autonomous of past and present social structures since legal systems have their own forms of self-reproduction—say, through internal discussions between judges, law professors and other legal experts, as well as through the use of legal transplants.[6]

This chapter takes the modest view that the precise effect of legal transplants depends on the circumstances of each individual case. However, it also presents a new idea as it suggests that a third type of reaction is possible: namely, that legal transplants work even 'better' in the transplant than in the origin country, here called 'overfitting legal transplants'. This can be thought of as a parallel to other cultural phenomena which are more popular abroad than at home. The structure of this chapter is as follows: it starts with two of these other cultural phenomena, namely, business cards in Japan and David Hasselhoff in Germany. Subsequently, it discusses the debate between the pessimists and optimists of legal transplants. The main sections then present the idea and try to develop categories of 'overfitting legal transplants'. Finally, the chapter discusses the wider implications of overfitting legal transplants for law-making and comparative law.

II. WHAT BUSINESS CARDS IN JAPAN AND DAVID HASSELHOFF IN GERMANY TEACH US

The history of modern business cards is not entirely clear, but it is commonly said that they derive from the following three sources.[7] First, starting in sixteenth-century England and France, bearer cards were used for legal notices, such as promissory notes or other obligations. Secondly, in seventeenth-century England, trade cards had the aim of advertising for a particular business, but they could also include further information, such as maps and price lists. Thirdly, in the same century in France, visiting cards had the purpose to announce the arrival of an important guest. These latter cards continued to be used as calling cards in Europe and North America until the nineteenth century. Later in that century, the three types of cards gradually merged into today's business cards.

It follows that modern business cards can be seen as a Western invention. They arrived in Japan in the late nineteenth century with the gradual open-

---

[6] For references see M Siems, *Comparative Law* (Cambridge, Cambridge University Press, 2014, forthcoming) 121–25.

[7] For the following see, eg 'The History of Business Cards: Four Centuries of Introductions' available at http://sagemedia.ca/articles/the-history-of-business-cards-four-centuries-of-introductions/; 'History of the Business Card', available at www.castleprint.co.uk/business_card_history_1.html.

ing of Japanese society to foreign influences.[8] In today's Japan business cards (*meishi*), and their correct use, are considered very important. For example, foreigners doing business in Japan are advised to present and receive them with both hands, to leave them on the table during a meeting, to place the card of the highest ranked person on top of the others, to not fold the cards and to store them in a smart leather case.[9]

A similar culture exists in other Asian countries, but not in the Western world:

> Today business cards are so ubiquitous that in some countries they are traded with no formality or consequence, serving as nothing more than an internationally recognized way to exchange contact information or a handy bit of paper on which to jot a note. In other nations, however, particularly in Asia, the cards are regarded as an extension of the individual to be treated with honor and respect. The exchange of cards is attended with great ritual and a breach of protocol can give serious offense.[10]

Parallels to this 'more popular abroad' phenomenon can be found in modern pop music. When, in the late 1980s, the US actor David Hasselhoff, well-known from the TV series *Knight Rider* and *Baywatch*, started his music career, he did not manage to get any single in the top 100 of the US charts—nor had much success in most other countries of the world. In Germany, however, as well as in Austrian and Switzerland, he was soon regarded as one of the greatest pop stars. Hasselhoff's single 'Looking for Freedom' made it to the top position of the German charts. He also had another top 10 single ('Is Everybody Happy?'), and two singles in the top 20 ('Crazy for You' and 'Do the Limbo Dance').[11]

Hasselhoff's success may seem inexplicable. Possibly, it may have mattered that Hasselhoff, while born in the US, is of German ancestry. But it can also be argued that it has to do with good timing and the fact that the German audience easily understood the title of his single 'Looking for Freedom' though not its substance (which simply dealt with a young man leaving home). It has been suggested is that the title of the song inadvertently captured the mood of the German public at the time of the fall of communism in 1989. As a BBC article explains:

> Barely a month after the fall of the Berlin Wall in November 1989, the city that had been divided by politics for more than 40 years was united in song. And leading the chorus of several hundred thousand voices was a man hitherto known to the rest of

---

[8] See 'History of "Meishi"—Visiting Cards and the Japanese Culture', available at http://www.geocities.jp/general_sasaki/history_meishi_culture.html.

[9] See, eg 'The Meishi: The Japanese Business Card', available at www.freebusinesscards.com/articles/the-meishi-the-japanese-business-card–28.html; 'Japan—Language, Culture, Customs and Etiquette', available at www.kwintessential.co.uk/resources/global-etiquette/japan-country-profiles.html.

[10] 'The History of Business Cards', above n 7.

[11] See http://www.charts.de/artist.asp?name=David+Hasselhoff.

the world for driving a talking car: David Hasselhoff, star of the hit 80s TV series *Knight Rider* . . . For that seminal concert, on New Year's Eve 1989, Hasselhoff stood atop of the partly-demolished wall and belted out a tune called Looking for Freedom . . . Hasselhoff, who by now was appearing in Baywatch, scooped a clutch of top German music awards and went on to become one of the country's biggest selling artists of the 90s.[12]

A similar phenomenon is that of the 'big in Japan' effect. This is meant to refer to the situation that some pop and rock bands from the US and Europe have been more successful in Japan than in their home countries.[13]

Thus, overall, it can be seen that it is possible that cultural phenomena— such as business cards and pop songs—may be more popular abroad than at home. Possibly, in the examples of business cards and Hasselhoff, it mattered that the foreign phenomenon reflected certain features of the transplant society in question—hierarchy and ceremony in the first example, and desire for freedom and change in the second one. Of course, it could also be argued that Hasselhoff simply had good luck. Thus, it may be difficult to draw any firm advice from these examples on how to make foreign ideas 'super effective' abroad.

The question raised in this chapter is whether there may be similar examples in law, ie legal transplants that work better abroad than at home. Before doing so, however, the following section will discuss how this view is related to the disagreement about the working or failure of legal transplants in the current literature.

III. LEGAL TRANSPLANTS: THE BIG DEBATE IN A NUTSHELL

Comparative lawyers have developed taxonomies of different types of legal transplants, including categories on the relative success or failure of the transplant in question.[14] To get a clear picture of the main arguments, the following focuses on the two extreme positions, namely the 'pessimists' on the one side and the 'optimists' on the other.[15]

The pessimist view of legal transplants comes in two variants. On the one hand, there is the postmodern view that legal transplants are largely irrelevant.

---

[12] 'Did David Hasselhoff Really Help End the Cold War?', 6 February 2004, available at http://news.bbc.co.uk/1/hi/3465301.stm.

[13] But see also G De Launey, 'Not-so-big in Japan: Western Pop Music in the Japanese Market' (1995) 14 *Popular Music* 203.

[14] Eg M Cohn, 'Legal Transplant Chronicles: The Evolution of Unreasonableness and Proportionality Review of the Administration in the United Kingdom' (2010) 58 *American Journal of Comparative Law* 583; W Twining, 'Social Science and Diffusion of Law' (2005) 32 *Journal of Law and Society* 205–7. See also O Kahn-Freund, 'On Use and Misuse of Comparative Law' (1974) 37 *Modern Law Review* 6 (continuum of legal transplants: some legal rules can be transferred by 'mechanical insertion' while other rules may be rejected, similar to the failed transplant of a kidney).

[15] For more details see Siems, above n 6, 195–200.

This is based on the position that law is not only about the words that can be found in legal texts. Rather, one needs to consider that 'meaning is a function of the application of the rule by its interpreter'.[16] Such an interpretation is always subjective and shaped by the larger cognitive framework of a particular country, in particular its culture and mentality.[17] As a result, it is argued that a legal rule cannot survive the journey from one legal system to another one unchanged since, 'as the meaning of the rule changes, the rule itself changes'.[18]

On the other hand, critical legal scholars argue that legal transplants are often harmful to the incoming legal system. This line of reasoning may be based on the relationship between the old and the new law, with the result that legal transplants should really be called 'legal irritants'.[19] But, more frequently, it is argued that the negative effect is due to the mismatch between the foreign law and the domestic social, economic, cultural and political environment. Thus, according to this view, legal transplants typically do not work, for example, due to lack of enforcement, sidelining or general unsuitability.[20]

The optimists argue at the descriptive level that even mindless legal borrowing 'is the name of the legal game'.[21] In particular, such borrowing is said to happen in private law, where rules and concepts 'can survive without any close connection to any particular people, any particular period of time or any particular place'.[22] On the other hand, there is the more normative view that legal transplants can help countries to address major economic and social problems. Thus, we are told that comparative lawyers should aim to 'increase intellectual interaction and borrowings',[23] denouncing opposition as 'parochialism'.[24]

To be sure, the optimists are not saying that any rule will under any circumstances work without any problems in the transplant country. Rather, it is seen as important to design legal transplants in a smart way.[25] For example,

---

[16] P Legrand, 'What "Legal Transplants?"' in D Nelken and J Feest (eds), *Adapting Legal Culture* (Oxford, Hart Publishing, 2001) 57.

[17] Ibid, 68 ('law as a culturally-situated phenomenon').

[18] Ibid, 61; see also P Legrand, 'The Impossibility of Legal Transplants' (1997) 4 *Maastricht Journal of European and Comparative Law* 111. Similarly, W Menski, *Comparative Law in a Global Context*, 2nd edn (Cambridge, Cambridge University Press, 2006) 5 ('law is much more than a body of rules that can simply be imposed on others').

[19] G Teubner, 'Legal Irritants: Good Faith in British Law or How Unifying Law Ends Up in New Divergences' (1998) 61 *Modern Law Review* 11.

[20] *Cf* NHD Foster, 'Comparative Commercial Law: Rules or Context?' in E Örücü and D Nelken (eds), *Comparative Law: A Handbook* (Oxford, Hart Publishing, 2007) 273–74.

[21] A Watson, *Law, Society, Reality* (Lake Mary, FL, Vandeplas, 2007) 5. See also A Watson, *Legal Transplants: An Approach to Comparative Law*, 2nd edn (Athens, GA, University of Georgia Press, 1993).

[22] A Watson, 'Legal Transplants and Law Reform' (1976) 92 *Law Quarterly Review* 81.

[23] Sir B Markesinis, 'Our Debt to Europe: Past, Present and Future' in Sir B Markesinis (ed), *The Coming Together of the Common Law and the Civil Law* (Oxford, Hart Publishing, 2000) 49.

[24] E Buscaglia and W Ratliff, *Law and Economics in Developing Countries* (Stanford, CA, Hoover Institution, 2000) 31.

[25] See G Frankenberg, 'Constitutional Transfer: The IKEA Theory Revisited' (2012) 8 *International Journal of Constitutional Law* 563 (laws need to be stripped of their social context

this may consider the need to ensure 'complementarities between the new law and pre-existing legal institutions',[26] ie that a transplant is more likely to be successful if two legal systems are based on a similar conceptual understanding of the law—say, because they belong to the same legal family.[27] Reference may also be made to research in political science on the key conditions for the transferability of policies—for example, that countries need to be ideologically and psychologically compatible.[28]

Empirically, the optimists can refer to the fact that most, if not all, legal systems have managed to incorporate ideas from various parts of the world: clearly, '[n]o legal system is entirely a prisoner of its own past traditions'.[29] But even the optimists tend to argue that, at best, legal transplants work almost as good as in the country of origin. Thus, the frequently used category is that of a 'cost-saving transplant', namely a foreign law is transplanted since the benefits of the imported rule exceed the costs of designing a new law on their own.[30] In this respect, the following sections of this chapter suggest that it is possible to go further.

IV. OVERFITTING LEGAL TRANSPLANTS: THE IDEA

The term 'overfitting' is borrowed from statistics, where it means that a model has more explanatory variables than necessary. For example, there may be a causal relationship $A + B = X$, but if we use the model $A + B + C + D = X$, the actual 'fit' is even better.[31] In the current context, the analogy is that in the origin country the law works well (X) due to A and B, ie $A + B = X$, but in the transplant country there is an 'overfit' because further factors (C and D, ie again $A + B + C + D = X$) make it work even 'better'.

before they can be recontextualised in the recipient country); H Xanthaki, 'Legal Transplants in Legislation: Defusing the Trap' (2008) 57 *International and Comparative Law Quarterly* 659 (distinguishing between 'transplant concept', 'transplant term' and 'transplant comparative research design'); E Örücü, 'Law as Transposition' (2002) 51 *International and Comparative Law Quarterly* 205 (transposition always in need of refinement).

[26] K Pistor, 'The Standardization of Law and Its Effect on Developing Economies' (2002) 50 *American Journal of Comparative Law* 97, 98.

[27] See, eg D Berkowitz, K Pistor and J-F Richard, 'The Transplant Effect' (2003) 51 *American Journal of Comparative Law* 163.

[28] See L Hantrais, *International Comparative Research: Theory, Methods and Practice* (Basingstoke/New York, Palgrave Macmillan/St Martin's Press, 2009) 133–39.

[29] TT Arvind, 'The "Transplant Effect" in Harmonization' (2010) 59 *International and Comparative Law Quarterly* 81.

[30] JM Miller, 'A Typology of Legal Transplants: Using Sociology, Legal History, and Argentine Examples to Explain the Transplant Process' (2003) 51 *American Journal of Comparative Law* 845. See also R Michaels, 'Make or Buy—A New Look at Legal Transplants' in H Eidenmüller (ed), *Regulatory Competition in Contract Law and Dispute Resolution* (Munich, Beck, 2013) 27; P Grajzl and V Dimitrova-Grajzl, 'The Choice in the Lawmaking Process: Legal Transplants vs Indigenous Law' (2009) 5 *Review of Law and Economics* 615.

[31] But note that in statistics (and econometrics) this is not actually seen as desirable, ie there should not be an 'overfit' of the model.

The subsequent section will discuss what, in the context of legal transplants, factors C and D could be. To start with, though, it also needs to be clarified what it can mean that law 'works better'. Roger Cotterrell distinguishes between two positions: someone who regards 'law as culture' will regard a transplant as successful when the law is consistent with the environment of the transplant country, whereas someone who regards 'law as an instrument' will do so when the law has the intended effect.[32] But it may also be said that both types of success are connected, since the effect of the transplanted law depends on the way it fits into the society of the transplant country.

As far as the transplanted law is more effective than in the origin country, this does not provide a normative justification for the transplanted law. For example, assume that in a country with a moderate climate there is a form of punishment that withdraws support for heating in winter. If a country with a colder climate transplants this form of punishment, this punishment works better, ie it is an overfitting legal transplant. Yet this does not provide any normative arguments in favour or against this form of punishment.

A related point is to consider that imported laws may benefit some groups more than in the origin country but, as a result, also be more harmful to other groups. For example, a law protecting creditors very effectively would, naturally, be a disadvantage for debtors. Thus, again, there can be an overfit, but it does not provide a justification for this law being adopted. It also shows that it may be necessary to identify different categories of overfitting legal transplants.

V. CATEGORIES AND TENTATIVE EXAMPLES

The first, and most intuitive, category of an overfitting legal transplant is the situation that the policy which the transplant aims to pursue is pursued even more effectively in the transplant country than in the origin country, given the particularly favourable political, cultural or socio-economic conditions of the transplant country.

The law as it relates to the board structure of companies may provide two examples. The typical distinction is between countries with just one board of directors ('one-tier countries'), those with a management board and a supervisory board ('two-tier countries'), and countries that let companies choose between these two models (eg France and Italy). In addition, in some of the two-tier countries, such as Germany, some members of the supervisory board have to be employee representatives.[33]

---

[32] R Cotterrell, 'Is There a Logic of Legal Transplants?' in Nelken and Feest, above n 16, 79.
[33] On board models see, eg PL Davies and KJ Hopt, 'Corporate Boards in Europe—Accountability and Convergence' (2013) 61 *American Journal of Comparative Law* 301; C Jungmann, 'The Effectiveness of Corporate Governance in One-Tier and Two-Tier Board Systems' (2006) 3 *European Company and Financial Law Review* 426.

When the People's Republic of China enacted a company law in the early 1990s it adopted the German two-tier model, including the idea of employee representatives.[34] It can be suggested that this is an overfitting legal transplant, since employee involvement in companies makes even more sense politically in a socialist country such as the PRC than in a social market economy such as Germany.

The other example is that of the European company (SE, *Societas Europaea*). This is a special form of company available to cross-border businesses in the EU.[35] In terms of board structure, the SE law leaves it to the companies to decide between the one- and two-tier models. This rule is apparently based on French and Italian law, but it can be suggested that it even more appropriate for the European company since it is a smart way to accommodate the diverse structures and preferences of European businesses.

The second category refers to the situation where the particular mix between old and new law creates a benefit which goes beyond that of the origin country. The way old and new law relate to each other has also been discussed in the literature on legal transplants. For instance, according to Brian Tamanaha, 'transplanted laws and legal institutions provide a new resource of power in society for individuals to resort to as a means to escape from, or with which to contest, the traditional order and social understandings';[36] and Michele Graziadei cites psychological research, according to which higher mental functions incorporate new into previous material—and legal transplants can be thought of as an example of such a process.[37]

An example may be the law of countries with mixtures between civil and common law, such as South Africa and Scotland. It may be said that the civil law may have the benefit of a scholarly and conceptual approach to law, whereas the common law may have the benefit of being pragmatic and flexible.[38] Thus, the advantage of such mixed legal systems may be that they combine the best of both worlds, ie being pragmatic but also trying to incorporate more scholarly legal concepts, say, for the benefit of legal consistency (and, possibly, 'objectivity in law'[39]).

Other examples may refer to more specific mixtures between legal rules that derive from different models.[40] An overfit may arise where more than one area of law protects the same interests. For example, both the law on secured interests and insolvency law aim to protect creditors. Just having a well-developed

---

[34] See C Liao, *The Governance Structures of Chinese Firms: Innovation, Competitiveness, and Growth in a Dual Economy* (Heidelberg, Springer, 2009) 87–88.

[35] See http://ec.europa.eu/internal_market/company/se/.

[36] BZ Tamanaha, *A General Jurisprudence of Law and Society* (Oxford, Oxford University Press, 2001) 120.

[37] M Graziadei, 'Legal Transplants and the Frontiers of Legal Knowledge' (2009) 10 *Theoretical Inquiries in Law* 723, 736–37.

[38] See discussion in Siems, above n 6, 44–48.

[39] J Husa and M Van Hoecke (eds), *Objectivity in Law and Legal Reasoning* (Oxford, Hart Publishing, 2013).

[40] Such 'vertically divided legal systems' are fairly common. See Siems, above n 6, 89–92.

law on secured interests may not, however, lead to a good level of creditor protection if the creditors are not protected in case of insolvency. Thus, if a country that already has a good insolvency law transplants legal rules from a country with merely a good law on secured interests, this may be regarded as an overfitting legal transplant.

Thirdly, there is the situation where the transplant fulfils an additional purpose in the transplant country. This additional purpose could be the symbolic value of a particular foreign law. The literature on legal transplants also discusses a similar phenomenon of 'legitimacy-generating transplants',[41] namely where a particular foreign model is considered as prestigious, or because it is seen as a signal for a desired turn towards modernity.[42]

A good example is the role of the common law in Hong Kong since, for lawyers from Hong Kong, being part of the common law helps them to maintain a difference from mainland China. For instance, a recent newspaper article reports on a dispute of whether not only barristers but also solicitors are allowed to wear a wig in court. It states that '[s]ince Hong Kong was handed back to China in 1997, some say the wig has taken on importance as a symbol of an independent judiciary', quoting a Hong Kong lawyer stating that 'it's a tradition that really dignifies our profession, especially in the context of our commitment to uphold the city's justice'.[43] It is likely that similar arguments play a role when legislators and judges from Hong Kong transplant elements of English law today, thus potentially contributing to an overfit.

Alternatively, the additional purpose could be that the legal transplant triggers additional extralegal changes. This is also of general relevance for the relationship of the fit of a legal transplant with current conditions, since a transplant may be 'geared to fitting an imagined future'.[44] Transplants of human rights law can provide an example. For instance, the Bill of Rights of the South African Constitution of 1996 was influenced by its European and North American counterparts, and the South African Constitutional Court has also considered the case law of other countries. These transplants are said to have worked well,[45] not only for the protection of individual rights

---

[41] Miller, above n 30, 854.

[42] See, eg C Milhaupt and K Pistor, *Law & Capitalism: What Corporate Crises Reveal About Legal Systems and Economic Development Around the World* (Chicago, Chicago University Press, 2008) 209; U Mattei and L Nader, *Plunder: When the Rule of Law is Illegal* (Oxford, Wiley-Blackwell, 2008) 19–20, 142.

[43] 'Wigged Out: Hong Kong's Lawyers Bristle Over Horsehair Headpieces', *Wall Street Journal*, 30 April 2013, available at http://online.wsj.com/news/articles/SB10001424127887324743704578444422350608136.

[44] D Nelken, 'Comparatists and Transferability' in P Legrand and R Munday (eds), *Comparative Legal Studies: Traditions and Transitions* (Cambridge, Cambridge University Press, 2003) 437, 456. See also D Nelken, 'Towards a Sociology of Legal Adaptation' in Nelken and Feest, above n 16, 20 (relevance for periods of revolutionary and post-revolutionary nation-building).

[45] For the following see J Fedtke, 'Constitutional Transplants: Returning to the Garden' (2008) 61 *Current Legal Problems* 49; DM Davis, 'Constitutional Borrowing: The Influence of Legal Culture and Local History in the Reconstitution of Comparative Influence: The South African Experience' (2003) 1 *International Journal of Constitutional Law* 181.

but also as a means of reconciliation and transitional justice in post-apartheid South Africa.[46]

A transplant can also be economically beneficial because it reduces the transaction costs that arise from differences between legal systems.[47] Here, the overfit may follow from the fact that the transplant country has a smaller economy than the origin country. For example, if Jamaica adjusts its company law to the US model, it may benefit from increased US investment, whereas there would be no corresponding incentive for the US to transplant Jamaican company law. This may even be the case where the transplanted law is not actually very useful for the protection of investors: thus, even 'legal placebos'[48] can be overfitting legal transplants.

Fourthly, the overfit may be about legal rules and institutions which are more durable in the transplant than in the origin country. This may be the case in some former colonies as far as the former colonisers have subsequently abandoned or loosened certain traditions. For example, as already mentioned, in Hong Kong, certain common law traditions may be taken more seriously than in England today. With respect to civil law countries, a well-known example is by John Henry Merryman on 'the French deviation'.[49] In his article, Merryman shows that French judges had soon disregarded the strictness of the French Civil Code of 1804, creating judge-made law (even though it was not officially called that). In contrast to this, the courts of Latin American countries did not regard it as acceptable to deviate from the strong separation of powers between legislators and judges, as positioned by their French-based civil codes.

Another example is that of local employment offices to review dismissals in the Netherlands. These originate from the German occupation in the early 1940s. In Germany these offices were abandoned after the end of the Second World War, but in the Netherlands they are said to have persisted 'as instruments for the rebuilding of the economy, specifically for the maintenance of employment and the continuity of industrial production'.[50] They are also seen as a good fit for the Netherlands, as its legal system relies more on filters and alternatives to courts than the German one.[51]

The fifth and final category refers to ideas about legal reform that have not been adopted in their countries of origin but have been implemented abroad.

---

[46] See also the relevance of human rights in the South African Truth and Reconciliation Commission, http://www.justice.gov.za/trc/hrvtrans/index.htm.

[47] Cf eg U Mattei, *Comparative Law and Economics* (Ann Arbor, MI, University of Michigan Press, 1997) 94, 219; K Pistor, 'The Standardization of Law and Its Effect on Developing Economics' (2002) 50 *American Journal of Comparative Law* 97.

[48] For this idea see A Aviram, 'The Placebo Effect of Law: Law's Role in Manipulating Perceptions' (2006) 75 *George Washington Law Review* 54.

[49] JH Merryman, 'The French Deviation' (1996) 44 *American Journal of Comparative Law* 109.

[50] A Jettinghoff, 'State Formation and Legal Change: On the Impact of International Politics' in Nelken and Feest, above n 16, 112.

[51] See, eg E Blankenburg, 'Civil Litigation Rates as Indicators for Legal Culture' in D Nelken (ed), *Comparing Legal Cultures* (Aldershot, Dartmouth, 1997) 41.

Thus, it may also be suggested that, here, we may not have legal transplants in a narrow sense, but cultural transplants akin to the examples of business cards in Japan and Hasselhoff's music in Germany.

The most famous example in this category is Jeremy Bentham's idea from the early nineteenth century to codify the common law. This was more successful in some of the British colonies than in England. In pre-independence India, codification concerned procedural rules as well as substantive law,[52] and these laws have also impacted on the colonial laws in Africa.[53] In the mid-nineteenth century, the American lawyer David Dudley Field also followed Bentham's idea and drafted a Code of Civil Procedure, which was initially adopted by the state of New York and which has influenced today's Federal Rules of Civil Procedure and the corresponding state laws.[54]

A recent example from civil law countries is the suggestion by the German professor Karsten Schmidt to replace the Commercial Code with a Business Enterprise Code. In 1998 the German lawmaker did not follow this advice in a major reform of German commercial law. However, a few years later, the Austrian lawmaker adopted Schmidt's proposal and enacted a Business Enterprise Code (*Unternehmensgesetzbuch*), in force since January 2007.[55]

VI. IMPLICATIONS FOR LAW-MAKING

The idea of overfitting legal transplants shows that foreign models can work very well, ie they are not only a second-best solution for lawmakers that lack the time or skill to draft their own laws. Interestingly, in some of the examples of the previous section the overfit occurred in the case of involuntary transplants (see the fourth and fifth categories): thus, if the conditions are favourable, transplants can work better than expected, even if they are not based on a deliberate borrowing by the transplant country.

But one should also not be naive about the effect of legal transplants. It has already been mentioned that the mere fact that legal transplants may work very well does not provide a normative justification for this particular set of legal rules (*cf* the withdrawal of heating example). Drawing lessons from comparative law is a complex endeavour, as explained elsewhere in more detail.[56] In particular, it may often be difficult to design a rule that deliberately aims to

---

[52] Eg Criminal Procedure Code 1861; Civil Procedure Code 1908; Penal Code 1860; Contract Act 1872.

[53] See, eg Menski, above n 18, 462.

[54] See, eg GA Weiss, 'The Enchantment of Codification in the Common Law World' (2000) 25 *Yale Journal of International Law* 505; K Zweigert and H Kötz, *An Introduction to Comparative Law*, 3rd edn (Oxford, Oxford University Press, 1998) 242–43.

[55] See M Siems, 'The Divergence of Austrian and German Commercial Law—What Kind of Commercial Law Do We Need in a Globalised Economy?' (2004) *International Company and Commercial Law Review* 273.

[56] See M Siems, 'Bringing in Foreign Ideas: The Quest for 'Better Law' in Implicit Comparative Law' *Journal of Comparative Law*, forthcoming.

achieve an overfit: rather, in some of the examples mentioned in the previous section the overfit seems to be more a result of serendipity. Some scepticism towards the ability to predict the effect of a particular legal design is also in line with the more general research about the relationship between legal and economic development, since there is no clear evidence about the direction (if any) of this causal relationship and the types of legal rules that may matter.[57]

Despite these caveats, it is suggested that lawmakers can draw the following lessons from the possibility of overfitting transplants. First, a lawmaker contemplating a legal transplant needs to consider which variant of overfit, as outlined in the previous section, may be applicable. In particular, it may be helpful to think outside the box, since the benefit may be related to something that does not exist in the same way in the origin country (see the third category above). Secondly, making the right choice requires good information about the substance of the legal rules that are to be transplanted since, while this chapter suggests that an overfit may be possible, this does not deny the risk of ineffective or harmful transplants. Thirdly, it is crucial to decide on how exactly the law is transplanted. For example, drafting the transplanted law in relatively general rules can have the benefit of accommodating possible differences between the origin country and the transplant country. Lawmakers also have to decide on whether, in addition to the legal rules, they need to emulate other elements of the foreign legal system, such as its legal education, methods and mentality. Fourthly, it has rightly been said that the process of legal reform and development may be more important than the substance of the transplanted rules.[58] Specifically, this has to consider how the new law interacts with the previous one since this can potentially contribute to an overfit (noted in the second category, above), but can also be a reason for its rejection.

In addition, the possibility of overfitting legal transplants is relevant to the debate about regulatory competition and the harmonisation of laws. On the one hand, regulatory competition seems to be a good tool to identify the best rules—and it is then at least possible that, in another country, these rules have not only a positive effect but work better than in the origin country. On the other hand, the idea of overfitting may support the harmonisation of legal rules, since it shows that outside influence on the domestic legal system does not necessarily have a negative effect. Indeed, the debate about the desirability of legal transplants and harmonisation is often conducted along similar lines.[59]

The EU in particular can be seen as an interesting testing ground for future research on overfitting legal transplants. The EU publishes scoreboards on the way Member States implement directives,[60] and those may be seen as indica-

---

[57] For the discussion see M Siems and S Deakin, 'Comparative Law and Finance: Past, Present and Future Research' (2010) 166 *Journal of Institutional and Theoretical Economics* 120.

[58] R Peerenboom, 'Toward a Methodology for Successful Legal Transplants' (2013) 1 *Chinese Journal of Comparative Law* 4.

[59] See, eg P Legrand, 'Against a European Civil Code' (1997) 60 *Modern Law Review* 44.

[60] See, eg http://ec.europa.eu/internal_market/scoreboard/performance_by_governance_tool/transposition/index_en.htm.

tors for the fit of particular rules in different legal and socio-economic systems. There is also some interaction between EU law and the law of the Member States. For example, when the Advocate General or the Court of Justice of the European Union puts special emphasis on the precedents from particular Member States, this may also be seen as an indicator for the fit of a particular EU directive with the law of this Member State.

VII. CONCLUSION

Legal transplants are sometimes compared to wine: a type of grape can be transplanted outside its native terrain, but the wine will be a bit different—as is said to be the case for transplanted law.[61] Yet, continuing with the analogy, the fact that the wine is a bit different does not mean that it will be inferior; rather, a skilful wineproducer may choose the terroir of the vineyard such that the wine may even be better (however this may be defined) than the original one. It was the aim of this chapter to show that a similar phenomenon may also exist in law.

Since this idea of such overfitting legal transplants is a new one, this chapter has tried to set the scene in outlining possible categories and examples, and how lawmakers may be able to make use of them. The five categories are: (i) a policy which is particularly favourable to the political, cultural or socio-economic conditions of the transplant country; (ii) a particularly favourable mix between old and new law; (iii) an additional purpose that the transplant fulfils in the transplant country; (iv) legal rules and institutions which are more durable in the transplant than in the origin country; and (v) ideas about legal reform which have been adopted abroad but not in their countries of origin.

These categories are closely related to core topics of legal methodology in general and comparative legal studies in particular. For example, the way a foreign legal rule is received in the transplant country crucially depends on how the relevant legal actors—legislators, judges, legal scholars, etc—understand and implement these rules.[62] Moreover, in comparative law in particular, recent scholarship has often been sceptical about treating rules in a merely instrumental way: according to Mark Van Hoecke, 'comparative law research may only be carried out meaningfully if it also includes the deeper level of underlying theories and conceptions'.[63] Thus, the quest for overfitting legal transplants is not about finding quick 'silver bullets', but about carefully understanding why domestic and foreign laws differ, and how a subsequent legal transplant may affect the former legal system.

---

[61] Arvind, above n 29, 66. See also G Watt, 'Comparison as Deep Appreciation' in PG Monateri (ed), *Methods of Comparative Law* (Cheltenham, Edward Elgar, 2012) 91–96 ('horticultural metaphor').

[62] For the role of communication in the making and legitimation of law see M Van Hoecke, *Law as Communication* (Oxford, Hart Publishing, 2002).

[63] Van Hoecke 'Legal Cultures, Legal Paradigms and Legal Doctrine', above n 2, 191.

This chapter started with the example of business cards in Japan. It explained that business cards arrived in Japan in the late nineteenth century with the gradual opening of Japanese society to foreign influences, and that in today's Japan they are considered more important than in Western countries. Around the same time, Japan also transplanted many legal rules from European countries, in particular from Germany,[64] though some argue that this has only led to a 'façade of Western law'.[65] Thus, future research may compare these parallel developments of specific cultural and legal transplants—how and why their effects may differ, and what this can teach us about the 'method and culture' of comparative law.

---

[64] See, eg JM Ramseyer, 'Mixing-and-Matching Across (Legal) Family Lines' (2009) *Brigham Young University Law Review* 1701.

[65] HW Ehrmann, *Comparative Legal Cultures* (Englewood Cliffs, NJ, Prentice Hall, 1976) 47. See also the references in M Siems, *Convergence in Shareholder Law* (Cambridge, Cambridge University Press, 2008) 258–59.

11

'Ius commune', Comparative Law and Public Governance

ALAIN WIJFFELS

I N THE FOLLOWING pages, written in honour of Mark Van Hoecke (and in memory of the various occasions on which our professional paths have crossed ever since he subjected me to my first oral university examination as a fresher, back in 1972), I would like to emphasise two related issues with regard to the historical and jurisprudential relevance of *ius commune*. The first of these issues can be summarised as the relevance of *ius commune* for comparative legal studies. The second issue raises the importance of the *ius commune* tradition for public governance. In the scholarly corpus of legal-historical studies, these issues have certainly not been entirely disregarded. However, comparatively little of the insights on those issues has percolated to the mainstream text-books on legal history, and therefore to legal studies in general. I can hardly hope to reverse that tendency in a single contribution to this volume, but, considering the readership which one expects will take notice of a collection of articles offered to Mark Van Hoecke, at least this essay may help to bring those issues to the attention of all those interested in legal scholarship beyond the narrow (and ever-narrowing) circle of specialised legal historians.

I. *IUS COMMUNE'S* MANY MEANINGS

The avowed purpose of this essay therefore requires a brief explanation of what is meant here by *ius commune*—without attempting to give a definitive and comprehensive definition of such a notoriously polysemic phrase. At a first, descriptive, level, *ius commune* refers to the Roman law and canon law as they were taught from the Second Middle Ages onwards in most universities (as a rule, in separate law faculties). Implied in this first (and provisional) definition is that one is not simply referring to the textual basis of medieval Roman and canon law teaching, but also to the doctrinal tradition which that

147

teaching generated, and even to the legal learning thus conveyed to law gradu-ates who became legal professionals in various areas of legal practice. It is often said (and I have occasionally written it myself, parroting eminent writers before me) that the phrase *ius commune* was used because everywhere in the Latin West the same curricula based on Roman and canon law were followed in the law faculties, and that the law taught in (Western) European universi-ties was therefore substantially the same everywhere. The laws taught in the universities appeared in stark contrast to the innumerable particular laws of local and regional customs and of statute law from different authorities—for which not even the conventional metaphor of a patch-work is adequate, since many of those particular laws would partly overlap one another. That second meaning of *ius commune* may well be justified from a historian's point of view, but it is less likely that it reflects how it was understood by contempo-raries, although there is of course a link between the phrase *ius commune*, as it was used by medieval legal scholars, and its differentiation from particular laws by legal historians. Even in medieval times, the concept (and sometimes, the phrase) 'common law' (in Latin) was not exclusively referring to Roman–canon law; it could also be used to refer to a law generally applicable within a specific territory or jurisdiction. Such a law would therefore be a *ius com-mune in loco*, ie a territorial common law, which was, from the perspective of Roman law scholarship, a particular law. The *ius commune* of university scholars had (in theory) a more universal vocation.

The difficulty for the modern lawyer to apprehend this second meaning of *ius commune* lies in the fact that it referred to something which belonged, on the one hand, to legal methods and legal theory, and, on the other, to posi-tive law. When the phrase *ius commune* was used by late-medieval scholars (whether in their academic work or in the course of their consultations on behalf of authorities or private parties involved in specific controversies), it served almost invariably as a concept which enabled the author to deal with a particular law. This could be in order to solve a conflict of laws, to determine whether a specific customary or statutory rule was applicable in a particular situation, and also in order to construe a customary or statutory rule. In addi-tion, though it was by no means in all cases the main purpose of bringing in the concept of *ius commune*, it would justify the actual application of a rule of Roman or canon law, and in such a case all the doctrinal issues and contro-versies which could be associated with that rule would inevitably be brought into the argument, adducing even more textual and doctrinal authorities from Roman and canon law scholarship.

At this stage, the legal historian should briefly explain to the reader who is not a professional legal historian that, besides the phrase *ius commune*, other phrases are commonly used in legal historiography which can only be regarded to some extent as equivalent concepts. One of these is that of 'learned law', although it should immediately be pointed out that it is far less common in English than the phrases (of which the English expression is usually no more than a feeble attempt at translation) used in German legal-historical schol-arship *gelehrtes Recht*, or *droit(s) savant(s)* in French. The latter expressions obviously refer to the fact that Roman law and canon law were primarily developed in the law faculties, whereas the particular laws were not. The university environment of formal law studies also meant that they followed the characteristic features of scholarly (one may even say, until the sixteenth century, scholastic) studies in general. The reference to *ius commune* as a scholarly law does not mean that the law taught in the universities remained aloof from legal practice. There was, however, broadly speaking, until modern times, a real contrast between the law of the universities and the particular laws of customs and statutes in the sense that, but for a few exceptions, the latter produced hardly any autonomous legal scholarship. As a result, legal scholarship remained a monopoly of academic Roman and canon lawyers throughout the late Middle Ages. That, in turn—and it may be one of the most underrated aspects of that chapter in our legal history—meant that all the fundamental concepts and principles—let's say a 'legal theory' in a very broad sense, as the whole set of notions and principles which make a system of positive law operational—were almost exclusively devised by Roman law and canon law scholars. The extensive use of *ius commune* learning for apply-ing a coherent system of legal authorities in the context of legal pluralism, or rules of a due process of law (in legal proceedings, but also for the medieval equivalent of executive action) or interpretative rules, and many other meta-juristic functions of legal principles other than rules of substantive law, were practically all governed by the learning of academic lawyers, and therefore also rooted in the latter's legal culture. Only from the sixteenth century onwards did particular laws inspire legal scholarship in their own right, but by then, and until the codification era, the main pattern of legal scholarship had been established in the academic Roman–canonistic tradition.

In English, the standard expression for the *ius commune* tradition (the phrase *ius commune* itself has become more familiar in recent decades) is that of civil law. Civil law, as a literal translation of *ius civile*, originally referred in ancient Roman law to that body of rules which applied specifically to Roman citizens. In medieval times, it was often used to refer to Roman law in general (as a *pars pro toto*), thus the English phrase civil law has some-times become synonymous to Roman law itself, especially when referring to the Roman law tradition from the Middle Ages onwards. After the English Reformation, when canon law faculties and education were suppressed in Eng-land, the expression civil law (and civil lawyers) was informally broadened so as to include (reformed) canon law (and the civil lawyers' presumed expertise in canon law). In more recent times, the use of the phrase civil law in English has undergone even further semantic changes. In a comparative law context, it is often used to refer to various legal systems which are deemed to have been strongly influenced by (early modern and nineteenth-century) Roman law scholarship, as opposed to the legal systems which are deemed to be based on the English common law. A twist in the tale of those shifting meanings is due to the (mis)conception which purports that the latter meaning of civil law derives from the French civil code (which was partly based on early modern Roman law scholarship). Moreover, somewhat confusingly, in even more recent times, the phrase civil law is increasingly used, as in present-day continental European legal systems, in order to refer to a branch of private law. In the latter sense, most of contemporary English civil law is based, paradoxically, on common law rules.

The distinctions are blurred even more by present-day references to *ius commune* as an undifferentiated historical category supposed to entail a body of law (mainly Roman law) throughout (continental) Europe previous to the era of national codifications. Especially when supporters of a greater legal integration within the EU use the phrase, the pre-nineteenth-century *ius commune* is sometimes presented either as the roots of the present-day European legal systems (having somehow survived under the layer of national codifications during the nineteenth and twentieth centuries) or as a more abstract reminder that, before the legal systems of the nation-states were established as national legal systems, the various European countries had shared a common legal system, or at least a common legal culture. One way or the other, the historical reference simply serves as a stepping stone to forward the notion of European law as a 'new *ius commune*'. It is a typical example of how a historical category is being used largely out of context. As a historical notion of reference, *ius commune* not only has, as has already been pointed out, different meanings (some going back to medieval and early modern law, some as constructs of different historiographic approaches), but, even when one considers *ius commune* as a body of positive (and mostly substantive) legal rules, most authors still overlook the essential transformations *ius commune* underwent when, over the centuries, it was cast in different moulds of thinking, each time producing a distinctive brand of legal methods. Although, each time, more or less the same textual sources, mainly drawn from Justinian's compilations, were recycled, the outcome was a new framework of legal thinking. Each time, the theoretical and practical relationship between Roman–canon law and particular laws was redefined.

Finally, the very meaning of *ius commune* in contrast to particular laws was itself the scholarly construct of academic *ius commune* as learned law. It has been argued that even the labelling of normative social patterns in terms of 'customary law' during the transition from the early to the late Middle Ages was itself a construct imposed by scholars of Roman and canon law. In any case, when faced with the diversity of laws within the territory of a polity and the ensuing jurisdictional complexity, late-medieval legal scholars devised a doctrine which enabled them to differentiate between different categories of laws and their authority, and to articulate a methodical framework which laid down the principles according to which each category of law was to be applied and construed. A fundamental distinction was thereby that between *ius commune*, which mostly (but, as already noted, not invariably) referred to the Roman and canon law traditions, and *iura propria* (the term of art for particular laws). It was a characteristic move of academic legal scholars to draw the distinction, which subsequently enabled them to 'call the shots' as regards the relationship between the two types of laws. In short, the strategy consisted in acknowledging the primacy of a *ius proprium* rule in relation to a *ius commune* rule, but the further elaboration of the relationship was over-all more favourable towards the *ius commune*, which meant that the primacy of *ius proprium* was subverted and overturned, so as to pave the way for a more extensive application of *ius commune* in practice. This was achieved by almost systematically working out rules of evidence, on the need to state a specific rule of law a party wanted to rely upon, on the assumption of the *curia novit iura* principle, on interpretation—and so on—which facilitated the use of *ius commune*. However, as in so many other aspects of *ius commune* scholarship, the device was flexible, leaving practitioners in every case the latitude to take into account the specific balance of power between the interests which would be protected by the application of a *ius commune* rule and those interests which were expressed in the *ius proprium* rule. The great strength of *ius commune* was that it was in almost every respect the general default system of law, and that its agents could operate it with a sufficient degree of discretion in order to support, undermine or deflect the application of *iura propria*.

II. *IUS COMMUNE* AND COMPARATIVE LEGAL STUDIES

Whatever meaning is given to any notion of common law—whether *ius commune* or any other form of common law—it always necessarily implies legal pluralism: there is no point in styling a set of principles and norms as 'common' unless there is some diversity of principles and norms for which the common set has been worked out. A common law always aims at transcending and to some degree controlling the various laws within its ambit. That process requires the common law to elaborate notions and principles which enable it to assemble the different ('particular') laws into a homogeneous structure. The process of homogenisation, however, can only be effective if the proper nature and purpose of any particular law is not exaggeratedly distorted. This was achieved in the medieval *ius commune* tradition by working out concepts and principles which were sufficiently abstract to allow some leeway in their application, so that its users had a reasonable degree of discretion to apply policy considerations which made it possible to take into account the interests at stake and to deal with conflicts of interests.

For most historical common law models, the purpose was not to compare different particular legal systems, though occasionally such a comparison could nonetheless occur. One of the best-known examples is that of the early modern *droit commun coutumier* in France, which different authors tried to achieve through different means; for some, the method consisted in drawing common or comparable features from individual customs, an approach which necessitated a comparison between different customs within the realm. Sixteenth-century French legal literature shows how those comparative experiments could still be carried out along different lines: some authors would propose general principles or rules of law which were deemed to form a common core of law shared by various customs within the realm; others would draw converging principles from the most elaborate written custom of the realm, *viz* the custom of Paris, which could, moreover, benefit from a substantial and well-documented case law (in particular of the Paris Parlement); however, any somewhat sophisticated comparative approach by such authors would inevitably also borrow concepts and principles from the *ius commune* tradition.

Today, comparative law is seen by some authors as one of the most appropriate methods for establishing a common European law in some areas—the construct of 'European private law', which was strongly developed at the end of last century, was in many ways the result of a scholarly comparative law analysis of national legal systems within Europe.

In 2005, the Canadian comparative lawyer Patrick Glenn published a monograph *On Common Laws*, in some ways a spin-off from his successful textbook *Legal Traditions of the World*. Glenn's approach to common laws—he correctly emphasises the plurality of common laws in various legal traditions—may perhaps betray (as in *Legal Traditions*) a propensity to turn a blind eye to the less uplifting side of most legal systems, but his analysis of a common law's characteristics, based on a vast array of secondary literature, may help legal historians to reconsider conventional ideas on *ius commune* and other models of common laws. The key concept in Glenn's interpretation of various historical forms of common law is that of a common law's inherent 'relational' character. The term refers to legal and jurisdictional diversity, in the sense that Glenn rightly emphasises that a common law's identity is always at least partly defined by the coexistence of particular laws, and sometimes also by its *modus vivendi* with other, concurrent common laws. However, Glenn also analyses common laws (such as the Roman law-inspired medieval and early modern *ius commune*) in a very unimperialistic fashion. Drawing partly on the subsidiarity of common law rules, Glenn appears to deny a common law's ability to impose itself as an obligatory normative system. Moreover, because common laws are not deemed to be created by a legislator, he suggests that a common law cannot properly speaking be abolished, and that therefore 'it never dies'—or at least, that even after a period of evanescence, it can be revived. Apart from the fact that this seems to be an over-optimistic view of the history of many common laws—including the *ius commune* referred to in the present essay—because it tends to ignore or downplay the resistance historically successful common laws often met on their way, it is a view which fails to explain satisfactorily why, after having defined common laws as a category *sui generis* and different from particular laws, essentially the same condition (*viz* the existence of a formal lawmaker) should apply for abolishing both a particular law and a common law. In Glenn's benign approach to legal traditions, the pendulum may have swung back too far away from the old-fashioned and over-positivistic notion of 'reception' of Roman law in a now bygone legal historiography.

While legal historians may regret that Glenn largely ignores the policies and strategies which influenced and shaped the complex interface between a common law and particular or other common laws, that may precisely be a fresh incentive for revisiting those forms of interface: the result may be useful for a reappraisal of historical forms of common laws, and it may also update legal historiography's contribution to current debates on how any common law—for example, in Europe—should be understood with regard to national and other particular legal systems. Historical common law studies therefore necessarily entail a comparative legal-historical approach, and the need to differentiate between the methods which legal scholars and practitioners applied at the time in elaborating and applying a common law, on the one hand, and the critical historical method required to assess any legal common law method of the past, on the other. The key to that critical assessment by comparative legal history methods lies in a combination of conceptual tools and a historical *Interessenjurisprudenz*, ie a historical appraisal of the conflictual and concurrent interests which existed and developed in the interface between different laws.

III. *IUS COMMUNE* AS A MATRIX OF PUBLIC GOVERNANCE

When, from the late-eleventh and twelfth centuries onwards, academic Roman law studies were initiated in the West, soon followed by canon law studies largely adopting the pattern of Roman law teaching, the concept and purpose of those studies were from the start—independently from general intellectual and cultural considerations—very practical. The primary concern and interest for those studies was to provide a conceptual framework for public governance and to train future lawyers who would become the executives of that system of governance. This was particularly obvious in the case of the early generations of university-trained canon lawyers, from about the mid-twelfth century onwards. The church, as the sole global actor in Latin Christianity, wielded enormous economic, social, political and ideological interests, cutting across the borders of territorial entities. It required a sophisticated system of government which could control the whole organisation and at the same time ensure effective local administration. During the final centuries of the Western Roman Empire, the church had already modelled its territorial organisation on that of the imperial system, and those ecclesiastical structures had more or less managed to survive throughout the early Middle Ages. After the Gregorian Reformation, the church was able to develop autonomously its own governance system and to form its own executive and administrative staff at all levels of that system. During the golden age of canon law (roughly from the mid-twelfth century until the second half of the thirteenth century), several popes, many bishops and a large number of the church's executive directors and managers were drawn from the graduates of the canon law faculties. To some extent, the trend was emulated by secular powers, too. Cities (at first, mainly cities from Northern and Central Italy) would, despite having a different concept of their tradition and of the foundation of political legitimacy, also take advantage of the public governance techniques offered by Roman law studies and further developed by canon law studies. Municipal polities were relatively open to the system and culture of those legal studies as instruments of government, and therefore willing to recruit law graduates because of their expertise in those instruments. Territorial rulers, too, when faced with more complex demands of administration than their feudal experience and vassals could provide, would increasingly rely on university law graduates to assist them in their administrative tasks. Those tasks included both administration in the sense of government executive action and administration of justice (the characteristic *Polizey und Justiz* of late-medieval and early modern government powers).

During the early modern centuries, the judicial tasks associated with government—especially in the courts of territorial rulers and of other largely self-governing polities—were (on the European continent) mostly in the hands of professional lawyers educated in law faculties. In the political bodies which advised the prince or the rulers of a polity, legal professionals also continued to take up key positions, although the picture differs considerably from one country to another. Legal thinking and legal concepts also notoriously played an important part in early modern political theories, although it should be acknowledged that the emancipation of political theory from theology did not entail the other established academic disciplines—the arts or law—succeeding in recovering or incorporating political theory as an exclusive branch of their own expertise. Early-modern political theories were largely able to develop independently from the university institutions and traditions, but nevertheless remained bound by cultural and intellectual conventions led by classical and Biblical historical models and references. The latter ensured (even long after the *Ancien Régime*) that political thinking, despite all national differences, continued to draw from a widely shared European ideological background.

It is commonly argued that, during the early modern period, public law developed to such an extent autonomously in different countries and jurisdictions that it ceased to be part of the European *ius commune* tradition. One of the least satisfactorily answered questions in legal history is precisely why, during the transition between the Middle Ages and the seventeenth century, the civil law tradition largely lost its ascendancy over public law in many European countries. The very different political developments which emerged from the Reformation and Counter-Reformation, and from civil wars such as the religious wars all over northwestern Europe, the Dutch Independence War, the Thirty Years' War in Germany, the conflict between Royalists and Parliamentarians in England, the mid-seventeenth century War of the Fronde in France, all resulted in a distinctive reshaping of the main institutions of public governance in each country. In most countries, apart from some older and more recent fundamental documents, the workings of those political institutions were to some degree governed by various kinds of constitutional conventions. The default value of the civil law tradition in this area was in most cases very weak. Germany was perhaps one of the most important exceptions, although even the complex body of public law of the Holy Roman Empire and its doctrinal constructs no longer systematically drew their inspiration from the Roman civil law tradition as a common European legal tradition.

Early-modern legal science established the main typology and systematisation of law in branches and sub-branches, the foundation of a legal methodology which both in most curricula of law schools and in mainstream legal thinking remains applicable today. During the seventeenth and eighteenth centuries, each branch or sub-branch of the law thus systematised was characterised in legal literature by a mixture of civil law and the particular laws of the specific jurisdiction under discussion. In some areas of the law, such as the law of contracts, the importance of civil law was usually much stronger; conversely, in other areas, such as family property issues, the particular laws often carried more weight. In that context, it is fair to say that, for many, if not most, public law issues, a particular jurisdiction's political institutions and constitutional conventions increasingly played a much greater role at the expense of civil law expertise. Characteristically, the eighteenth-century phrase *Droit public de l'Europe* referred not to a common body of domestic constitutional laws largely shared by the various political systems in Europe but, rather, to the normative system governing international relations between European powers. When the *Droit public de l'Europe* did occasionally include rules of a specific country's constitution, for example with regard to dynastic succession, these were invariably rules specific to a particular country but, for the sake of the European balance of power, were given the additional authority of being incorporated in the law of nations. Significantly, whereas, in early-nineteenth-century civil codes, *ius commune* doctrines of the early modern period are often easily recognisable in the coeval written constitutions which appeared in different continental countries (and which can be regarded as very abridged—and incomplete—codifications of the new public law), it is much more difficult to recognise any particular direct contribution from pre-revolutionary *ius commune*. Nineteenth-century constitutional law literature, even much less than nineteenth-century private law literature in those countries where a civil code had been introduced, seemed to confirm that public law doctrines had entirely broken away from the civil law tradition.

Yet, the history of early modern political theories may sometimes have obfuscated key developments and areas of public law where civil law doctrines inherited from the later Middle Ages may have exercised a decisive influence.

The legal-historical background of early modern so-called 'absolute power' may be one example. The eponymous feature of early modern absolutism is usually (and correctly) linked to the formula 'legibus solutus' and to the early modern concept of sovereignty as an exclusive supreme political power within a polity. However, absolute power was already a concept (and term of art) in late-medieval doctrines, and has been likened by at least some jurists of the civil law tradition to the concept of 'extraordinary power'. In late-medieval doctrine, the distinction between ordinary and extraordinary power should perhaps mainly be understood as a functional distinction in the exercise of public governance, rather than as a political ideology or a distinct form of government. It was understood that, under normal circumstances, a ruler would exercise his powers in the 'ordinary' way, which essentially meant following the laws and conventions of his polity. Under exceptional circumstances, however, he could make decisions which departed from the laws and conventions, for example by ignoring vested rights of an individual or corporation, and, if the circumstances justified it, that extraordinary exercise of his powers would be valid. Late-medieval civil law doctrines produced a great deal of literature in order to define what justification was required for switching from the ordinary to the extraordinary mode of government—provided that the latter would always have to remain exceptional and temporary. This was the late-medieval jurists' attempt to 'restrain the irrestrainable', *viz* to maintain the exercise of power *legibus solutus* within legal bounds. In the late-medieval political context of the Italian peninsula, where those doctrines were first elaborated in the law faculties, the relations of power were such that the distinction between what was ordinary and extraordinary in the exercise of power more or less had a basis in political reality. For example, during the last centuries of the Middle Ages, Italian cities could all the more easily accept the Emperor's nominal supremacy precisely because it was largely nominal (the Pope's position was already much more problematic for many Italian cities). In domestic political relations, often knocked off balance by the rivalries between opposing factions, the distinction could be useful in order to legitimise (also *a posteriori*) measures taken by a regime at a time of extreme political unrest. What happened from mainly the sixteenth century onwards, also beyond Italy, was that a new type of ruler who succeeded in imposing his supreme power in a polity would be able to identify himself with the 'general interest' of the polity to such an extent (the civil law also being instrumental on this issue) that, in pursuing his policies, he could more and more often be justified in exercising his extraordinary power. Terminologically, one may recognise in some countries a similar phenomenon in the area of criminal law: the late-medieval doctrine made a distinction in criminal proceedings between a stage in those proceedings which was the 'ordinary' way of proceeding (and which largely followed the standard pattern of civil proceedings, ie adversarial and written, hence also more lengthy) and the possibility of switching to an 'extraordinary' way of proceeding (where those safeguards could be left out). By the sixteenth century, in some jurisdictions (as, for example, in many territories of the Low Countries), the 'ordinary' criminal proceedings had become the exception while the 'extraordinary' proceedings were routinely applied in the vast majority of cases, but the term 'extraordinary' was nevertheless maintained for what had in fact become the usual procedure. Similarly, one may argue that, referring to the late-medieval terms of *potestas ordinaria* and *potestas extraordinaria*, the characteristic early modern sovereign had acquired a position in which the exercise of his extraordinary power, ie the *potestas absoluta*, was becoming the usual exercise of government. In early modern public law, the late-medieval terminology may then have been largely jettisoned, but the legal justification of the 'absolutist' ruler's exercise of power implicitly remained, and thus also some largely invisible doctrinal foundation stemming from the *ius commune* tradition.

Another feature of early modern public governance where the civil law tradition inherited from the Middle Ages remained more prominent was that of the practice of the central and supreme courts. Although the principle of separation of powers was never fully carried out until the end of the *Ancien Régime*, delegated forms of central or supreme justice, especially in the territories ruled by sovereign monarchs, were already well established by the end of the Middle Ages. In most countries, the organisation and functioning of those central and supreme courts gave the administration of justice, even without an independent judiciary in the modern sense, at least a distinct legal hallmark. Judicial tasks remained therefore an essential part of the public governance system, and were at the same time rooted in a growing autonomous tradition of legal standards. For the *Ancien Régime*, those developments in different countries are all the more striking because the sovereign often retained or developed his own prerogative system of justice, which, depending on the political situation, could sometimes clash with the regular courts—as, notoriously, in France under the absolutist monarchy. Nevertheless, in very different political contexts—and to different degrees— the institutions of the prerogative justice borrowed devices from the regular courts (such as rules ensuring a due process of law) in order to enhance the quality and credibility of their own adjudicating practice. Thus, even the justice administered by those political bodies close to the ruler contributed, paradoxically, to the development of the rule of law. (It should be added, for the sake of a balanced argument, that, conversely, the courts sometimes borrowed techniques from their political counterparts—and competitors— and also that they were not in all cases immune from political pressure and strategies in their decision-making process). The history of these general developments could vary from one country to another, again, depending on the political history in each country, but the parallels need to be emphasised, as they point to structural comparisons which can be made between, for example, the Parlements and sovereign courts in France, on the one hand, and the King's Council on the other; in the Empire, between the Reichskammergericht and the Reichshofrat; or, in the Southern Netherlands, between the sovereign courts and the Privy Council. This is another feature of *Ancien Régime* public governance that shows that the heritage of *ius commune* was still alive on the eve of the revolutionary developments which would redraw the outlines of Western constitutional systems. Even if (and precisely because) rulers such as Napoleon saw the law they enacted primarily as an instrument of power, constitutional restraint of absolute power nevertheless prevailed: the rule of law tradition, of which the emphasis on the principle of legality was a modern form in the wake of codifications and written constitutions, remained at the heart of the concept of an efficient and fair public governance.

IV. NO LESSONS FROM THE PAST

In this brief essay, I have tried to emphasise that the Roman–canonistic *ius commune* tradition (i) provided a theoretical and methodological prerequisite for handling the legal complexity which included a diversity of both particular and common laws, including creating a comparative basis for those different systems; and (ii) that, as a matrix and practical instrument of public governance developed in the Middle Ages, it retained, albeit less visibly than in areas of private law, a degree of common foundation of public law in diverging political systems during early modern times.

The late-medieval and early modern *ius commune* is no longer a direct model for contemporary forms of common law, and certainly not for public governance in the twenty-first century. Its long history until the codification era has nonetheless profoundly affected the structure, the principles of functioning and the language of our Western legal systems. Twentieth-century history has shown how fragile all those *acquis* may be under the pressure of a totalitarian regime, but has also shown their resilience and capacity to withstand such pressure. I am not sure whether that is what Glenn meant when he wrote that common laws never die; besides, the historian can never assume that the values attributed to public governance in our present-day democratic societies belong to an irreversible advance of mankind. However, the history of *ius commune* shows that the basic values of a legal culture can be transmitted to an era when that legal culture has undergone a wholesale metamorphosis. No amount of legal science, however, can be decisive in procuring such a result unless those basic values are carried and defended by jurists who remain at the centre of public governance: in the courts, but also at the heart of government.

Further Reading

Since the editors encouraged the contributors to be bold and free from conventional constraints, I have refrained from adding footnotes to what is essentially an essay based on an ongoing reassessment of the historical material I have been working on for more than a quarter of a century in the course of both my research and teaching. Some essential ideas I have already developed in earlier publications, although, in some cases, my presentation at the time now looks a little stale or *passé*. Among the articles written specifically for readers who are not legal historians are: 'Aux confins de l'histoire et du droit: la finalité dans le débat sur la formation d'un nouveau ius commune' (1998) 207 *Revue d'Ethique et de théologie morale 'Le Supplément'* 33; 'European Private Law: A New Software Package for an Outdated Operating System?' in M Van Hoecke and F Ost (eds), *The Harmonization of European Private Law* (Oxford, Hart Publishers, 2000) 101–16; 'Qu'est-ce que le *ius commune?*' in A Supiot (ed). *Tisser le lien social* (Paris, Editions de la Maison des Sciences de l'Homme, 2004) 131–47 (also in A *Wijffels* (ed), *Le Code civil entre* ius commune *et droit privé européen* (Brussels, Bruylant, 2005) 643–61); 'Droit privé européen, *ius commune* et "seconde constitution" de l'Europe' (2003 [= 2005]) 1 *Annuaire de droit européen* 820; 'Le *ius commune* européen: mythe ou référentiel indifférencié des discours sur la formation d'un droit européen?' in B Bernabé and O Camy (eds), *Les mythes de fondation et l'Europe* (Dijon, Éditions Universitaires de Dijon, 2013) 87–101. A less hermeneutically written, but more critical, assessment of *ius commune* as a 'small world' is: '*Orbis exiguus*. Foreign Authorities in Paulus Christinaeus's Law Reports' in WH Bryson, S Dauchy and M Mirow (eds), *Ratio decidendi. Guiding Principles of Judicial Decisions. Vol 2. Foreign Law* (Berlin, Duncker und Humblot, 2010) 37–62. The shift of my interests linking *ius commune* to public governance is comparatively recent, due to changes in my teaching and research commitments. A few very tentative pages reflecting that shift are included in my textbook for law undergraduates: *Introduction historique au droit. France—Allemagne—Angleterre* (Paris, Presses Universitaires de France, 2010).

It would be excessively tiresome to give an extensive bibliography of works which have provided me with materials and insights for some of the developments I mention—apart, of course, from my own ongoing work on primary sources—but a few innovative and readable monographs should nevertheless not be left unmentioned. I have used Patrick Glenn's books for several years as standard reading material for some of my undergraduate and graduate courses in legal history and comparative law; the one closest to the topic of this essay, and at the same time a goldmine for bibliographical references, is HP Glenn, *On Common Laws* (Oxford, Oxford University Press, 2005). On late-medieval political theories, including the distinction between *potestas ordinaria, extraordinaria* and *absoluta*, I often refer to K Pennington, *The Prince and the Law, 1200–1600. Sovereignty and Rights in the Western Legal Tradition* (Berkeley,

University of California Press, 1993). For the early modern developments, a short but incisive study is D Quaglioni, *La Sovranità* (Rome, Laterza, 2004). A recent study gives a fresh view on the relationship between the judiciary and government in France, both during the *Ancien Régime* and during the nineteenth and twentieth centuries, taking into account for the earlier centuries the civil law tradition: J Krynen, *L'État de justice. France, XIIIe–XXe siècle. Vol 1. L'idéologie de la magistrature ancienne* (Paris, Gallimard, 2010), *Vol 2: L'emprise contemporaine des juges* (Paris, Gallimard, 2012). A general overview through the looking-glass of central and supreme courts is CH van Rhee and A Wijffels (eds) *European Supreme Courts. A Portrait through History* (London, Third Millennium Publishing, 2013).

12

Things Being Various: Normativity, Legality, State Legality

SEÁN PATRICK DONLAN

> World is crazier and more of it than we think,
> Incorrigibly plural. I peel and portion
> A tangerine and spit the pips and feel
> The drunkenness of things being various[1]

I. INTRODUCTION

DEBATES SURROUNDING THE concept of 'law', or the utility of such a concept, are not new. The search for the meaning of 'law' has long been an important part of Western thought, but, with a few important exceptions, most contemporary jurisprudes appear profoundly uninformed by historical and comparative analyses. Seeking universal concepts of law, legal philosophers often seem ignorant of, or uninterested in, conceptual universes beyond their own time and place. The standard of state law has been an especially important model, both explicitly and implicitly. Eschewing comparative analysis, across either time or place, jurists have generated through it an idealised concept rooted in the legal and governmental forms with which they are most familiar. For the Western past and for much of the global present, however, the metric of state law is inappropriate.

State law is, in fact, a relatively novel and recent normative form even in the West, though one particularly successful at colonising and dominating its rivals. As a model, it has impoverished our professional and public discourses on law for much of the last two centuries—the period of the state's maturation as a meaningful political form. The belief in law's necessary marriage to the state has distracted us from a deeper, more public, past convention

---

[1] L MacNeice, 'Snow' in *Poems* (Faber & Faber, 1935).

161

that might be more useful for the present and, indeed, for the future. Laws and legal institutions, identified as such, preceded the state. In fact, a unified system of national state common laws is the historical exception rather than the rule. Before the rise of the state, laws existed and competed both with rival legal regimes and with other forms of normativity. When it did arise, the law of the state was parasitic on an already established, conventional concept of law, as well as, more importantly in practice, pre-existing legal institutions.

This recognition of law's origins in more general, if institutionalised, norms in an age before the state and its laws has important benefits for legal study. It suggests that any meaningful understanding of 'law' requires comparative and historical analysis. It suggests that this comparative-historical analysis and methodology must be broadened to capture social norms (norms) that do not qualify as legal norms, either as conventionally understood (laws) or by the standard of the state (state laws). That is, legality, including state legality, must be set within normativity more generally.[2] Indeed, where possible, our focus as scholars should be on normative communities rather than narrowly legal or political institutions, and our ability to generate an accurate picture of the complex normativity of a place remains insufficient without attention to the degree to which the principles of a normative or legal order are implemented in practice and alter over time. This comparative and historical analysis will not, however, provide a neat picture of discrete and mutually exclusive units of norms, laws and state laws. Instead, any deep focus on the wide spectrum of normativity will reveal a wide variety of hybrid, dynamic forms. Any investigation of this hybridity seeks, at best, to capture a normative snapshot that alters as soon as it is taken.

The standard of state law is so theoretically dominant and practically important that it is easy to be distracted by its gravitational pull. In a series of papers over the last few years, I have sought to promote a more holistic, relational analysis of the legal-normative 'hybridity' of different time-spaces. In this work, the comparative enterprise was explicitly defined as a close reading of normative-legal complexity. In articulating this approach with contemporary examples in mind, I made use of modern conventions to distinguish between what I called 'legal hybridity' and 'normative hybridity'. In doing so, I attempted to bracket any deeper conceptual analysis that might distract from that study. However, this concession, the use of bifurcated categories, is itself distorting for a more general theory of normativity. In any event, my use of 'hybridity' is related to two interconnected axes of investigation. The first, employing modern conventions, was between (i) non-state norms (ie both normativity and legality independent of the state) and (ii) state laws (state legality). A second axis focuses on the gap between the titular principles and the actual practices of normative and legal orders (an interrelated assemblage

---

[2] 'Legality' here merely refers to having to do with law, rather than with the more complex notion of the 'principle of legality' related to the 'rule of law'.

of norms). While I have created confusion by adopting this approach, the study of this hybridity, along with the diffusion of norms and laws that creates the various hybrids, points towards the need for a historical, comparative and institutional theory that sets research on legality within the wider matrix of normativity.

II. CONCEPTS

Jurisprudence, in the sense of legal philosophy, can often seem to operate backwards. An ideal conceptualisation of 'law' defines in advance what counts as such or what fails to meet its requirements. Actual practices are measured by preconceived, abstract formulations. These are frequently products of presentist perspectives, thin and whiggish histories, and limited cultural horizons. Context is lost. In such an approach, any neologism (eg 'wal') is as meaningful a conceptual choice as 'law'. Speculation of this sort will be idle until jurists have a better idea of the lived practices of the past and the present, both in the West and beyond. To be meaningful, this requires investigation of the understandings of law that are internal to both those engaged in formulating the meaning of the practices in some official or even philosophical sense and those engaged in the practices but external to such debates.

Grossly simplifying the complex, the relationship between words and the world around us is always bridged by convention. 'Norms', in the sense of normative valuing, are standards of oughtness or appropriateness, of right claims and conduct. This usage in English and many other European languages is long established, but originally grew out of the Latin *norma*, a craftsman's tool used to create right angles. In this sense of oughtness, norms and the normative communities that maintain them are a universal aspect of human existence. We are, we might say, normative animals. Both in our use of terminology as well as in its lived forms, we can express normativity in radically diverse ways. But our terms need not be universals; instead, they denote specific, if complex, conventions with which the relevant community is familiar. And conventions have histories—they are contested and change. Anomalous uses may appear. 'Law' and its cognate forms across the West are no different. They have no essence or fixed meaning. Their significance comes from convention, from collective experiences and common opinion.[3]

---

[3] At least in the vast majority of cases, norms believed to be universal must be little more than a projection of a community's internal values beyond itself, to reify its standards of appropriateness and excellence. This might even be true for 'justice' itself. While some minimal human goods and values may exist across time and space on the basis of generally common human inclinations, these are so extraordinarily plastic and so profoundly altered in different normative contexts that nominally common elements are invariably thin. This includes law, though its institutionalisation results in a greater level of autonomy vis-à-vis both other norms and the order from which the legal regime developed.

Given the long history of the term 'law' and the manner in which second-ary meanings can arise over time, the concept for which it stands is admittedly polyvalent rather than univocal. Nevertheless, there remains an identifiable focal or central meaning. For centuries, 'law' has, across the West, stood for norms of specific institutions structured in specific ways in specific times and places. It was a subset of more general normativity, an institutional normative order attended to or overseen by individuals trained in the conceptual vagaries and vocabulary of an established, meaningfully substantive normative order. In this construction, legal orders are a product of intellectual and institution formalisation.[4] In this way, law (legality) is distinguished from both less organ-ised—but no less meaningful or valuable—instances of social normativity and the narrower, derivative form of state law (state legality). The associated West-ern folk concept of law was employed to distinguish laws from customs, both within Europe and beyond. However, this conceptualisation of law is neither a universal, scientific category nor an inherently superior form of normativity. A place without law simply manages its norms differently. Indeed, Western 'law' is not the only complex intellectual and institutional form of normativity; others very similar to our own have existed, and exist now.[5] In addition, our concept of law, if not always its related practices, has been exported around the globe over the course of centuries of Western colonisation and hegemony.

But we need to be careful. It is one thing, for example, to liken the concepts behind the terms for 'apples', 'oranges' or 'pears' in different languages. It is quite another to equate complex forms of normativity without distinction. Removing normativities, including laws and state laws, from their specific contexts kills what makes them live and meaningful for their communities. To claim that one is merely a particular version of the other confuses our unique conventions with universal constants. Comparatists know, of course, the value of finding commonalities, but a common core between concepts in different traditions remains distinct from the original concepts. This third, usually more abstract and bloodless, conceptualisation may drain the original two of the distinctive elements that gave them local significance. Like their descriptions, meanings are thick. It is in this sense that efforts to validate non-Western forms of normativity by labelling them 'law' are often misplaced. As a descriptive matter, the promiscuous use of 'law' for just any concept or form fails to appreciate its encultured, conventional application. While such efforts are often meant to prescribe a kind of moral and political equivalence

---

[4] This is not, or so I suggest, an empty formalism. If the king's law was always law even if unjust, there were substantive requirements that denied legal status to forms otherwise indistin-guishable. That is, there was a requirement of some minimal accepted authority and external, and culturally specific, substantive metrics that distinguishes law from the rules, institutions and sanctions of banditti. This external measure was no doubt fine and sometimes difficult to maintain in practice. It could be quite vague, part of the wider European culture, not least Christianity.

[5] It is tempting, for example, to equate well-developed Chinese forms that predate our own with law. There is probably little harm in this. There may even be a positive gain in recognising that our concept, or very similar concepts, may be found elsewhere.

between Western laws and other law-like norms, this ironically makes the Western concept of law an absolute metric for others. It thus assimilates non-Western or non-standard forms of normativity to a dominant, hegemonic meaning linked to Western ideas and institutions. It is, ironically, a type of conceptual colonisation.

III. CONVENTIONS

Convention, including conceptual conventions, is necessarily a product of time and place. In short, Western legal history since the fall of Rome is a movement from *ius* to *lex*: that is, from a sense of rightness, closely associated to the meaning of norm and often with respect to social mores, to the posited rule of a political authority. In this, there is a repetition of sorts of what happened within Rome over its long life. That story, however, would distract us too much here. For now, it is enough to note that a very rough and revisable typology of normative institutionalisation in the West can be created for the period after the fall of Rome. The picture painted will lack precision, but will capture the overall truth of the development of institutionalised normativity. This spectrum of institutional forms is closely connected to the political movement towards the modern nation-state over time. This movement need not, however, be unidirectional. Later forms never entirely displace earlier, simpler orders. And if this development need not be universal, our Western story has parallels elsewhere.

Inchoate and inconsistent, implicit social norms can be rationalised through language, itself another normative ordering, to general principles or more specific rules. This is as much a question of practice as principle, and happens organically over time as regularities are sought in norm creation and application. In this way, normativity is instantiated in tradition, from a large variety of (i) implicit and non-institutionalised normative practices and orders to ever-more institutionalised forms. If a bright line cannot be drawn, the creation of a (ii) 'normative regime' can be seen as the inclusion of a minimal level of specialisation—perhaps largely in personnel—in creation, however conscious, and/or application, whatever the content. The further shift to a (iii) 'legal regime' that meets the institutional threshold is obviously significant. The formalities that historically led to the recognition of normativities as 'law' include specialisation in personnel, training and language, the last of these assisted by the introduction of writing and archives that allowed an institutional memory of authorised or authentic norms to be maintained over time and space.

But this type of legality, like normativity, took plural forms. Normative and legal ordering was multicentric, with disparate competing centres of power and persuasion. Legal regimes only rarely sought, and still less often expected, to govern their rivals. The ability to legislate or adjudicate authoritatively—to have 'jurisdiction' or the ability to 'speak the law'—was contested for centuries. Indeed, looking at Europe in the period after the fall of the Roman Empire, there were for centuries multiple contemporaneous normative and legal regimes coexisting and overlapping in the same geographical space and at the same time, though often affecting different individuals. Even after Roman law was rediscovered through Justinian's *Digest*, it was only one such regime. For a long time, the legal regimes of Europe included multifarious folk laws, local and particular *iura propria*, the romano-canonical 'learned laws', and other transterritorial *iura communia* (including feudal law and perhaps the *lex mercatoria*). A complete picture of this normative landscape would require us to add numerous other normative and legal regimes, not to mention other non-institutionalised normative practices and orders.[6] Further, norms and laws could be bent by the practical pressure of power: here from the king, there from the local aristocracy, there from the church.[7]

When they finally develop late in Western history, states and their laws are still more formally institutionalised. (iv) 'State legal regimes' make the novel claim to sovereign dominance or exclusivity. Other normative orders and regimes were seen, at least in increasingly important theories of state sovereignty, as reliant on the sufferance of the state. Gradually legality began to be equated with state legality. Finally, the modern Western (5) 'state legal systems' of the nineteenth century were able to make such claims comparatively more meaningful while also threading together the diverse legal regimes that persisted into a single national common law, though earlier ideas and institutions might continue to exist within reformed structures and substantive law.[8] While the last half-century has brought many changes and the future promises more, this modern legal world persists and remains dominant, at least in legal terms.

IV. COLONIES

Examples of historical hybridity are easy to find, particularly in colonial contexts, where the diffusion of norms and laws leaves a hybrid easier to recognise than in the old world. For example, just after the turn of the nineteenth cen-

---

[6] The former regimes included numerous summary and discretionary jurisdictions of 'low' justice, arbitration of different sorts, the internal jurisdiction of non-state corporate bodies like guilds, and a wide variety of other alternative methods of dispute resolution. These lesser jurisdictions arguably affected more people more of the time than did royal or common laws. They were everywhere in communication with, though differentiated from, less institutionalised normative orders. But family decision-making, religious mediation, blood feuds, duelling and vigilantism, among other forms, must also be included. The boundaries between these orders and the law was porous.

[7] If the triumphalist dominance of its 'common law' often obscures English legal hybridity and diffusions, this kaleidoscopic motion was, and is, no less true of the Anglo-American legal traditions.

[8] The equity courts, for example, in the sense of the English Courts of Chancery, continues to have a subterranean existence in English law although all of that substance is now lumped below the historically inappropriate label 'common law', which had, in fact, been the laws of the courts of common law specifically, excluding equity, ecclesiastical law, manorial law and so on.

tury, the area that is now the American state of Louisiana was divided between two territories, the American Territory of Orleans and Spanish West Florida. The former made up most of what would become the state, though it was only a small piece of the vast area ('La Louisiane') obtained by the United States in the Louisiana Purchase (1803). It had been French, then Spanish for lengthy periods. Although its people were overwhelmingly Francophone throughout this period, it was held by Spain at the time of the French Revolution. The impact of that event, cataclysmic in the old world, was hardly felt in the new. In the early nineteenth century, La Louisiane was very briefly French again before its sale to the United States. A flood of Anglophone immigration, including many lawyers ignorant of the traditions of local law, followed.

Bordering Orleans, Spanish West Florida extended from present-day Louisiana, through Mississippi and Alabama, to Florida. It had been French and then British, before Spain captured and obtained it as a result of the American Revolution. For almost 40 years it was ruled by the Spanish alongside their Louisiana territory. The laws of both were French and Spanish colonial variants of the *ius commune*. In contrast to Spanish Luisiana, and in addition to significant Amerindian and slave populations in both West Florida and Luisiana, the former was largely settled by Anglophones. Although Spanish control was increasingly contested by the United States, West Florida remained Spanish until the second decade of the new century. By the early nineteenth century, the diffusion of different populations and legal traditions into Orleans and West Florida had created unique legal and normative hybrids.

Within a decade after Americans obtained authority over Orleans, a complex hybrid of continental private laws, Anglo-American criminal law and American public laws (distinct from that of England) was established. A sectional 'mixed jurisdiction'—as we call it now—was formed.[9] The territorial legislature decided to redact its private law, the Governor eventually assented, and the *Digest of the Civil Laws Now in Force in the Territory of Orleans* was promulgated in 1808. Published in French, it drew its substance from the laws in force, a Spanish colonial variant of the *ius commune*. Much of its form, however, including the use of the French language, was drawn from the *projet* to the Code Civil (1804). Neither merely doctrine (legal scholarship) nor merely declaratory, the *Digest* only abrogated those laws that contradicted it. This represented a substantial shift towards positive laws, in contrast to

---

[9] Of course, the Anglo-American and continental traditions were themselves diverse, and differed in significant respects from their common modern forms. The former was still dominated by the flexible and variable methods of the *ius commune* and pre-modern digests that functioned as restatements of the law rather than modern codes. The hyper-formalism of the exegetical school had not yet secured its pre-eminent position, even in France. And with Anglo-American law, England was yet to create a united court structure. Neither in the United States nor in England was there a binding system of *stare decisis*. Precedent remained persuasive. In general, the positivism that made these changes possible was not yet dominant, even though it was in the ascendancy. A failure to understand how different this legal context was from later periods has marred Louisiana legal history for a long time.

either the rule of jurist's doctrine or judge-made law, though codal, exegetical positivism was never embraced. Jurisprudence, both before and after, also showed continuity with the private law before the arrival of the Americans.

But the private laws of the Orleans Territory were almost immediately filtered through hybrid Anglo-Spanish procedures as Anglophones appeared as judges and advocates. Criminal law and procedure quickly became Anglicised. Trial by jury and *habeus corpus* were easily received. Commercial law slowly shifted to American laws. This post-revolutionary, post-colonial legal hybridity was also mirrored by competing extralegal normative rules and orders. For example, the American Governor himself participated in a duel in 1807 with a political enemy. The age of honour, a non-state normativity that had its own norms and adjudicators, was not dead. The Orleans Territory is admittedly a special case, given the explicit complexity of its legal origins, but other legal traditions, in both the old world and the new, contained similar, often much deeper, complexities. To some degree, greater unity would be established across the nineteenth century, but all Western jurisdictions were complex. As with present jurisdictions, those of the past would be best understood through a relational study of normativity, legality and state legality.

West Florida was similarly complex. Spain's complex municipal and colonial laws formally applied, but there was little access to either legislation or doctrine. Also, like the population as a whole, its minor magistrates tended to be Anglophones. The result seems to have been that the widespread Spanish tolerance of local custom meant that ordinary adjudication in West Florida could reflect, albeit indirectly, Anglo-American laws. Outside of the courts, too, Anglophones sought to push the official laws towards norms and laws with which they were more familiar. In any event, by 1810, the American state had forcibly annexed West Florida (arguing that it had been included in the Louisiana Purchase). In 1812, when the Orleans Territory became the state of Louisiana, the westernmost districts of West Florida were tacked on, providing a significant injection of Anglo-Americans broadly versed in continental law. The two territories, whose histories had been entangled for so long, were united. Their laws and peoples, of diverse origins, formed a new hybrid. It was one of many.

V. HYBRIDS

My attempt to encourage jurists to see the comparative enterprise as a close reading of normative-legal complexity, in both the past and the present and in both principle and practice, has been conducted in the language of 'hybridity'. This was done because competing conceptualisations, especially those of 'legal pluralism' and 'mixed legal systems', were each limited and partial in practice. So why 'hybridity'? In its origins, the Latin word *hibrida* referred to a wild boar/pig mix. A 'hybrid' is still commonly seen as a complex individual entity, a singularity, from two parents. More recently, the term has become far broader in application. This more elastic meaning can be productive. In 'post-colonial studies', for example, the concept of 'hybridity' serves as part of a critique of binary, reified thinking about cultures and their members. It emphasises the deep and dynamic complexity of individual identities in colonial and post-colonial contexts. But 'hybridity' is rarely used in legal and normative scholarship. When employed by comparatists, it is synonymous with the 'mixity' of state laws, ie the coexistence of diverse, discrete state legal traditions within a single jurisdiction. It is a common, but minor, usage, a rhetorical relief from the use of 'mixed'. I have suggested instead that 'hybridity' may be used as a constructive term-of-art in a holistic, relational analysis of the legal-normative complexity of different time-spaces.

This sense of 'hybridity' is admittedly related to the scholarship of both empirical and radical 'legal pluralism'. But many legal pluralists show little real interest in state law, the conceptual analysis of 'law' or the established conventions related to these subjects. Their focus is typically limited to non-state norms, and they often adopt an overbroad and overly casual, unconventional use of 'law'. While the result is close to what is argued here—a division of normativity, legality and state legality—the legal pluralist's concept of 'law' excludes almost nothing. It is also often portrayed as something universal rather than encultured. In addition, 'radical', 'critical' or 'post-modern' legal pluralists correctly emphasise that individuals, not institutions, are the constant, if incremental, creators of both norms and laws. But this descriptive focus on individuals as the nexus of various normativities emphasises an almost chaotic kaleidoscope of normative complexity. It obscures meaningful commonalities. Like language itself, the meaning of normativity and legality is relational rather than merely individual; a solipsistic law makes no more sense than a private language. The aggregative normativity and legality of corporate communities and their institutions must be taken seriously. This is, of course, the natural concentration of much legal and social science. Accepted as working generalisations, as useful shorthands that allow us to get work done, this communal or institutional focus need not involve reification, deny individual possibility or ignore complexity. It offers, however, a manageable viewpoint from which to understand legal-normative creation and negotiation. Indeed, an individual focus might blind us to these wider patterns of normative influence. Finally, we must attend to the larger forces that drive subjects in their choices. Individuals do not generate norms *ex nihilo*. They may be little more than flotsam and jetsam in a hurricane.

If my sense of 'hybridity' is wider in practice than 'legal pluralism', or so I argue, it is considerably broader than the discussions of explicit and relatively discreet combinations of legal traditions identified as 'mixed legal systems'. Even at their most expansive, comparatists and mixed jurists are still essentially positivistic. They make only occasional forays into culture. There is little discussion about the gap between black letter law and their actual application.

My focus is the deeper complexity shot through every aspect of normative and legal ordering. There is little science to this. Assigning labels to the different fragments of an order, no less than the order itself, is always an approximation that will fail to capture the nuances of actual practice. They are never closed, never static.[10] Norms, whether legal or non-legal, are always in flux, stabilised only—though profoundly—by the weight and inertia of convention, of traditions and practices, as well as by the purposes served by the norms. Without giving up a belief in talking sensibly about complexity, I have tried to recognise that norms and laws always exist in a complex and fluid web that can only very roughly be captured in the language of pan-national legal and normative movements.

Finally, the analysis of normative and legal hybridity, understood in this way, goes hand-in-hand with the study of normative-legal 'diffusion', the movements over time that generate normative-legal complexity. The discussion of diffusion is, of course, common among comparatists. A bewildering and occasionally enlightening vocabulary exists for this: 'receptions', 'transplants', 'transfers', 'contaminations', 'irritants', 'migrations' and the 'transfrontier mobility of law'. I have little to add here except to note that William Twining has been especially aware of the importance of looking beyond state law in the process of diffusion, as well as in the utility of existing social science discussions about normative transfers.[11] In short, hybridity is, as I define it, a historical, comparative and institutional theory that sets research on legality within the wider matrix of normativity. It does so by looking at the complexity of (i) non-state norms (ie both normativity and legality independent of the state) and state laws (state legality), and (ii) the gap between the titular principles and actual practices of normative and legal orders.

VI. CORPORA

As noted, the standard of state law is both so theoretically dominant and practically important that it is easy to be distracted by it. Reflecting important conventions of the past two centuries, the state may be used, not unreasonably, to mark the border between the legal and the non-legal.[12] However, the use of state ratification to establish the law/non-law boundary has been, for

---

[10] In this way, hybridity challenges the dissection of plural and dynamic traditions into discrete, closed 'families', 'systems' or 'circles' and undermines commonly held and conjoined beliefs in legal nationalism and positivism, legal centralism and monism.

[11] See, eg W Twining, 'Diffusion of Law: A Global Perspective' (2004) 49 *Journal of Legal Pluralism* 1.

[12] Such a distinction is meaningful, defensible and accepted in practice by jurists, many social scientists and the public. And state laws are distinct, at least in practice, from other norms. For much, though admittedly not all, of the world, the modern state and state legal systems play a critical role that should not be ignored. While we may find that norms are encircled and hemmed in by the state, we may also find that state laws act 'in the shadow of' very meaningful non-state norms.

me, a merely practical maoneuvre. Accepting this simplistic bifurcation was an attempt to bracket or set aside deeper and passionate philosophical debates in the interests of generating useful data, but the use of a simple legal/non-legal division is inappropriate for a more general theory of normativity. Instead, as a method of comparative analysis, hybridity marries conceptual and empirical models from the legal and social sciences to investigate the principles and practices of (i) state legality (including those of customary and religious origin) and (ii) lived non-state norms. The latter contains both normativity and non-state legality, especially non-state justice systems. Using modern conventions, I referred to these rather roughly as 'legal hybridity' and 'normative hybridity'; they might be better labelled 'state hybridity' and 'non-state hybridity'.

Defined in this manner, the focus is on the origins and organisation of the rules and principles of an order, regime, system or corpus of law. 'State hybridity' obviously includes mixed legal systems. This category is itself quite large, including many of the present legal systems in the world. These mixed systems, including some quite exotic hybrids, were often the result of Western political expansionism and the diffusion of its laws. Especially through colonialism, Western laws came into contact with numerous other legal and normative traditions: Asian, Hindu, Islamic, a wider variety of customary traditions, etc. Some of these were already complex hybrids, but the addition of Western laws—either by imposition or through borrowing under Western hegemony—further complicated the normative-legal spaces of much of the world. The result, globally, are a number of coherent and connected, though never closed, legal traditions. These are both meaningfully national and pan-national. Indeed, far-flung jurisdictions, including many post-colonial states, continue to look to their mother tradition for guidance. But context and local significance is everything. While it may be necessary to make simplistic taxonomic classifications for pedagogical and professional purposes, it is mistaken and deeply Eurocentric to assume, for example, that India is best classified as an Anglo-American system or that China is best classified as belonging to the continental legal traditions without recognising the practical importance of the different contexts and the presence of additional, competing traditions, Western and non-Western, within law and without.

Indeed, drawing deeply on comparative legal history and the extensive comparative literature on the processes of diffusion, the recognition of legal hybridity extends much further. All state laws are examples of what social scientists call 'state' or 'weak legal pluralism'. Even here, however, the legal 'system' remains unified, at least in theory. Jurisdictional conflict is handled, either formally or informally, by state institutions whose recognition or ratification, when it comes, effectively converts the rules and decisions of other orders (including state-sanctioned customary orders) into state laws. This need not happen explicitly; the complex and varied ingredients of a legal tradition may lie hidden below state law's superficial surface. As noted, Europe's multifarious legal traditions, not least those of England, were forever in motion towards new permutations and momentary equilibria. While these ancestors may have little continuing control over their progeny, the recognition of historical hybridity alerts us to the complexity of even the most ordinary, and apparently autochthonous, system.

Just as importantly, neither the state nor those laws that preceded the state have ever had normative exclusivity. There has been no—and is now no—unified and pure normative or legal space, controlled respectively by an all-embracing state or society. Instead, laws and norms always rest within the wider web of what social scientists call 'strong' or 'deep legal pluralism', the totality of normative orders and more diffuse normative influences. As noted, this wider 'non-state hybridity' is often referred to in contemporary social science as 'legal pluralism' or, more recently, 'normative pluralism'. Legal pluralists usually mean to capture the interaction of state laws and semi-autonomous non-state normative orders that lack the sanction of the state. In practice, the focus of such analysis is usually on non-state norms beyond the West, often in the shadow of a failed and imported state and frequently with a hint of cultural essentialism. Indeed, with the laudable aim of insisting on value parity between Western and non-Western forms, legal pluralists have attacked the jurist's narrow focus on the state and the politics of colonialism and hegemony they saw linked to it. This has often succeeded in making scholars sensitive to similarities between non-state norms and state laws, but the blurring of these categories has also often confused jurists, arguably dissuading many from engagement.[13] The language of legal pluralists and their allies—'everyday law', 'implicit law', 'living law', 'ubiquitous law', 'unofficial law' and even 'law in brief encounters'—jumbles enlightening metaphors with established meanings and conventions. The suggestion that any normative order is a legal order is ultimately unhelpful and undermines pluralist insights.

VII. ACTION

So, all contemporary normative and legal traditions are hybrid creations, an ongoing gumbo of nominally native elements and new, often borrowed, features. In addition to this type of hybridity, however, a second type exists. It is obvious, but too essential not to recognise. Normative and legal orders of various types can be distinguished on the basis of their titular principles and actual practice. That is, current discussions of hybridity can focus on an order, regime or system. But understood in this sense, the image presented may appear static and coherent. Complexity will seem an aspect of the order's past and, however unintentional, an impression of unity will be suggested.

---

[13] Understandably, perhaps, jurists are often more interested in legal norms than social norms. In fact, both comparative lawyers and legal historians, reflecting their disciplinary training and a more general conventional use of 'law', use 'legal pluralism' as a synonym for what 'state hybridity'.

But hybridity also involves, indeed is still more concerned with, the varying interpretations and applications of such rules and principles and their effects on these standards over time. It reveals that these approximations, or reifications, are never the whole story. With respect to both normative and legal orders, there may be a significant divide between its overt understanding or self-understanding and the often covert, unarticulated realities of its practice (without denying that principle and practice influence each other dialectically).

But this analysis of legal and normative practice should not focus only on internal considerations and professional activities. Even internal decision-making is increasingly affected by all manner of global norms, a fact with which legal theory is struggling to come to grips with. And these are external to national state laws, and to law itself. The public interpretation and application of law, or obstruction to application, is critical to my approach. Legal and normative consciousness is, in fact, as important as codes or case law. Indeed, because the influences on legislation, adjudication and legal consciousness go beyond considerations merely internal to an order, it is necessary to include still more diffuse normative and practical influences. Dominant political, economic and ideological forces and power relationships inevitably impact on legal and normative practices of norm-generation and interpretation. While these may be seen as external, such influences are secreted in the interstices of internal practices. This can be both local and global. Diffusion, for example, occurs not on the basis of rational choice, but under the influence of cultural prejudice and political, economic and ideological hegemony.

This focus on practice is obviously able to draw on numerous, well-established approaches to law that underline the complexity of the most ordinary law and legal system; the gap between the 'law in books' and the 'law in action'.[14] If the latter is not merely meant to be vulgar behaviourism, it must actually concern itself with what William Ewald called the 'law in minds'.[15] Similarly, Rodolfo Sacco's theory of 'legal formants' goes beyond the inevitable slippage of legal interpretation. Instead, he underscores the considerable diversity in the interpretation of state laws, a complexity frequently rooted in practical, professional differences among those interpreting the law (especially judges, jurists and legislators).[16] Contrary to appearances, there is no single legal norm in a coherent and neatly hierarchical system, not even in the most apparently monolithic tradition. A number of other modern schools of legal philosophy—perhaps especially post-modern legal theory, critical legal studies and various schools of hermeneutics—provide many of the same conclusions.

---

[14] R Pound, 'Law in Books and Law in Action' (1910) 44 *American Law Review* 12.

[15] See, eg 'Comparative Jurisprudence (I): What Was it Like to Try a Rat?' (1995) 143 *University of Pennsylvania Law Review* 1889.

[16] R Sacco, 'Legal Formants: A Dynamic Approach to Comparative Law (Installment I of II)' (1991) 39 *American Journal of Comparative Law* 1; R Sacco, 'Legal Formants: A Dynamic Approach to Comparative Law (Installment II of II)' (1991) 39 *American Journal of Comparative Law* 343.

In each of these instances, the insistence on context significantly problematises the concept of closed and discrete systems of rules.

These theories are primarily rooted in law and legal practice. They understandingly focus on the role of legal actors expounding on doctrine or interpreting enacted laws and the jurisprudence produced in adjudication.[17] The analysis of texts is a large part of this type of legal study, though is not the whole of it. The complexities of interpretation and application are often less obvious in normative traditions that are more oral than written. Failing to redact norms may disguise the variable content, or indeed vacuity, of a normative order. Where it is appropriate to talk of sustained development in any direction, this often occurs *sub silentio*, without individual intention or explicit acknowledgement. The absence of texts, and often the multiplication of applicable languages and cultures, significantly complicates an understanding of such traditions. On the other hand, the process of writing down norms, whether social or legal, has often significantly altered their meaning and application. This was true both in the European past as well as in Europe's colonial encounters with other legal and normative traditions. Both at home and abroad, redaction has often had the effect of placing elites, both juristic and legislative redactors and adjudicators, in a more powerful position. Of course, actual public practices and legal and normative consciousness are still more important. The deep focus on normativities in practice, both 'in action' and 'in minds', is at the heart of hybridity as a comparative enterprise.

VIII. CONCLUSION

The model of state law has impoverished our professional and public discourses on law for much of the last two centuries. Laws and legal institutions preceded the state and a unified system of national state common laws. This recognition of law's origins in more general, if institutionalised, norms in an age before the state and its laws has important benefits for legal study. It is both critical and constructive. It suggests that meaningful understanding of 'law' requires a close and holistic comparative and historical analysis. It suggests that comparative method must be relational, broadened to capture a thicker image of normative-legal hybridity: normativity, legality and state legality.

Further Reading

Additional information on my work in comparative law can be found in the following: "'Our Laws are as Mixed as our Language": Commentaries on the

---

[17] Indeed, law reports, whatever their formal status as sources of law, can be important to this scholarship, functioning as (unscientific) case studies of normative application.

Laws of England and Ireland, 1704–1804' (2008) 3 *Journal of Comparative Law* 178; '"All This Together Make Up our *Common* Law": Legal Hybridity in England and Ireland, 1704–1804' in E Örücü (ed), *Mixed Legal Systems at New Frontiers* (Wildy, Simmonds & Hill, 2010); 'Comparative Law and Hybrid Legal Traditions: An Introduction and Histories of Hybridity: A Problem, a Primer, a Plea, and a Plan (of Sorts)' in E Cashin-Ritaine, SP Donlan and M Sychold (eds), *Comparative Law and Hybrid Legal Traditions* (Schulthess, 2010); 'Remembering: Legal Hybridity and Legal History' (2011) 2 *Comparative Law Review* 1; (with M Brown) (eds), *The Law and Other Legalities of Ireland, 1689–1850* (Ashgate, 2011); 'The Mediterranean Hybridity Project: At the Boundaries of Law and Culture' (2011) 4 *Journal of Civil Law Studies* 355; 'Book Review of E Melissaris, *Ubiquitous Law: Legal Theory and the Space for Legal Pluralism* (2009)' (2012) 25 *Canadian Journal of Law and Jurisprudence* 177; 'Clashes and Continuities: Brief Reflections on the "New Louisiana Legal History"' (2012) 5 *Journal of Civil Law Studies* (US) 67; (with B Andò and D Zammit), '"A Happy Union"?: Malta's Legal Hybridity' (2012) 27 *Tulane European and Civil Law Forum* 165; 'Book Review of Mariano Croce, *Self-Sufficiency of Law: A Critical-Institutional Theory of Social Order* (2012)' (2013) 47 *Law & Society Review* 988; 'Book Review of Aldo Schiavone, *The Invention of Law in the West* (2012), tr J Carden' (2013) 1(2) *Comparative Legal History* 291; 'Entangled Up in Red, White, and Blue: Spanish West Florida and the American Territory of Orleans, c1803–1810' in T Duve (ed), *Entanglements in Legal History: Conceptual Approaches* (Max Planck Institute for European Legal History Global Perspectives on Legal History Series, 2013); 'To Hybridity and Beyond: Reflections on Legal and Normative Complexity' in M Mattar and V Palmer (eds), *Mixed Legal Systems, East and West: Newest Trends and Developments* (Ashgate, forthcoming); 'The Ubiquity of Hybridity: Norms and Laws, Past and Present, and Around the Globe' in Mancuso and T Io Cheng (eds), *The New Frontiers of Comparative Law* (LexisNexis, forthcoming); 'Everything Old is New Again: Stateless Law, the State of the Law, and Comparative Legal History' in S Van Praagh and H Dedek (eds), *Stateless Law: Evolving Boundaries of a Discipline* (Ashgate, forthcoming); (with L Heckendorn-Urscheler), 'Introduction' in Donlan and Heckendorn-Urscheler (eds), *Concepts of Law: Comparative, Jurisprudential, And Social Science Perspectives* (Ashgate, forthcoming).

13

Against Method?

H PATRICK GLENN

P
AUL FEYERABEND FAMOUSLY wrote in his *Against Method*
that 'anything goes', a proposition unlikely to fare well in the legal profession.[1] Yet the argument is directed against the idea of 'a' scientific
method, which would be rigorously followed across a wide range of scientific
endeavours. Feyerabend sought to show that methodological principle was
frequently and historically deviated from, and that this was the only guarantee of human progress. We find the same notion of 'a' or 'the' comparative
method often used in law, essentially to contrast with a nameless method of
simple application of state law. Yet the history of comparative law is not one
of adherence to a methodological norm but rather one of deviation and variety. There is no comparative method.

This conclusion is in no way incompatible, however, with a variety of comparative methods over time and with deviation from each of them.[2] Indeed,
the recoverable history of comparison in law reveals a preoccupation with
principles of method, though no consistency in their application. This preoccupation with method may have more to do today with a carryover from the
hard sciences and with the autonomous character of a discipline of comparative law than with any general methodological rigour. This cannot be said,
however, to represent a principle of 'anything goes', since there are often
unwritten principles of argumentation and proof which are departed from
only at a cost. This is implicit in the 'deep' comparative law which Mark Van
Hoecke has so eloquently argued for.[3]

Comparison in law has therefore often been associated with outstanding
practitioners of legal thought, whether they are recognised as comparativists

---

[1] P Feyerabend, *Against Method*, 3rd edn (New York, Verso, 1993) 14.

[2] See, eg PG Monateri, *Methods in Comparative Law* (Cheltenham, Edward Elgar, 2012). It is
often therefore said that there are as many methods of comparative law as there are comparativists, or at least as many methods as there are concepts of comparative law.

[3] See, eg his 'Deep Level Comparative Law' in M Van Hoecke (ed), *Epistemology and Meth-
odology of Comparative Law* (Oxford, Hart Publishing, 2004) 165; M Van Hoecke, 'Islamic
Jurisprudence and Western Legal History' in J Nielsen and L Christoffersen (eds), *Shari'a as
Discourse: Legal Traditions and the Encounter with Europe* (Farnham, Ashgate, 2010) 45.

or not. In a sense, they are bound together by an appreciation of the law as diverse though, as might be expected, there are exceptions. Differences are therefore accepted as normal while impurity or hybridity may be seen as a wholesome and even necessary variety.[4] It is at least acknowledged, while the notion of a comparative method or methods is an implicit rejection of notions of incommensurability.[5] Problems of incomprehension can thus be overcome, given appropriate method or methods.

The variety and ubiquity of comparison in law appears best illustrated not through theoretical analysis but through examination of some of its most famous exemplars. These vary greatly both in their method and in their association with disciplines other than comparative law, but the root process of comparison is present, to a greater or lesser degree, in all of them.

I. THE COMPARISON OF LAW IN THE PHILOSOPHY OF LAW

It may appear surprising to locate the comparison of law within an abstract- and universalist-prone discipline of the philosophy of law, but it has been surprisingly present in many of the discipline's most distinguished representatives. In some instances it is faint indeed, but HLA Hart's *The Concept of Law* was explicitly stated to represent both a sociological enquiry and a concept of law which was adequate to explain the variety of laws conforming to the principles announced. An entire chapter is devoted to 'The Variety of Laws'.[6] A more recent exponent of some of Hart's ideas does not hesitate to speak of '[a]ll legal systems', which are then stated to be potentially incompatible and unable to acknowledge other claims to supremacy.[7] Joseph Raz also speculated on causes for the incomprehension of other legal orders, in writing that 'our ability to compare options depends on the nature of our social practices, which may "run out" leaving us with no grounds of comparison'.[8] Hans Kelsen also wrote in a very informed way about the law of different places in advancing a universalist concept of positive law, based on a basic norm which was presumed for all societies.[9] It might even be said that the more

---

[4] For this as a general thesis, even beyond law, W Schmidgen, *Exquisite Mixture: The virtues of impurity in early modern England* (Philadelphia, University of Pennsylvania Press, 2012), privileging difference and discontinuity.

[5] See HP Glenn, 'Are Legal Traditions Incommensurable?' (2001) 49 *American Journal of Comparative Law* 133.

[6] HLA Hart, *The Concept of Law*, 3rd edn (Oxford, Oxford University Press, 2012) vi. Though for Hart's comparative method not showing 'the slightest familiarity with the writings of comparative lawyers' see AWB Simpson, *Reflections on* The Concept of Law (Oxford, Oxford University Press, 2011) 160 ('comparative law might as well have never been invented').

[7] J Raz, *The Authority of Law. Essays on Law and Morality* (Oxford, Clarendon Press, 1979) 119.

[8] J Raz, 'Facing Up: A Reply,' (1989) 62 *Southern California Law Review* 1220.

[9] See notably his *General Theory of Law and State* (Cambridge, MA, Harvard University Press, 1945), notably at 29 (citing Lord Brougham's *The British Constitution*) and 281 (citing FJ Goodnow's *The Principles of Administrative Law of the United States*), and *The Communist Theory*

startling the universalist character of the claim the greater is the necessity to assert compatibility with apparently different forms of legal order, as proof of universality. The actual comparison may be of the thinnest variety, however, untroubled by questions of method, since the overall object is one of coherence and intellectual consistency rather than exploration of possible variance.

It is therefore interesting that a recent excursus in the field of legal philosophy was very critical of the entire field of contemporary legal philosophy in proposing a general jurisprudence as a means of 'understanding law from a global perspective'.[10] William Twining accords a major place in the understanding of law to 'Southern voices' as a means of correction of what he perceives as the faults of legal philosophy, as generally understood.[11] In a broadly similar manner, François Ost and Michel van de Kerchove propose to found their philosophical notion of movement from a pyramidal concept of law to one of legal networks by concentrating on an emerging 'reality' of several domains of law (constitutional, commercial, penal, international) and across legal systems.[12] We are seeing here philosophical works which, under the pressure of current events, accord a larger and larger place to the grounding of their reflections on observable phenomena in different societies. They are recognisably philosophical in character, but the presence of comparison appears more present than it was a half-century earlier.

It is true that the level of comparison in these works is not high, but it has been judged adequate by the authors for purposes of presentation of their respective themes. The method of comparison is not an obvious preoccupation, since there is often little of it. We see here an underlying notion that the method and depth of comparison is variable according to the objectives pursued. This should be confirmed by examining radically different use of comparison.

II. THE COMPARISON OF LAW IN SOCIOLOGY AND ANTHROPOLOGY OF LAW

The disciplines of sociology and anthropology are fully attentive to societal difference. The entire notion of culture is used to sharply distinguish one

---

of Law (London, Steven, 1955). For his universalist concept of posited law, H Kelsen (M Knight trans), *Pure Theory of Law* (Berkeley, University of California Press, 1967).

[10] W Twining, *General Jurisprudence: Understanding Law from a Global Perspective* (New York, Cambridge University Press, 2008), notably at ix (for Western traditions of academic law with rich heritage but which 'appear to be generally parochial, narrowly focussed, and unempirical, tending towards ethnocentrism'). See also B Tamanaha, *A General Jurisprudence of Law and Society* (New York, Oxford University Press, 2001), notably ch 8 for a 'typology of kinds of law'.

[11] Twining, ibid, ch 13.

[12] F Ost and M van de Kerchove, *De le pyramdide au réseau?* (Brussels, Facultés Universitaires Sant-Louis, 2002), notably at 12 (for a 'monde qui a changé') and 20 (citing traditional customary law, islamic law).

society from another, though there are now efforts to emphasise 'transcultural' or 'intercultural' phenomena. In all cases, the attention to the observable opens the door wide to comparative observation.

This is perhaps not evident in some intra-cultural studies which have become classics in the field, such as Bohannan on the Tiv,[13] Gluckman on the Barotse[14] or Moore on custom on Kiliminjaro,[15] but these works were all written for Western readers and comparison is an unstated but constant phenomenon in the enterprise. Hoebel's work on 'primitive man' is even expressly subtitled as a 'study in comparative legal dynamics',[16] while Norbert Rouland's writing on current legal anthropology is rich in comparative observation.[17]

Such anthropological writing shares with more contemporary sociology a constant concern with method. As 'social sciences', each is constrained inevitably to scientific method, with an unstated object of discovering the truth of the phenomenon they examine. The existence of such a truth is implicit in the disciplines, though there are often iconoclasts. It is a truth statement that law is found in action and not simply in books. The discovery of truth is one which entails an appropriate methodology, ideally permitting falsification, in the same way that the hard sciences have developed scientific method in pursuit of the truth of the physical world.

To the extent that legal comparison is of observable social phenomena, it is therefore often seen as a subfield of anthropology or sociology. The comparison of texts, though they are observable, enjoys an unenviable reputation as an essentially sterile exercise, even though philology or textual analysis outside of law is an eminently respectable activity. The methods and depth of comparison are once again dictated by the overall objectives pursued and their epistemological foundations, as in the philosophy of law. The same can be said of the comparison of law in economics.

III. THE COMPARISON OF LAW IN ECONOMICS

An entire subfield of economics has now developed which uses legal origins and legal traditions to explore the relative efficiency of different laws in reaching economic objectives.[18] The basic proposition that certain legal traditions,

---

[13] P Bohannan, *Justice and Judgment among the Tiv* (London, Oxford University Press, 1957).

[14] M Gluckman, *The Ideas in Barotse Jurisprudence* (New Haven, Yale University Press, 1965).

[15] S Falk Moore, *Social Facts and Fabrications: 'Customary Law' on Kiliminjaro, 1880–1980* (Cambridge, Cambridge University Press, 1986).

[16] E Hoebel, *The Law of Primitive Man: A Study in Comparative Legal Dynamics* (Cambridge, Harvard University Press, 1961).

[17] N Rouland (trans P Planel), *Legal Anthropology* (London, Athlone, 1994).

[18] For the debate, with robust criticism, M Faure and J Smits (eds), *Does Law Matter?* (Cambridge, Intersentia, 2011); S Deakin and K Porter (eds), *Legal Origin Theory* (Cheltenham, Edward Elgar, 2012); R Michaels, 'Symposium' (2009) 57 *American Journal of Comparative Law* 765. See also the reports of the World Bank, which accept the thesis of inefficiency, notably of a French, codified tradition (*Doing Business in 2013*, 10th edn, available at

broadly defined, are more economically efficient that others is contested on many grounds. It is said that legal sources do not drive economics, that there are national differences which destroy any general conclusion on the efficacy of broad traditions and that such general conclusions must inevitably be based on errors in the understanding of national laws. The debate is vigorous and, though the objections appear overwhelming, the discussion has placed at the centre of attention the alleged performance of different laws from the perspective of an assumed objective. It is a comparative exercise that has almost in its entirety involved the comparison of different laws, in terms of their formal content or in terms of survey appreciations of their effect.

The debate on the truth value of the conclusions reached is therefore a classic debate of methodology and whether the methodology used is adequate to support the conclusion reached. The methods are quantitative and, to the extent that survey data is used, sociological. Unlike philosophers of law, whose comparative method is near to non-existent, and qualitative social scientists, whose comparative method is implicit in examination of specific realities in the field, the economists who maintain the significance of legal origins are almost totally preoccuped with broad questions of the method of legal comparison—how laws and jurisdictions are best grouped, how to measure the effect of different laws, how to gauge compliance and non-compliance, and so on. The methodological preoccupation is directly linked to the empirical and normative claims which are being made and their contemporary significance. It is concentrated exclusively on state laws and generally economic indicators, and is a by-product of contemporary capitalism.

The specialised disciplines of legal philosophy, legal sociology, legal anthropology and law and economics are all, however, relatively recent ones, and it is possible to perceive comparison in law beyond their confines, both in terms of time and in terms of perspective or overall objective.

IV. THE COMPARISON OF LAW IN THE CONSTRUCTION
OF NATIONAL LEGAL SYSTEMS

The comparison of laws played a fundamental role in the construction of national legal systems from, say, the sixteenth century. As with comparison of laws in legal philosophy, legal sociology, legal anthropology and economics, it was not known as comparative law. With the benefit of hindsight we may

http://www.doingbusiness.org/~/media/GIAWB/Doing%20Business/Documents/Annual-Reports/English/DB13-full-report.pdf); strongly contested by French doctrinal sources and still more generally. See Association Henri Capitant, *Les droits de tradition civiliste en question* (Paris, Société de Législation Comparée, 2006) (questioning the fundamental notion of a causal link between economic development and sources of law, pointing out errors of law in the analysis of French law, insisting on virtues of codification); and for a US critique, K Davis and M Kruse, 'Taking the Measure of Law: The Case of the *Doing Business* Project' (2007) 32 *Law & Social Inquiry* 1095 (for weak empirical base, again questioning the causal relation to development).

now call it comparative law, but it was a particular form of it, which may be described as constructivist univalence in its most fundamental characteristic. It was constructivist (and not constructive or presumed) because its primary objective had become the construction of a national set of laws which, itself, would do away with the necessity of further comparison. It therefore sought to eliminate the various normative orders existing on actual or potential state territory in favour of a single, exclusive and univalent solution for each perceived problem. The elimination of contradiction, and therefore the principle of the excluded middle, played a large part in the national codifications of law.[19]

In Europe there was a large process of examination of Roman, canon and customary law, as well as their Jewish or Islamic counterparts, for purposes of construction of national law.[20] It relied on a method which had been used by both Justinian and Gratian, in sifting through a vast range of sources in search of that which was seen as worthy of preservation.[21] This process of mining of existing, known law for purposes of construction also occurred in the US, and is now a well-known phenomenon of law reform in most jurisdictions.[22] It was necessarily accompanied in many jurisdictions with varyingly effective forms of accommodation with chthonic or indigenous law, preceding the arrival of European settlers in many places.[23] This process of accommoda-

---

[19] See H Kelsen (trans C Eisenmann), *La théorie pure du droit* (Paris, Dalloz, 1962) 274 ('la norme fondamentale assure l'unité de ces normes dans leur pluralité. Cette unité s'exprime aussi dans le fait qu'un ordre juridique peut être décrit en propositions de droit qui ne se contredisent pas'); for the importance of the principle of non-contradiction in the construction of national codifications, D de Béchillon, 'L'imaginaire d'un Code' (1998) 27 *Droits* 173, 182; and for the absence in general of contradictions within national codifications, G Gavazzi, *Delle antinomie* (Turin, G Giappichelli, 1959) 106.

[20] See generally HP Glenn, 'The Nationalist Heritage' in P Legrand and R Munday, *Comparative Legal Studies. Traditions and Transitions* (Cambridge, Cambridge University Press, 2003); A Wijffels, 'Arthur Duck et le *ius commune* européen' (1990) *Revue d'histoire des facultés de droit et de la culture juridique* 193 (notably for the influence of English civilians on English law); and for French law, J-L Thireau, 'Le comparatisme et la naissance du droit français' (1990) *Revue d'histoire des facultés de droit et de la culture juridique* 153. For John Selden's expertise in Jewish law, J Rosenblatt, *Renaissance England's Chief Rabbi: John Selden* (Oxford, Oxford University Press, 2006) ('rabbi' in honorific sense).

[21] For Gratian's need to overcome previous 'incoherencies', A Padovani, 'The Metaphysical Thought of Late Medieval Jurisprudence' in E Pattaro (ed), *A Treatise of Legal Philosophy and General Jurisprudence*, vol 7 (Dordrecht, Springer, 2007) 95.

[22] For US reliance on civil or Roman law well into the twentieth century see, eg P Stein, 'The Attraction of the Civil Law in Post-Revolutionary America' (1966) 52 *Virginia Law Review* 403; M Hoeflich, *Roman and Civil Law and the Development of Anglo-American Jurisprudence in the Nineteenth Century* (Athens, GA, University of Georgia Press, 1997); R Helmholz, 'Use of the Civil Law in Post-Revolutionary American Jurisprudence' (1992) 66 *Tulane Law Review* 1649; J Langbein, 'Chancellor Kent and the History of Legal Literature' (1993) 93 *Columbia Law Review* 547; M Reimann (ed), *The Reception of Continental Ideas in the Common Law World* (Berlin, Duncker & Humblot, 1993); and for the Americanisation of German abstraction, S Riesenfeld, 'The Influence of German Legal Theory on American Law: The Heritage of Savigny and His Disciples' (1989) 37 *American Journal of Comparative Law* 37 (notably on German influence on Llewelyn, giving 'secured transactions' as an example of borrowing of abstract concept of civilian origin).

[23] RA Williams Jr, *The American Indian in Western Legal Thought. The Discourses of Conquest* (New York, Oxford University Press, 1990).

tion, or the lack thereof, assumed a much lesser order of priority in the minds of lawyers than the process of national, univalent, legal construction in both public and private law. States had to be constructed, and in many cases there was nothing considered adequate for limiting the imposition of their laws.

Codification and the emergence of the notion of stare decisis marked the end of this process, since they both signalled a turning away from residual or supplementary sources of law and an exclusivist concentration on current sources of state law. In some continental jurisdictions, such as Prussia, Spain and Switzerland, citation of non-state sources of law was prohibited by formal enactment. 'L'autorité de l'État ne souffre point le vide',[24] it was said, and state authority was even required to eradicate all other sources of normativity. If comparison was fundamental to the construction of states and their national legal systems, it was not privileged for an ongoing role in their functioning. The method of its use had become one of political choice in the ultimate legislative process, and functional comparison became a widely accepted methodology, dictated largely by immediate law reform objectives.[25] The comparison of laws thus became subject to eventual political control and the rise of internally directed systems theory. Paradoxically, this diminished national role was accompanied by the rise of the formal discipline of comparative law.

V. THE COMPARISON OF LAW AS A TAXONOMIC PROJECT

It is frequently said that the discipline of comparative law has its origins in the major conference on comparative law held in Paris in 1900. It is important to note that the comparison of law has been with us at least since the time of Justinian, so the crystallisation of an autonomous discipline is but one step of many. Yet the birth of a scientific concept of comparative law had important consequences for its methods in a time of allegedly scientific development of autonomous national laws. What place was left for a process of comparison once the national legislature, or supreme court, had spoken with final authority?

The answer was one of the science contemporaneous with the times. Just as comparative anatomy and comparative biology had revolutionised these disciplines and led them to a broader and more detailed understanding of their

---

[24] D Nordman, 'Problématique historique: des frontières de L'Europe aux frontières du Maghreb (19e siècle)' in *Frontières: Problèmes de frontières dans le tiers-monde* (Paris, L'Harmattan, 1982) 19.
[25] See notably R Michaels, 'The Functional Method of Comparative Law' in M Reimann and R Zimmermann, *The Oxford Handbook of Comparative Law* (Oxford, Oxford University Press, 2006) 339, though at 342 'many' functional methods; M Graziadei, 'The Functionalist Heritage' in P Legrand and R Munday, *Comparative Legal Studies: Traditions and Transitions* (Cambridge, Cambridge University Press, 2006) 100, notably at 109 on quantity of 'facts' left out of functional analysis though, at 125, 'very successful.'

objects of study, so comparative law could undertake a similar, taxonomic appreciation of the emerging national legal systems. Functional comparison could also contribute to this broad task of understanding. Yet this was not so much a matter of legal practice, even of preparing the ground for legislative or judicial intervention, as one of pure science, with no immediate practical consequences. In keeping a window open on the world, in the face of claims of national sovereignty, comparative law could be seen as a noble endeavour—the disinterested appreciation of all state laws, *à toute fin utile*.

It was certainly a method of comparison, that of binary, eventually uni-valent, taxonomy (a national legal system is in one legal family or another), which was conditioned by the circumstances of its time. State law presumed to create all the law that was necessary. Comparative law accepted this total-ity of state law and sought to render the different national legal orders into static members of 'legal families', a biologically derived language which is still prominent in discussion of different laws and which is entirely compatible with the autonomous and sovereign concept of a national legal system.[26] This method of comparative law must be said to have been less successful than that of its unnamed predecessor. There was much disagreement on the definition of legal families, very little actual taxonomic endeavour. It contributed to a static and flat concept of comparative law, of very little utility or interest for legal practitioners or the vast majority of legal academics (to say nothing of students). It was complemented in its commitment to state legal orders by a neighbouring discipline of private international law, which through the nine-teenth and most of the twentieth centuries rejected any notion of comparison of domestic laws (at least private ones) in favour of a highly questionable pro-cess of seeking the natural 'seat' of legal relations, even complex ones, in a single state order. Again, the commitment to state law was largely complete. It even resulted in national rules of geographical allocation of legal problems, in preference to any comparative analysis of the reach or adequacy of state rules. It was said that there are 'conflicts' of laws, based on their simple dif-ference, a remarkably belligerent attitude which by itself largely precluded any larger process of comparison and conciliation.[27]

Autonomous disciplines of comparative law and private international law exist today, such as they do, largely because of these nineteenth- and twenti-eth-century ideas of the exclusivity of state law. There was therefore a need

---

[26] See HP Glenn, 'Vers un droit comparé intégré?' (1999) *Revue internationale de droit com-paré* 842, with references. The most recent and comprehensive plea for taxonomic comparative law is that of L Constantinesco, *Traité de droit comparé*, particularly vol 3, *La science des droits comparés* (Paris, Economica, 1983).

[27] Cf HP Glenn, 'La conciliation des lois: Cours général de droit international privé' in *Recueil des Cours* (The Hague, The Hague Academy of International Law, forthcoming); and for the application of private international rules d'office or von Amts wegen, on the part of the judge, eliminating party agreement as a means of conciliation of legal differences, HP Glenn, 'Harmo-nization of law, foreign law and private international law' (1993) 1 *European Review of Private Law* 43.

to ensure this exclusivity by eliminating the comparison of laws to the extent possible (except as an academic exercise or for purposes of national improvement) and extending the territorial reach of state law even to the international case. The events of the late twentieth and early twentieth-first centuries, however, are already demonstrating the limited and inadequate character of this view of the sources of law, and giving rise to new and more active forms of the comparison of laws.

VI. THE COMPARISON OF LAW AS A SEARCH FOR EQUILIBRIUM

Today the number of states in the world is approaching 200, an increase of some 125 since the founding of the United Nations in 1946. There are no more empires, representing great social diversity in spite of their often reprehensible methods. Much is therefore expected of states, and there has been a great increase in their activity at the international level. If doctrinal discussion has previously concentrated on sovereignty and the autonomy of states, the accent today has turned towards collaboration and necessary interdependence. This is why Ost and Van de Kerchove speak of networks rather than pyramids.[28] Van Creveld counted some 123 international organisations in 1951; the number had increased to 395 in 1985 and is well beyond that number today.[29] There were almost none when Savigny wrote in mid-nineteenth century. The state is therefore today one of collaboration, and its independent role in international relations has greatly diminished.[30] It chooses to integrate itself into thicker and thicker networks, since sovereign isolation is no longer compatible with the welfare of national populations. National borders are therefore increasingly permeable, particularly to people and information, and there is discussion of 'Entgrenzung',[31] 'déspatialization',[32] 'Deterritorialisierung'[33] or

---

[28] Ibid, in Section I above.

[29] M van Creveld, *The Rise and Decline of the State* (Cambridge, Cambridge University Press, 1999) 382. For a large historical perspective on the growth of international connections during the same period, E Rosenberg (ed), *A World Connecting, 1870–1940* (Cambridge, Belknap Press of Harvard University Press, 2012).

[30] See, eg J Guillaumé, *L'affaiblissement de l'État-Nation et le droit international privé* (Paris, LGDJ, 2011) 228; see also H Buxbaum, 'Transnational Regulatory Litigation' (2006) 46 *Virginia Journal of International Law* 306 ('deterritorialization' of sovereign authority, disaggregation of its elements into networks, emphasis on participation in transnational regimes). For the 'trading state' which must trade for the needs of its population, R Rosecrance, *The Rise of the Trading State* (New York, Basic Books, 1986) 15 (no state able to achieve self-sufficiency). Guillaumé concludes that macroeconomic interdependence leads to juridical interdependence; above, this note, at 5.

[31] U Beck and C Lau, *Entgrenzung und Entscheidung: Was ist neu an der Theorie reflexiver Modernisierung?* (Frankfurt, Suhrkamp, 2004).

[32] JB Auby, *La globalisation, le droit et l'État* (Paris, Montchrestien, 2003) 15.

[33] R Michaels, 'Welche Globalisierung fur das Recht? Welches Recht für die Globalisierung?' (2005) 69 *Rabels Zeitschrift für ausländisches und internationales Privatrecht* 525, 541.

'aterritorialité'.[34] Even war would have become 'post-territorial'.[35] The Hegelian notion of war as the ultimate expression of national identity suffers an inevitable decline in these circumstances.[36]

What place is there for the comparison of laws in these contemporary circumstances, and according to what methods? Given a declining role of national boundaries, it can only become a more frequent phenomenon, in the hands of a growing number of people. This recalls the origin of the world 'compare', as a combination of the Latin words 'with', or cum (com), and 'pare', or peer or equal. Comparing in its origins, freed of nineteenth-century nationalism, would thus involve a process of existing with a (presumed) equal and using, in precise circumstances, the methods which are suitable for that objective.[37] This is not a method of 'anything goes' but a recognition that the comparison of laws has always varied in its methods according to circumstance. It does have implications for an autonomous discipline of comparative law, but there is nothing to prevent ongoing work and the association of those whose primary interest is in the diversity of laws. There are benefits of a larger field of practitioners.

It is, moreover, already the case that the field of comparison of laws is expanding in its ambit. The most visible evidence of this is in the field of what is known as 'judicial dialogue', as judges from different states increasingly meet, discuss and compare national solutions.[38] There are different national nuances in this process, but it appears to be a universal phenomenon, even in the US, where it has recently created a vigorous debate.[39] The use of comparative sources is even more widespread in international or regional courts.[40] The European notion of a 'margin of appreciation' granted to EU Member States entails a Europe-wide ascertainment of national solutions in order to deter-

---

[34] G Agamben (trans V Binetti and C Casarino), *Means without End: Notes on Politics* (Minneapolis, University of Minneapolis Press, 2000) 23.

[35] W Opello Jr and S Rosow, *The Nation-State and Global Order* (Boulder, Lynne Rienner, 2004) 252 (feeble intensity, non-state actors).

[36] G Hegel, *Philosophy of Right* (New York, Cosmos, 2008) 330 (international law subservient to will of state), 334 (conflicts resolved by war absent agreement).

[37] See HP Glenn, 'Com-paring' in E Örücü and D Nelken (eds), *Comparative Law: A Handbook* (Oxford, Hart Publishing, 2007) 91.

[38] G Canivet, 'Trans-judicial Dialogue in a Global World' in S Muller and S Richards, *Highest Courts and Globalisation* (The Hague, Hague Academic Press, 2010), notably at 24 for use of websites facilitating judicial collaboration, 27 for 'juridical cosmopolitanism' and 34 for programmes of judicial exchange.

[39] For the phenomenon generally, U Drobnig and S van Erp, *The Use of Comparative Law by Courts* (The Hague, Kluwer, 1999); and for some 3000 law review articles on the subject in the US, though judges in the US Supreme Court continue the practice, R Alford, 'Lower Courts and Constitutuional Comparativism' (2008) 77 *Fordham Law Review* 647.

[40] See, eg C Steer, 'Legal Transplants or Legal Patchworking? The Creation of International Criminal Law as a Pluralistic Body of Law' in E van Sliedregt and S Vasiliev (eds), *Pluralism in International Criminal Law* (Oxford, Oxford University Press, forthcoming); M Bobek, *Comparative Reasoning in European Supreme Courts* (Oxford, Oxford University Press, 2013); R Titiriga, *La comparaison, technique essentielle du juge européen* (Paris, L'Harmattan, 2011), notably at 29 on the challenge of 'invisibility of comparison.

mine the nature of the margin of appreciation which is established. There is often complaint that comparative citing of sources in courts does not meet the standards of a rigorous discipline of comparative law, but the work of courts is not the work of academics. A judgment is not a research application, but conforms to different criteria. The need for an expansion of reasons for judgment has been expressed by recent writing in political theory.[41]

The discipline of private international law is also becoming more susceptible to the comparison (rather than conflict) of laws. There are a number of examples of this. Legislative codification of private international law now frequently uses result-selective tests, which involve comparison of laws to reach a particular decision. The judge must decide which national solution provides the acceptable level of protection for the consumer, child or employee.[42] National laws thus become the stuff of solutions which are guided by an overriding material solution. The French Court of Cassation has decided, moreover, that the entire process of choosing a national law to control the results of a case can be abandoned if the two laws are 'equivalent' in character.[43] The judge is free to conclude within the cadre of the two laws. The task of establishing the equivalence of the two laws is thus left to legal practice, and there is no necessity for the judge to refer the case to one or another of the national laws which are present in the case, in the absence of an affirmation of controlling difference. Comparison is also controlling in California, where the notion of 'comparative impairment' has been explicitly adopted by the Supreme Court of California, and some form of comparative examination of the territorial reach of laws is implicit in all notions of interest analysis, laws of 'immediate application, (of the forum or of a third state) or 'special connections' (*Sonderanknüpfungen*).[44]

This type of comparison of laws can be seen to have its own logic, which would even be an example of 'new' forms of logic which are presently being advanced. In place of a binary opposition, one member of which must be chosen by virtue of logical principles of non-contradiction and the excluded middle (A or not-A, the law of France or the law of England), it becomes possible to work with both laws, now seen as equivalent and no longer presumed

[41] A Sen, *The Idea of Justice* (Cambridge, Belknap Press of Harvard University Press, 2009) 394 ('the need to accept the plurality of reasons that may be sensibly accommodated in an exercise of evaluation').

[42] S Symeonides, 'Material Justice and Conflicts Justice in Choice of Law' in P Borchers and J Zekoll, *International Conflict of Laws for the Third Millenium* (Ardsley, NY, Transnational, 2000) 125.

[43] See Civ 1ère 13 avril 1999 (Compagnie royale belge), *Revue critique de droit international privé* 1999, 698, *Bulletin civil* 1999.I no 130, 85. For further jurisprudence in this sense, in the last 20 years, H Gaudemet-Tallon, 'Le pluralisme en droit international privé: richesses et faiblesses (le funambule et l'arc-en-ciel)' (2005) *Recueil des cours* 9, 340; H Gaudemet-Tallon, 'De nouvelles fonctions pour l'équivalence en droit international privé?' in *Le droit international privé: esprit et méthodes, Mélanges en l'honneur de Paul Lagarde* (Paris, Dalloz, 2005) 306; B Fauvarque-Cosson, *Libre disponibilité des droits et conflits de lois* (Paris, LGDJ, 1996) 233.

[44] For comparative impairment, W Baxter, 'Choice of Law and the Federal System' (1963) 16 *Stanford Law Review* 1.

to represent binary opposition or conflict. The solution becomes multivalent[45] in the sense that the eventual solution shares some of the features of both laws, or is limited to its precise facts so as to leave each law complete in its potential application to future cases. The same process is more and more evident in other cases of 'conflict'—of rights, for example, or between personal and state laws within countries, where there is no possibility of geographic localisation as a solution to the claims of application of different laws or different principles.[46]

In this wider process of comparison of laws, involving a more detailed and precise form of logic, comparison becomes recognised as an essential feature of law. In its academic manifestations it may thus even be seen as 'ordinary legal scholarship'.[47] It would therefore become an essential element in the reconciliation of peoples and of their laws.[48]

VII. CONCLUSION

Over time and space and discipline, there have been different types of resort to foreign law, for different objectives and therefore with different methods. There is thus no single method of comparative law, but varying objectives and methods. This is a salutary phenomenon, since the comparison of laws has been constantly present, in varying forms, as an affirmation of the willingness of lawyers to learn from the experience of others.

[45] For this phenomenon in the 'new' logics, D Gabby and J Woods (eds), *The Many Valued and Nonmonotonic Turn in Logic* (Amsterdam, North Holland, 2007); and for the logic of lawyers having long resisted the mathematisation of logic and so-called rules of non-contradiction, excluded middle, in spite of their importance for national legal construction, S Toulmin, *The Uses of Argument* (Cambridge, Cambridge University Press, 1958).

[46] For the number and importance of states having accepted a formal 'statut personnel' not governed by state law, HP Glenn, *The Cosmopolitan State* (Oxford, Oxford University Press, 2013) 149 (32 listed); to which must be added the problem of reconciliation of the exercise of religious laws guaranteed by the of freedom of religion expressed in national constitutions.

[47] See, eg S Smith, 'Comparative Legal Scholarship as Ordinary Legal Scholarship' (2011) 5 *Journal of Comparative Law* 331.

[48] On the management of human diversity as one of the pressing problems of the contemporary world, United Nations Development Program (UNDP), *Cultural Liberty in Today's World: Report on Human Development 2004* (New York, UNDP, 2004), notably at v for inclusive, culturally diverse societies as 'pre-condition' for other social objectives.

14

Comparatively Speaking: 'Law in its Regulatory Environment'

ROGER BROWNSWORD

I. INTRODUCTION

I N AN IMPORTANT article, Mark Van Hoecke (together with Mark Warrington) argued that comparative lawyers should broaden their horizons by reviewing the law in its context—this signifying that comparatists should depart from, and go beyond, the traditionally narrow doctrinal 'law as rules' approach.[1] In the spirit of Van Hoecke's progressive comparativism, this present essay advances the idea that law should be placed not simply in its general context but specifically in the setting of the relevant 'regulatory environment'. Put simply, the idea is that, if it is laws that we wish to compare,[2] then we should be comparing not 'out-of-context law A' with 'out-of-context law B', but 'law A in its regulatory environment' with 'law B in its regulatory environment'—or, perhaps, 'law A as one element in the larger regulatory environment' with 'law B as one element in the larger regulatory environment'.

The essay is built on three principal propositions. The first proposition is that those who are researching the law might find it fruitful to frame their inquiries by reference to the concept of the 'regulatory environment'. So framed, the questions that we might otherwise ask about, say, the effectiveness or the legitimacy of a particular law, would become questions about the effectiveness or legitimacy of that particular law situated in the larger

---

[1] M Van Hoecke and M Warrington, 'Legal Cultures, Legal Paradigms and Legal Doctrine: Towards a New Model for Comparative Law' (1998) 47 *International and Comparative Law Quarterly* 495. Of course, there is more than one way of reading 'law in context', with more than one emphasis, and many articulations of what is encompassed by 'context'. On this latter point, Van Hoecke and Warrington take a very broad approach, saying that, by 'context', we should understand 'not only the material context of sociology, history, economy, but also the ideological context of the law and what could be called the "juridical way of life"' (532).

[2] If we read Alan Watson literally, perhaps comparatists should not be comparing laws, or even comparing anything. See A Watson, *Legal Transplants*, 2nd edn (Athens, GA, University of Georgia Press, 1993) 4: 'Comparative Law cannot be primarily a matter of drawing comparisons'.

regulatory environment. The second proposition is that, while this framing might prove to be fruitful for both domestic and comparative legal inquiry, its utility and appropriateness might vary depending on the purpose of the particular inquiry. The third proposition is that, by attending to the regulatory environment and, particularly, to the full range of regulatory modalities (both normative and non-normative instruments), we might identify an important new line of inquiry for comparatists (and, indeed, chiming in with another theme of Van Hoecke's article, for non-comparatists).[3] This new inquiry concerns not particular laws, nor even particular laws in their larger regulatory environment, but the regulatory environment itself, and particularly the changing 'complexion' of that environment as regulators abandon traditional legal instruments in favour of non-normative technological fixes.[4] To put this in other words, progressive comparatists might track the 'hardening' of regulatory environments as laws give way to architecture, design and various kinds of technological and biological coding.

The elaboration and consideration of these propositions is in three parts. In the first part of the chapter, the focus is on the nature of law, the nature of the regulatory environment, the range of regulatory modes and the relationship between these various concepts. In the second part, moving from the first to the second proposition, the focus is on the purposes of legal inquiry (domestic and comparative) and how they might be facilitated by framing the questions relative to the concept of the regulatory environment. Finally, in the third part, a new line of inquiry for comparatists is sketched. This inquiry, with a forward-looking trajectory, focuses on the use of modern technologies as regulatory tools, designing places, products and (possibly) even people in ways that enable regulators to steer their regulatees towards desired regulatory objectives.

II. LAW AND THE REGULATORY ENVIRONMENT

According to Van Hoecke, one of the questions that should be considered by comparatists is 'What is law?'[5] As is well known, in mainstream jurisprudential debates, the concept of law is contested in two principal dimensions. First, there is the historic disagreement about the connection between law and morals (which, stated very simply, divides legal positivists and legal idealists). Whereas legal positivists deny any necessary conceptual connection between

---

[3] Van Hoecke and Warrington, above n 1, 497, where Van Hoecke and Warrington remark that, by undertaking comparative law inquiries, we become 'aware of the elements which are influencing the law at all levels'.

[4] For the 'complexion' of the regulatory environment see R Brownsword, 'Lost in Translation: Legality, Regulatory Margins, and Technological Management' (2011) 26 *Berkeley Technology Law Journal* 1321.

[5] Van Hoecke and Warrington, above n 1, 520–22.

law and morals, legal idealists insist upon it.[6] Secondly, there is a more recent debate about where we find law (which, again stated simply, divides pluralists and, for want of a better term, 'Westphalians'). Whereas pluralists deny any necessary limitation of law to the top-level institutions and ordering activities of nation states (for pluralists, law can be found just about anywhere), Westphalians insist upon this limitation—for Westphalians, law is hard and high.[7] These positions can be combined and finessed to yield many particular conceptions of law (and legal order and legal system, and so on).[8] However, they all tend to operate on the agreed premise that law is a normative ordering phenomenon, signalling what the subjects of law ought or ought not to do. As Lon Fuller famously expressed this shared point of departure, law is to be understood as the enterprise of subjecting human conduct to the governance of rules.[9]

It is also a shared assumption that the principal functions of law are to channel behaviour, to settle disputes and to allocate authority. This idea is best expressed in Karl Llewellyn's law-jobs theory.[10] However, Llewellyn (with his pluralist inclinations) invites jurists to reflect on the many different strategies that groups have employed to order their affairs and to settle their disputes. Although much of the post-Llewellyn literature focuses on the many different strategies for dispute settlement,[11] the recent and highly influential work of Lawrence Lessig, recognising important developments in information and communication technologies, has put the basic repertoire for performance of the channelling function into the spotlight. According to Lessig, there are four principal channelling modalities (or modes of regulation): the law, social norms, the market and architecture (or code).[12] The wearing of seat belts is one of Lessig's illustrative examples, thus:

> The government may want citizens to wear seatbelts more often. It could pass a law to require the wearing of seatbelts (law regulating behavior directly). Or it

[6] For one of the seminal exchanges see HLA Hart, 'Positivism and the Separation of Law and Morals' (1957–58) 71 *Harvard Law Review* 593; see also LL Fuller, 'Positivism and Fidelity to Law—A Reply to Professor Hart' (1957–58) 71 *Harvard Law Review* 630.

[7] See, eg J Klabbers, A Peters and G Ulfstein, *The Constitutionalization of International Law* (Oxford, Oxford University Press, 2009); A Halpin and V Roeben (eds), *Theorising the Global Legal Order* (Oxford, Hart, 2009). For a critical review see R Brownsword, 'Framers and Problematisers: Getting to Grips with Global Governance' (2010) 1 *Transnational Legal Theory* 287.

[8] My own position is a rationally grounded legal idealism with an inclination towards pluralism. See D Beyleveld and R Brownsword, *Law as a Moral Judgment* (London, Sweet and Maxwell, 1986) (reprinted Sheffield, Sheffield Academic Press, 1994).

[9] LL Fuller, *The Morality of Law* (New Haven, Yale University Press, 1969) passim.

[10] KN Llewellyn, 'The Normative, the Legal, and the Law-Jobs: The Problem of Juristic Method' (1940) 49 *Yale Law Journal* 1355.

[11] For an accessible overview see S Roberts, *Order and Dispute* (London, Penguin, 1979); and, more recently, L Rosen, 'Comparative Law and Anthropology' in M Bussani and U Mattei (eds), *The Cambridge Companion to Comparative Law* (Cambridge, Cambridge University Press, 2012) 73.

[12] L Lessig, *Code and Other Laws of Cyberspace* (New York, Basic Books, 1999) ch 7; L Lessig, 'The Law of the Horse: What Cyberlaw Might Teach' (1999) 113 *Harvard Law Review* 501, 507–14.

could fund public education campaigns to create a stigma against those who do not wear seatbelts (law regulating social norms as a means to regulating behavior). Or it could subsidize insurance companies to offer reduced rates to seatbelt wearers (law regulating the market as a way of regulating behavior). Finally, the law could mandate automatic seatbelts, or ignition-locking systems (changing the code of the automobile as a means of regulating belting behavior). Each action might be said to have some effect on seatbelt use; each has some cost. The question for the government is how to get the most seatbelt use for the least cost.[13]

Smart regulators will seek out the optimal mix of the various instruments that they have in this extended repertoire, but let us pause to emphasise one point. The law is just one possible element in this mix—no doubt, it is glaringly obvious that this is so, but in a community of lawyers (with a legal doctrinal gaze) it warrants repetition. There is more than one way of channelling behaviour; and, in any particular case, the law does not have to bear all, or even any, of the regulatory burden.

Potentially, with Lessig's identification of architecture and 'code' as channelling instruments, we open up a third dimension of contestation, namely whether law is to be understood to be normative alone or also non-normative. If we limit the concept of law to a normative phenomenon, then law operates exclusively through signals that convey what ought, or ought not, to be done (whether as a matter of duty or as the effective exercise of a power). However, if we allow that law might also be instantiated where the signals channel behaviour in a non-normative way, then it is possible that technological fixes (signalling what can and cannot be done) will also qualify as legal phenomena. With an increasing regulatory reliance on technological instruments, this point of contestation is likely to assume some importance.

Turning from law to regulation, we again find a concept that is contested in more than one dimension. In the way that the state-centric concept of law is contested by pluralists, there is a parallel debate in relation to the concept of regulation. Precisely how we might differentiate between 'regulation' and 'governance', let alone 'hard' and 'soft' law, is problematic.[14] It is also moot whether regulation extends beyond interventions that are intended to correct market failures to policies that are not focused on the economy.[15] However, the general idea is that regulation performs what Llewellyn calls the channelling function by steering and guiding the conduct of regulatees. It is also commonly assumed that regulators, having made their initial channelling intervention, will take steps to monitor compliance and correct non-compliance. Hence, as Julia Black puts it, we think of regulation as 'the sustained and focused attempt to alter the behaviour of others according to standards

---

[13] Lessig, *Code and Other Laws of Cyberspace*, ibid, 93–94.

[14] *Cf* LA Kornhauser, 'Governance Structures, Legal Systems and the Concept of Law' (2004) 70 *University of Chicago-Kent Law Review* 355.

[15] For two background visions of regulation (one as an infringement of private autonomy justified only by considerations of economic efficiency, the other as a much broader collaborative enterprise) see T Prosser, *The Regulatory Enterprise* (Oxford, Oxford University Press, 2010) ch1.

or goals with the intention of producing a broadly identified outcome or outcomes, which may involve mechanisms of standard-setting, information-gathering and behaviour-modification'.[16]

In many cases, as seems to be implicit in the common understanding, the assumption is that the initial regulatory intervention will be in the form of setting a standard (with, concomitantly, a normative signal). However, unless the concept of regulation (possibly along with the concept of law) is to be limited to the use of normative signals, there is no reason why regulation should not also feature non-normative technological signalling instruments.

This conceptual confusion and contestation notwithstanding,[17] we talk quite comfortably about the importance of getting the 'regulatory environment' right—right for financial services, right for innovation, right for health care and patient safety, right for the European single market, right for small businesses, and so on. But how should we conceive of the 'regulatory environment'?

Perhaps the most helpful starting point is to think about the regulatory environment as a signalling environment, in much the same way that we think about the setting for road traffic or for the railways. Just as, on the roads and railways, red lights signal 'stop' and green lights signal 'go', regulators may signal that certain conduct is prohibited (red light), or permitted or required (green light always indicating at least permitted and, in some contexts, required). Given that the purpose of the signals in a transport context is to reduce the risk of injury, both to oneself and to others, we might read compliance with the signals as both prudentially and morally indicated. In other words, there are mutually reinforcing reasons for compliance: first, there is the prudential reason that it is in one's own interest to comply; and, secondly, there is the moral reason that one respects the interests of others by complying. In principle, though, regulators might back their signals in a way that draws on exclusively moral or exclusively prudential, or mixed moral and prudential, reasons. Stated formally, regulators might seek to engage the practical reason of their regulatees by employing either the register of moral reason (signalling that some act, x, categorically ought or ought not to be done relative to standards of right action) or the register of prudential reason (signalling that some act, x, ought or ought not to be done relative to the prudential interests of regulatees), or a combination of these registers.

Now, in modern road transport settings, various kinds of technologies might be employed to advise drivers that they are either non-compliant or at risk of non-compliance—for example, roadside signs might flash a warning that the vehicle is exceeding the speed limit, an overhead motorway gantry might

---

[16] J Black, 'What is Regulatory Innovation?' in J Black, M Lodge and M Thatcher (eds), *Regulatory Innovation* (Cheltenham, Edward Elgar, 2005) 1, 11.

[17] J Black, 'De-centring Regulation: Understanding the Role of Regulation and Self-Regulation in a "Post-Regulatory" World' (2001) 54 *Current Legal Problems* 103.

advise that it is time to take a break or a vehicle equipped with the appropriate sensors might caution the driver against proceeding when affected by drink or drugs. In all these cases, the signals are normative (various acts ought or ought not to be done) and the regulatory register can be read as having both prudential and moral elements.

It is a feature of technologically enabled regulatory environments, however, that they do not always stop at advice. Sometimes, the technology simply disables an act.[18] On modern railway trains, for example, it is not possible for passengers to open the carriage doors until the guard has released the central locking system.[19] Similarly, smart cars might be disabled on sensing alcohol or drugs in the driver; and they will be designed so that they always comply with the speed limits.[20] Where environments are technologically controlled in this way, the regulatory signal is no longer normative and we have a quite different regulatory register. This is the register of practicability or possibility. Here, regulators signal that it is not reasonably practicable to do some act, x, or even that x simply cannot be done (that is, it is impossible to do x)—in which case, regulatees reason not that x ought not to be done, but that x cannot be done (either realistically or literally). In other words, in place of prescription, we have only possibility.[21]

Taking stock, we can treat any particular regulatory environment as having (in principle) two dimensions. First, there is the normative dimension: here, regulators seek to guide the conduct of regulatees; standards are set; prohibitions, permissions and requirements are signalled; regulators employ prudential or moral, or combined prudential–moral, registers to engage the practical reason of regulatees; and various kinds of technology might be used to reinforce the standards and the signals. Secondly, there is the non-normative dimension: here, regulators target a certain pattern of behaviour; various kinds of technology (product design, architecture, and the like) are used to channel regulatees in the desired way; and the only register employed is that of practicability/possibility.

There are doubtless many questions that we might ask about this concept of the regulatory environment, but an obvious one is: how do we draw the limits or boundaries of any particular regulatory environment? If we start with the regulators' view, they will want (i) a class of regulatees (it could be a broad class or quite a narrow one) (ii) to act in a certain way (iii) in some defined zone (which again could be broad or narrow). For example, while

---

[18] See, eg M Hildebrandt, 'Legal and Technological Normativity: More (and Less) than Twin Sisters' (2008) 12.3 *TECHNE* 169; R Brownsword, *Rights, Regulation and the Technological Revolution* (Oxford, Oxford University Press, 2008).

[19] See J Wolff, 'Five Types of Risky Situation' (2010) 2 *Law, Innovation and Technology* 151.

[20] See E Schmidt and J Cohen, *The New Digital Age* (New York, Alfred A Knopf, 2013) 25: 'Google's fleet of driverless cars, built by a team of Google and Stanford University engineers, has logged hundreds of thousands of miles without incident'.

[21] R Brownsword, 'Whither the Law and the Law Books: From Prescription to Possibility' (2012) 39 *Journal of Law and Society* 296.

regulators want their regulatees, whoever they are and wherever they are, to respect the physical well-being of one another, they will have more focused schemes for safety on the roads, for health and welfare at work, and for the safety of patients in hospitals, and so on. Accordingly, in many cases, the regulatory environment will be multilevel: in the normative dimension, there will be background standards of general application, but in many cases the foreground standards will be specific to particular persons or particular places, or both; and, in the non-normative dimension, technological management might be quite general (as when the state applies filters and blocks in relation to online content),[22] but will often be local and particular. Obviously, the regulatory environment will lack coherence unless the signals that are given at various levels are compatible and harmonised. So long as one set of regulators (or their delegates) fill out the regulatory scheme, there is no excuse for regulatory incoherence. However, problems can arise where regulators are in competition with one another.

This last remark prompts some reflection on the position of regulatees where they face contradictory signals. Occasionally, where traffic signals are faulty, traffic officers will attempt to control an intersection. For motorists, this can be confusing. Similarly, some motorists develop their own unofficial rules of the road (for example, using their headlights to signal a direction), which then might present some drivers with a dilemma: do they follow the official rules and their signals or do they follow the unofficial code and its signals? What we have here is not a competition between two top-down regulators but an exercise in bottom-up self-regulation coming into tension with the background top-down standards and signals. This is a phenomenon that is far from uncommon: we see it, for example, whenever a regulatee community sets up its own rival code or culture (whether this is drivers, file-sharers, bankers, doctors or sports people).[23] In these cases, the regulatory environment lacks overall coherence and, depending on the balance of power and influence, there is likely to be a degree of top-down regulatory ineffectiveness.

How, then, should we capture the essence of a 'regulatory environment' (if, indeed, this is a meaningful question)? Although we can say that we are conceiving of a signalling environment that is designed to channel group conduct, it needs to be recognised that there is a great deal of variety in particular instantiations. Whilst some environments are regulated in a top-down law-like fashion (with regulators clearly distinguishable from regulatees), others are more bottom-up, more self-regulatory (with regulators and regulatees much

---

[22] See, eg TJ McIntyre, 'Child Abuse Images and Cleanfeeds: Assessing Internet Blocking Systems' in I Brown (ed), *Research Handbook on Governance of the Internet* (Cheltenham, Edward Elgar, 2013) 277; I Brown and CT Marsden, *Regulating Code* (Cambridge, Mass., MIT Press, 2013) ch 5.

[23] On the last mentioned see R Brownsword, 'A Simple Regulatory Principle for Performance-Enhancing Technologies: Too Good to be True?' in J Tolleneer, P Bonte and S Sterckx (eds), *Athletic Enhancement, Human Nature and Ethics: Threats and Opportunities of Doping Technologies* (Dordrecht, Springer, 2012) 291.

less sharply defined as such) and more reliant on informal standards. Moreover, while some regulatory environments are reasonably stable and well-formed, others are unstable, overlapping, conflictual, and so on. And, crucially for present purposes, in some regulatory environments technology insinuates itself as a regulatory instrument, even to the point in some instances of replacing the normative (moral and prudential registers) with a non-normative register of practicability/possibility. No doubt there is a great deal more to be said about the concept of a regulatory environment, but, for present purposes, this suffices.

III. THE REGULATORY ENVIRONMENT AND COMPARATIVE LAW

If our cognitive interest is in the adequacy or acceptability of a particular national law, it seems to me that we cannot satisfactorily engage with the issues unless we put that law in context—which, I suggest, means setting that law in the relevant regulatory environment. It is easiest to see why this is so where our interest is in the (in)effectiveness of a particular law, but it also applies where our inquiry concerns the legitimacy of the law.

To start with (in)effectiveness, there are many reasons why laws might fail to fulfil their purposes. Sometimes, it is the lawmakers or law enforcers themselves that are responsible—for example, they might be corrupt or prey to more subtle forms of capture, or they might lack resources; or it might be that they are not as competent or smart as they need to be.[24] At other times, the problem lies beyond the local legal system—for example, there are well-known problems arising from regulatory arbitrage and from tax havens; and one of the major lessons of the last 20 years is that global and regional trade agreements, in conjunction with the development of the online world, have significantly reduced the effective influence of local regulators.[25] However, for present purposes, it is the response of those to whom the laws apply that is most obviously relevant. One law-in-action study after another suggests that laws fail to work not only when they engage with the habitual criminal classes, but also when they encounter professional, business or generational cultures of non-compliance.[26] In such cases, it is the larger regulatory environment that offers the appropriate explanatory framework for the ineffectiveness of particular laws.

Suppose that our interest is in a particular criminal law, a law that prohibits x. Within the criminal justice system, we might find that there is already some resistance to full enforcement of the law. For example, the police might tolerate some deviation (as with road traffic offences), prosecutors might decline

---

[24] For a discussion see R Brownsword and M Goodwin, *Law and the Technologies of the Twenty-First Century* (Cambridge, Cambridge University Press, 2012) chs 11–12.

[25] Brownsword and Goodwin, ibid, ch 14.

[26] Ibid, ch 13.

to proceed where they judge that it is not in the 'public interest' to do so (as with assisted suicide or some low level offensive online speech) and, even where the evidence is compelling, juries might decline to convict. In all these cases, informal norms develop which qualify the full-blooded application and enforcement of law x; and these norms need to be set alongside law x in the larger regulatory environment.[27] At the same time, as the law-in-action literature suggests, there might be cultures of non-compliance within the group at which law x is aimed, so that peer pressure or guidance within this group channels individual conduct in a way that resists, deflects or distorts the intentions of law x. To understand the impact of law x, to assess whether law x is unfit for purpose, the inquiry needs to be framed in a way that takes account of the regulatory environment into which law x is projected and of which it is now a (less than wholly effective) part.

Similar considerations apply where the law in which we are interested permits x. For example, there has been much discussion about whether laws that permit the harvesting of human organs from the recently deceased would be more effective in increasing the supply of organs if organ donation were to be predicated on opt-out rather than opt-in. Other things being equal, we might reasonably expect an opt-out scheme to produce more organs for transplantation than if the scheme were opt-in. However, once we place the proposal for opt-out in the larger regulatory environment, we might find that it makes little or no difference because the informal medical code is to respect the wishes of the deceased's relatives (effectively giving the relatives a veto) and because community norms do not yet treat donation as a matter of obligation. Again, if we are to understand how a change in a law of this kind might impact, we need to reckon with the larger regulatory environment.[28]

In many instances, resistance to a particular law and, concomitantly, non-compliance rests purely on a calculation of self-interest—for example, there might be a good business case to be made for polluting the environment or ignoring a patent restriction. However, in other cases, resistance is more principled, paradigmatically so in cases of conscientious objection. This leads to questions concerning the legitimacy of particular laws.

Where our cognitive interest is in the legitimacy of a particular law, it is perhaps not quite so obvious why we should place our inquiry in the context of the larger regulatory environment. Indeed, there might be some instances where we can, without more, condemn the legal position as categorically illegitimate—for example, if we judge that a particular law violates human rights or human dignity, we might not need to refer to the larger regulatory envi-

---

[27] *Cf* P Roberts, 'Comparative Law for International Criminal Justice' in E Örücü and D Nelken (eds), *Comparative Law: A Handbook* (Oxford, Hart, 2007) 339, 359.

[28] Understanding the regulation of (permitted) euthanasia in Belgium and the Netherlands is a case in point. See M Adams, 'Doing What Doesn't Come Naturally. On the Distinctiveness of Comparative Law' in M Van Hoecke (ed), *Methodologies of Legal Research* (Oxford, Hart, 2011) 229.

ronment (although, if we were to so refer, we might find that the violation
is ameliorated or exacerbated by that environment). In other cases, though,
we cannot make a rounded assessment unless we have the full picture. For
example, many contract and consumer lawyers have been critical of the Commission's recent preference for maximum harmonisation directives. Where the
national jurisprudence is strongly protective of the interests of consumers,
it is understandable that commentators should be critical of directives that
impose lower standards of protection. However, if we place the body of law
that is targeted at the consumer marketplace in Europe (a mixture of minimum and more recent maximum harmonising directives in conjunction with
national laws) in the larger regulatory environment, we will surely find that,
even though directives can be copied out, they do not copy across into practice in the same way. In some parts of the consumer marketplace, suppliers
will be so anxious to retain their custom and reputation that they will give
consumers a better deal than the law requires (and even maximum harmonisation measures do not prohibit this); by contrast, at the other end of the
market, vulnerable consumers will be exploited by rogue traders for whom the
legal requirements (whether in a minimal or maximal form) are there to be
ignored. This does not mean that those who criticise the move to maximum
harmonisation do not have an important point (particularly bearing on questions of local democracy). Rather, it means that, once we place these laws in
the larger regulatory environment, we find that the signals and the associated
practice are more complex.[29]

Having restricted the discussion thus far to inquiries in relation to national
law, it is time now to suggest that, for comparatists too, inquiry might be
enriched by attending to the regulatory environment. For example, when comparisons are made between the English law of contract and civilian law, one
of the striking differences is the way in which the former permits 'abusive'
termination for breach.[30] Whereas the civilian systems rely on doctrines such
as good faith and abuse of right to control such opportunistic action, English
law—at least, until fairly recently—seemed to be perfectly happy to license
such action. Comparatists have been quick to caution that simply transplanting the doctrine of good faith and fair dealing would not be the answer.[31]
However, my point is a rather different one. It is that, if this particular part
of English law were to be placed in the larger regulatory environment, it
would not be at all surprising to find that commercial people, sector by sector,
have their own understanding of what is and is not acceptable. For example,
contractors in the shipping sector might have a very different view to those

---

[29] Cf R Brownsword, 'Regulating Transactions: Good Faith and Fair Dealing' in G Howells
and R Schulze (eds), *Modernising and Harmonising Consumer Contract Law* (Munich, Sellier,
2009) 87.

[30] See, eg R Zimmermann and S Whittaker (eds), *Good Faith in European Contract Law*
(Cambridge, Cambridge University Press, 2000).

[31] See G Teubner, 'Legal Irritants: Good Faith in British Law or How Unifying Law Ends up
in New Divergences' (1991) 61 *Modern Law Review* 11.

whose business is in construction or in sales.[32] Once we interrogate the regulatory environment, we are likely to find that the norms that actually guide day-to-day dealing are quite different to the rules that have achieved notoriety in the law books.[33]

That said, there are many different comparative projects, some more pragmatic and practical than others, and there are many potential lines of comparative inquiry—from plain curiosity to projected transplantation (to improve the local jurisprudence) or harmonisation, from studies of legal effectiveness to questions of legitimacy, and so on. It might well be that the utility of framing questions by reference to the regulatory environment differs from one kind of comparative project to another, from one line of inquiry to another. We can take this a little further by checking the relevance of the regulatory environment to a number of comparative law purposes and projects helpfully identified by Esin Örücü.[34]

Örücü highlights seven purposes for comparative lawyers. First, the object of the exercise is to 'improve and consolidate knowledge of the law and understanding of the law in context'.[35] By juxtaposing the unknown with the known, comparatists aim 'to sharpen awareness and cognition of the legal, social and cultural environments in which we live'.[36] Secondly, the project is to group legal systems, to classify them (together with legal cultures and traditions) so that they are available for comparison. The third purpose of comparative lawyers is both pedagogic and political—to broaden the mind of the law student which, in turn, promotes tolerance. Fourthly, comparatists might be assistants in the process of law reform, offering legislators 'a pool of models from which to choose'.[37] A fifth purpose for comparative law research is to 'provide a tool of interpretation for judges by making them aware of foreign solutions to similar problems, when there are none at home'.[38] Sixthly, comparatists can make various contributions on the international legal stage, whether in drafting or interpreting instruments or teasing out universal or generally recognised principles. Finally, there are various kinds of harmonising or unifying projects that call on the skills and knowledge of comparatists including, in Europe, the articulation of European codes or the identification of common cores.

If we set aside the purposes in Örücü's inventory that are pedagogical and political, the central claim of this chapter is that we cannot understand law

---

[32] *Cf* S Deakin and J Michie (eds), *Contracts, Co-operation, and Competition* (Oxford, Oxford University Press, 1997).

[33] For a seminal study of the gap between the law-of-contract-in-the-books and business practice (the law-in-action) see S Macaulay, 'Non-contractual Relations in Business: A Preliminary Study' (1963) 28 *American Sociological Review* 55.

[34] E Örücü, 'Developing Comparative Law' in Örücü and Nelken, above n 27, 43, 53–56.

[35] Ibid, 53.

[36] Ibid, 54.

[37] Ibid, 55.

[38] Ibid.

without using the regulatory environment as the relevant context. Moreover, any attempt to deliver effective legislative reforms or to aid judicial interpretation is liable to founder unless the regulatory environment has been properly taken into account—and this applies whether the arena for reform or interpretation is domestic, regional or international. With regard to projects that aim to harmonise or unify laws, this is surely a futile exercise if the resulting laws are out of kilter with the local regulatory environment.[39] As Mathias Reimann[40] remarks: 'even today, prestigious comparative law projects can remain remarkably uninterested in the sociological dimension of law. The current efforts to unify European private law on the (quasi-)legislative level provide the perhaps most striking as well as disconcerting example'.[41]

Granted, we have not yet found a role for the regulatory environment where the comparative law purpose (the second in Örücü's list) is to classify legal systems; however, the way in which the regulatory environment comes to shape this kind of project will become clear in the next part of the chapter.

IV. A NEW LINE OF INQUIRY FOR COMPARATISTS

Near the end of his widely cited book, *Legal Transplants*, Alan Watson gathers together some concluding reflections.[42] The twelfth such reflection reads:

> [L]aw like technology is very much the fruit of human experience. Just as very few people have thought of the wheel yet once invented its advantages can be seen and the wheel used by many, so important legal rules are invented by a few people or nations, and once invented their value can readily be appreciated, and the rules themselves adopted for the needs of many nations.[43]

Turning this round somewhat, we can say that, just as emerging technologies are found by a few vanguard nations to have potential as regulatory tools, so their value is appreciated and soon these techno-regulatory instruments are adopted by other nations. In this case, however, law is more liable to be set aside than to be borrowed or transplanted.

To return to Lawrence Lessig's seminal work, it is now a commonplace that regulators have at their disposal a variety of regulatory instruments, including various technological instruments, or (in an ICT context) 'code'.[44] While

---

[39] *Cf* the critique in L Niglia, *The Transformation of Contract in Europe* (The Hague, Kluwer Law International, 2003).

[40] M Reimann, 'Comparative Law and Neighbouring Disciplines' in Bussani and Mattei, above n 11. 11.

[41] Brownsword and Goodwin, above n 24, ch 13. See, too, R Brownsword, 'The Theoretical Foundations of European Private Law: A Time to Stand and Stare' in R Brownsword, H Micklitz, L Niglia and S Weatherill (eds), *The Foundations of European Private Law* (Oxford, Hart, 2011) 159.

[42] Watson, above n 2.

[43] Ibid, 100.

[44] L Lessig, *Code and Other Laws of Cyberspace*, above n 12.

intelligent use of these instruments (such as CCTV, DNA profiling, GPS locating and tracking devices, DRM technologies, and so on) should improve the chances of achieving the regulatory purposes, there might nevertheless be questions about the acceptability of their application and use. The immediate questions are about the infringement of privacy or the compromising of human dignity, or the like. For present purposes, however, it is the legitimacy of using technology as a regulatory instrument that is at issue; and this raises what I call a question of the 'complexion' of the regulatory environment.

The material legitimacy concerns here are rooted in the idea that, in a moral community, people try to do the right thing (meaning that they take account of the legitimate interests of others), ie they act for the right reason. So long as technological tools are used to amplify the prudential signal that it is in the self-interest of regulatees to comply—because the technology will detect non-compliers—there is some threat to the conditions for moral community. However, it is when code and design leave regulatees with no option other than compliance that the legitimacy of the means employed by regulators needs urgent consideration. The problem here is that, even if we concede that the technology channels regulatees towards right action, the technologically secured pattern of right action is not at all the same as freely opting to do the right thing. Moral virtue, as Ian Kerr protests, cannot be automated.[45] Expressing this concern in relation to the use of 'digital locks', Kerr says:

> [A] generalized and unimpeded use of digital locks, further protected by the force of law, threatens not merely [various] legal rights and freedoms but also threatens to significantly impair our moral development. In particular, I express deep concern that digital locks could be used in a systematic attempt to "automate human virtue"—programming people to "do the right thing" by constraining and in some cases altogether eliminating moral behaviour through technology rather than ethics or law. Originally introduced to improve the human condition, digital locks and other automation technologies could, ironically, be used to control our virtual and physical environments in unprecedented ways, to eliminate the possibility for moral deliberation about certain kinds of action otherwise possible in these spaces by disabling the world in a way that ultimately disables the people who populate it. Not by eliminating their choices but by automating them—by removing people from the realm of moral action altogether, thereby impairing their future moral development.[46]

Applying this analysis to the case of honest action, Kerr detects the irony that

> an ubiquitous digital lock strategy meant to "keep honest people honest" is a self-defeating goal since it impairs the development of *phronesis*, stunts moral maturity and thereby disables the cultivation of a deep-seated disposition for honesty. Woven

---

[45] I Kerr, 'Digital Locks and the Automation of Virtue' in M Geist (ed), *From 'Radical Extremism' to 'Balanced Copyright': Canadian Copyright and the Digital Agenda* (Toronto, Irwin Law, 2010) 247.
[46] Ibid, 254–55.

into the fabric of everyday life, digital locks would ensure particular outcomes for property owners but would do so at the expense of the moral project of honesty.[47]

The point is that the shift from law (or ethics) to technological instruments changes the 'complexion' of the regulatory environment in a way that has deep moral significance. Instead of guiding regulatees by prescribing what ought or ought not to be done, regulators might wholly depart from the normative register by signalling what can or cannot be done. To comply or not to comply is no longer the question for regulatees; the only question is what in practice can be done.

That said, it surely cannot be right to condemn all applications of technological management as illegitimate. For example, modern transport systems incorporate safety features that are intended to design out the possibility of human error. Should we object to this? Or, again, should we object to the use of regulating technologies that replace a failed normative strategy for securing the safety of patients who are taking medicines or being treated in hospitals?[48] Nevertheless, we need to monitor the cumulative impact of regulators resorting to such instruments;[49] and, of course, there is much to debate about the transparency, reversibility and location of these technological 'fixes' for non-compliance. In both specialist regulatory circles and the public square, we need to be talking about the acceptability of 'techno-regulation'.[50]

For comparatists, several new lines of inquiry are implicit in these remarks. Let me sketch just two possible new directions for comparative inquiries.

First, in relation to their classificatory projects, instead of thinking about families of legal systems, comparatists might address the families of regulatory environments.[51] In this chapter, I have highlighted the distinction between normative and non-normative signalling (and, concomitantly, normative and non-normative regulatory environments). Looking to the future, it is the normative and the non-normative that are the candidate families, and we need to know how far regulators both at home and abroad are making use of

---

[47] Ibid, 292.

[48] For the weaknesses of traditional regulatory approaches see E Jackson, *Law and the Regulation of Medicines* (Hart, Oxford, 2012); B Goldacre, *Bad Pharma* (London, Fourth Estate, 2012). For some reservations about the use of design in order to improve patient safety see K Yeung and M Dixon-Woods, 'Design-Based Regulation and Patient Safety: A Regulatory Studies Perspective' (2010) 71 *Social Science and Medicine* 502.

[49] K Yeung, 'Can We Employ Design-Based Regulation While Avoiding Brave New World?' (2011) 3 *Law, Innovation and Technology* 1.

[50] See R Brownsword, 'What the World Needs Now: Techno-Regulation, Human Rights and Human Dignity' in R Brownsword (ed), *Human Rights* (Oxford, Hart, 2004) 203; R Brownsword, *Rights, Regulation and the Technological Revolution* (Oxford, Oxford University Press, 2008). For one sign of a growing awareness of this concern see V Mayer-Schönberger and K Cukier, *Big Data* (London, John Murray, 2013) 162: 'Perhaps with such a [big data predictive] system society would be safer or more efficient, but an essential part of what makes us human—our ability to choose the actions we take and be held accountable for them—would be destroyed. Big data would have become a tool to collectivize human choice and abandon free will in our society.'

[51] Cf R Brownsword, 'Code, Control, and Choice: Why East is East and West is West' (2005) 25 *Legal Studies* 1.

technology-reliant channelling strategies. We can be pretty sure that regulators will keep an eye open for the effectiveness of these strategies, but we need to understand how these approaches are justified, if at all, and whether, indeed, they can be viewed as legitimate.

This first line of inquiry might be pushed one stage further. It will be recalled that I have said that, in principle, coding can be embedded in places, products and people. For some time, the non-normative family is likely to rely on the coding of products and places. However, what if it becomes possible to code people in the way that robots are programmed? Irrespective of the mental experience of these coded persons, as regulatees the channelling signals are now internal. This departs from the model of a regulatory environment that I have developed because regulatees are no longer responding to external channelling signals. At this point, if we continue to have a cognitive interest in channelling, we might need to elaborate a new framing approach. Instead of the regulatory environment, maybe coding (of products, places and persons) is our future frame, these codes all being non-normative, in stark contrast to what, as lawyers, we are accustomed to think of when we refer to (normative) codes. In this new technologically managed world, even the common law countries would employ 'codes' to channel the conduct of regulatees.[52]

Secondly, the ideals of legality (as a simple notion of due process) and, likewise, of the rule of law assume that standards are promulgated and then faithfully applied and prospectively enforced—there is, for example, no secret or retrospective rule book. In other words, the assumption is that we are engaging with a normative form of channelling. When Fuller proclaims the virtues of legal ordering (as against brute power or managerial command), he assumes that we are dealing with a normative order.[53] However, once non-normative channelling strategies are employed, it is quite unclear how the virtues of normative legal ordering can be translated, if at all.[54] For example, in a non-normative regulatory environment, what does it mean to insist that the rules as administered should be congruent with the rules as declared? Does it now mean that what is treated as impossible (as a non-option) really should be impossible? If so, what is the virtue in that? Once again, comparatists might assist us in understanding whether and, if so, how the ideals of legality can persist in a quite different non-normative regulatory environment.[55]

To this, some might object that, if the drift away from normative ordering and legality is so important, there is no reason why comparatists should bear the burden of highlighting the significance of the complexion of the regulatory environment and the increasing use of technological instruments. Surely, non-

---

[52] For a provocative discussion of the environment as engineered 'atmosphere' (understood as the 'varying measures of normativity and space that appear simultaneously in the lawscape') see A Philippopoulos-Mihalopoulos, 'Atmospheres of Law: Senses, Affect, Lawscapes' (2013) 7 *Emotion, Space and Society* 35.

[53] Fuller, *The Morality of Law*, above n 9.

[54] Brownsword, 'Lost in Translation', above n 4.

[55] Brownsword and Goodwin, above n 24, chs 2 and 12.

comparatists, too, should have these questions on their intellectual agenda. Indeed, they should. Moreover, this is just the point that Mark Van Hoecke was making when he observed that, by reflecting on the nature of comparative inquiry, researchers would sharpen their sense of the purpose of any kind of legal inquiry. Progressive comparatists are also progressive non-comparatists.

V. CONCLUSION

In one of the great, albeit fictitious, comparative essays of the nineteenth century, Samuel Butler describes the way in which the Erewhonians had seemingly taken a retrograde step by destroying their machines.[56] Moreover, in this once quite technologically sophisticated society, Butler reports such strange practices as treating criminals as sick (and deserving sympathy) and the physically ill as blameworthy and in need of correction. Butler's brilliance lies not so much in presenting the Erewhonians in a light that invites ridicule but in sowing the seeds of the idea, at any rate in twenty-first century readers, that these technophobes in their distant land might actually be a whole lot smarter than we first appreciated.

For, what is becoming increasingly clear in the early years of the twenty-first century is that the acceleration in technological development, aided and abetted by globalisation,[57] while expanding our options, at the same time diminishes the set of actions that are technologically unmediated. The development of modern online environments presents a cornucopia of new options but also channels us towards online information gathering, online interacting (communicating) and online transacting. In another age, these are actions that would have taken place face-to-face without technological support. If these (and many other) actions—even the act of reproduction—can be technologically mediated, the same must be true of the ordering of social life. Once the technology is in place, the situation is not irreversible, but in most places the Erewhonian strategy of destroying the machines is unlikely to appeal.

These modern technologies have one obvious bearing on comparative lawyering: quite simply, in the online world, the territorial boundaries that define the legal systems to be compared are not present in the same way; in the online world, here is there and there is here.[58] In a rapidly changing world, progressive comparatism implies that we must get to grips with a context that is in

---

[56] S Butler, *Erewhon* (London, Penguin, 1935).

[57] *Cf* R Cotterrell, 'Seeking Similarity, Appreciating Difference: Comparative Law and Communities' in A Harding and E Örücü (eds), *Comparative Law in the 21st Century* (London, Kluwer, 2002) 35, who remarks that 'In a world of globalizing tendencies, it is necessary to distinguish carefully different components of law's social environment' (53). Whilst Cotterrell's interest is in different kinds of communities (and, concomitantly, different kinds of social environment), my point is that, in the twenty-first century, comparatists need to be factoring into this context similar and different uses of technology as a regulatory tool.

[58] Seminally see DR Johnson and D Post, 'Law and Borders—The Rise of Law in Cyberspace' (1996) 48 *Stanford Law Review* 1367.

constant flux but where the trajectory is increasingly and relentlessly techno-logical.[59] My point, in this chapter, is that we need to rely on the concept of the regulatory environment to interrogate not only the law as it is but also the law as it is becoming—and, in particular, the shift from normative chan-nelling such as it is to non-normative channelling strategies.

Famously, Basil Markesinis lamented that comparative law, having failed to excite the imagination of students and practising lawyers, is still searching for an audience.[60] If progressive comparative lawyers can help us to under-stand the place of law in a rapidly changing world of converging info-, bio-, nano- and neuro-technologies,[61] and particularly the changing complexion of the regulatory environment, their subject might yet find an audience with law students and legal practitioners—but, more importantly, it might engage the attention of populations worldwide who value having a voice in the articula-tion of their regulatory environments.[62]

---

[59] *Cf* Schmidt and Cohen, above n 19.

[60] B Markesinis, 'Comparative Law—A Subject in Search of an Audience' (1990) 53 *Modern Law Review* 1.

[61] For provocative 'big picture' overviews see, eg P Baldi, *The Shattered Self—the End of Natu-ral Evolution* (Harvard, MIT Press, 2001); J Garreau, *Radical Evolution* (New York, Broadway Books, 2005). Looking forward see, eg M Kaku, *Physics of the Future—The Inventions That Will Transform Our Lives* (London, Penguin Books, 2011); for an extended sense of our history see TF Taylor, *The Artificial Ape* (New York, Palgrave MacMillan, 2010).

[62] See R Brownsword, 'The Shaping of Our On-Line Worlds: Getting the Regulatory Environ-ment Right' (2012) 20 *International Journal of Law and Information Technology* 249.

15

The Importance of Institutions

JOHN BELL

I N *LAW AS Communication*, Mark Van Hoecke pointed out 'We can indeed tell different stories about the law . . . Every simplification means that one does not give a full account of (legal) reality, but nevertheless such simplifications are necessary to enable us to 'see' any reality, to understand it, to grasp it'.[1] That modesty typifies Mark's contribution to legal scholarship. He has been careful not to claim too much for his own contribution and he has valued the contribution of others. The result is that he has created a community of scholarship which has been able to flourish beyond his own retirement. This reflection aims to complement Mark's own ideas with a greater focus on the institutional aspect of law. Mark has sought to combine an interest in legal theory and comparative law, and this essay is in the same vein, though with a greater focus on what interests a comparative lawyer rather than on what interests a legal theorist. For the purposes of comparative law, I would wish to argue that law is best seen as an institution. The reason is that the concept of an institution captures a number of significant distinctive features about a legal system, and these features provide an agenda for comparative law. Mark Van Hoecke's own preferred focus of 'law as communication' is very useful if the focus of our attention is the way that law guides conduct. But if we want to understand the distinctive features of a legal system, then we need to focus on the nature of law as a social institution. There are a variety of accounts of the nature of law as an institution. This essay suggests that, at least from the point of view of the legal theory adopted by a comparative lawyer, the law is best seen as involving not only legal norms, but the institutional context in which they are embedded—the organisations, procedures, personnel and ethos which make it work. These are the features which explain why legal systems differ.

---

[1] M Van Hoecke, *Law as Communication* (Oxford, Hart Publishing, 2002) 2, 5.

I. WHY DOES THE INSTITUTION MATTER?

In his reflections on comparative law, Pierre Legrand[2] has tried to argue for a different form of legal theory than that conventionally presented by works on legal convergence in Europe. At root, he has two arguments. First, the comparatist must reject 'law-as-rules' as impoverished. If we take public law as an example, we must not look at whether European legal systems have rules on 'proportionality' or 'legitimate expectations', but try to understand how legal systems approach the control of government through such concepts. Secondly, 'I claim that meaningful comparative work demands . . . [that] an understanding of law or of an experience of law other than one's own can only arise from thorough contextualism'.[3] Mitchel Lasser[4] has described this second feature as the belief that 'immersion' in a particular legal system is an essential part of conducting comparative law, especially where one may be trying to seek out the unstated and unconscious assumptions on which those within the system operate. Given the importance of the institutional features of law, this aspect of the legal method takes on an increased importance in comparative law and legal theory. Understanding law and how legal systems work requires us to look beyond the rules that are applied. If we think in Van Hoecke's terms about communication, we have to look not just at the individual acts of communication by legislators and judges, but at the system and processes of communication in which they operate. A legal theory needs to capture the institutions and not just the norms.

If we step back and think about the function of law, the distinctive contribution of law is solving problems through rules and through institutions. Van Hoecke follows Fuller in suggesting that there are two major issues which are governed through law: structuring society and facilitating the life of an individual.[5] Law helps not only to set out the conditions and limits for the exercise of public power (structuring competences and processes of decision-making), but also to provide a scheme of legitimating public power—if power is exercised in certain ways, then it becomes socially acceptable.[6] Now, in one sense, the powers exercised by the state or by an individual pre-exist the law. So Van Hoecke is right that an important function of the law is to provide a scheme for legitimising the exercise of power. But, if we step back and look at the law as a social institution, then we can see that law creates a distinctive way of dealing with social problems. It reduces complexity in social life by offering an ordered system of rules, principles and procedures within which

---

[2] P Legrand, 'Public Law, Europeanisation and Convergence: Can Comparatists Contribute?' in P Beaumont, C Lyons and N Walker (eds), *Convergence and Divergence in European Public Law* (Oxford, Hart Publishing, 2002) 225.

[3] Ibid, 229.

[4] M Lasser, *Judicial Deliberations. A Comparative Analysis of Judicial Transparency and Legitimacy* (Oxford, Oxford University Press, 2004) 10–11.

[5] Van Hoecke, above n 1, ch 4.

[6] Ibid, 63.

problems can be resolved. To go back to Van Hoecke's concern with public power, law is concerned with who is given the power to make a decision (or is seen as legitimate in making it) and how this is done.[7] Thus, a decision by a public authority to allow an individual to build an extension to his house confers legitimacy on that action and enhances the freedom of one individual after due consideration of the interests of other individuals. But that conferral of permission/legitimacy is not the result of a chaotic survey of local opinion or a collection of votes sent in by text message or Twitter. The law determines who should make the decision and by what process, including who is to have a say in the decision-making. Lawyers value not only doing the right thing, but doing it repeatedly and consistently. So the key to a legal solution is to develop routines and rules that will deliver the right solution repeatedly and (in a certain way) without thinking. Such routines are embedded in agreed procedures and institutions. At the same time, there needs to be flexibility to adjust to the unforeseen and unfair.[8] So it is not just rules and outcomes that matter, but the framework of institutions and processes within which rules are enacted and applied and outcomes are achieved, reviewed and improved.

II. WHAT COUNTS AS AN INSTITUTION?[9]

If institutions matter, what counts as an 'institution'? The jurisprudential literature contains a number of definitions, each of which has a particular purpose in mind. Van Hoecke helpfully defines law as 'an institutionalised normative system'.[10] By contrast, there are the formal institutions, the specialised bodies which are authorised by the law to make rules and to adjudicate upon them. These two 'levels' have two aspects, structures and procedures.[11] In describing these, he draws particularly on Hart's concept of primary and secondary rules, the secondary rules being particularly relevant to the determination of the competence and legitimacy of decisions by law-making and adjudicating bodies. Van Hoecke also draws on Hart for what he describes as 'sociological institutionalisation', by which he means 'the acceptance of the legal system by the people to whom it is meant to apply'.[12] The formal institutionalisation and the sociological institutionalisation are necessary for the existence of a legal system. However, Van Hoecke also suggests that a developed system will have a professional institutionalisation which will help in the development of the system: 'A fully developed legal system embodies three categories of legal professions: professional lawmakers (members of Parliament), professionals of

---

[7] Ibid, 21.

[8] Zenon Bankowski argues that we need to keep in tension the demands of law and love: *Living Lawfully* (Dordrecht, Kluwer, 2001).

[9] See J Bell, *Judiciairies within Europe* (Cambridge, Cambridge University Press, 2006) 6–12.

[10] Van Hoecke, above n 1, 21.

[11] Ibid, 22.

[12] Ibid, 24.

the administration of justice (eg judges) and professionals of legal doctrine (eg legal academics)'.[13]

By contrast, in his work on law as 'institutional fact', MacCormick was predominantly interested in legal reasoning. Drawing on Searle's conception of 'institutional fact',[14] Weinberger and MacCormick pointed out[15] that law is not a set of 'natural facts' that can be inspected directly; rather, it is an interpretative reality under which certain physical events take on a special significance. An institutional fact is a fact, which we invest with meaning within a particular set of social relations because it performs a particular function. Thu,s in law, agreed perceptions turn a set of facts into a 'trial'—the situation in which one person sits on a raised platform while another person stands silently in front of him and yet two others argue facing the person seated. That assignment of meaning to natural facts depends on collective intentionality, not just the wishes or views of a particular individual observer or actor.[16] The legal point of view gives meaning to events and processes. That legal point of view is expressed in ideas, and MacCormick was interested in how the ideas used in legal rules and principles fitted together. He defined an 'institution' as a bundle of interconnected rights, duties, values and norms, such as a 'trust' and a 'contract'.[17] The contract is not just one rule, but a range of interconnected rules held together by principles and values. He was concerned that we should not focus on the individual rule or normative statement, but we needed to understand how an individual rule or legal idea had resonance in relation to other legal ideas. This embedding of ideas is an important feature of the law as a system of norms. The understanding of particular concepts arises from an understanding of the connections between the ideas which lawyers use to explain and justify legal decisions. MacCormick's account illuminates our understanding of 'law as a system of rules' and how we interpret them. This is an analysis of legal doctrine which explains how the legal community creates the institutional reality, which individuals can then use legal concepts to explain. But the institutional system and practices precede the ideas. For that reason, we need to start with a different conception, one much closer to Van Hoecke's approach to legal institutions.

The institutional system secures the predictability which law exists to provide. Such a system consists in a set of organisations (such as courts and legislatures), a set of people (judges, lawyers, prison warders) and a set of procedures (trials, transfers of land, making wills or enacting legislation). Van Hoecke is right that the specialised people who are involved may only become professionalised at quite a late stage in legal development, as the social insti-

---

[13] Ibid, 26.

[14] JR Searle, *The Social Construction of Reality* (London, Allen Lane, 1995) 47.

[15] N MacCormick and O Weinberger, *An Institutional Theory of Law* (Dordrecht, Kluwer, 1986) ch 3.

[16] Searle, *The Social Construction of Reality* 46.

[17] MacCormick and Weiberger, above n 15, 9–13, 49–74.

tutions of law become more sophisticated. For example, professional judges may develop late, as they did in Sweden.[18] But the distinctive functions are part of the foundation of a legal system. The organisations, the people to service them and the processes through which they operate are the guarantee of the predictable legal system which delivers the outcomes which the rules are designed to achieve. These are the institutional aspects of a legal system which can implement legal rules, engage in legal reasoning and thus make use of 'institutional facts (in legal reasoning)' which MacCormick describes. In the modern era, the important thing is the translation of political decisions and debates into a routine of government. Politicians have visions and ideas. They want actions and results. Law is part of the bureaucratic structure which enables this to happen. Action does not result from soundbites or political communiqués; it results from patient implementation by lots of people, judges and administrators, over many years. Bureaucratic routines can deliver results by the action of officials, but results delivered in particular by those outside government depend on the law. For example, the vision of a Europe without (internal) frontiers has taken over 50 years. There needed to be processes by which the big vision is translated into decisions on specific steps to be implemented in specific timescales. Those processes require procedures by which decisions can be made, even when not everyone is fully happy. Legislative and judicial processes have achieved that, and most pre-date the specific legal rules. The institutions provide the framework within which the functions of law operate.

In work with David Ibbetson, I have expanded a little on this framework function of legal institutions and how they relate to the idea of law as a system of rules. We related institutions to legal reasoning by suggesting that

> Legal institutions, ie the framework within which the law operates, including the following: the formal canons of reasoning used by judges and officials to translate linguistic formulations into actual decisions on particular sets of facts; 'legal style', which we might define in terms of the judges' and officials' perceptions of their own roles within the system; legal practices, ways of doing things (especially lawyers' craft skills) which are often inherited and are based on just how it has happened to be convenient to do things; and the legal process. Related to these are what might be described as 'legal culture', a set of beliefs and attitudes (implicit and explicit) which give meaning to and condition activity.[19] Many of these are inherited from tradition and are consciously transmitted, eg by legal education, but they can be forcibly changed, as occurred in continental Europe with the advent of codification or in England with the enactment of the Human Rights Act in 1998.[20]

---

[18] Bell, *Judiciaries within Europe*, above n 9, 253–54.

[19] The term is used in a variety of different ways: see J Bell, *French Legal Cultures* (London, Butterworths, 2001) ch 1.

[20] J Bell and D Ibbetson, *European Legal Development. The Case of Tort* (Cambridge, Cambridge University Press, 2012) 45.

At the level of rules, we argued that there is an interplay between the legal doctrine (interpreting the rules) and the legal outcomes (the way the law is applied and the consequences for people) which may lead to a more precise formulation of the rule or even a change in it. This feedback loop takes place within the parameters of the legal institutions and legal culture, which influence the way the feedback operates. In turn, this legal system operates within the context of a non-legal ways of resolving the problems. In this chapter, I want to expand on the place of legal institutions and legal culture as a foundation of the legal system in relation to Mark Van Hoecke's analysis of law as communication.

III. LEGAL INSTITUTIONS AND COMMUNICATION

The institutional framework of law sets the parameters within which legal reasoning takes place. Mark Van Hoecke makes much of the importance of legal interpretation in his work *Law as Communication*.[21] His purpose was to challenge the focus within legal theory on legal *argumentation*, which treats law as a matter of winning an argument, rather than achieving social purposes. For him, interpretation is about identifying what lawmakers are seeking to achieve and how they are to find it.[22] Van Hoecke is thorough in his account of legal methods and shows the various options which are commonly recognised. He recognises that the choice of methods requires legitimation, and that this choice is often debated among judges and academics.[23] These facts are correct, but I think they show that an account of law needs to give more prominence to the institutional framework. If law is a process of communication, both within the legal community (from legislators to judges and others applying the law or advising on it) and outside it (from legislators and judges to the subjects of the law), then we need to pay attention to who determines the approach to interpretation and how this approach is transmitted. It may be that the communication of legal norms is the primary function of the law, but the communication on how to read the law is an important secondary set of standards, which Van Hoecke's account only hints at, in part because his account of institutions is too focused on the vocabulary and categories set out by HLA Hart. Interpretation is a practice which is developed by the members of a legal community. As Vogenauer has shown,[24] interpretative principles vary at different periods within a particular legal community, as well as between different legal communities. Vogenauer argues that, though the constitutional status of the judge in relation to the legislator may be fixed by means of a

---

[21] Van Hoecke, *Law as Communication* 134–171.
[22] Ibid, 127.
[23] Ibid, 171.
[24] S Vogenauer, *Die Auslegung von Gesetzen in England und auf dem Kontinent* (Tübingen, JCB Mohr, 2001).

legal rule, in practice it is determined in relation to numerous legal, political and social circumstances.[25] Features such as the burden of reform for the legislator and the need to keep the law up to date have an impact on the role the judge performs in fact, because there is a pragmatic decision to be made about how law reform is achieved. There may also be legal and political cultural features, such as the importance attached to legislative texts as instruments of rational reform of the law in the Enlightenment period.[26] Modern attachment to human rights allows the judge a greater power to adjust the text of the statute than would have been acceptable in the Enlightenment. There is an inevitable tension in relation to the best way to resolve the tension between these different factors, a tension which is crystallised in the rules on interpretation.[27] The contemporary style is set by the legal community of the day and is then transmitted by professional teaching and practice. Legal education will transmit the expectations of legal reasoning and the practice of the courts will reinforce this by refusing to accept what they take to be inappropriate arguments. This aspect of communication is the result of developments in the legal profession.

So a study of legal interpretation as part of the process of communicating legal norms needs to provide an account of the legal professions and their interaction. Vogenauer[28] argues that it is rare for legal systems to adopt new interpretative methods through open deliberation. That is seen by practitioners as too theoretical. However, changes can be made through the handling of individual cases, which are then systematised. So any account has to give a picture of how the different parts of the legal community relate to each other and set the tone for the practice of interpretation.[29] The issue is not simply a matter of contemporary problem solving, but it involves relationships to experiences in the past. The function of legal professions is not just to run the current legal system, but to transmit the lessons and crafts of the past. The new entrant is apprenticed to learn the craft and can then adapt it for the future. But it is those cumulated experiences from the past which often shape the legal institutions and professions of the present and especially differentiate one legal system from another.

IV. THE PLACE OF INSTITUTIONS

In *The Impact of Legal Institutions and Professions*, Paul Mitchell and his colleagues[30] also specifically examine the role of legislators, judges and academics

[25] Ibid, 167, 1287.
[26] Ibid, 657–58, 1293–94.
[27] Ibid, 1314.
[28] Ibid, 19.
[29] See A Paterson, *The Law Lords* (London, Macmillan, 1982) 56–65.
[30] P Mitchell (ed), *The Impact of Legal Institutions and Professions* (Cambridge, Cambridge University Press, 2012).

in the development of tort law. They consider that, although, constitutionally, legislators may have very wide discretion, they operate in practice within a significant number of constraints. Changes in tort law often require significant work, which is a low political priority, so others within the legal community take the lead on law reform. Decisions are often made in response to a crisis or the surfacing of a sensitive issue, and early action is needed. The processes of legislative change often involve drawing on the work of committees which have had the time to deliberate and consult on issues before they produce proposals. Legislative reform may also be the result of comparison with other cognate countries, and may draw on the insights of judges, academics and non-lawyers. Although the terse judicial decisions of many continental systems make it difficult to identify such influences on their decision-making, there is some evidence to show that individual judges have an influence on legal development, even in these countries. In many cases the individuals in question have been academics, so there is external evidence of their personal opinions. Academics may contribute to doctrinal writing through their textbooks and articles.[31] However, it is in their legislative committee work and in their roles within the judiciary that less publicised routes of significant influence can be identified in a range of different legal systems. The three professionalised groups Van Hoecke identifies contribute to the law-making process. Through each of these three groups, a particular legal system is made open to other legal systems, and it is that porosity of legal systems which it is important to emphasise. One legal system sits in relation to other legal systems, just as much as it sits in relation to non-legal schemes of values and practices. The story of the legal system is not just the communication and reception of rules, but the shaping of the processes of rule formulation, rule interpretation and rule application by the institutions and procedures of the legal system. An understanding of both legal change and legal differences requires an understanding not only of rules and concepts, and their language and interpretation, but also the way these are moulded.

V. WHICH INSTITUTIONS?

I have argued elsewhere[32] that a legal culture is composed of a number of key elements. Legal actors engage in activities which lead to consequences. They then reflect on these consequences, and modify the norms and standards which define how the activities are to be conducted in the future. It is not simply that applying norms is a single act of communication; it is a regular process of communication on which the actors reflect. As Vogenauer makes clear in his account of legal interpretation, the key legal actors are socialised within both legal and non-legal communities, and operate within institutions. It is

---

[31] Ibid, 6–8.
[32] Bell, *French Legal Cultures*, above n 19, 21–2; Bell, *Judiciaries within Europe*, above n 9, 11.

thus important to understand what these institutions are, and here we can build on Van Hoecke's account.

The building block of a legal institution is an organisation whose mission is to play a part in the operation of the law: in drafting or enacting rules, in advising or applying rules. At a primary level, that organisation has specific functions in relation to the process of communicating legal norms to subjects. To perform its function, it will have routines and procedures by which its activities take place, and it will be staffed by individuals from appropriate roles or professions. Julia Black uses the term 'interpretative community' in the distinctive sense of a given set of actors coming together to interpret rules and give them meaning, developing a shared meaning to legal rules.[33] It seems to me that this concept of 'community' is helpful in drawing attention to the common purpose in which the different actors are engaged.

In addition to functions, there is the procedure for interpreting and applying the legal norms. There are, in particular, procedures by which the individual can make use of the legal norms, eg to write a will or to enforce a right through the courts. There are rules which define who is a judge, or a registry for land transactions and practices which relate to their training. These contextual features are very significant not only for the way in which the law operates, but also for differences between legal systems. To take a very simple example, a common European rule may have substantially different outcomes depending on the institutional structure of the country in which the rule is being applied. A country with a long delay before a case is heard will provide a different outcome for an applicant, as might a legal system with different ease of access to the courts or traditions of legal interpretation.

At a secondary level, there are ways in which the legal actors are trained or educated to perform organisational tasks, such as interpreting the law. They are formed into a community not only by acquiring knowledge, but also, in some sense, by being socialised into the ethos of the organisation—ensuring that they are able to carry out the tasks in the appropriate way. This notion of an ethos is captured by what David Ibbetson and I described as a 'legal culture'. It is necessary not only that the primary functions of an organisation are defined and its operational rules, but that there is a shared sense of how this should be done. For example, the education of lawyers in legal methods ensures that they will read statutes correctly. The rules have been best described as traditions of good practice, rather than legal rules.[34]

At a tertiary level, there is the relationship in a country between legal and non-legal institutions. For example, in public law, there are at least two sets of non-legal institutions, political and administrative, and these institutions shape the character of how the law works, the law setting a framework around how

---

[33] J Black, *Rules and Regulators* (Oxford, Clarendon Press 1997) 30. I am grateful to Yseult Marique for this reference.

[34] J Bell and G Engle, *Cross on Statutory Interpretation*, 3rd edn (London, Butterworths, 1995) 38–43.

they work. The legal institutions are the principal ones which a theory of a legal system has to consider, but the understanding of legal change requires understanding of the relationship to non-legal institutions, as Teubner makes clear.[35] It is this relationship to non-legal institutions which the work of Paul Mitchell and his colleagues admirably captures in relation to the development of tort law.

VI. HOW FAR DO INSTITUTIONS EXPLAIN DIFFERENCES?

My suggestion that law is structured deeply around national institutions has significant explanatory power for comparative law and also has consequences for legal theory. To take an example, when asked to talk to a French audience about comparisons between civil service employment in England and France, I rapidly discovered the difference between the respective institutions. There were no books (then) on English civil service employment law. I had to resort to borrowing a copy of the 'Civil Service Handbook',[36] the internal guidance leaflet of the civil service. Noting the importance of civil service litigation in the French administrative courts, I set about trying to discover the English equivalent, only to be defeated by the fact that most of the civil service litigation is handled by means of internal boards within the service, rather than by formal courts. There was a radically different culture to the use of 'law' (in the sense of specifically legal institutions) in the two civil service systems.

Even when we look at legal norms in the way Van Hoecke does, however, much comparative law focuses on the way the same legal rules are applied in different countries. But to do that task, and since we need to go beyond description to provide explanation, we need to understand the organisational context in which they operate. Both the common law and the French Civil Code have operated in different legal systems and produce different results. For example, the common law reluctance to give compensation for economic loss produces different rules in England than in Australia and the US.[37] The French Civil Code was adopted in a number of European countries in the wake of the military victories of Napoleon in 1805. Yet, once the countries became independent again, they adopted their own approach. For example, the Dutch not only used the concept of 'fault' for delictual liability within Articles 1382 and 1383 Code civil, but also the concept of 'unlawfulness'. Here, the Dutch legal community drew on its affinity to the German legal communities and the range of ideas circulating among them.[38] The result is that

[35] G Teubner, *Law as an Autopoietic System* (Oxford, Blackwell, 1993) ch 5.

[36] J Bell, 'English Law and French Law—Not so Different?' (1995) 63 *Current Legal Problems* 95.

[37] KM Hogg, 'Negligence and Economic Loss in England, Australia, Canada and New Zealand' (1994) 43 *International & Comparative Law Quarterly* 116.

[38] See N Jansen (ed), *The Development and Making of Legal Doctrine* (Cambridge, Cambridge University Press, 2010) 80–83, 165–76.

the same text took on different interpretations. The same is true of Article 1384 of the same code, which has been interpreted in radically different ways in France and in Belgium. These are examples of a pervasive phenomenon— legal norms require interpretation, and interpretation is the act of a legal community. There are debates or concerns which are significant in one community that are not significant in another. Some of the differences are about the ideas and values adopted in different legal communities; others, however, are about the institutional structures. For example, conceptions of a 'fair trial' differ where the paradigms of a criminal trial differ. The English common law tradition developed its rules and ideas around trial by jury—the adversarial presentation of evidence by prosecutor and defence to a previously uninvolved jury of lay people—and thus the distinct process of the collection of evidence and investigation by others (in recent centuries the police).[39] The French and many other civilian traditions developed around the active involvement of a member of the judiciary in the investigation process (the *juge d'instruction*), and the fundamental continuity between the investigation and the trial process—the evidence produced in the investigation is used as the basis for the trial (often only before other judges). The importance for the common lawyer of cross-examination at trial is perplexing to someone who is used to sorting out conflicts of testimony by a confrontation of witnesses before the investigating magistrate in a pre-trial hearing.[40] The criminal procedure example helps us to understand that it is not just the organisations (investigatory and trial bodies) and the procedures (rules of evidence) that form the context for the legal norm, but that there is an ethos, a set of values, which goes with the way in which they operate. We thus need to understand the legal norms as being nested within organisations, procedures and the ethos of values by which they are interpreted and applied.

It would be wrong to view legal institutions (organisations and groups of people) and their ethos or legal culture as rigidly fixed. Here it is useful to draw lessons from the work of Christoph Knill.[41] He compares the implementation of a number of EU policies in the environment and public information areas. His conclusion, however, is that a study of institutions does not provide a full explanation. In particular, he identifies a difference between a 'static' institution and one that is 'dynamic': in the latter case, change may be easier to take on board. There is a danger in much of the writing on 'legal tradition' or 'legal culture' that one treats these ideas as immutable, but they are in fact constantly evolving, so it is important to see particular features of a legal system within the context of that evolution. Furthermore, the bureau-

---

[39] See J Hodgson, *French Criminal Justice* (Oxford, Hart Publishing, 2005) ch 7; D Salas, 'The Role of the Judge' in M Delmas-Marty and JR Spencer, *European Criminal Procedures* (Cambridge, Cambridge University Press, 2002) 506–21.

[40] Indeed, the idea of the concentrated 'trial' moment is not really appropriate to describe the French system.

[41] C Knill, *The Europeanisation of National Administrations* (Cambridge, Cambridge University Press, 2001) esp 201–12.

cratic institution is not the only agent of change—there are other groups with power outside the legal system, such as lobby or pressure groups, which may influence the extent to which a particular reform seen as acceptable. (They exercise pressure in positive or negative directions to encourage change.) Thus, one needs to study the nexus of institutions, both public and private, within which legal institutions operate. Indeed, there is the question of how central the institution is to achieving change. Knill identifies three forms of Europeanisation: (i) through institutional compliance (making an institution change what it does); (ii) through changing domestic opportunity structures (eg by making certain restrictions illegal, though not requiring positive action from the state, there may arise pressures for change to take best advantage of the new liberalised market); and (iii) through framing domestic beliefs and expectations (giving a climate in favour of certain policies). Only the former sees the law as central to achieving the objective. Going back to the civil service example, the English system did not give a central place to law in setting the framework for how the civil service operates.

Knill's insights are important for comparative law. Much of what we study is in terms of legal rules or legal institutions. Knill's research suggests that the institutional specificity of each country needs to be understood and included in any account. That specificity is not limited to the legal institutions themselves, but must embrace the domestic context of pressures within which they operate. Why the English civil service law is so minimal can be explained not just by reference to civil service culture, but also by the role of parliament and unions. By contrast, the role of purges in the public service gives a greater political edge to French civil service relations.[42]

But Knill also helps us to understand the importance of studying the exercise of discretionary power (or Hart's 'power-conferring rules', if you prefer, to which Van Hoecke gives so much space). We need to understand the incentives to make decisions in particular ways and how the law serves to shape those incentives (not just dictate them). The context for the exercise of discretionary power may well be distinct from one system to another. At the same time, the lesson of Knill's third form of Europeanisation (changing the climate of opinion) is very important for breaking down the national specificity of legal approaches. The EU is not the only supranational influence. The Organization for Economic Co-operation and Development (OECD) is a major body for creating a climate of ideas. It undertakes studies and its national ministers agree statements of good practice, which are then influential. For example, practices of transparency in public administration has led to national legislation in a number of countries at different times. The OECD reports are presented as neutral, but often they argue that certain actions will be more 'efficient' or have produced benefits of 'modernisation'.[43] Hence, the OECD argues that

---

[42] On purges see V Wright, 'L'épuration du Conseil d'Etat en juillet 1879' (1972) *Revue d'histoire moderne et contemporaine* 621.

[43] See www.oecd.org especially on themes of public organisation and economic performance.

'Public sector modernisation is no longer an option, but a necessity. It will help governments respond to changing societal needs and maintain competitiveness in an uncertain international environment'.[44] The importance of these external institutional sources in changing the value climate in which national law operates is important. It provides justifiable common reference points to discussion of whether legal systems are converging on particular areas. It is justifiable because national ministers or civil servants are agreeing on policies at an international level and are then trying to implement them through legal and extralegal means when they get home.

VII. CONCLUSION: WHAT THEORY FOR COMPARATIVE LAW?

The suggestion in this chapter is that, at least to be helpful for comparative law, legal theory needs to provide an account of the institutions of the law within which Van Hoecke's communication of norms operates. Van Hoecke has given us some pointers to what a theory of the institutions of law would include, and this chapter has sought to develop from that basis.

The chapter takes for granted that the methodology for comparative research is concrete, problem based and involves 'immersion'. It is not rule focused, but seeks to understand the local context within which the problems handled by the law are shaped and operated. For this, one needs to study legal institutions both as organisations which have traditions and ways of handling problems and as bodies within which discretionary decisions are made under certain constraints and pressures. These institutions operate not just at one moment, but over time. As a result, any account has to examine the professions which ensure the persistence of institutions, and hand on the accumulated skills and knowledge. In this way, the law can continue to operate over time as a organisation which is able to provide distinctive solutions. However, the institutions need to be seen as potentially dynamic and open to external (often non-binding) influences, which may come from supranational organisations and non-legal institutions. Legal theory can offer us a framework within which to understand the dynamics of a legal system and how it operates the function of law as communication. Comparative law can then build on it by asking how those dynamics operate in the concrete situations of specific legal systems, and how those dynamics differ between legal systems.

---

[44] Publicity for its report 'Modernising Government—the Way Forward' (OECD, 2005).

16

Live and Let Die: An Essay Concerning Legal-Cultural Understanding

JØRN ØYREHAGEN SUNDE[1]

I. WHAT IT IS ALL ABOUT

LAWYERS EXERCISE POWER on behalf of the state by determining the rights and duties of the legal subjects. Legal method is an important instrument to avoid arbitrary use of this power. In a time of internationalisation of law, legal method must be supplied with legal-cultural knowledge and analysis to fulfil its task in the legal system. This chapter discusses how this can be done in practice.

First, I will explain how legal culture can be both a phenomenon and an instrument of legal analysis, and describe the character of the internationalisation of Norwegian law. Secondly, I will give an everyday example of the need for and actual use of a legal-cultural understanding of law for practising lawyers today. Thirdly, I will show why research on and communication of legal-cultural knowledge must be immediately applicable to law in action. Fourthly, I will attempt to give a manageable definition of and a clear-cut criterion for the kind of legal-cultural analysis law in action demands. All in all, my aim is to give life to a practical approach to legal culture, rather than attempt to become a well-versed insider of any legal-cultural dimension of the law.[2]

[1] I am much indebted to professors Per Andersen, Dirk Heirbaut and Dag Michalsen for their comments and corrections.
[2] See here K Lemmens, 'Comparative Law as an Act of Modesty: A Pragmatic and Realistic Approach to Comparative Legal Scholarship' in M Adams and J Bomhoff (eds), *Practice and Theory in Comparative Law* (Cambridge, Cambridge University Press, 2012) 302–25.

II. LEGAL CULTURE AS AN INSTRUMENT FOR ANALYSING LAW FOR EVERY PRACTISING LAWYER

Legal culture is a label we give characteristics of law not as it is defined, but rather how it is understood and applied in the practices of groups of the legal subjects. In Norway, law has been understood differently at different points in time. In 1274, it was understood as all of the rules that were applied to decide right and wrong action or non-action, and that was enforced by state institutions. In 1814, it was understood as legislated provisions. As a result, the rule of law was understood and practised differently in different times. This affected how the court system was organised, how law was produced, etc.

Legal culture is thus a social phenomenon. By studying and acquiring knowledge about this phenomenon, we can also use it an instrument to dissect, analyse and understand law. To understand law in this sense, as a product of legal culture, is no different than understanding law by examining its method. Legal method as an instrument to transform different kinds of legal material into legal rules is a phenomenon that can be detected, but that can also be cautiously used as an instrument to enhance this process.

In a time when the internationalisation of law, at least in Norway, is working its way to the same level of transnational law as in the High Middle Ages,[3] there is a great need for legal-cultural analysis. Norway became a part of the EU in legal affairs with the agreement concerning the European Economic Area with the EU in 1992.[4] This agreement came into force in 1994, and the European Convention on Human Rights became a part of Norwegian Law in 1999.[5] As a result, Norwegian law can be catagorised in three ways: law produced within Norwegian jurisdictional borders; law produced within the jurisdictional borders but based on sources produced outside these borders; and law produced outside Norwegian jurisdictional borders.

The first category is law based on filling the lacunas of, altering or rejecting existing Norwegian law without any treaty-based obligation to do so. Such law can be found in the revision planned in 2013 of the 2002 provision on child bullying,[6] or the Supreme Court decision of the same year on labour insurance.[7] The second category is law legislated or applied by Norwegian courts and administration, based on sources of law produced outside Norwegian jurisdictional borders, due to treaty-based obligations. Such a law is, for example, the Act on Product Liability of 1988,[8] based on an EU directive

---

[3] Norges offentlige utredninger (NOU) (Norwegian Public Reports) 2012: 2 Utenfor og innenfor (Oslo, Departementenes servicesenter, 2012) 135.

[4] Lov om gjennomføring i norsk rett av hoveddelen i avtale om Det europeiske økonomiske samarbeidsområdet (EØS) m.v. (Act on EEA in Norwegian Law) of 27 November 1992 no 109.

[5] Lov om styrking av menneskerettighetenes stilling i norsk rett (Act on Promoting Human Rights in Norwegian Law) of 21 May 1999 no 30.

[6] Lov om grunnskolen og den vidaregåande opplæringa (Act on the Primary, Secondary and Tertiary Education) of 17 July 1998 no 61, § 9a–3.

[7] Decision by the Norwegian Supreme Court of 21 October 2013, case no 2013/221.

[8] Lov om produktansvar (Act on Product Liability) of 23 December 1988 no 104.

of 1985.[9] The third category is law made and applied outside Norwegian juris-dictional borders with no formal direct effect on Norwegian law, but which in practice can still be used by the legal subject to predict what the law in action will be in the future. In a Norwegian context, this would be, for example, the decisions passed by the European Court of Justice (ECJ).[10]

We know that, until 2012, EU law influenced 9 per cent of all administra-tive decrees and 29 per cent of all Norwegian legislation passed by Parliament, even if only 2.5 per cent of the acts passed consisted solely of EU law.[11] Since EU law is incorporated through legislation, direct references to this source of law are found in only a few per cent of the Supreme Court decisions between 2000 and 2012.[12] The European Convention on Human Rights, on the other hand, left its mark on 15 per cent of all Supreme Court decisions between 2000 and 2012,[13] rather than on the legislation. The dark horse in the race for internationalisation of Norwegian law is the decisions passed by the public administration. There is reason to believe that the application of EU law makes administrative agencies the largest handler of Norwegian law produced within but based on sources of law produced outside Norwegian jurisdictional bor-ders. However, no data is available on how much of the total law application done by public administration is influenced by the internationalisation of law. I would nevertheless estimate that between 15 and 20 per cent of all Norwegian law in action today belongs either to the category of law produced within but based on sources produced outside Norwegian jurisdictional borders or the category of law produced outside Norwegian jurisdictional borders.[14]

The Norwegian Product Liability Act of 1988, based on an EU directive from 1985, has previously been used as an example of Norwegian law pro-duced outside Norwegian borders. There are noticeable differences between

---

[9] Council Directive, 85/374/EEC of 25 July 1985 on the approximation of the laws, regulations and administrative provisions of the Member States concerning liability for defective products.

[10] See, eg the decisions by the Norwegian Supreme Court published in *Norsk Rettstidende* (Oslo, Den Norske Advokatforening, 2011) 609–21 and in *Norsk Rettstidende* (Oslo, Den Norske Advokatforening, 2010) 944–46 for the direct effect of ECJ decisions on Norwegian law. Accord-ing to the EEA agreement, ECJ decisions have no effect in Norway, but this is then not the law in action.

[11] See NOU 2012:2: 127–31 and 882–84.

[12] An overview of cases where substantial EEA- and EU law has been discussed in the Nor-wegian Supreme Court 1994–2010 is given by HH Fredriksen, *EU/EØS-rett i norske domstoler* (Oslo, Europautredningen, 2011) 16–17, but see also 12–16.

[13] This number is based on a search for references to the European Human Rights Conven-tion and protocols, EU directives and the EEA agreement in Supreme Court decisions (including both appeals on procedure and on substantial law) from 2000 to 2010 in the legal database Lov-data (http://www.lovdata.no/). The part of the search concerning European human rights was conducted by Morten Nadim for his article 'Large and Small Systems—Development in argu-mentation in the Norwegian Supreme Court 1970–2010' [2014] *Retfærd* 1.

[14] See the discussion in House of Commons Library, 'How Much Legislation Comes from Europe?', research paper 10/62 (13 October 2010), available at http://www.parliament.uk/briefing-papers/RP10-62.

the Norwegian[15] and English[16] implementations of the EU directive on product liability.[17] This is not a sign of a reluctance to implement but, rather, a sign of legal-cultural decoding, and shows an awareness of certain characteristics in Norwegian and English tort and civil procedure laws that are due to legal culture. It is therefore an example of the legal-cultural decoding that is needed when applying law based on sources produced outside jurisdictional borders or law produced outside jurisdictional borders. In the case of Norway, the internationalisation of law has grown massively since 1988. In addition, legal-cultural decoding is done today not only by the legislator, but by all who practise law. Following is an example.

III. IMAGINE YOU VENTURE INTO A LEGAL-CULTURAL LANDSCAPE

Imagine you are a judge in the European Court of Human Rights (ECtHR) in Strasbourg in 2012. Your chamber receives one of the rather rare Norwegian cases, this time concerning retroactive legislation and protection of property.[18] The question at stake is: could the Norwegian Parliament issue an act that (i) de facto makes perpetual all temporary land lease contracts already entered into and, in addition, (ii) severely limits the lessor's right to link land rent to the market value of the leased land? You begin your preparation by reading selected parts of the Norwegian Supreme Court decisions from 2007 that finally decided the case nationally.[19]

The core legal question in the case as it appeared in the Norwegian court system was whether or not a law on land-leasing contracts was contrary to the Norwegian Constitution of 1814, and hence subject to judicial review. The first thing you notice is that this question was dealt with within the ordinary court system, simply because in Norway there is no constitutional court and few extraordinary courts.[20] This means that, at first, a single judge in one of the 66 first-level courts decided the case and performed the judicial review.[21] The case would next have been decided by three judges in one of the six appeal courts, if it was not appealed directly to the Supreme Court.

[15] http://www.lovdata.no/all/nl-19881223-104.html.

[16] Consumer Protection Act of 1987, http://www.legislation.gov.uk/ukpga/1987/43.

[17] This was the theme for the grand master thesis by E Mohn, 'Product Liability—Strictly Speaking—A Comparison of Norwegian and English Product liability, with Focus on the Concept of Strict Liability, the Development of this Legal Area and the EU's Influence, in a Legal Cultural Context, University of Bergen (2012, unpublished), supervised by the author of this article.

[18] European Court of Human Rights, *Case of Lindheim and Others v Norway*, application no 13221/08 and 2139/10, judgment 12 June 2012.

[19] *Norsk Retstidende* (Oslo, Den norske advokatforening, 2007) 1281–305 and 1306–08.

[20] The only extraordinary courts in the Norwegian court system are the 34 Land Dispute Courts and the Labour Court at the first level, and the five Land Dispute Courts dealing with facts, and not law, at the second level.

[21] There are several examples that acts have been found unconstitutional at this bottom level of the court hierarchy in Norway, eg *Norsk Retstidende* (Oslo, Den Norske Advokatforening, 2010) 1445–72.

The second thing you notice is that the ordinary courts are competent to perform a judicial review if there is a conflict between the Constitution and an Act of Parliament. Due to their political dimension, such cases are argued before all 20 judges in a plenary session when the case reaches the Supreme Court.

As you keep on reading the decisions from the Norwegian Supreme Court, you notice that there are explicit references to several sources of law. This is a feature of Norwegian legal culture that can be traced back at least to the mid-eighteenth century. The Constitution is treated as a living legal instrument, and hence as a source of law, as in the American constitutional tradition. There are also references to several single Acts of Parliament, a quite obvious source of law. There are, however, no references to codes, because the last code for Norway, issued for the Norwegian kingdom by the Danish-Norwegian king, dates from 1687,[22] and only six articles are still in force. There are also several references to preparatory works,[23] which are a source of law in Norway, as in all the Nordic countries. There are also several references to decisions by the Supreme Court itself, which is treated as precedent and is the second most important source of law. The same applies to decisions from the ECtHR, which in Norwegian law is treated as precedent, whether or not Norway is a party to the decisions.[24] The references to legal literature are few and, even if it is regarded as a source of law, it is of minor importance. That does not apply to considerations of fairness, which play a major role in the decision you read. For instance, in paragraphs 112 and 113 in the Supreme Court decision, you find a discussion of the retroactive effect of the act of Parliament. The argument is that, since the lessor could imagine that the government would one day regulate land-leasing contracts in a way that affected the lessor's right to negotiate the land rent, 'it must lie within the freedom granted to the legislator under Article 97 of the Constitution to regulate matters in this way' without the regulation being dismissed as retroactive, and hence unconstitutional and inapplicable in the case.[25] The discussion, then, is not on the principle of retroactive laws, but rather on fairness.

The vagueness of both the Norwegian Constitution of 1814 and the European Convention of Human Rights, and the specific character of the case law of the Norwegian Supreme Court and the ECtHR, leaves room for fairness arguments. There is, however, nothing extraordinary about the fairness arguments in this case, as they are a relevant source of law.[26] The Norwegian

---

[22] A code for the Danish kingdom was issued in 1683, and was model for the code for the Norwegian kngdom in 1687.

[23] The preparatory works consists of all the official documents that prepare the ground for a new piece of legislation.

[24] I Helland, *Rulings of the European Court of Human Rights as a Legal Instrument—a Comparison between German and Norwegian Law* (Bergen, Universitetet i Bergen, 2012) 411–12.

[25] ECtHR, *Case of Lindheim and Others v Norway*, judgment 12 June 2012 (15).

[26] 'Reelle hensyn' literally means 'actual considerations', and includes a whole group of different kinds of arguments, the function of which in Norwegian law today is to secure a fair

Supreme Court uses the fairness argument quite often, and makes explicit references to it surprisingly often. In Norwegian legal theory, this group of arguments is embedded in the legal source 'reelle hensyn', which is one of seven legal sources acknowledged in Norwegian law. Since 1996,[27] the Supreme Court has made explicit references to this legal source in 224 of the 2738 cases they have decided.[28] The annual average of such references is 13 of 161 cases, which is 8.2 per cent of the decisions passed every year.[29] In criminal cases, fairness arguments are used less frequently since the Norwegian Constitution of 1814, § 96 states the rule of law principle in criminal cases: 'reelle hensyn' are referred to in 49 of 1361 cases, which is 3.6 per cent. Since 1996, the Norwegian Supreme Court has made explicit references to fairness in 175 of 1377 civil cases, or 12.7 per cent of the time. Next to the abundance of legal sources explicitly referred to, the rather extensive use of fairness arguments, even to some extent in criminal cases, is a striking characteristic of Norwegian legal culture.

As you read the decisions of the Norwegian Supreme Court, and as a judge in the ECtHR you notice these characteristics of Norwegian law, to which a Norwegian lawyer would pay scant attention, you venture into a legal-cultural landscape in which you will remain throughout the case. This is seen by the fact that characteristics of Norwegian law such as juridical review or the abundance of legal sources are not questioned by the ECtHR. However, the judges on the Norwegian Supreme Court also ventured into a legal-cultural landscape in this case. Knowing that the cases could end up in Strasbourg, they based their argumentation partly on case law from the ECtHR, and they avoided the strangest element of the Norwegian culture, which is the open and explicit reference to fairness through references to 'reelle hensyn'.[30] The lawyers appearing before the ECtHR had also taken legal culture into consideration, and adjusted their argumentation by fitting fairness arguments into the balancing test, which they linked to the principle of proportionality so often exercised by the ECtHR. Hence, all professionals involved in this case ventured into a legal-cultural landscape, with the consequences this implies.

outcome of the case. See also I Helland and S Koch, 'Methodische Grundlagen der juristiscen Entcheidungsfindung im norwegischen Privatrecht' (2013) 3 *Zeitschrift für Europäisches Privatrecht* 610, which describes 'reelle hensyn' as 'verschiedene Würdigunsgeschichtpunkte, die oftmals wie reine Billigkeitswägungen mit Bezug auf den konkreten Fall wirken'.

[27] 1996 is chosen as a breaking point, since the criminal procedure was changed by law. Since 1996, the Norwegian Supreme Court has decided about an equal numbers of civil and criminal cases every year; prior to this, the court would decide more than three times the number of criminal cases.

[28] The statistics on references to 'reelle hensyn' as a legal argument by the Norwegian Supreme Court were produced by my assistant Haakon Skogstad, with some additions to the statistics added by my assistant Stine Idsø.

[29] In 1997, 1999, 2001, 2004 and 2007, the Norwegian Supreme Court made such explicit references to fairness in more than 10% of the cases it decided, while this was done in less than 5% of the cases in 2008 and 2010.

[30] G Mathisen, 'From Rendezvous to Relationship' in JØ Sunde and KE Skodvin (eds), *Rendezvous of European Legal Cultures* (Bergen, Fagbokforlaget, 2010) 203.

There are not many judges in the ECtHR, and the number of clerks preparing the cases is not large. The same goes for the Norwegian Supreme Court, and the number of Norwegian lawyers appearing before the ECtHR or other internationals tribunals. The case used as an example here is, however, only representative of the role of legal culture in European law today, not the extent to which it plays that role. As already stated, a fair estimate, though still only an estimate, is that 15–20 per cent of law practised in Norway today has its origin in sources produced outside Norwegian borders. European human rights are one such source, not only as they are expressed in the European Convention on Human Rights, but especially as they are developed by the ECtHR. Even more important is EU law, both the directives and the case law from the ECJ, since the Agreement on the European Economic Area from 1992 gives Norway a status that resembles an EU Member State where legal affairs are concerned. To this we must, however, also add UN and WTO law as (minor) contributors to the internationalisation of Norwegian law.

These sources of law are produced outside Norwegian borders, but applied within and turned into law in action here. This is done by the courts, as in the case we have just studied. With their approximately 79,000 decisions in the first instance, 3,000 in the second instance and 150 in the Supreme Court as the third and last instance,[31] the courts are, however, actually the least important contributors in turning law produced outside the Norwegian borders into law in action within the borders. As noted, the champion of the internationalisation of law in Norway, as in the rest of Europe in the area of Eurolegalism,[32] is the administration.[33] Important fields of Norwegian law, such as competition law and labour law, are today almost pure EU law, and sources of an endless flow of administrative decisions. Administrative decisions in Norway are one of seven acknowledged sources of law. Regardless of the fact that they possess this status, however, such decisions are law in action, determining the legal rights and duties of the citizens. This means that everyone from the lawyers working in public administration in local counties, to the Ministry of Justice and Public Security, to the lawyers employed in local, regional, national and international businesses and to the judges in courts at all levels apply law originating from legal sources produced outside Norwegian borders. Hence, they are all spending time every week in a legal-cultural

---

[31] The number of court decisions is taken from the Norwegian Courts Administration's Annual Report for 2012, http://aarsmelding.domstol.no/. The number of cases dealt with by the first instance includes approximately 1100 cases decided by the Land Dispute Courts and approximately 40 cases decided by the Labour Court.

[32] See RD Kelemen, 'Eurolegalism and the European Legal Field' in A Vauchez and B de Witte (eds), *Lawyering Europe—European Law as a Transnational Social Field* (Oxford, Hart Publishing, 2013) 245; see also CC Eriksen, *The European Constitution, Welfare States and Democracy—the Four Freedoms vs National Administrative Discretion* (London, Routledge, 2012) 2–3, 169–73.

[33] There are no administrative courts in Norway, and administrative disputes are dealt with by the administration, often with a possibility for appeal to the courts.

landscape even though they are not elite lawyers in the ECtHR, the Norwegian Supreme Court, or other international or national institutions.

Knowledge of legal culture cannot tell them exactly where the legal path runs through the landscape; that is still a question of legal method. Knowledge of legal culture can, however, give them the ability to read the landscape, in order to see what to take into consideration when seeking the legal path. Legal-cultural knowledge is needed when law produced outside national borders is intended to be reframed in a new cultural context before it is applied, in a way that achieves the flexibility that secures the same effect under various conditions. This is the case, for instance, with some EU law, the major source of the internationalisation of Norwegian law. As stressed by Mark Lawson:

> In a European polity made up of different national cultures, invoking complex regulatory structures, no law can stand independently of the cultural and functional context into which it is to be applied . . . The diversity of national polities has often led to attempts to provide the national level with some flexibility in incorporating EU law obligations in the domestic realm, where new cultural and political factors may require rules to be re-framed precisely in order to give force to their original meaning.[34]

In this situation, legal-cultural knowledge is of great importance when discovering the legal path in the legal-cultural landscape. At other times, the intention is for the law produced to be applied in the same manner in different countries. In other words, the aim is that legal culture shall have no effect on the application. To apply the law in the same manner, it must, however, be understood in the same way. This implies, first, that the norms are not only translated, but also legal-culturally decoded by the applier, and, secondly, that the manner in which they are actually applied is legal-culturally recoded to make it possible for the producer and/or the keeper of the norms to evaluate the application. Hence, legal-cultural knowledge is an essential instrument in the reduction of the role of legal culture.

IV. IMAGINE PRACTISING LAW IN A LEGAL-CULTURAL LANDSCAPE

Imagine you are a recent graduate in law, working for the Norwegian Immigration Appeals Board, a board that decided over 18,700 cases in 2012.[35] In every single case, both Norwegian law based on sources produced outside Norwegian jurisdictional borders and Norwegian law produced outside Norwegian jurisdictional borders are of relevance. It is a long way from your

---

[34] M Dawson, 'Soft Law and the Rule of Law in the EU' in A Vauchez and B de Witte (eds), *Lawyering Europe—European Law as a Transnational Social Field* 224, 238.
[35] http://une.no/Statistikk/Behandlede-saker/.

desk in an open office landscape to the office of the experienced lawyers who work as judges in the ECtHR in Strasbourg. Nevertheless, you are in the same situation: you have to venture into a legal-cultural landscape, and you do so every day. Further, you engage in this adventure as a practising lawyer, not as a scholar; you have, on the one hand, a duty to understand the law relevant for the case and, on the other, limited knowledge and time at your disposal.

It could be claimed that, next to scholars, only the elite jurists in the national ministries of justice and the supreme courts need to possess such legal-cultural knowledge. However, the internationalisation of politics, which is an important backdrop to the internationalisation of law, has not yet produced the kind of political bodies that can make international codes of law that could (at least in theory) reduce the amount of discretion needed under the application of law. In addition, variation in languages makes it impossible to apply a legal method centred on deduction from terminology, and no alternative legal method has been developed that enables us to identify, link and deduce with certainty from a body of provisions regardless of legal terminology, to (again, at least in theory) reduce the amount of discretion needed under the application of law. With an increased internationalisation of law, it is instead the courts and administrative organs that to an increasingly greater degree produce and unify law through their actual practice. This is the same on both the international and national levels.

This is a worrying fact. As a citizen, I am willing to render a judge in the ECtHR the power to decide legal issues complicated by the legal-cultural factor. I am willing to do so because the judge is experienced, and he is surrounded by a staff of able clerks. The same goes for the judges on the Norwegian Supreme Court. However, the newly graduated lawyer on the Norwegian Immigrant Appeals Board is in quite a different situation. However, the matters decided there and in other administrative organs are no less important, and at times perhaps even more important, than those decided by the ECtHR.

This shows that, for practising lawyers, such as the new graduate on the Norwegian Immigrant Appeals Board, legal culture is not metaphysics, but a part of his everyday work, influencing the law in action produced, just as is legal methodology. In Norway, this situation has come about because the internationalisation of law gave law a legal-cultural dimension. Before the internationalisation of Norwegian law from the 1990s on, legal methodology had been an instrument to unify law and create equality before the law and legal certainty. Now legal methodology must be given a new dimension that matches the dimension law has been given. The legal-cultural model is an instrument that enables us to amend a legal-cultural dimension when studying and practising law.

V. LEGAL CULTURE AND THE PRACTICE OF
LAW IN NORWAY SINCE THE 1990S

The whole idea of operating with the term 'legal culture' is the acknowledgement that law is more than words. A pressing question is then: where do you stop if the aim is to go beyond? Mark Van Hoecke and Mark Warrington deal with this problem in their 1999 article 'Legal Cultures, Legal Paradigms and Legal Doctrine: Towards a New Model or Comparative Law'. In the outset of the article, they state that '[o]ver the past decade especially, many writers have emphasised the need for a broad approach to the subject of comparative law, thereby moving it beyond the 'law as rules' approach of traditional legal doctrine'.[36] Among the different approaches to law as more than rules, they choose the legal-cultural approach. They then go on to ask:

> How may we grasp 'legal culture'? What makes one 'legal culture' different from another? It is easy to agree that law is more than just statuary rules and court decisions. But how do we determine, describe and compare the specific way in which values, practices and concepts are integrated into the operation of legal institutions and interpretation of legal texts?[37]

The authors not only raise the question, but set out to answer it. They do so by, among other things, continuing the line of thought Franz Wieacker puts forth in his article 'Foundations of European Legal Culture',[38] and of Konrad Zweigert and Hein Kötz in their *An Introduction to Comparative Law* (though these discuss legal families and not legal culture), by defining and investigating a group of elements that play a key role in the character of a legal culture.[39] In doing so, Van Hoecke and Warrington created a basis for legal-cultural analysis,[40] and opened up for a concrete approach to legal culture at a time when legal culture brought about by the internationalisation of law is no longer a pressing matter merely for scholars and elite lawyers, but for every practising lawyer.[41]

---

[36] M Van Hoecke and M Warrington, 'Legal Culture, Legal Paradigms and Legal Doctrine: Towards a New Model for Comparative Law' (1998) 47 *International Comparative Law Quarterly* 495.

[37] Van Hoecke and Warrington, ibid 513.

[38] F Wieacker, 'Foundations of European Legal Culture (1990) 38 *American Journal of Comparative Law* 19.

[39] K Zweigert and H Kötz, *An Introduction to Comparative Law*, 3rd edn (Oxford, Oxford University Press, 1998) 67–72.

[40] When dealing with how to conduct legal-cultural studies, this article is not mentioned by either R Cotterrell, 'Comparative Law and Legal Culture' in M Reimann and R Zimmermann (eds), *The Oxford Handbook of Comparative law* (Oxford, Oxford University Press, 2006) 710–37 or D Nelken, 'Legal Culture' in JM Smits (ed), *Elgar Encyclopedia of Comparative Law* (Cheltenham, Edward Elgar, 2006) 372–81.

[41] See A Vauchez, 'Introduction. Euro-lawyering, Transnational Social Fields and European Polity-Building' in A Vauchez and B de Witte (eds), *Lawyering Europe—European Law as a Transnational Social Field* 1.

As we have seen, an operationalising approach to legal culture is more necessary today than even in 1999. My ambition is to follow the same line as Van Hoecke and Warrington. The first step is to define legal culture as ideas and expectations of law made operational by institutional or institution-like practices.[42] This definition is designed to capture the interplay between institutions and intellectual structures. To obtain detailed knowledge of this interplay, each structure can be split up into legal-cultural elements. There are several such elements, but in my research and teaching I have chosen to focus especially on the six that have proven most useful when conducting legal-cultural analysis: (1) conflict resolution, (2) norm production, (3) idea of justice, (4) legal method, (5) professionalisation and (6) internationalisation.[43] It must be noted that the following treatment of the institutions and intellectual structures, and the six legal-cultural elements, is just a preliminary sketch.

The institutional structure of a legal culture, in short, comprises the institutions where law is shaped through different practices.[44] The most basic institutions are those that settle conflicts, simply because conflict resolution (1) is society's most basic demand of its legal system. It is through conflict resolution that peace and security can dominate society. Norm production (2) is an activity that has gradually been at least partly emancipated from conflict resolution. Originally, legal norms were produced by deciding cases; each time a conflict was resolved, a norm was produced. As time went by, these norms were reused in similar cases, and case law appeared. Case law could, however, also be systemised and developed by a lawmaker, who then could go on to legislate independently from court practice and, by doing so, create a new institutionalised practice within law. The last move in this process would be codifications of law. It is in this way that legislation became a dominant method of producing legal norms.

The production and application of legal norms does not take place in an intellectual vacuum; rather, there are several intellectual factors that dictate how norms are made and applied. The most basic is the idea of justice (3). As with conflict resolution, justice is a basic demand directed towards law. Conflicts resolved arbitrarily, for instance by drawing straws, are better than unsolved conflicts, and thus this has been a means of solving conflicts in desperate situations. However, conflict resolutions that are considered just have a much higher degree of legitimacy than those that are considered unjust or arbitrary, and will therefore be accepted more often and extensively. It must

---

[42] This account is based on the more detailed account of the subject in J Øyrehagen Sunde, 'Champagne at the Funeral—An Introduction to Legal Culture' in Sunde and Skodvin, above n 30, 11–28.

[43] For an actual use of the model for a historical analysis see J Øyrehagen Sunde, 'Daughters of God and Counsellors of the Judges of Men—A Study in Changes in the Legal Culture in the Norwegian Realm in the High Middle Ages' in S Brink and L Collinson (eds), *New Approaches to Early Law in Scandinavia* (Turnhout, Brepols, 2014) 135–83.

[44] In non-state societies these institutions are extremely weak, but might still, with terminological generosity, be called institutions.

be kept in mind that what is considered just is not constant, but varies from place to place and time to time. Further, the idea of justice might well vary between legal fields. Nevertheless, there will be a dominating idea of justice, dependent on the time, place or field of law. This will be the point of departure when considering what is just.

To make an idea of justice operative—that is, to solve a specific case in accordance with an idea of justice—a legal methodology (4) is required. A legal method is simply the manner in which ideas of justice are transformed from values and various sources of law into legal rules used to settle a specific conflict. One task for a legal method is to create a fairly tight framework for the otherwise uncertain process of going from legal raw material to refined legal rule, making it intersubjective.

While lawyers and non-lawyers might share an idea of justice, legal method appears with an increased professionalisation (5) of law, and is more and more specialised. First, professionalisation means that those who handle law on behalf of society spend more and more of their time on legal issues. Secondly, it means that there are special criteria to fulfil before one can be trusted with the position of handling law.[45] All kinds of professionalisation have the same effect: they afford lawyers an internal view of law. This implies that good law in the eyes of the professional becomes more and more a question of internal correlation, while good law for the non-professional is still a question of justice in the individual case.

Internationalisation (6) is used here in relation to all kinds of influence of legal technologies and norms produced outside jurisdictional borders. As society changes, law must change to be able to fulfil its obligation in conflict resolution. Only in exceptional cases can law be changed based on mere experiment; normally, legal reforms are based on experience. The main sources for deriving knowledge from experience are history and comparative law. The extensive use of comparative law when reforming law makes law a social and cultural nomad. In a Norwegian context, law has continuously been influenced by legal technologies and norms from outside the jurisdictional borders that exist at any given time, with the period 1945–85 as the low point. With change as the reason for this continuous internationalisation, it is no surprise that the internationalisation has contributed to changing how law is perceived inside the borders it has crossed.

This preliminary and sketch-like dissection of legal culture illustrates that such culture has both an institutional and an intellectual structure. The institutional structure consists of the institutions settling conflicts and producing norms, whereas the intellectual structure consists of the ideas and expectations that shape the law. This is the heart and soul of a legal culture, and the result of the dissection could be used as a model. Even though a model is never

---

[45] Such criteria can be a good reputation, practical legal experience or a legal education.

more than the mere shadow of what it is supposed to reflect, this model of legal culture can be used as a point of departure for legal-cultural analysis.

As an example of such actual use, we can imagine the judge in the ECtHR during the preparations for the case concerning property rights and land leasing in Norway in 2012. He asks his clerk why the discussion in the Norwegian Supreme Court concerning retroactive laws is more about fairness than about principles of law. To investigate and communicate the complex answer to the question, the clerk applies the legal-cultural model. He first explains the structure of courts in Norway, the core of the present system of conflict resolution. As is evident from the case, the Norwegian Supreme Court is producing precedent on top of a very stringent hierarchy of courts and is therefore able to unify considerations of fairness in Norwegian law. By doing so, it makes them rather predictable. The clerk then turns to norm production, and explains that the fact that there is no effective code in force in Norway has given room for a variety of legal sources, fairness being one, to fill the loopholes of law when there is no system from which to deduce.

The clerk goes on to inform the judge that the expectation in Norway that law must be fair means that predictability must often yield when the result is unfairness, resulting in an idea of justice where predictability is where you start and fairness is often where you end. That is made possible by a legal method with the aforementioned variety of legal sources, and the role of fairness among them. This is not that surprising, the clerk continues, taking into consideration the role of professionalisation in Norwegian law. Fifty years ago there were still only nine ordinary professors, with 90 students in law graduating annually, meaning that the professional element of a more predictability-focused method and a more rigid and systematic legal method never had a large audience in Norway. Finally, the clerk says, the international input to Norwegian law has been altered and applied to fit these expectations, as the transformation of EU Directive 85/374 to a Norwegian act on product liability from 1988 illustrates. The judge then nods and is satisfied, though not because he now has a complete understanding of Norwegian legal culture; far from it—the clerk has given a very superficial answer to a question of great complexity. But he now knows enough to get on with the work on the case without being distracted by all its particularities, and to expand his knowledge, if necessary. That is one function of the legal-cultural model.

VI. IMAGINE THE FUTURE FOR LEGAL CULTURE AS AN ANALYTICAL INSTRUMENT

There is a great need for legal-cultural knowledge in a world where a peripheral country such as Norway faces a situation where probably between 15 and 20 per cent of the law in action originates from legal sources produced outside its borders. In this situation, it is useful to operationalise legal-cultural knowledge and add it as a new dimension to legal method, in the same way national law is given a new dimension by including law based on legal sources produced outside jurisdictional borders and law produced outside such borders. We must give life to a practical approach to legal culture, and abandon the ambition of becoming a well-versed insider of any legal-cultural dimension of the law at stake.

17

Policy and Politics in Contract Law Reform in Japan

SOUICHIROU KOZUKA AND LUKE NOTTAGE[1]

I. INTRODUCTION

C ONTRACT LAW HAS traditionally been a popular subject for comparative law scholarship. It generated, for example, the monumental study into contract formation, led by Professor Rudolf Schlesinger at Cornell University in the 1960s, which in turn developed into the search for 'the common core of European private law' centred on the University of Trento.[2] A related development in comparative law methodology is Professor Rodolfo Sacco's theory of 'legal formants'—aspects of statute law, case law, scholarly commentary and any other aspects that lead to a specific result being achieved within a particular legal system. One of Sacco's central insights was that the relative weight of a particular legal formant is complex, sometimes borrowing from another formant within a particular country, and frequently evolving. Another insight is that a legal formant in one country (such as a legislature) often borrows from a legal formant in another (such as a codification or statutory enactment), which can in turn perturb the interaction of legal formants in the receiving country.[3]

Sacco's methodological approach opens up a rich field of comparative research into the complicated interactions among institutions charged with

---

[1] A longer version of this chapter, providing more details on the content of Japan's contract law reform proposals rather than the process and interest groups involved, is available at ssrn. com/author=2360343. We thank Prof Maurice Adams for suggesting the fruitful parallels with the comparative law methodology developed by Prof Rodolfo Sacco.

[2] See www.jus.unitn.it/dsg/common-core/approach.html and (comparing other methodological approaches in recent private law harmonisation debates) L Nottage, 'Convergence, Divergence, and the Middle Way in Unifying or Harmonising Private Law' (2004) 1 *Annual of German and European Law* 166.

[3] R Sacco, 'Legal Formants: A Dynamic Approach to Comparative Law (Installment I of II)' (1991) 39 *American Journal of Comparative Law* 1, especially 21–26, 30–34; R Sacco, 'Legal Formants: A Dynamic Approach to Comparative Law (Installment II of II)' (1991) 39 *American Journal of Comparative Law* 343, 394–401.

enacting legislation, the judiciary, legal academics and other institutions (such as law firms, and even businesspeople who actually exchange contract terms or resolve disputes),[4] which can influence how legal issues are resolved in fact. However, the main applications have been to determine how already given statutory provisions, judgments or scholarly interpretations play out in practice across different countries.[5] Less attention has been paid to how such legal formants interact to generate new legal norms. Yet this focus helps detect the relative power and specific interests associated with different groups within a particular legal system.

This chapter adopts the latter approach, concentrating on Japan in the context of its now well-advanced proposals for the first comprehensive revision of contract law provisions since enactment of its Civil Code in 1896.[6] The approach enables us to analyse the process of new norms being generated as contests over the formation of legal formants within one country. Such contests may be affected by some institutional settings: for example, the strong role of (seconded) judges in the official reform discussions supporting the proposals that provide for significant scope for discretionary application of some key principles of contract law. The process and its institutional backgrounds, in turn, may suggest that the new Code provisions are likely to be applied by the judiciary rather differently from similar provisions found in international instruments, which itself implies the existence of legal formants behind the provisions seemingly common to other countries. The following analysis of the Japanese situation should also be instructive in considering how contract law reform processes may evolve in other countries, although of course the legal formants there (such as the roles played by the legislature or legal academics compared to judges) may prove to be very different.

Large-scale contract law reform in Japan started as an (ostensibly) academic project in 2006, and has been officially considered by a working group of the Legislative Council (*hosei shingikai* or LC) under the aegis of the Ministry of Justice (MoJ) since October 2009.[7] Despite the historic political turnover in September 2009, with the Democratic Party of Japan (DPJ) taking power after almost uninterrupted rule by the Liberal Democratic Party (LDP) since 1955, the principles of the private draft revisions derived from the lengthy academic project on contact law have remained largely unchanged. The return to power of the LDP in December 2012 made little difference either. Apparently, contract law is too technical an agenda for political initiative to exert significant influence.

---

[4] L Nottage, 'Planning and Renegotiating Long-Term Contracts in New Zealand and Japan: An Interim Report on an Empirical Research Project' [1997] *New Zealand Law Review* 482.
[5] See, eg Sacco, 'Legal Formants (Installment II of II)', above n 3 350–58.
[6] H Ishikawa, 'Codification, Decodification, and Recodification of the Japanese Civil Code' (2013) 10 *University of Tokyo Journal of Law and Politics* 61, 63–64.
[7] See www.moj.go.jp/ENGLISH/ccr/CCR_00001.html.

On the other hand, particularly among legal professionals, there has been much politicking over the contract law reform process. Experienced lawyers in practice—especially in small law firms—have opposed changing the contract law rules that they are familiar with, while bureaucrats at the MoJ (including judges seconded by the Supreme Court of Japan) have tried to produce some elements of reform after many years of deliberations. Thus, this chapter will suggest that contract law reform is largely unaffected by macropolitics but is quite strongly influenced by micropolitics, possibly because the contest over the legal formants is more a subject for the latter than for the former.

We also briefly explore this tension in the context of other law reform initiatives in Japan as well as abroad. There are significant parallels particularly with the EU,[8] where academic leadership coalesces with bureaucratic incentives to promote comprehensive contract law reforms, even when the legal profession and the business sector remain quite lukewarm. This comparative perspective also offers insights for the prospects of the Australian government's discussion paper released in April 2012, investigating the pros and cons of undertaking various types of contract law reforms in Australia.[9]

II. JAPAN'S CIVIL CODE REFORM PROJECT

A. The Process

A driving force behind Japan's ongoing contract law reform process has been Takashi Uchida, who resigned in 2007 as Professor of Civil Law at the University of Tokyo in order to lead the LC's working group now charged with recommending specific reforms. At the first working group meeting, one member reportedly suggested that deliberations should proceed 'without paying too much attention to "the Basic Policy for the Law of Obligation Reform" (draft proposals by [the] Japanese Civil Code (Law of Obligations) Reform Commission)' because it had been confirmed that the working group's deliberations should start 'from zero'.[10] However, the draft proposals (DP) of that semi-private Reform Commission (RC),[11] along with a detailed five-volume commentary written by its members (the Basic Policy),[12] were clearly intended to frame the subsequent debate in the formal working group arena.

---

[8] See, eg J Rutgers, 'European Competence and a European Civil Code, a Common Frame of Reference or an Optional Instrument' in A Hartkamp, M Hesselink, E Hondius, C Mak and CE du Perron (eds), *Towards a European Civil Code* (Alphen aan den Rijn, Kluwer, 2011) 311–32.

[9] See www.ag.gov.au/Consultations/Pages/ReviewofAustraliancontractlaw.aspx.

[10] See www.moj.go.jp/content/000056871.pdf, 4.

[11] Available in English at www.shojihomu.or.jp/saikenhou/English/draftproposals.html.

[12] Civil Code (Law of Obligations) Reform Commission, *Shokai: Saikenho Kaisei no Kihon Hoshin [Introduction: The Basic Policy in Reforming the Law of Obligations]* (Tokyo, Shojihomu, 2009). See also generally A Kamo, 'Crystallization, Unification, or Differentiation? The Japanese Civil Code (Law of Obligations) Reform Commission and Basic Reform Policy (Draft Proposals)' (2010) 24 *Columbia Journal of Asian Law* 171.

Uchida had been the primary force behind the establishment and lengthy deliberations of the RC. It had 35 members—almost all professors, which is one reason why Uchida refers to it as a private or academic study group.[13] (Another reason is that the meetings of the group did not take place in the MoJ and were not funded by it or other government sources—as explained in Section III.D below.) However, the RC did end up with Uchida as an official of the MoJ, after he resigned from the University of Tokyo, taking a five-year appointment as a senior advisor to the MoJ's Headquarters for Reform of Business-related Basic Legislation from October 2008. The Commission also included one official throughout its 260 meetings held from October 2006 to April 2009 (namely Takeo Tsutsui, a judge seconded to the MoJ by the Supreme Court of Japan), as well as a succession of shorter-term nominees from the MoJ (ending in Joji Dando, another seconded judge). Both were later appointed to the MoJ's formal working group, along with 13 of the 32 professors from the RC (including Uchida).

Two other (more obviously) private study groups were formed in response to the MoJ's announcement in 2006 that it was considering initiating a formal review of the Civil Code's provisions on contract law. The largest was led by Masanobu Kato, a prolific professor of civil law who retired to Sophia University in Tokyo from Nagoya University. Although four of his group's 21 professors were subsequently appointed to the LC's working group, two of those four were also members of the RC anyway. Kato was one of eight members of the 21 professors who also served on the RC, but he was not among the four from his study group subsequently appointed to the working group, even though he had been Uchida's senior (*sempai*) at graduate school at the University of Tokyo Law Faculty. Kato has become an increasingly vocal critic of Japan's present contract law reform project.[14]

The MoJ's working group was formally established in October 2009, six months after the RC's Basic Policy was released—and just one month after the LDP lost power in a general election. The LC is Japan's main legislative reform body, with various subcommittees or working groups, depending on the area of law, though each main ministry has its own law reform council and the LC's operations rely heavily on part-time appointments of law pro-

---

[13] T Uchida, 'Contract Law Reform in Japan and the UNIDROIT Principles' (2011) *Uniform Law Review* 705, 708–09; see also T Uchida, *Saikenho no Shin-jidai—'Saikenho Kaisei no Kihon Hoshin' no Gaiyo [A New Era for the Law of Obligations: An Overview of the 'Basic Plan for Reforming the Law of Obligations']* (Tokyo, Shoji Homu, 2009) 36–48. Of the 33 professors, 26 were civil law scholars (including Uchida), five were commercial law scholars and two were civil procedure scholars. See the list in Appendix A of the longer online version of this chapter.

[14] M Kato, *Minpo (Saikenho) Kaisei [Reform of the Civil Code (Law of Obligations)]* (Tokyo, Nihonhoryonsha, 2011). For a list of members of his study group see Appendix C of the longer online version of this chapter.

fessors.[15] The LC's Working Group on the Civil Code (Law of Obligations) comprised 37 core members:[16]

- 18 professors (all professors of law, including 13 from the previous RC);
- four judges;
- six officials (comprising Uchida, a former professor; four judges seconded by the Supreme Court to the MoJ; and a sixth official in the Cabinet Legislative Bureau (*naikaku hosei kyoku*), also a seconded judge);[17]
- four practising lawyers (*bengoshi*, one each from the four largest bar associations in Japan);
- three nominees from the business sector (including two in-house counsel); and
- one specialist each in consumer and labour union affairs.

As an official law reform body, and in contrast to the RC, summaries of views expressed at the working group's meetings were subsequently made publically available.[18] As with draft primary and secondary legislation, it has also provided opportunities for 'public comment'. Deliberations have taken longer than envisaged, partly because of the 'triple disasters' that struck northeastern Japan on 11 March 2011,[19] but also by some unexpectedly intractable discussions over contract law principles. Nonetheless, the working group issued an Interim Summary of Issues (*ronten seiri*) in April 2011 and an Interim Report (*chukan shian* or IR) on 26 February 2013.[20] A Final Report is due by early 2014, and a Bill may be introduced into Parliament later that year.

B. The Substance of the Proposals

The semi-private RC's detailed DP, released in 2009, in places only slightly modified or simply rephrased the current text of the Code. However, it also recommend some substantial changes, including:[21]

---

[15] On the LC and other Councils within Japan's very 'vertically divided administrative system' see Ishikawa, above n 6, 75–76.

[16] For a list of the working group's members see Appendix B of the longer online version of this chapter.

[17] The Bureau advises the government on the constitutionality of draft legislation or other technical legal issues. Ishikawa, above n 6, 76 mentions the view that the Bureau 'practically monopolizes the authority of official interpretation of the Constitution, and [Japan's] extreme judicial passivism strongly depends on the bureaucratic power and capability' of the Bureau.

[18] See, eg www.moj.go.jp/ENGLISH/ccr/CCR_00002.html.

[19] See generally, eg R Samuels, *3.11: Disaster and Change in Japan* (New York, Cornell University Press, 2013); S Butt, H Nasu and L Nottage (eds), *Asia-Pacific Disaster Management: Comparative and Socio-legal Perspectives* (Berlin, Springer, 2014).

[20] The Interim Report is available (in Japanese), with a helpful summary (*gaiyo-tsuki*) and detailed Supplementary Explanations (*hosoku setsumei*), at www.moj.go.jp/shingi1/shingi04900184.html.

[21] Kamo, above n 12.

- codifying the unwritten but generally accepted principles of the Civil Code;
- elaborating the principle of good faith in relation to contracts;
- discarding the idea that 'initial impossibility' makes a contract null and void;
- adopting a unitary concept of 'nonperformance' instead of three categories of default (nonperformance, delay in performance and imperfect performance), as well as departing from a fault-based contractual liability system;
- limiting the scope of damages from nonperformance by foreseeability rather than by adequate 'causal link' (*soto inga kankei*);
- allowing the avoidance of a contract when there is serious misperformance, whether the debtor is liable or not;
- simplifying the prescription regime;
- requiring all assignments of receivables to be filed in order to be effective vis-à-vis third parties;
- integrating the Consumer Contracts Act, and the parts on commercial contracts in the Commercial Code, into the Civil Code; and
- considering the possibility of abandoning the influence of the 'Pandekten' system (German-style codification), involving the general provisions (*Allgemeiner Teil*) being set out in the first part of Japan's Civil Code.

The list suggests that a large part of the DP proposed giving explicit expression to legal formants that already exist in the Japanese law of contracts but have remained largely uncodified. Such unwritten legal formants include well-established case law and, to a lesser extent, foreign and international contract law principles supported by a majority of academics. It may worth noting that the prevailing view in Japan affirms the status of court precedents as a source of law, despite the fact that Japan largely still follows the continental European civil law tradition.[22] Further, the study of foreign laws has always had significant influence on the development of Japanese law.

Although phrased as a 'Basic Policy' (*kihon hoshin*) for the Civil Code reforms, the DP and their commentary reveal a tension.[23] One underlying policy seems to be consensualism. This was mainly introduced under the influence of the common law tradition, mediated by way of international instruments (in particular, the UN Convention on Contracts for the International Sale of Goods, or CISG).[24] A strict view of consensualism adopts the 'classical' view of contract law[25] as serving to enforce what the parties have promised to each

---

[22] Matsumoto, 'Adjusting an "Imported" or "Received" Law: An Approach from "Precedent" in Japanese Law' in E Hondius (ed), *Precedent and the Law* (Brussels, Bruylant, 2007).

[23] S Kozuka, 'Project for a Reform of the Contract Law in Japan and its Impact on Franchise Agreements', available at papers.ssrn.com/sol3/papers.cfm?abstract_id=2408038.

[24] Acceded to in 2008: see generally H Sono, 'Japan's Accession to the CISG: The Asia Factor' (2008) 25 *Zeitschrift für Japanisches Recht/Journal of Japanese Law* 195; N Kashiwagi, 'Accession by Japan to the Vienna Sales Convention (CISG)' (2008) 25 *Zeitschrift für Japanisches Recht/Journal of Japanese Law* 207.

[25] See generally I Macneil, 'Adjustment of Long-Term Economic Relations under Classical, Neoclassical and Relational Contract Law' (1978) 72 *Northwest University Law Review* 854; L

other. Consensualism was reflected in the proposed new system of liability for misperformance, replacing Japanese law's traditional 'fault-based system' that examines both an 'objective element' (non-performance) and a 'subjective element' (intention to breach or fault) before affirming the debtor's liability.

Yet the DP are sometimes inclined toward judicial intervention, aimed at regulating contracts fairly. One proposal was for some rules in the Consumer Contracts Act 2000 to be adopted as more general rules applicable also to contracts between businesses. It even went so far as to propose a list of unfair terms applicable to all contracts, besides the more comprehensive list for consumer contracts.[26] These proposals apparently presumed a guiding policy that the contracts must be sufficiently regulated through judicial intervention.

The IR of February 2013 lists numerous proposed amendments under 47 headings, also lined up largely in the order of the current Civil Code. The LC's working group generally accepted the RC's recommendations regarding restatements of well-established case law and other general principles. A 'loose consensualism' (or 'neoclassical' theory of contract)[27] has also largely survived. For example, the seller's strict liability for latent defects (*kashi tampo sekinin*) shall no longer be a special type of liability, but rather will generate certain remedies based on the concept of the seller's misperformance.[28] Yet various proposed amendments turn on 'the meaning of the contract' (*keiyaku no shushi*), for example regarding claims for specific performance, or 'the aim of the contract' (*keiyaku no mokuteki*), for example regarding avoidance of the contract after a serious breach. This opens scope for judicial intervention, and the IR also proposes various protections for weaker parties. For example, going beyond the DP, the IR proposes that a clause in a standard contract that the other party cannot reasonably anticipate ('surprising terms') shall not be binding as part of the agreement.[29]

The strong parallels between the DP and the IR proposals are unsurprising, given the timeline and overlapping membership of the RC and the working group, respectively, outlined above. However, some of the RC's more ambitious proposals were frustrated. The IR did not make even tentative suggestions to revise the general structure of the Civil Code, or to directly incorporate many provisions from the Consumer Contracts Act or the Commercial Code. Other DP suggestions met resistance from practising lawyers and were withdrawn before the IR was published. For example, the RC proposed replacing the fault-based system with a distinction between risks undertaken and not undertaken

---

Nottage, 'Tracing Trajectories in Contract Law Theory: Form in Anglo-New Zealand Law, Substance in Japan and the United States' (2013) 4(2) *Yonsei Law Journal* 175, available at ssrn. com/abstract=2270889.

[26] DP, Rules 3.1.1.33 and 3.1.1.34.
[27] Macneil, above n 25.
[28] IR, Item 36-4.
[29] IR, Item 30-3.

by the parties. However, the phrase 'events undertaken in the agreement' disappeared from the IR; 'events attributable to the debtor' has been reinstated.[30] Nonetheless, a match-up of the DP against the IR shows two major trends.[31] On the one hand, most of the DP's proposals survived in some form, although the number of proposed amendments was reduced. On the other hand, differences between the DP and IR proposals are fewer regarding the general provisions on contractual obligations (*keiyaku soron*) compared to proposals addressing specific types of contract (*keiyaku kakuron*) set out in the Civil Code, such contracts of sale or mandate (agency). One implication could be that there is more chance of achieving major amendments within the LC process if there are more comparative reference points, especially provisions and principles based on international instruments such as CISG and the UNIDROIT (International Institute for the Unification of Private Law) Principles.

III. TENTATIVE INTEREST GROUP ANALYSIS OF THE CIVIL CODE REFORM PROCESS

An interesting feature of Japan's ongoing contract law reform process is that it has maintained momentum, and even quite specific proposals, despite the dramatic loss of political power by the conservative LDP in the September 2009 general election, followed by the equally dramatic loss by the DPJ in the December 2012 election. The Civil Code reform project seems to have been largely ignored, or offered some muted support, by both main sides of politics.

This is somewhat surprising. First, after all, the DPJ campaigned before 2009 as a party more concerned about protecting consumers, and even small business operators facing off against the larger elite firms ostensibly favoured by the LDP. Thus, it might have been concerned that the RC's initial draft proposals envisaged new 'mandatory rules' for the Civil Code that insufficiently protected consumers (regarding fraud or mistake, for example), or inadequate 'default rules' (making it less likely, for example, for agreed terms in a consumer contract to be held void as unfair under the Consumer Contracts Act 2000). The DPJ might also have preferred stronger new provisions on misrepresentations or other issues potentially beneficial to small businesses in dealings with larger competitors. However, the LDP had also increasingly appealed to the consumer vote, as evidenced by enactment of that Act in 2000 as well as reforms to consumer credit and product safety regulation in 2006.[32] It has also long been protective of smaller businesses, anyway.

---

[30] IR, Item 10-1(2). Compare DP, Rule 3.1.1.63(1).

[31] See our comparison chart (in Japanese) available at blogs.usyd.edu.au/japaneselaw/2013/06/minpo.html.

[32] See L Nottage, 'Consumer Rights in Japan' in P Haghirian (ed), *Japanese Consumer Dynamics* (New York, Palgrave Macmillan, 2010) 31–60; see also L Nottage and S Kozuka, 'Lessons from Product Safety Regulation for Reforming Consumer Credit Markets in Japan and Beyond' (2012) 34(1) *Sydney Law Review* 129.

Secondly, the DPJ had positioned itself as more opposed to aspects of 'market fundamentalism', allegedly exposed by the global financial crisis of 2008 and more influential among LDP politicians. The DPJ might have been more cautious about law reform proposals that could have promoted further moves towards deregulation, favouring (especially financial sector) firms over the general populace. Ryan argues that this occurred with 2004 and 2006 enactments concerning the law of trusts, suggesting indeed that:[33]

> The omission of the civil trust from [that] reform process may be explained by the sublimation of the goals of grassroots reformers to the fiscal and macroeconomic goals of the State and the sectional interests of its influential clients in the finance sector. This lopsided impact on the reform process might be traced to the composition of the Trust Reform Committee of the [LC].

Combined with the DPJ's calls for a new relationship with the bureaucracy, one allowing for greater weight to be given to political leadership,[34] in late 2009 one might have expected some hesitation about proceeding apace with a Civil Code reform process initiated in 2006 under an LDP government, and/or some DPJ pressure on the MoJ to appoint working group members representing more diverse views than those proposed particularly by the RC.

Yet there is little evidence of such politicisation. This may have been due to the momentum already generated informally (particularly via the RC) for Civil Code reforms, their more technical nature, and the many other pressures on the new DPJ administration—particularly as it sought to assert its authority over other parts of the bureaucracy.[35] Nor it is easy to discern significant shifts, linked to the DPJ's political preferences, in the evolution of proposals from the RC (finalised in April 2009) compared to the working group's Statement of Issues (in May 2011) and especially the proposals found in its IR (in February 2013).

While politicians are primarily interested in the statutory rules that will affect the distribution of assets within a society, jurists (including judges, MoJ bureaucrats, legal academics and attorneys) are much more concerned about the contents and forms of various legal formants. Thus, micropolitics likely influencing various interest groups have led to considerable momentum and continuity throughout the Civil Code reform process so far, as outlined below. Such micropolitics—as contests over legal formants—were nevertheless still framed by the bureaucratic system underpinning the Civil Code and neighbouring fields of law. Indeed, as one recent commentator has noted

---

[33] T Ryan, 'The Trust in an Ageing Japan: Has Commercialisation Precluded the Trust from Reaching its Welfare Potential?' (2012) 7 *Asian Journal of Comparative Law* 197, 220–21.

[34] See generally, eg Samuels, above n 19.

[35] Other examples of the DPJ making more attempts to politicise law reform proposals but not succeeding concern broadcasting regulation and corporate law reform: see blogs.usyd.edu.au/japaneselaw/2013/01/political_change_versus_law_re.html.

more generally, modernising contract law through this 'recodification' can be achieved:[36]

> [O]nly within the framework of the traditional bureaucracy. In this sense, it can be said that the structure of a law rather than its contents is strongly influenced by the characteristics of the political system.
>
> The present situation is far removed from the situation in the nineteenth century, in which the Civil Code and other codes were codified together on the forceful initiative of the government.

A. Officials

One key concern for the MoJ in recent years has been to come up with a major new law reform project after concluding several large-scale revisions, such as corporate law in 2005.[37] In particular, reforms in the latter field showed the fragility of the LC as Japan's major law reform body: some earlier corporate law reforms had instead emerged as Members' Bills (*gi'in rippo*), supported by the Ministry of Economy, Trade and Industry in their drafting and preparatory study groups (*kento kai*) outside the regular *shingikai* processes. The LC had also been sidelined somewhat during the Judicial System Reform process implemented over 2001–04, although the related headquarters established within the Cabinet had included some secondees from the MoJ as well as other government departments.

Maintaining the LC was important for consistency and coordination in law-making, in light of persistent factionalism within the central government bureaucracy. Each major ministry or agency generally still operates a *shingikai* or similar deliberative council to promote law reforms—despite efforts since the Koizumi era to bypass some of those, by centralising more power especially in the Cabinet Office.[38] Sometimes the LC had also played a significant 'tie-breaker' role, as seen for example during the complex enactment process for the Product Liability Law of 1994.[39] For these reasons, promoting large-scale Civil Code reforms through the MoJ can be viewed as promoting the public good in Japan.

It may have been for a somewhat similar reason that changing the fundamental structure of the Civil Code was not pursued seriously in the LC's working group. If the Civil Code were to incorporate the Consumer Contracts Act, for example, the MoJ could not have avoided becoming involved in jurisdictional disputes with the Consumer Affairs Agency, newly established

---

[36] Ishikawa, above n 6, 79.

[37] See generally L Nottage, L Wolff and K Anderson (eds), *Corporate Governance in the 21st Century: Japan's Gradual Transformation* (Cheltenham, Edward Elgar, 2008).

[38] See generally T Shinoda, 'Japan's Cabinet Secretariat and its Emergence as Core Executive' (2005) 45 *Asian Survey* 800.

[39] L Nottage, *Product Safety and Liability Law in Japan: From Minamata to Mad Cows* (London, Routledge Curzon, 2004) ch 2.

in 2009.[40] Absorbing parts of the Commercial Code might not have entailed outright disputes with other government agencies, as there is no doubt that the Commercial Code falls within the jurisdiction of the MoJ. However, it could have triggered arguments about the definitions of 'commercial' or 'business' as opposed to 'civil' or 'personal', thereby embroiling the MoJ in practical and philosophical controversies. For the MoJ to maximise its own institutional benefit throughout the process, it therefore seems very important that the basic structure of the Civil Code should remain largely intact despite other amendments. Thus, Japan's 'vertically divided administrative system' continues to cast a significant shadow on the law reform process.[41]

In addition, establishing and managing the working group also achieved more direct benefits for the MoJ. It was able to secure budget and personnel allocations for a major project, even though central government has been subjected to significant annual cuts particularly over the last decade. The MoJ also maintained higher status associated with key figures in this law reform process (as in several others associated with LC) being seconded judges from the Supreme Court of Japan.

B. Judges

The Japanese judiciary is also under pressure, in difficult macro-economic circumstances, to demonstrate that it is providing value for money to taxpayers. For example, the Supreme Court played a very visible role in designing and advertising the new quasi-jury (*saiban'in*) system, enacted in 2004 and implemented from 2009, as a centrepiece of criminal justice reforms.[42] The Civil Code project arguably provided another opportunity to contribute to a law reform issue of potentially far-reaching public interest.

Admittedly, this contribution did arise in a less visible way. This was partly due to the inevitably more technical and complex nature of proposals for revising contract law provisions. The general public will also be generally unaware that, in addition to the (four) judges serving on the working group, five others were seconded by the Supreme Court to the MoJ or the Cabinet Legislative Bureau—and therefore appear as officials on the working group records, not as judges. Nonetheless, other members of the working group and many within

---

[40] On the growing importance of consumer protection law and policy, including establishment of the Agency in 2009 see Nottage, 'Consumer Rights in Japan', above n 32.

[41] See generally Samuels, above n 19 and specifically Ishikawa, above n 6, 77, who had predicted that: 'while the unity of bureaucratic elites in every branch of government facilitates administrative and legislative coordination, it is not easy to draft a statute with multiple purposes that bestrides more one presiding ministry . . . special laws different in nature from the Civil Code, such as the laws for consumers or merchants, could not easily be integrated into the Civil Code, even by a major reform of the Civil Code'.

[42] K Anderson and L Ambler, 'The Slow Birth of Japan's Quasi-Jury System (Saiban-in seido)' (2006) 21 *Zeitschrift für Japanisches Recht/Journal of Japanese Law* 55.

the legal profession are probably aware that at least some of those 'officials' are seconded judges, contributing to this major new law reform project. After all, there is a longstanding tradition of the Supreme Court sending judges to work at the MoJ in various capacities.

One somewhat controversial example involves judges being seconded to the MoJ's litigation department, which is primarily responsible for defending the government in public law litigation.[43] Secondments are generally for 2–3 years, but sometimes can be for much longer periods. They are considered important in providing new experiences and perspectives for judges, who usually begin a lifelong career in the judiciary after successfully completing a (still very difficult) national legal examination (*shiho shiken*), followed by a year-long traineeship. But secondments, especially to posts charged with law reform activity within the MoJ, also form an established part of elite-track career progression within the judiciary. The Supreme Court administrators (led by judges themselves) need to manage almost 3,000 judges nationwide, and seem to believe that the best judges are those who can not only decide cases, but also develop and demonstrate other skills—such as contributing to law reform.

Secondment to the MoJ to work on projects like the Civil Code reform may also allow the judiciary to frame more judge-friendly legislation. What that means probably varies considerably depending on the area of law, but two somewhat conflicting possibilities come to mind regarding contract law. On the one hand, judges are likely to be attracted to legislative provisions that are easy to implement, such as specific rules—especially those that already reflect established judicial practice through case law developments. This should allow quicker disposition of heavy caseloads, and greater predictability may even reduce the need for plaintiffs to file suits. On the other hand, particularly if more politically charged aspects are involved, judges may prefer more general provisions that allow greater scope to be subsequently molded to changing socio-economic circumstances.

By meeting both needs of the judiciary, the IR suggests a very significant victory for the judiciary in the contest over contemporary legal formants in Japan. Restatements of the principles and case law, or even a loose form of consensualism, are beneficial to judges as they givew them an express basis for justifying court decisions. By upgrading the case law (itself an important legal formant) into codified rules, judges can now claim that they are not creating a rule based on personal preference, but rather that their decisions are the inevitable outcome of applying the provisions set out in the Civil Code. At the same time, the proposed reforms in the IR contain various provisions that allow the court to exercise discretion in applying these rules, such as determining

---

[43] L Nottage and S Green, 'Who Defends Japan? Government Lawyers and Judicial System Reform in Japan and Australia' (2011) 13 *Asian-Pacific Law and Policy Journal* 129. See also generally, eg H Itoh, *The Supreme Court and Benign Elite Democracy in Japan* (Burlington, VT, Ashgate Publication, 2010).

'the meaning of the contract' or 'the aim of the contract'.[44] In identifying and interpreting relevant facts, the Japanese judiciary will continue to enjoy sufficient freedom to reach solutions that it considers just and equitable,[45] thereby maintaining the considerable trust it enjoys from the general public.[46]

It should also be noted that the judges' techniques of identifying and interpreting the facts are another type of legal formant. This arises in particular due to the existence of an official manual published by the Legal Research and Training Institute[47] dealing with the theory of *yôken iijitsu* (literally meaning 'facts to be proven'), guiding the judges (and hence lawyers before the court) towards a stylised approach to finding the facts.

Thus, the reform proposed in the IR should satisfy judges by giving them advantages in the formation or maintenance of legal formants in two ways. A similar victory for judges in Japan's recent contests over legal formants can be observed in 2011 reforms to the (German-inspired) Code of Civil Procedure, regarding the jurisdiction of Japanese courts in international cases.[48]

C. Academics

The professoriate may have viewed a revitalisation of the LC, through the Working Group on Civil Code Reforms, as an opportunity for a renewed sense of achievement and potential contribution to the public good. Perhaps in order to compete with *shingikai* or other law reform bodies in different parts of the government, the MoJ had sometimes involved fewer law professors in recent LC initiatives, such as reforms to trust law.[49] Substantively, moreover, some involved in the present working group process will be attracted to the scope to advance issues they have raised about some broader themes, such as the relationship between private and public law generally,[50] and underlying visions of contemporary society arguably implicit or pursuable in contemporary civil law.[51]

---

[44] See Section II.B above.

[45] See generally A Pardieck, 'Layers of the Law: A Look at the Role of Law in Japan Today' (2013) 22(3) *Pacific Rim Law and Policy Journal* 599.

[46] See generally JO Haley, *The Spirit of Japanese Law* (Athens, GA, University of Georgia Press, 1998).

[47] The Institute runs a (now one-year, state-subsidised) training programme, managed by the Supreme Court for those who have passed the difficult national legal examination, for eventual qualification as a judge, public prosecutor or practising attorney.

[48] D Yokomizo, 'The New Act on International Jurisdiction in Japan: Significance and Remaining Problems' (2013) 34 *Journal of Japanese Law* 95.

[49] See Ryan, above n 33, 221.

[50] See, eg K Yamamoto, 'The Role of Private Law in a Constitutional System' (2004) 1 *Kyoto Journal of Law and Politics* 45.

[51] For example, A Omura, *Minpo Kaisei o Kangaeru [Thoughts on Reforming the Civil Code]* (Tokyo, Iwanami Shinsho, 2011) argues that the goal of the reform should not be consensualism but rather a society supported by 'contracts with justice' (163).

More generally, legal academics involved both in the working group and its predecessors (such as the RC) may have felt a vindication of the largely very doctrinal—but often comparative, and occasionally more contextual—approach to civil law scholarship in Japan.[52] This style, particularly the comparative law orientation, has come under growing pressure from the professionally oriented postgraduate 'law school' system, which was also inaugurated in 2004 as part of the Judicial System reforms.[53] The Civil Code reform projects, prompted in part by major recent amendments in Germany and France, as well as developments in international contract law, suggest the continuing validity of comparative law approaches. A significant feature of the working group deliberations has been extensive reference to comparative and international law sources. As occurs traditionally in other law reform projects in Japan, if a clear global standard emerges, this would have a powerful influence on the debate and recommendations.[54] However, it would be interesting to determine what would happen if such recommendations were to conflict with the above-mentioned law reform preferences, particularly of the judiciary.

The IR satisfied academics by upgrading into (draft) codified provisions some rules found in foreign and international contract law, which the academics (at least) believed to constitute a legal formant. However, it did so, skilfully avoiding possible conflicts between the interests of academics and judiciary, by taking up the academics' suggestions for importing some partly foreign concepts, which in practice would be used only exceptionally. The proposed new rules on change of circumstances, the defence of inadequate assurance of performance, and provisions on unfair exploitation would not be used frequently, so judges should not be bothered by them in their daily activities. Yet, for Japanese academics, it does not matter whether these concepts are used frequently or not; what matters to them is that such rules come to be expressly stated in their own Civil Code. Some professors may even derive personal benefit from the adoption of the new concepts, as practitioners—until

---

[52] From a German perspective, Japan's civil law scholarship appears distinctly more contextualist: see G Rahn, *Rechtsdenken und Rechtsauffassung in Japan* [*Legal Thought and Conceptions of Law in Japan*] (Munich, CH Beck, 1990). But everything is relative: it seems more focused on black letter law than US law, in particular: L Nottage, 'Changing Contract Lenses: Unexpected Supervening Events in English, New Zealand, US, Japanese, and International Sales Law and Practice' (2007) 14(2) *Indiana Journal of Global Legal Studies* 385. This is arguably underpinned by longstanding interest in contract law theory, especially in the US: Nottage, 'Tracing Trajectories', above n 25.

[53] See generally D Foote, 'Introduction' in D Foote (ed), *Law in Japan: A Turning Point* (Seattle, University of Washington Press, 2007); see also critiques such as L Nottage, 'Build Postgraduate Law Schools in Kyoto, and Will They Come—Sooner *and* Later?' (2005) 7 *Australian Journal of Asian Law* 241.

[54] Regarding product liability law reform in Japan, see, eg Nottage, *Product Safety and Liability Law*, above n 39, ch 2. Indeed, as mentioned above (Section II.B), this pattern helps explain why more of the DP's proposals seem to have been survived in the IR in regard to amendments concerning general principles of contractual obligation (*keiyaku soron*). Japan may be particularly open to borrowing from abroad, but it is far from unique. The prestige associated with imitating legal developments abroad is a major attraction noted by comparative law scholars: Sacco, 'Legal Formants (Installment II of II)', above n 3, 398–99.

they finally get accustomed to them—will need academic writings for guidance in those exceptional cases when they may have to invoke the new provisions.

In sum, the interests of the professoriate seem generally to have aligned quite neatly with the bureaucratic coalition (centred on the MoJ and the Supreme Court) strongly in favour of contract law reforms in Japan. However, although Uchida has been able to bring them on board, academics are probably less keen on large-scale reform due to the pressures on legal education generally created by the law school initiatives over the last decade. Further, some leading civil law scholars have not been included in the working group or its predecessor RC: notably, Professor Kato. He has publically objected not only to the way in which the working group got underway, but also its alleged focus on developments abroad. Instead, perhaps appealing to the judges on the working group, Kato has emphasised the need for the Civil Code reforms to hew more closely to case law and doctrinal perspectives indigenous to Japan.[55]

D. Law Firms and Bar Associations

Practising lawyers, who now number almost 30,000 as a result of the law school-related reforms since 2004,[56] divide into three main sub-interest groups. For example, international law firms are now very well established in the Tokyo market, able to hire *bengoshi* qualified to give advice on Japanese law and to share profits (not just costs) with foreign partners qualified in the law(s) of their home jurisdiction(s). They are likely to welcome Civil Code reforms that make Japanese contract law more transparent and familiar for their foreign clients, as well as Japanese clients doing business abroad who may seek to incorporate Japanese law as governing their contractual relationships. New provisions closer to contemporary contract law models overseas also make it easier for international firms to attract and deploy (often younger) lawyers from their offices in other jurisdictions—it should take less time to bring them up to speed with any issues arising under Japanese law. However, much of the work of international firms (for example, in cross-border financial transactions) is likely to remain largely governed by English or New York contract law. This may explain why these firms have not been very visible in the Civil Code reform deliberations so far.

While similar considerations apply to Japan's largest domestic law firms with extensive cross-border practices or otherwise advising on financial transactions,[57] they may be even happier with Civil Code reforms. After all,

---

[55] Kato, above n 14.

[56] M Abe and L Nottage, 'Japanese Law' in JM Smits (ed), *Encyclopedia of Comparative Law* (Cheltenham, Edward Elgar, 2012) 462–79.

[57] See, eg B Aronson, 'The Growth of Corporate Law Firms and the Changing Role of Lawyers in Japan' (2008) 26 *Zeitschrift für Japanisches Recht/Journal of Japanese Law* 33; Asian Legal Business, 'Asia's 50 Largest Law Firms of 2011' (Thomson Reuters, 16 April 2012), available at asia.legalbusinessonline.com/surveys-and-ranking/asias-50-largest-law-firms-of-2011/108186.

much of their recent growth has come from hiring *bengoshi* who have gone through the new law school system, and those students are already and increasingly exposed to the discussions and proposals emanating from the RC and the working group. Japan's larger law firms will also have the capacity to research and disseminate information about new contract law provisions, along with practical implications. Major Civil Code reforms therefore offer an opportunity to consolidate their competitive advantage over smaller firms, which still comprise the bulk of legal practitioners in Japan.[58]

Smaller firms, especially sole practitioners and those outside the Tokyo area focused more on domestic matters, are therefore quite likely to oppose large-scale reforms. Older *bengoshi*, in particular, will be more reluctant to have to invest in learning about new provisions and their origins or applications—although some (for example, those specialising mainly in family law) may instead see the amendments as an opportunity to update their knowledge of contract law and move into a new practice area. It was quite natural that the bar associations showed strong resistance, which succeeded partly in pushing back some novel ideas and reinstating the old concepts that their members are more accustomed to. Conversely, the MoJ made some compromises in order to pursue the reform despite the reluctance of lawyers with practices. The lobbying of the latter was not insignificant, but the tactics of the former appear to have been far better calculated.

These differences in positions among practising attorneys derive from their potential power to influence the formation of legal formants after the new Civil Code is in force. However, the differences may still play out during deliberations in the working group, which includes *bengoshi* from Japan's four largest bar associations.[59] For example, the Osaka Bar Association covers firms with a smaller scale and/or less exposure to cross-border transactions. Nonetheless, even the latter can sometimes be led by *bengoshi* from larger or more internationally oriented law firms. More generally, such firms are already providing client briefings on the Civil Code reform proposals. Already, partly in response to the RC's recommendations in 2009, publications edited by some of the large bar associations have revealed significant engagement with the reform discussions.[60]

---

[58] See, eg M Nakazato, JM Ramseyer and EB Rasmusen, 'The Industrial Organization of the Japanese Bar: Levels and Determinants of Attorney Incomes' [2006] *Harvard Law and Economics Discussion Paper* 559, available at ssrn.com/abstract=951622.

[59] None of the four *bengoshi* representatives on the working group come from Japan's 'Big Four' or other large law firms.

[60] See, eg Osaka Bar Association, *Minpo (Saikenho) Kaisei no Ronten to Jitsumu (Jo) (Ge)* [*Issues and Practice in Reforming the Civil Code (Law of Obligation)*], 2 vols (Tokyo, Shoji-homu, 2011).

E. The Business Sector and General Public

It is difficult to ascertain the interests of the business sector overall regarding the Civil Code reforms. Most firms and even industry associations probably remained completely unaware that the working group had commenced deliberations in late 2009, apart from legal publishers—especially Shoji Homu, which funded the semi-private RC over 2006–09.[61] The IR generated more media coverage in February 2013, but even this was short-lived and not very extensive. After all, the IR comprised an interim set of recommendations, mostly on quite technical issues of contract law. Corporate legal department staff are more likely to understand the topics and their significance, but there is still a struggle in Japan to catch the attention of senior managers, compared to in-house counsel abroad.[62]

Among industry groups, perhaps the strongest concerns about the ongoing reform project come from the financial services industry. One aspect relates to the proposed provisions protecting the weaker party—consumers (probably somewhat better off than under the Consumer Contract Act)—but possibly also SMEs (small and medium enterprises; for example, new provisions on pre-contractual information disclosure). A much more significant worry, though, has been new proposals for assigning receivables (*saiken joto*). This, however, is a relatively discrete topic, which might well be deferred to a subsequent round of amendments to the Civil Code. A similar pattern of leaving out more controversial issues from bills tabled in parliament is commonplace in Japan, as indeed it is in many countries, although Japanese officials and legislators are quite diligent in later revisiting such deferred topics.

Under these circumstances, one would not expect peak industry groups—even those comprising larger corporations as opposed to SMEs (represented mainly by the Nippon Keidanren)—to strongly oppose the concept of Civil Code revisions. Indeed, some such corporations may welcome reforms to consolidate a competitive advantage over smaller rivals, created by aligning contract law rules in Japan with those that larger firms may be increasingly familiar with abroad.

The general public will be even more uninformed or uninterested, particularly given more high-profile everyday concerns, such as the macro-economic situation and the aftermath of the 2011 disasters in Japan. There is also less scope, compared to, say, corporate law, for a scandal to blow up in the field of contract law that could dramatically increase the salience of the reform process in this field. Overall, therefore, this leaves the field open for specific

---

[61] See bizlawbook.shojihomu.co.jp/contents/list/index.html and the longer online version of this chapter.

[62] T Kitagawa and L Nottage, 'Globalization of Japanese Corporations and the Development of Corporate Legal Departments: Problems and Prospects' in W Alford (ed), *Raising the Bar: The Emerging Legal Profession in East Asia* (Asian Legal Studies Program, distributed by Harvard University Press, Cambridge, MA, 2007) 201–85.

interest groups to advance their own agendas in Civil Code reforms—especially the MoJ officials, judges and academics.

IV. CONCLUSIONS

Overall, the somewhat conflicted sub-interest groups within the community of lawyers and various business sectors in Japan, as well as the lack of knowledge and interest on the part of the general public about the Civil Code, mean that a strong bureaucratic coalition (of MoJ officials and judges)—mobilised and supported by key legal academics (especially Professor Uchida)—has been able to develop and maintain considerable momentum in advancing the reform process. The outcome so far includes proposals that give heavy weight to existing judicial practice, while partly accommodating some recommendations by academic members of the working group, many of whom had served on the prior semi-private study group. There are significant parallels with other recent reforms involving the LC within the MoJ.[63]

Such micropolitics have been much more important than macropolitics, namely the DPJ achieving electoral victory in September 2009, followed by defeat in December 2012. Although one view might be that this reflects the relative inexperience of the DPJ, it is hard to imagine that even a more experienced party would have had much influence in injecting more macropolitics into the reform discussions, especially given the major impact of the RC in framing the debates (and even the membership) of the working group established in October 2009.

From a comparative perspective, the process and the (yet to appear) final outcome of the reform uncover the relative power of various interest groups in maintaining or contesting traditional legal formants. In Japan, the importance of academic champions of law reform in the relatively technical area of contract law, working closely with officials, is characteristic of contract law reforms in civil law jurisdictions like Germany and France. This is also a feature of proposals long debated in the EU, now taking concrete form in the proposed regulation on a common European sales law.[64]

In common law countries, especially those in the English law sub-tradition, such as Australia, the professoriate still struggles to throw off a sense that legal academics remain a very junior partner compared to practising lawyers—and especially the judiciary.[65] Even in the US, where law professors enjoy a higher status, a team led by the highly respected Professor Richard Speidel failed to complete a large-scale reform of the Uniform Commercial Code's Article 2 on

---

[63] Yokomizo, above n 48.

[64] See generally Nottage, 'Convergence, Divergence, and the Middle Way', above n 2, and more recently ec.europa.eu/justice/contract/.

[65] See, eg (then High Court of Australia Justice) D Heydon, 'Threats to Judicial Independence—The Enemy Within', Lecture Night (23 January 2012), available at www.innertemple.org.uk/downloads/members/lectures_2012/lecture_dyson.pdf, 14.

sales law.[66] Other interest groups, particularly within the larger and more powerful legal profession still characteristic of common law jurisdictions, perhaps
combined with somewhat greater macropolitics, tend to impede comprehensive and long-term reform initiatives in fields such as contract law that remain
largely based on case law.

This does not bode well for the possibility of contract law reforms in Australia, mooted by the federal Attorney-General's Department in a discussion
paper released in April 2012, followed by considerable public consultation. The
most promising next step would be a referral to the Australian Law Reform
Commission, possibly jointly with counterparts in major states like New South
Wales.[67] In addition to full-time commissioners—usually drawn from among
professors, judges and leading lawyers—there is scope to appoint part-time
and/or fixed-term commissioners, who might include professors or others
specialising in contract law who are capable of championing a more comprehensive and therefore long-term reform inquiry. But the Department has still
not released any follow-up communications, and recent reforms to consumer
law[68] as well as arbitration law[69] suggest that the government is becoming
increasingly unwilling to risk losing political control by referring law reform
proposals to an independent advisory body like a Law Reform Commission.

That view from Australia casts in a more favourable light the recent attempts
in Japan to keep the LC relatively insulated from political pressures, as well
as the impetus from academics and officials (including seconded judges) to
develop and maintain momentum in large-scale reforms to contract law. At
least this ambitious process has been initiated, and discussions have been both
rigorous and vigorous—including a few strong dissenting voices, like that of
Professor Kato. There will still be significant opportunities for broader public
input and debate, including perhaps some macropolitics, once the working
group issues its Final Report in 2014 and when a reform Bill is finally presented to the Japanese Parliament.

[66] See R Hyland, 'American Private Legislatures and the Process Discussion' in A Hartkamp,
M Hesselink, E Hondius, C Mak and CE du Perron, *Towards a European Civil Code* (Alphen
aan den Rijn, Kluwer, 2011) 71–90, especially 80–81.

[67] See L Nottage, 'The Government's Proposed "Review of Australian Contract Law": A Preliminary Positive Response', Sydney Law School Research Paper 12/49 (2012), available at ssrn.
com/abstract=2111826, with an updated version forthcoming in M Keyes and T Wilson (eds),
Codifying Contract Law (Aldershot, Ashgate/Dartmouth, 2014).

[68] L Nottage and J Malbon, 'Introduction' in J Malbon and L Nottage (eds), *Consumer Law
and Policy in Australia and New Zealand* (Sydney, Federation Press, 2013) 3–38.

[69] L Nottage, 'Addressing International Arbitration's Ambivalence: Hard Lessons from Australia' in V Bhatia, C Candlin and M Gotti, *Discourse and Practice in International Commercial
Arbitration* (Aldershot, Ashgate/Dartmouth, 2012) 11–44.

18

The Eurocrises and What Socio-legal Studies Could Do about Them, or: Comparing European Pluralisms from Legal Cultural Approaches

JOXERRAMON BENGOETXEA[1]

ARK VAN HOECKE has always shown interest in multidisciplinary approaches to legal phenomena, going beyond the purely dogmatic approach. In his contribution to the Benelux–Scandinavian Symposium held at Antwerp in 1983, he called for judges 'to consult the theory of law, which in turn will make an abundant use of research in the field of sociology of law' if they were to interpret and apply the law adequately.[2]

The aim of this contribution in honour of Mark is to invite socio-legal scholarship to analyse current events and explain the links between the different types of Eurocrisis that are currently haunting Europe: the crisis of the euro currency and the Eurozone, the economic crisis linked to stagnation or even recession (depression?) in many sectors of the economy throughout the EU, the welfare state crisis also in the EU, but especially in the Southern countries, the crisis of social integration and multiculturalism in the whole of Europe, the political crisis in many European states and in the EU as a 'polity', the institutional crisis in the EU, even the crisis of international cooperation

---

[1] This work was produced in the framework of Grupo de Investigación consolidada GIC07/86 and UFI 11/05, both on European integration and of project der2010-19715, on fundamental rights after the Lisbon Treaty (subprogram juri of the Spanish del Ministry for Science and Innovation). It was finalised in the context of my visiting professor scheme at the Centre of Excellence on the Foundations of European Law and Polity, University of Helsinki.

[2] 'The Utility of Legal Theory for the Adjudication of the Law' in A Aarnio and M Van Hoecke (eds), *On the Utility of Legal Theory: Proceedings of the Benelux–Scandinavian Symposium, Antwerp, 1983* (Tampere, A-Tieto Oy, 1985) 106.

and humanitarian aid. Obviously, relations between these crises are not linear nor directly causal, but rather supra-systemic and nodal.

If such socio-legal research and analyses are undertaken, and if they are duly disseminated, at least law- and policy-makers can be more aware of their systemic connections; civil society will have better understanding of the issues affecting them, and perhaps judges will be able to understand the impact of such crises and systemic disruptions and adjustments on citizens' rights and try to find innovative solutions.[3]

I. EUROZONE CRISIS

The dominant factor is captured under the heading 'structural reforms', a euphemism for austerity, ie the thinning out of state finances and budgets and the culture of cuts, zero debt and ever-higher costs of borrowing. This has generated a widespread sense of panic concerning access to basic welfare services and chances of sustained employment, and therefore loss of quality of life. Arguably, the sense of panic is not (yet) so great as to generate a clear cross-party and cross-European consensus on the way to implement such harsh structural reforms. Only recently the French government has voiced concern at the aggressive recommendations made by the European Commission concerning the structural reforms that France would need to make regarding, for example, its pension system and retirement age (June 2013). But a broad consensus would have to deal with many more reforms, including the redistribution of wealth in society, access to welfare and basic common goods. These are concerns that social sciences and law should address providing with interpretative as well as normative frameworks for assessment.

The 'Eurocrisis' has been the main point on the agenda for most major summits since 2010, not only the summits of the European Council or the Eurozone Group, but also international summits like the G8 (Camp David, USA, mid-May 2012) or the G20 (Los Cabos, Mexico, mid-June 2012).[4] This

---

[3] An interesting example of how these processes can interact is to be found in the judgment of the Court of Justice of the EU in Case C-415/11 *Aziz*, delivered on 14 March 2013, not yet reported.

[4] See point 11 of the Summit Declaration: 'Against the background of renewed market tensions, Euro Area members of the G20 will take all necessary measures to safeguard the integrity and stability of the area, improve the functioning of financial markets and break the feedback loop between sovereigns and banks . . . we welcome Spain's plan to recapitalize its banking system and the Eurogroup's announcement of support for Spain's financial restructuring authority. The adoption of the Fiscal Compact and its on-going implementation, together with growth-enhancing policies and *structural reform and financial stability measures*, are important steps towards greater fiscal and economic integration that lead to sustainable borrowing costs. The imminent establishment of the European Stability Mechanism is a substantial strengthening of the European firewalls.' Towards the completion of the EMU concrete steps are needed 'towards a more integrated financial architecture, encompassing banking supervision, resolution and recapitalization, and deposit insurance. Euro Area members will foster adjustment through *structural reforms to strengthen competitiveness in deficit countries* and to promote demand and growth in surplus

Eurocrisis, affecting an important number of EU Member States, is an unprecedented mix of public debt crisis, banking crisis, zero or negative growth, mortgage-based private debt crisis, high unemployment, a radical diet imposed on the public expenditure of the welfare state, a public sector crisis, failed institutional design and credibility/confidence crisis. Nothing much is really expected from these types of summit meetings, even when newcomers to the club or leaders seeking re-election come with seemingly fresh ideas to stimulate growth and employment.

Linked to the Eurocrises, recent events in Europe give us an impression of social disintegration, political disorientation or lack of vision, institutional fatigue—even a concept failure. National politicians posing as European leaders try to give a serene impression of having things under control, as if following the EU treaties and applying pre-established rules will help solve the crises. European federalists think it is high time to take a new, bold step in the process of European integration. That only a political and fiscal union, with a common or shared macroeconomic policy-making, can save the euro is a generally accepted formula, a variant of the commonplace that if the euro goes the EU fails.

Yet a naive faith in greater and ever closer integration is not enough to make up for faulty institutional design. Meanwhile, Eurosceptics are raving. What might have started off as a financial crisis now risks sliding into dangerous widespread populist, totalitarian and anti-immigrant positions, and provoking technocratic and market interferences into politics. 'Well, too bad! *Bon débarras!*' they seem to say. Nevertheless, this poses serious challenges to democracy and pluralism.

II. INSTITUTIONAL CRISIS AND SPEECH ACTS

Interestingly, the EU Treaties do not provide any way out of the euro. This possibility was not, apparently, even contemplated. The euro was probably thought to be an irreversible project. Ever since the Maastricht Treaty was adopted, the idea was that respect of the convergence criteria would ensure stability by preventing excessive borrowing and debt, uncontrolled inflation and ultimately default. A few years later, however, after the first wave of the financial crisis and the Greek rescue, saving the euro became the new mantra, and talk of splitting up the Eurozone along a North/South divide (with Ireland counting as South), although not on the institutional agenda, has indeed been

countries. The EU members of the G20 are determined . . . to support growth . . . through completing the European Single Market and making better use of European financial means, such as the European Investment Bank (EIB), pilot project bonds, and structural and cohesion funds, for more targeted investment, employment, growth and competitiveness, while *maintaining the firm commitment to implement fiscal consolidation to be assessed on a structural basis*. We look forward to the Euro Area working in partnership with the next Greek government to ensure they remain on the path to reform and sustainability within the Euro Area.' (emphasis added).

the subject of serious discussion, not only in political and entrepreneurial milieu, but also in academic circles. It takes European leaders quite a lot of effort and time to step in and defend the euro.

This wave was apparently reversed when Mr Draghi, President of the European Central Bank, made a warning to financial speculators and uttered the following speech act at a news conference on 2 August 2012: 'It is pointless to bet against the euro—it is pointless to go short on the euro . . . You do not go back to the lira or the drachma or whatever'. These important illocutionary acts were made

> a week after telling the world that the ECB would do 'whatever it takes' to save the euro union . . . suggesting that the ECB might buy the bonds of countries like Spain and Italy if they committed to tough measures to reduce deficits and revamp their economies.[5]

Saving the euro, buying state bonds subject to conditionality and ensuring stability were the turning point during the summer of 2012. These statements produced greater effect than the series of measures and instruments adopted by the Eurozone and the EU to rein in financial speculation. Until such date default, collapse or failure were *l'air du temps*.

The banking and financial sector collapse might have been at the epicentre of the crisis tsunamis. It was all a problem of banks having engaged in risky operations especially on derivatives. After the collapse of Lehman Brothers, many other banks faced severe liquidity problems—some even solvency problems. Instead of letting such 'bad' banks fall completely, as Iceland did, most Member State governments went to the rescue of the major banks by massively injecting capital originating in taxpayers' budget. For a time, even major bankers praised these apparently Keynesian moves on the part of the governments. The EU institutions and the Commission state aid and competition experts looked away. Not unexpectedly, some Member States started experiencing difficulties, having increased their debt and emptied their treasuries. They needed to borrow. This further increased their public debt and deficit. After receiving the necessary capital injections to ensure liquidity, all of a sudden Member States had to become austere again; no more public spending. Re-regulation of the banking sector was no longer urgent, and the banks resented interference in their business.

The apparent insensibility of Germany, which insisted on cuts—austerity—and reforms before ECB bond-buying and other forms of 'Europe-wide solidarity' could be activated, leaving aside the issuing of Eurobonds, which even the OECD supports, added to individualistic attitudes of Member States aiming to protect their financial industries ('the City') at all costs and opposing measures like the tax on financial transactions, leads one to think that something more than a clash of economic analyses—Keynesianism v Chicago school—is going on. This smacks of protectionism and national interests.

---

[5] L Thomas Jr, 'Central Banker Facing a Test', *New York Times*, 28 August 2012.

III. FROM ECONOMIC TO POLITICAL CRISIS AND BACK AGAIN

Politics and the economy are very closely connected. The famous phrase credited to Bill Clinton—'it's the economy, stupid!'—could be turned around: 'but it is also politics!' Or, rather, it is the fear of not being re-elected if certain (seemingly wise but harsh) economic decisions, ie structural reforms, are made. 'And it is also the rule of law' one could add, after the immense relevance in the debate on the European Stability Mechanism of the German Constitution and the Federal Constitutional Court.[6]

Ireland, Hungary and the so-called PIGS (Portugal, Italy, Greece and Spain) have been in recession for some years, having hitherto experienced a boom (notably Spain and Ireland). Portugal and Ireland have received intervention or been rescued. Nevertheless, the Irish supported the new structural reforms of the euro in a referendum (60%, 31 May 2012). Even though Italy and Spain seem too big to rescue because of their respective huge public and private debts, Spain has already called for intervention measures, adopted by the Eurogroup on 10 June 2012, to redress its banking collapse, and might need to demand some form of 'mild rescue' in the future. Cyprus saw some sort of a bank run when it defaulted, and the measures initially adopted by the troika were a clear affront to the rule of law in suggesting that deposits under 100,000 euro might be compromised, in direct contravention of the deposit guarantee scheme directive. The political consequences are different in each cases, as mentioned below.

The bankruptcy of Greece, and the austerity and restructuring measures it needs first to decide and then to implement if it is to avoid 'Grexit' (euro exit), have already transformed Greek domestic politics, where the two main-

---

[6] Judgment of the Second Senate of the Federal Constitutional Court of 12 September 2012, rejecting the applications for an injunction brought against the German ratification of the Treaty on ESM, brought on the grounds of a violation of the overall budgetary responsibility of the German Bundestag, entrenched in constitutional law through the principle of democracy (Arts 20(1) and (2) and 79(3) of the German Constitution GG). Admittedly, the authorisation in Art 136(3) TFEU to establish a permanent mechanism for mutual aid between the Member States of the euro currency area changes the present design of the economic and monetary union in such a way that it moves away from the principle of the independence of the national budgets which has characterized the monetary union so far. However, the ratification of the Treaty is constitutional with the proviso that the ESM Treaty may only be ratified if at the same time it is ensured under international law that the limitation of liability set out under Art 8(5), sentence 1 of the ESM Treaty limits the amount of all payment obligations arising to the Federal Republic of Germany from this Treaty to its share in the authorised capital stock of the ESM (EUR 190 024 800,000) and that no provision of this Treaty may be interpreted in a way that establishes higher payment obligations for the Federal Republic of Germany without the agreement of the German representative. As elected representatives of the people, the members of the German Bundestag must retain control of fundamental budgetary decisions even in a system of intergovernmental governing. In this respect, the German Bundestag is prohibited from establishing mechanisms of considerable financial importance that may result in incalculable burdens with budget significance being incurred without the mandatory approval of the Bundestag. The Bundestag and Bundesrat will also receive the comprehensive information that they need to be able to develop an informed opinion.

stream parties have jointly lost 40% of the votes and failed to agree on an emergency government, while the neo-Nazi Golden Dawn threatens immigrants and warns gays they will be next to go—and obtained 21 seats (7% of the vote) in the one-day parliament that called for new elections for 17 June 2012. Hungary, also affected by the economic crisis, is altogether a special case: leaving aside the hard-line nationalist majority supporting the Viktor Orban government, there is also an anti-gypsy Movement for a Better Hungary (which got 17% of the vote) and a paramilitary Hungarian Guard; and the Council of Europe's Venice Commission 'For Democracy through Law' has on several occasions voiced concerns about the Hungarian constitutional process and outcome, but to no avail.[7] The Commission seems to have given up. The Council will not use the mechanism of Article 7 TEU. Romanian democracy is just as troubling, with a referendum held to oust the president failing only for insufficient voter turnout. In these two countries the political crisis seems to have silenced the economic one. Poland had its own political setback not so long ago.

In Spain, the official unemployment figures (25% overall, and 50% of the young) are not yet silencing the austerity mantra of the government: 'cut or be cut'.[8] This is presented as an imposition of the global markets, but the governing Popular Party (PP) did get a broad mandate in the November 2011 elections.[9] In Italy, an unelected President of the Government Council, Mario Monti, was imposed apparently out of the blue,[10] to try to decide and implement the necessary reforms. In that case, the signs were not of despair for the loss of democratic representation but, rather, of relief to see the disgraced *cavaliere* go. However, Monti was outmanoeuvered in his attempt to be re-elected, and a new political technocrat, Enricco Letta, replaced him, only for him to be replaced by Mateo Renzi. The three premiers after Berlusconi have failed to secure direct electoral mandate.

In France, the Front National had 6.5 million voters in the first round of the Spring 2012 presidential elections and the previous Sarkozy government tabled a proposal to rethink the Schengen system, and enable the re-establishment of internal frontiers on an ad hoc basis.[11] The day after the French elections, the

---

[7] Opinion nos 614/2011 (25–26 March 2011) and 621/2011 (17–18 June 2011)

[8] According to UNICEF, in 714,000 homes all of the adult members unemployed. There are 2.2 million children live below the poverty threshold (mostly in immigrant families and of young couples). The number of homes with no income increased by 120% between 2007 and 2010 ('Report on Spain 2012–2013').

[9] With the notable exceptions of Asturias, Basque Country and Catalonia, where the PP did not manage a majority. In the Andalusian Parliament elections of March 2012, however, the PP lost many of the votes it had gained in the general election of November 2011. On 11 September 2012, over one million demonstrators marched in Barcelona calling for outright independence. See http://en.wikipedia.org/wiki/2012_Catalan_independence_demonstration. Many observers have tried to establish a link between independence claims and the financial and economic crisis in Spain.

[10] Monti was first appointed a life senator so he could be elected as president of government council.

[11] According to the evaluation of the Schengen system made by the Commission in mid-May 2012, in the aftermath of the Arab spring revolutions of 2011 and with the ongoing crisis in

Dutch Freedom Party ceased to support the austerity-bent Dutch government and made it fall. However, in the elections of 12 September 2012 the party lost much of its support. These are only some of the political outcomes of, and erratic reactions to, austerity; the events indicate that there is a 'Crisis of European Democracy'.[12]

IV. A CRISIS OF SOLIDARITY, DOMESTIC AND EUROPEAN

In many countries, austerity measures and the Eurocrisis are eroding one feature Europeans felt most proud of until a few years ago: its diverse social safety nets (welfare, health, education, inclusion policies). The impact of welfare collapse on societal relations will be huge. This is a crisis of the social welfare systems, and therefore also a crisis of identity for Europe, because solidarity and the social model have been defining features of the EU. The street protests in many cities (15 million citizens in all of Spain; Athens; occupy movements throughout the UK; occasional riots in French *banlieux*) and many similar protests are a symptom of these crises and social imbalances, and of the lack of prospects for an unemployed young generation that is better educated than any before.

The erosion of the social model and of solidarity seems to mark an end to toleration. This malaise grows even more sombre if we direct our gaze at multiculturalism, another jewel of integrated Europe, together with peace, the rule of law and the single market. In a speech to the CDU youth, Chancellor Merkel spoke of the end of 'multi-kulti'.[13] UK Prime Minister David Cameron probably thought he had given multiculturalism its *coup de grâce* in

---

Syria, around 30,000 unlawful entries have been detected in the EU external frontiers in 2011, 75% of them on the Greek-Turkish border (Rhodope area). On 7 June 2012 the Danish Presidency of the Council agreed to proceed to a reform of the Treaty on the Functioning of the EU whereby the legal basis is modified for any decision to temporarily suspend the Schengen Agreement with no need to consult Parliament. In other words, reinforced inter-governmentalism and loss of supranational control dismantles Europe.

[12] This is the title of Amartya Sen's article in the *New York Times*, 22 May 2012, where the Nobel laureate holds: 'Perhaps the most troubling aspect of Europe's current malaise is the replacement of democratic commitments by financial dictates—from leaders of the European Union and the European Central Bank, and indirectly from credit-rating agencies, whose judgments have been notoriously unsound'. In more complex terms, J Habermas, *Between Facts and Norms* (Cambridge, MA, MIT Press, 1998) 150 provides the theoretical framework for this malaise: 'the constitutional state requires that the administrative system be kept free of illegitimate interventions of the factual strength of privileged interests'. Habermas does not say what follows when privileged interests prevail.

[13] 16 October 2010: 'We are a country which, at the beginning of the 1960s, actually brought guest workers to Germany. Now they live with us, and we lied to ourselves for a while, saying that they won't stay and that they will disappear one day. That's not the reality. This multi-kulti approach, saying that we simply live side by side and are happy about each other, this approach has failed, utterly failed': http://www.euractiv.com/culture/merkels-ethnic-remarks-add-fuel-fire-news-498867.

a speech to the Munich Security Conference a few weeks later.[14] One would find little to object to if the proclaimed failure of multiculturalism was provoked by a rejection of its implied ethical relativism and a celebration of a more interactive and hybrid interculturalism.[15] This might well be 'the age of plural equality', as Lawrence Friedman reminds us,[16] but, at the same time, anti-minority feelings and attitudes are taking place almost everywhere. Do we have the interpretative social science tools to understand these processes and the practical discourse to generate normative consensus on the steps to take?

Europe—especially, but not exclusively, Germany and Austria—has a tragic history of racism, suffered mostly by Jews and Roma, which coincided with a terrible financial and economic crisis, German WWI debt, mass unemployment and hyperinflation. We should never forget what happened. Historians and anthropologists can provide interesting guidance on the societal trends that led to totalitarianism in many European countries. Can we assume a democratic majoritarian resilience to absolute politics?

Anti-minority or anti-diversity feeling in contemporary Europe is now directed against Muslims and, again, Roma. A recent report by Amnesty International detected discriminatory trends (opinions and attitudes, but also adoption of legal norms forbidding certain attire or the construction of certain buildings) against Muslims in France, Spain, Belgium, Switzerland and the Netherlands.[17] The situation of the Roma, the only genuinely European minority, came to the fore with the projected mass expulsion of Romanian Roma from France in September 2010, which led to a (subsequently aborted) Commission infringement proceeding.[18] However, the predicament of the Roma in Hungary, Romania and other Central European countries is no better, as the many cases before the ECtHR show.[19]

---

[14] Cameron said that Western countries needed to confront extremism rather than pursue a 'hands-off tolerance' and that 'the doctrine of state multiculturalism' had encouraged segregation and failed to supply 'a vision of society' to which people want to belong: http://www.euractiv.com/culture/merkel-cameron-multiculturalism-failed-news-501945.

[15] As W Kymlicka points out, the influential 2008 White Paper on Intercultural Dialogue from the Committee of Ministers of the Council of Europe argues that inter-culturalism should be the preferred model for Europe because multiculturalism has failed. Kymlicka interprets that 'multiculturalism is offered up as a sacrificial lamb, a handy scapegoat for popular discontent, in the hope that this will undercut support for populist, anti-immigrant or anti-Roma, xenophobic parties'. See Kymlycka's reply to Meer and Modood in N Meer and T Modood, 'How does Interculturalism Contrast with Multiculturalism?' (2012) 33 *Journal of Intercultural Studies* 2.

[16] *The Human Rights Culture* (New Orleans, Quid Pro Books, 2011) 123: 'Plural equality and free choice are fundamental premises of the rights movement and of modern society in general'.

[17] http://www.amnesty.org/en/news/muslims-discriminated-against-demonstrating-their-faith-2012-04-23.

[18] The official dismantling of Roma camps in the Paris *banlieux* in the summer of 2012, together with special occupational training measures has replaced the expulsions by the Sarkozy government.

[19] See, eg *DH and Others v Czech Republic*, 47 European Human Rights Reports 3 and more generally, the European Court of Human Rights website's Press and Information factsheet on Roma and Travellers, March 2012.

Social solidarity is generally at stake, and the political and institutional locus where social solidarity is debated, decided and arranged—local or European—and where social inclusion is promoted—in other words, the 'social constitution'[20]—becomes a key factor in determining the forum of politics and legitimacy (the merging of people and polity), and ultimately of nation-building and of (de)construction of the demos.

The different dimensions of the current European crises—the financial–economic crisis and the social, political and multicultural crises—interact in different ways, which need to be studied, historically, comparatively and sociologically. As an example, the Council of Europe Commissioner for Human Rights Nils Muiznieks has called on Contracting States to consult proposed austerity measures with their citizens, with the occupy movements and with civil society in order to find ways out of the crisis. He considers it is necessary to fight for the fundamental rights of the most vulnerable groups, like youth, older people and homosexuals, and insists on the need to ensure immigrants' rights to education and nationality.[21]

Similarly, in a joint article, a number of European intellectuals call for the dismantling of two related dogmas—austerity and fortress Europe—and urge the European institutions to renew their aspiration to democracy, to social progress, to promoting equality between individuals and to protecting those who suffer most directly the forms of racial and social violence accentuated by the crisis.[22] Europe's duty to the less developed world should be added to these aspirations. It is a worrying symptom that decreases in internal solidarity and tolerance should be echoed by dwindling external aid and development cooperation, and also in its support for the Alliance of Civilizations,[23] for peace building and transitional justice.

These traits are detectable not only in far-right populisms, but also in mainstream political parties. And the attitudes and symptoms are not only to be found in the reactions to different values and forms of life claimed by religious or ethnic minorities. Fundamentalist and totalitarian attitudes are also displayed by the criticised groups when they oppose toleration and individual autonomy and critique within their groups. As Beck and Grande put it in *Cosmopolitan Europe*:

> Everything that the fundamentalists hate is to be celebrated and cherished as what is authentically European: the much lamented 'vacuum of meaning', the 'decadence',

---

[20] The term is forcefully contrasted with the economic, ordo-liberal, constitution by C Joerges, 'Democracy and European Integration. A Legacy of Tensions, a Re-conceptualization and Recent True Conflicts', Law Working Papers 2007/25 (European University Institute, 2007).

[21] Strasbourg press conference, EFE News Agency (25 May 2012).

[22] A Giddens, A Michnik, E Wiesel et al, 'L'Europe unie est un rêve, l'austérité et le rejet de l'immigré, un cauchemar', *Le Monde*, 28 May 2012.

[23] http://www.unaoc.org/. The riots, deaths and protests against US embassies worldwide following the publication on YouTube of a film called *The Innocence of Muslims*, apparently produced by Coptic Egyptians in California in mid-September 2012, show how such attempts are fragile but necessary.

the 'loss of the middle', the rejection of the metaphysical image of 'the' human being and 'the' European West. Why? Because the cosmopolitan-European character of a society consists in the fact that nobody lays down what is right and good and how people should live their lives as long as they do not harm others (105)

Populists and fundamentalists share many traits, and Europe as an enlightenment project and as an area of solidarity and peace is the worst nightmare for them.

V. POPULISM AND LEGAL PLURALISM

It is not easy to find common traits amongst the different populist parties that are gaining ground in European countries. To begin with, domestic politics and issues differ considerably from one Member State to another, and strategies to capture or retain electoral support often provoke odd demagogic stances on both mainstream and fringe parties. Nevertheless, a general reaction to Europeanisation and globalisation can be detected, together with a call for rebalancing power towards the national level. Europe does not have migration-friendly politics, but the anti-migrant feeling is another common trait of such populist parties and movements, and even mainstream parties have fallen prey to the discourse of 'crimmigration', restricting liberal values and rights concerns for nationals and regularised migrants. An anti-Islamic discourse is also a common trait of some such populisms.

The issue of populism brings to the fore another of the European crises. A less visible, but nevertheless important, ensuing phenomenon is that of new legal pluralism. In some countries, such as the UK, this issue is taken seriously, and discussions on ways to recognise or enhance the coexistence of normative systems and even legal orders are not reserved just to academia: they are in the media, in politics and on the street. Not so in mainland Europe, not even in France. In many European countries the issue of pluralism has recently been addressed under the perspective of regionalisation and federalism or subsidiarity, or more recently from an awareness amongst EU scholars of the clashes of legitimacy behind constitutional pluralism, a topic related to that of sub-state constitutionalism.

A new form of normative pluralism has nevertheless taken shape and is provoking interesting legal reactions. Historically, the issue of pluralism was one of sociologically, comparatively and historically minded legal scholars, like Mark Van Hoecke. Thus, in his work on Islamic jurisprudence and Western legal history,[24] Van Hoecke elaborates on an interesting contrast of pluralisms. It is well worth quoting him at length on this topic because he is quite exceptional in bringing together these diverse pluralities:

[24] M Van Hoecke, 'Islamic Jurisprudence and Western Legal History' in J Nielssen and L Christoffersen (eds), *Shari'a as Discourse. Legal Traditions and the Encounter with Europe* (Ashgate, Farnham, 2010) 45–55.

Western societies in the Middle Ages show a combination of local particularism with customary law, limited legislation at a regional level, universal canon law and legal science (based on Roman Law). In the 19th Century, a synthesis of this development, together with the new views on society, led to codifications. However, the rise of the national state also brought about a narrowing of legal systems and legal cultures to the borders of those states. In the course of the last few decades those national legal systems started to develop into the opposite direction again. There has partly been a process of regionalization, with regional parliaments, with relatively important competences, in many European countries (including Great Britain, France, Germany, Spain, Italy, Belgium), on the one hand, but more importantly a new universalism through European law, and most importantly (European) human rights, on the other. (p. 49)

. . . Today, however, a new legal pluralism has developed. Especially in Europe, the more sophisticated distribution of competences over regional, national and European authorities has created such a new form of legal pluralism. Moreover, non state legal systems and some of their rules have been increasingly recognized by national courts. This ranges from sports law of international sport organizations to religious rules of varying religions. By this, Western law has developed from personalism to territorialism and, today, again creating some space for person-bound legal rules (51)

The impact of plurality on the law and on politics is quite clear. An interesting debate is to what extent the universalism of human rights, and the different organisational and procedural arrangements Europe has managed to work out from an institutional view of law and conflict resolution, will provide widely accepted solutions to deal with normative pluralism. The role of lawyers and jurists in this sense, and even of legal scholars, is crucial, for we can generally allow ways of understanding, interpreting and integrating the diversity and autonomy of individuals and groups with societal needs for cooperation and peaceful conflict resolution.

VI. SOME CONCLUSIONS

Two important questions can be drawn from the gloomy narrative of Euro-crises. The first question to ask is whether there is any link (and, if so, what type) between the austerity measures being commended by, amongst others, global financial institutions, European institutions and neo-liberal think tanks and the rise of the populisms mentioned above. This is a fine question not only for social systems or conflicts theorists and methodologists,[25] but also for econ-

---

[25] For an analysis of these processes in the new Europe related to French and Italian populism, culture and security see M Berezin, *Illiberal Politics in Neoliberal Times* (Cambridge, Cambridge University Press, 2009).

omists and political scientists, even for legal anthropologists.[26] Interestingly, the European Commission denies any such link, though it does recognise the symptoms, blaming national leaders for them.[27]

The second question is of normative and constitutional prognosis: will a European people, a constituent demos, eventually conform as a result of these crises or will the state-national constitutional contexts or even the sub-state national settings remain as the natural forum of austerity and solidarity politics?[28]

There is a gradual development of a forum where the decisions required in order to weather the economic and financial crisis become effective and the social solidarity necessary for inclusive strategies to manage cultural diversity inspires harmonising measures. This forum is no longer exclusively national; it is both local and global, it is polycentric, and this is why finding the appropriate level to respond to the challenges is crucial, in true subsidiarity spirit.

We witness the waning of the nation-state as the main, perhaps even the only, forum of sovereignty, deliberation and decision-making on such issues of practical reason as toleration and solidarity. Some sectors find it difficult to accept this new setting of global, liberalised and individualist market models and risks, as they consider the EU to be, and feel attracted by the apparent comfort and security offered by nationalisms and populisms. Surely there ought to be alternatives between these extremes? And surely socio-legal scholars should be analysing these phenomena? Social science methodologies cannot remain strictly national.

Just as it becomes pressing to find ways out of the different economic, financial and political crises mentioned above, it becomes pressing to understand diversity within Europe, to analyse cultural plurality and the legal and moral claims and challenges that it generates on the legal systems (pluralism), on jurisdictions (transnational litigation) and on institutions at all levels—local, regional, state and supranational—and to see how the different responses at these levels themselves create a new pluralistic picture. It is necessary to study all dimensions and their interaction from a comparative law and society perspective, as Mark has called us all to do.

After all, the solutions to the crises cannot possibly be devised by only some and for only some of the better organised stakeholders, excluding large numbers of those affected, like the many minority groups excluded from full European citizenship. This is happening at a time when Europe risks becom-

---

[26] In this sense, the recent creation of a new department of legal anthropology under the guidance of Marie-Claire Foblets at the Max Plank Institute for Social Anthropology in Halle is a sign of hope.

[27] 'EU leaders share responsibility for the rise in popularity of anti-European parties, the European Commission said Monday [23 April, after the first round of French elections] but rejected the notion that austerity measures are contributing to the trend', available at http://euobserver.com/843/115994.

[28] This question is raised by P Krugman, 'Apocalypse Fairly Soon', *New York Times*, 18 May 2012.

ing selfish and excluding large parts of the world, abandoning internal and external solidarity. Our identity as Europeans, but also as immigrants, Muslims, Christians, atheists, agnostics, women, men, Basques, Flemish, Germans, Finns, Italians, Irish, Scots, Roma, etc, is at stake. And the critical discursive construction of this plural identity should be inclusive, tolerant and far removed from populism and chauvinist or exclusionary nationalism.

Surely, as practical jurists and also as socio-legal scholars, we need to be able to understand and explain these changes and to suggest innovative ways to ensure inclusion, tolerance and participation. We need to collaborate within the different interlocking laws understood as institutional normative orders[29] in order to find solutions that ultimately affirm and uphold human dignity, autonomy and self-determination, and also solidarity in society and between societies.

Populism—a mix of nationalism, Euroscepticism and xenophobia in Piris' words[30]—and anti-cosmopolitan feelings are in the air, and they are exacerbated by the decreased internal and external solidarity provoked by the economic and social welfare crises. The worst strategy is to play their game. Europeans should reinstate the values of toleration and seek inspiration from *l'âge des Lumières* or the Scottish Enlightenment.

The current European crises could also be an opportunity for the (cosmopolitan) peoples of Europe to take the bold step into a European federation, at least for those peoples of Europe that wished to take such a step to the avant-garde. This step involves economic–monetary and social integration–solidarity also at the European level, in other words, the reflective equilibrium between the economic and social constitutions and the federal and pluralist cultural dialogue between European citizens and European peoples inspired by the cosmopolitan legal order and human rights. These normative proposals are worth analysing and discussing as well.

---

[29] N MacCormick, *Institutions of Law* (Oxford, Oxford University Press, 2007).

[30] J-C Piris, *The Future of Europe: Towards a Two-Speed EU?* (Cambridge, Cambridge University Press, 2011) 104 mentions the following as populist threats to a number of European countries: Vlaams Belang, Danish People's Party, True Finns, Front National, Freedom Party, National Party and Sweden Democrats. He considers the two-speed Europe solution could be a means to fight the populist trend.

19

Comparing the Legitimacy of Constitutional Court Decision-Making: Deliberation as Method

TOON MOONEN

WITHIN THE FIELD of legal theory and legal philosophy, a major space has always been reserved for questions of legitimacy. It comes as no surprise that in some areas of law, such as constitutional law, these questions have been at the centre of debate for decades. The rise of constitutional courts as important players in this field is undoubtedly related to that. Nevertheless, whereas the legitimacy of the constitution is one thing, the legitimacy of constitutional review by court is quite another,[1] and the topic of this contribution may be different still: the legitimacy of constitutional law, defined as the result of decision-making by courts.[2] Especially in countries with relatively young constitutional courts, such as Belgium, questions in that regard still need adequate discussion. The mere fact that the Belgian court was only established when Mark Van Hoecke's first achievements in academia were already many years behind him and will celebrate its 30th birthday the very same day of his academic goodbye is the best evidence of his long and rich career. Drawing on his work, I will put forward the outline for an alternative theoretical method to assess the legitimacy of constitutional

---

[1] In general, nobody would argue that the political branches are not constrained by the constitution. One could, however, wonder—and many have in fact questioned—why democracies need constitutional review by the judiciary. Some have vigorously argued against it (see, eg J Waldron, 'The Core of the Case Against Judicial Review' (2006) *Yale Law Journal* 1346). I will proceed from the assumption that the main argument why societies have installed (or accepted) constitutional review by courts is based on the idea of checks and balances: because there is a risk of a chronically under-enforced constitution, politics cannot be the judge of its own activity.

[2] For those with a strong normative view on how constitutional review should be exercised, there may not be a real difference: doing it badly may then be considered worse that not doing it at all.

269

court activity. I will argue that constitutional courts, taking their existence as given, have the most to win in terms of legitimacy if they operate according to the principles underlying the idea of deliberative democracy. This approach eases comparison beyond national substantive particularities.

I. DEALING WITH CONSTITUTIONAL PLURALISM

The debate about the legitimacy of (the activity of) constitutional courts in a democracy is familiar. The question is how judges, who are not directly accountable to the citizens but are authorised to interpret the constitution and set aside the analysis of the democratically elected legislature, can justify their work in terms of democratic governance. Many would accept that today democracy is not only about majoritarianism, but is also about the conditions to provide each citizen with an opportunity to engage in the political process on equal footing. The challenge posed by constitutional review, then, is not as much its counter-majoritarian character, as it is classically dubbed, in the sense that it overrules majoritarian policy measures. Seen from this perspective, the threat of a *gouvernement des juges* is only troubling for those with a narrow conception of democracy. The challenge is in the delimitation of those conditions, which in practice form the outer limits of ordinary, majoritarian legislative discretion. This specification of the challenge may solve one problem; however, it confronts us with a daunting other one.

Of course, I am not contemplating scenarios here in which judges have explicit antidemocratic agendas or otherwise shadowy aspirations to power. Giving constitutional courts the mandate to determine, on the basis of a constitutional text, which guarantees the citizen precisely has and which he does not have, or how power is dispersed over various levels of government, nevertheless remains something of a leap of faith. The reason is that, whereas constitutional text may solve some problems in clear and straightforward ways, lawyers (and also linguists and political scientists) nowadays agree that it cannot provide concrete answers to all thinkable constitutional dilemmas. All who are somewhat familiar with legal theory, methodology of law and/or comparative law know about the existing diversity, throughout space and time, concerning democratically admissible approaches to constitutional interpretation.[3] Clearly, this

---

[3] A brief sketch is enough to illustrate the point. Argumentative approaches may include classical canons of legal interpretation, since they in principle take values as a criterion a democrat might find valuable, such as original or present consent, rationality or stability. Approaches may also involve more sophisticated argumentation patterns, such as by arguing that, for the sake of certainty, a constitution should as much as possible be considered to be a set of rules instead of standards. Some judges find particularly important the constitutional interpretation by elected branches of government. Others rely on more substance-oriented models of reasoning. In addition, many, if not most, will probably be willing to concede that in some difficult cases it is inevitable for judges—especially when relying on open-ended adjudicative tests—to take into account personal elements, based on an individual conception about what the constitution should provide in order for the citizen to be able to lead the 'good' life, thereby infusing

does not make comparative research on an international level any easier and, on the internal level, constitutional texts mostly do not provide guidelines on this. As a result, courts, and especially constitutional judges, take into account myriad factors when they determine constitutional meaning for the purposes of the review. More often than not, multiple solutions for the cases constitutional courts have to adjudicate are imaginable, and it is easy to see how citizens in a democracy reasonably disagree on what constitutes a good constitutional decision. They may reasonably disagree because, within the framework of a pluralist democracy, different politico-legal values can guide the exercise of constitutional review and lead to different outcomes. In fact, as Sunstein argues, democratic constitutional governance would be practically impossible if citizens did not accept the fact that they may agree on the theoretical outlines of good constitutionalism but disagree on their application, or agree on concrete cases but based on a variety of theoretical arguments. 'For arbiters of social controversies, incompletely theorized agreements have the crucial function of reducing the political cost of enduring disagreement.'[4] The absence of a hierarchy—or even agreement about the identification—of the interpretative criteria admissible under democratic constitutional government often makes discourses incomparable. Even if we are not willing to concede in theory that multiple approaches to constitutional interpretation are legitimately possible, at least in practice we observe that there is no consensus and no way of enforcing one above the other based on its intellectual merits only. In Michelman's words:

> To assert [reasonable interpretive pluralism] is to declare impossible a publicly reasoned demonstration of the truth about what it is everyone has reason to agree to in the matter of legal human-rights entrenchments and interpretations. Reasonable interpretive pluralism does not place truth in this matter beyond reasoned argument, or make it just a matter of opinion or desire or power; it makes it *politically* unavailable, in real political time, among people who, aware of human frailty and 'burdens of judgment,' all perhaps sharing belief that here is a truth on the matter, can neither all agree on what that is nor dismiss as unreasonable their opponents' positions.[5]

In real life, there is an abundance of democratically plausible theories about how a constitutional court should go about its business. If an interested layman asks what the constitution says on this or that particular question, one answer often follows: it depends. Moreover, most theorists themselves take

---

a dose of consequentialism and ideology into a decision. For a comparative view see, among the vast number of sources, eg J Goldsworthy (ed), *Interpreting Constitutions* (Oxford, Oxford University Press, 2006).

[4] C Sunstein, 'Constitutional Agreements without Constitutional Theories' (2000) 13 *Ratio Juris* 125. The absence of agreement does not diminish the system's own legitimacy per se. See also eg J Habermas, 'On Law and Disagreement. Some Comments on "Interpretive Pluralism"' (2003) 16 *Ratio Juris* 193.

[5] F Michelman, 'Human Rights and the Limits of Constitutional Theory' (2000) 13 *Ratio Juris* 71 (emphasis in original).

nuanced positions, trying to reconcile different perspectives, adding variables to their theory to ease out differences, thereby compromising to the extent that, even when questioned about constitutional philosophy, many would be forced to answer: that depends, too. Relatively speaking, some constitutional philosophies and solutions will be considered more or less appropriate than others in a particular space and time. But sometimes such an agreement will not exist. The problem is that if contending approaches depart from different premises about the weight of various elements of or the implications of democratic government for good constitutional decision-making, it is impossible to determine objectively which ones of these contentions are correct. As a result, it comes as no surprise that in reality many disagreements exist about the merits of a theory, but participants in those debates usually at least implicitly concede that more than one theory could reasonably compete within the same time and space without making the system for that reason alone undemocratic.

We are now confronted with a number of judges that may have different takes on constitutional philosophy and method, or, at least, different preferred outcomes, for whatever reason. As said, differences between interpretative theories can be relative, but they can also imply critical shifts in outcome. I do not propose a substantive normative theory of constitutional interpretation; neither do I argue that anyone will be as adequate as another. I do, however, propose that, in many situations, it will be impossible to conclude on that objectively. Claims about substantive legitimacy are often precarious for that reason, and comparison of legitimacy arguments between systems is difficult. Given that context, the goal of the previous observations was to set the stage for a different methodological approach to thinking about the legitimacy of the activity of a constitutional court.

II. LEGITIMACY AND THE CONSTITUTIONAL COURT'S AUDIENCES

I propose an approach of what constitutes legitimate judicial decision-making that rises above the pros and cons of particular interpretative approaches, since engaging in a seemingly unresolvable exchange of possible interpretative truths and nothing more is, from a legitimacy point of view, dissatisfying. Of course, this has been done before. In what follows, I will in particular start from Van Hoecke's model of circles of communicative legitimation of judicial decision-making, which he recently also applied to constitutional cases.[6] As he argues, '[j]ust as *law* is constantly made in and through legal practice,

---

[6] M Van Hoecke, 'Constitutional Courts and Deliberative Democracy' in P Popelier, A Mazmanyan and W Vandenbruwaene (eds), *The Role of Constitutional Courts in Multilevel Governance* (Antwerp, Intersentia, 2013) 183–97 (emphasis in original).

legitimation too is constantly achieved through deliberative communication'.[7] Decisions are increasingly legitimate, he continues, if they succeed in convincing increasingly larger audiences of their qualities. Starting from the parties to a case, those concentric communicative circles further concern the rest of the judicial apparatus, the professional legal audience, non-professional civil society and all citizens. Van Hoecke derives legitimacy precisely from the discussion and acceptance of judicial interpretations as authoritative in increasingly encompassing environments.[8] Most importantly, this process of convincing does not necessarily mean that everybody changes her mind on substantive methodology or outcome; it does mean that audiences accept that the court has taken a position that is reasonably permissible in view of any of the values a democracy under the rule of law cares about.

> Eventually, acceptance of decisions of constitutional courts in the society to which they apply is the ultimate touchstone for their legitimation. This does not mean that a majority should agree, but that a majority may accept the decision, and should not consider it to be clearly unreasonable or unacceptable.[9]

Van Hoecke's communicative circles can be easily identified if the theory is applied to constitutional courts. Given that no constitutional court depends on a single judge, for a start, the first circle of legitimacy would be the court itself: the more judges agree to the decision, the more internal legitimacy it has. On the next level, we find the parties to the case, which may include citizens, but overall also the government and potentially other societal actors acting as amicus curiae, including even, for example in federal states, other governments. Having them accept a concrete decision as legitimate is, of course, a serious accomplishment, and even more so if it can convince the professional community surrounding the court, including first and foremost the other high courts with some constitutional jurisdiction. In constitutional cases, it often also becomes a matter for academia and other specialised stakeholders to discuss, too, and especially Parliament. More often than is the case with ordinary adjudication, in constitutional matters the court makes a decision, the legitimacy of which is the topic of explicit discussion throughout the entire body politic of the state. Today, through the internationalisation of law and especially fundamental rights protection, one can also say that even transnational actors have become part of the communicative audience of a constitutional court, including supranational institutions, but potentially also foreign audiences. In

---

[7] M Van Hoecke, 'Judicial Review and Deliberative Democracy: A Circular Model of Law Creation and Legitimation' (2001) 14 *Ratio Juris* 420 (also integrated in M Van Hoecke, *Law as Communication* (Oxford, Hart Publishing, 2002) 172–78.

[8] Van Hoecke, 'Judicial Review and Deliberative Democracy', ibid, 418–23.

[9] Van Hoecke, 'Constitutional Courts and Deliberative Democracy', above n 6, 196. We would not even go so far as to consider the presence of a majority relevant; the difference between acceptance by a large minority may in practice not be much different from acceptance by a small majority. See about the importance of acceptability also Michelman, above n 5, 73.

that sense, the legitimacy of our own constitutional choices is not entirely independent from what people outside the polity may think.

Most case law will be somewhere on a sliding scale of legitimacy, theoretically ranging from decisions nobody considers democratically acceptable to those about which everybody in the interpretative community agrees were decided correctly and for the right reasons.[10] Clearly, as a result of this approach, legitimacy is no longer defined as the connection between what one believes to be the right method to deal with a case and how the court has decided. What matters is whether we are willing to accept that the constitutional court could have reasonably reached its decision.[11] In a sense, the threshold for the court to produce substantively legitimate constitutional law is lowered from what one thinks should be the right answer to what one can imagine any democrat could accept as the right answer.

Of course, one might object that this does not fundamentally change the picture. Some members of the audience may still consider a given solution—or an entire line of cases—to be overall less legitimate than desirable, regardless of whether they are willing to concede that others may reasonably think differently. Ending the story here would mean obfuscating the problem and not really solving it. Arguably, the problem is unsolvable if substantive 'correctness' somehow remains the nexus of legitimacy. Tying the legitimacy of the court's activity only to the result may thus not be helpful, and not even fair towards a court: if what is constitutionally good is a subjective matter, then the legitimacy of the court's activity is doomed to forever remain contested. Although I agree that it is perfectly fine to forever argue about what is constitutionally the good thing to do, it is another thing to intrinsically relate the whole of the court's legitimacy to the result of that argument.

This does not mean, however, that a constitutional court is ultimately excused more easily than before because in a democracy, if not anything, then at least 'many things go'. I argue that the lowering of the court's substantive legitimacy requirements (to what is a reasonably democratic solution, instead of the required solution) should be compensated by taking into account the efforts the court makes to achieve this threshold with its audience. The

---

[10] Given what I have said above about the irrelevancy of majoritarianism as such when deliberating about the content of constitutional values, the conclusion must be that a larger margin of legitimacy is preferable over a smaller one.

[11] Arguably, theories that are, in their premises or in their application, democratically irrational—because they donot relate to any value anyone considers worthy of attention under such government—could be rejected. Most actual competing approaches, however, cannot be rejected outright as democratically irrational because they appeal to values most would agree to be important for democratic constitutional government. Admittedly, people may disagree about what values serve constitutional democratic government in the first place. This raises particular problems, such as the practical observation that many in the audience might not have elaborate views on that, or the normative proposition that some approaches may be not be compatible with any conception of democratic governance, regardless of what the audience thinks. A hard core of democratic agreement is presupposed, if only because it is necessary to create a forum in which the court's audiences can authentically discuss the reasonableness of a decision. One needs some democracy in order to properly sustain it.

practical question, then, is how larger communicative audiences can be convinced, given all of the possible democratic arguments and approaches, that the constitutional court has made an acceptable decision. Such 'process legitimacy' cannot simply imply a referral to the fact that constitutional courts are usually composed through specific procedures, usually with parliamentary involvement, and with certain political, federal or institutional balances in mind. Although evidently necessary, it is unsatisfying to take such safeguards described above for granted, because they only guarantee a good basis for adequate process. They do not guarantee the process itself. The answer to this problem lies in an application of the principles of deliberative democracy to the process of constitutional court decision-making.[12]

III. ACHIEVING LEGITIMACY THROUGH DEMOCRATIC DELIBERATION

Since the 1980s, a variety of different theories have been proposed which have since been classified as relating to the concept of deliberative democracy. The field and scope of application of these are wide, so I will content myself here with a recent definition by Frankenberg. Deliberative democracy

> picks up, on the level of normative theory, liberal democracy's claim to legitimacy based on reasons—as distinct from a situationally contingent acceptance—and connects its key focus, not on a predetermined will but on the process of its formation, with participatory democracy's claim to popular participation.[13]

For deliberative democrats, discourse and the processing of arguments are more important in terms of legitimacy than voting and the counting of votes. Unlike other forms of democracy, the centre of the legitimacy of a decision is the way it is taken—more precisely, the extent to which all arguments presented have been the subject of a real, fair and qualitative discussion. Some authors have already discussed the connection between democratic deliberation and constitutional court activity. Mostly, the judge or the court is seen as a forum for, or a facilitator of, democratic deliberation. In that sense, Popelier and Alvarez propose that the success of a court in contributing to democratic deliberation in society depends on such parameters as individual access, the motivation of the decision, judgment flexibility and the capacity to test legislation against those constitutional norms that facilitate the democratic debate themselves.[14] Quite clearly, and importantly, locating the legitimacy of the

---

[12] In this chapter we do not elaborate on the merits and challenges of a deliberative approach to the ordinary democratic process in general.

[13] G Frankenberg, 'Democracy' in M Rosenfeld and A Sajo (eds), *The Oxford Handbook of Comparative Constitutional Law* (Oxford, Oxford University Press, 2012) 255.

[14] P Popelier and A Patino Alvarez, 'Deliberative Practices of Constitutional Courts in Consolidated and Non-consolidated Democracies' in Popelier et al, above n 6, 208–29. Public reasoning, and its relation to political philosophy, as a determinative factor for the legitimacy of constitutional

court's activity in the approval it can count on in its audiences—as opposed to measuring it against a specific normative theory—is by definition a valorisation of argumentation and deliberation. I further qualify the part of a constitutional court in democratic deliberation in two ways.

Before doing so, however, it is important to specify to which debate deliberation through a constitutional court actually contributes. One might be tempted to limit the scope of its influence to the ordinary policy debate (which is the mainstream object of deliberative democracy theory), but that is only part of the story at best. As we have seen, the deliberation for which the court is a forum principally concerns the constitutionally acceptable—or, in the context of the positive state, mandatory—nature of certain measures. The deliberation to which the court contributes is thus not simply a rationalised prolongation of the policy debate citizens might have contributed to by voting, rallying, lobbying or otherwise. On the contrary, the deliberation concerns whether it is constitutionally admitted, prohibited or (even) mandated to have that policy. As a result, and although a constitutional court decision has ordinary policy ramifications, the debate is principally one about the constitution. The difference may seem self-evident, but it is easily overlooked and has important consequences for the deliberative nature of the debate, first of all because it will instigate the participants to produce different kinds of arguments, but moreover because some of the choices the judges make are taken out of the realm of majoritarian policy deliberation altogether.[15]

A. The Court as an Actor in a Process of Deliberation

First, describing a constitutional court as a place of deliberation is only an adequate description of the overall process of constitutional determination if the decision of the court has some kind of a definitive character. This element can easily be overlooked, though in practice that is not usually the case. Quite often, a constitutional court is not the ultimate forum, but only one actor in a larger network of deliberating institutions. The organisational template of a democratic state may contain other actors, such as courts and advisory bodies, which also engage in constitutional interpretation without being

adjudication under circumstances of democratic pluralism has also been the object of elaborate theorizing in recent American political science literature. See, eg R den Otter, *Judicial Review in an Age of Moral Pluralism* (Cambridge, Cambridge University Press, 2009).

[15] Even a judge who would want to constitutionally affirm the policies of his personal ideological preference and outlaw the others is institutionally only capable of doing so in terms of a constitutional question, not in terms of policy preference. Especially if a judge would design a very specific policy, for example by recognising positive obligations from an abstract constitutional principle, his policy judgment is still framed as a constitutional requirement. This fact alone may be enough for many judges to draw a sharp line between constitutionally preferable choices and politically preferable choices, although the effect of both—a policy being installed or removed—is the same.

directly dependent on the previous assessment of the constitutional court. In systems of 'weak(ened) review', as it is described in Tushnet's vocabulary,[16] the court may even be an institution of constitutional deliberation in competition with the legislative branch itself. In those situations, an exchange of arguments takes place, or has to take place, between the institutions themselves. Arguably, the principles of deliberation could be applied to these contexts, meaning that the constitutional opinion of the constitutional court is an element of discourse, persuasion and search for consensus among all bodies involved.[17] More generally, many of the factors identified as influencing court decisions actually originate within the constitutional court's audience—other courts, political branches, but also doctrine—confirming the deliberative nature of the decision-making in a complex institutional context. The fact that the court decides in this way of course facilitates the acceptance within those audiences that we are looking for.

B. The Court Deciding Through Democratic Deliberation

Secondly, perhaps the most critical observation to be made is that, although constitutional courts may indeed be suitable fora for problems of constitutional interpretation, and thus attract arguments about constitutional governance from all corners of society, none of the actors raising those arguments are actually involved in the final decision-making about a problem. Citizens, governments, intervening parties or amici curiae argue to the best of their abilities and understandings, but, in the end, it is the court that decides. Contrary to what is the case in more conventional cases of deliberative decision-making, the arguments raised before the court are not necessarily intended to convince the other parties involved in the controversy. The court is not a moderator, easing the discussion and facilitating the finding of a solution among the participants. There is thus a degree of contradiction in saying that the court is a forum for democratic deliberation if the actors proposing the arguments are not the ones who will finally take a decision.

This observation does not render the assertion that constitutional courts contribute to deliberative democracy false, though it does call for an important qualification. Constitutional courts do contribute to a deliberative decision-making process concerning constitutional values if their own internal decision-making is also determined by qualitative deliberation, and if that argumentative deliberation can be tracked in the formal decision delivered by the court. The core of the argument of this chapter is that, if the substan-

---

[16] See, eg M Tushnet, 'The Rise of Weak-Form Judicial Review' in T Ginsburg and R Dixon (eds), *Comparative Constitutional Law* (Cheltenham, Edward Elgar, 2011); see also M Tushnet, 'Alternative Forms of Judicial Review' (2003) *Michigan Law Review* 2781.

[17] About interinstitutional deliberation see, eg J Tulis, 'Deliberation between Institutions' in J Fishkin and P Laslett (eds), *Debating Deliberative Democracy* (Malden, Blackwell, 2003) 200–11.

tive legitimacy of the court's activity is based on a deliberative exchange with its audiences, as I have argued above, then, in deciding in a deliberative way itself, the constitutional court has the best chance to convince the largest communicative circles around it, thereby increasing its overall legitimacy to the maximum possible. As Michelman concludes:

> a possible characteristic of the regime, in virtue of which everyone subject to it could abide by it out of respect for it, is that the regime's human-rights interpretations are in some way made continuously accountable to truly democratic critical re-examination, re-examination that is fully receptive to everyone's perceptions of situation and interest and, relatedly, everyone's opinion about true justice. If that is a true proposition, and if it further turns out that accountability to democratic critical examination is the *only* practically possible respect-worthiness-conferring virtue that a regime of human-rights interpretations might have in conditions of reasonable interpretive pluralism, we would then have explained how recourse to a democratic procedure can possibly confer normative legitimacy on a human-rights regime.[18]

Because constitutional courts are often composed in such a way that they represent a variety of approaches to the constitution and its place in accommodating 'the good life', in controversial cases, not all judges will be convinced by the same arguments. As a result, the disagreement existing in society, and which was brought to court, is likely to exist in the court too. Part of the legitimacy of its decision depends on whether the court takes on the responsibility to address in full all democratically rational arguments raised before it. Importantly, it should also reproduce that deliberative process in the decision it delivers. That final point is essential, because, although a court could deliberate qualitatively and then deliver a single-sentence decision, not being required to publicly account for the deliberation leaves the court's communicative audiences increasingly unconvinced and leaves the door open for less well-deliberated decisions.

IV. THE CHALLENGES FOR THE CONSTITUTIONAL JUDGE

If a constitutional court takes a deliberative approach, the chance that the inner communicative circles, consisting of other courts, advisory bodies and political institutions, will accept and incorporate the solutions of the constitutional court as the most appropriate way to think about the debate increases. Van Hoecke concludes that '[c]onstitutional courts have a privileged position in this communicative process, as they may authoritatively determine the

---

[18] Michelman, above n 5, 73 (emphasis in original). See also J Ferejohn and P Pasquino, 'Constitutional Courts as Deliberative Institutions: Towards an Institutional Theory of Constitutional Justice' in W Sadurski (ed), *Constitutional Justice, East and West. Democratic Legitimacy and Constitutional Courts in Post-Communist Europe in A Comparative Perspective* (The Hague, Kluwer, 2002) 27.

exact scope of constitutional rules and principles'.[19] Ideally, focusing on process and acceptance within societies rather than hard-to-objectivise substantive standards, the comparison of legitimate court activity is made easier methodologically. Unmistakably, though, however self-evident a deliberative approach to judicial decision-making may seem, it puts quite a heavy burden on the judges: it is an intellectually demanding responsibility.

First of all, it implies that a judge is open to potentially being convinced by others. Decision-making among actors unwilling to be persuaded under any circumstances may still be democratic and acceptable to some, but the process would amount to not much more than vote counting. That would not contribute to increase legitimacy; it would be a mere confirmation of the existing disagreements of opinion within the court's audience. Secondly, the eventual decision remains a group responsibility and effort because, even if a judge argued against the solution adopted, it is still her right, but also her duty, to have her arguments incorporated. This does not mean that the deliberation should, for that reason alone, lead to a compromise. Her arguments should be part of the deliberative process; it does not mean that the result should necessarily accommodate her position in some way too. Such an approach requires detachment from the judge: on a first level, she will argue on the merits of a case, and agree or disagree with the outcome of the deliberation; on a second level, she should be willing to think, along with the drafters, about how the decision as taken may be used to convince as much of the communicative audience as possible, either by making sure that the court shows the sceptics among them how it considered her arguments and why it eventually rejected them, or by making the court's principal argument as strong as possible. Thirdly, and paramount, the responsibility of the judge goes so far that it is her duty to consider if all democratically rational approaches and solutions are on the court's discussion table, especially if for some reason they were not (adequately) represented in court, and even if she feels not particularly attracted to it.

All that does not make the job of constitutional court judge any easier. It requires competent lawyers, skilled debaters, talkers but also listeners, and above all imaginative people capable of analysing what arguments go on in each of the court's communicative audiences. Imagination and empathy, moreover, are also requirements for the deliberative process between the judges itself, since empathic judges, often having done a great deal of deliberation already on their own,[20] can take the discussion easily and quickly to the right level. Authentic deliberation requires a judge to leave the comfort zone of her personal constitutional rights and wrongs, and forces her to grapple with the fact that the alternative methods of her colleagues may find reasonable support, and should thus be accounted for. It implies that an argument

---

[19] Van Hoecke, 'Constitutional Courts and Deliberative Democracy', above n 6, 196.
[20] See R Goodin, 'Democratic Deliberation Within' in J Fishkin and P Laslett (eds), *Debating Deliberative Democracy* (Malden, Blackwell, 2003) 54–79.

cannot be ignored during debate or in the decision, and that, if an argument is rejected, it should be the best version of it. Anything else will give way to the challenges that the deliberation has not been fair and reasonable, thus putting pressure on the legitimacy of the decision.

Taking into account the necessary independence from the legislature to avoid corruption of the process in view of bare policy concerns, Zurn is convinced about the comparative advantages of separate and specialised constitutional courts.[21] It seems, however, that institutional organisation is not even the most important determinant of a court's practical potential to embody this kind of qualitative deliberative constitutional discussion. Practically, as long as a constitutional court and its audience refrain from embracing its role in democratic constitutional governance, decisions may not reflect the deliberative dialogue sought. Of course, such reluctance is not hard to understand.

> In a well-functioning constitutional democracy, judges are especially reluctant to invoke philosophical abstractions as a basis for invalidating the outcomes of electoral processes. They are reluctant because they know that they may misunderstand the relevant philosophical arguments, and they seek to show respect to the diverse citizens in their nation.[22]

Especially in those systems that are, for reasons of federalism or the heterogenic composition of society, de facto consensus democracies (so-called consociational systems),[23] such as Belgium, public and highly deliberative decision-making may seem naive or illusionary, or at least it is put under great pressure.[24] The possibility to convince, or the willingness to be convinced or to recognise the reasonableness of a particular unwanted solution, may indeed be jeopardised to a greater extent than in other contexts. Nevertheless, in those societies, the court's audiences know—and many would even approve—that decisions could only be reached through the art of complicated compromise. Deliberation does not require compromise, but neither does it exclude it. The publicly translated deliberation that can be expected from such courts can be exactly about the interests at stake and the search for a workable compromise.

The reason why consociationalism cannot be an excuse for lower standards of qualitative judicial deliberation is one of democratic accountability. As said, most agree today that democratic governance is not only about direct electoral accountability, so there is no reason why a constitutional court would not accept its role of real decision-maker, even though it is clearly a role of a different kind than the political branches, and accountable in a different way.

---

[21] C Zurn, *Deliberative Democracy and the Institutions of Judicial Review* (New York, Cambridge University Press, 2007) 274–300. In any case, he would like to see the courts complemented by other institutional and civic fora for constitutional debate.

[22] Sunstein, above n 4, 127.

[23] On this topic see also, eg A Lijphart, 'Constitutional Design for Divided Societies' (2004) *Journal of Democracy* 96; A Lijphart, *Democracy in Plural Societies: A Comparative Exploration* (New Haven, Yale University Press, 1977).

[24] See also Popelier and Patino Alvarez, above n 14, 204–05.

The point about accountability, however, is most essential: in the absence of a vote, the judges of a constitutional court have to be otherwise accountable, and I argue that they can do this through a deliberative decision-making attitude and openness about the decision-making process. It will probably be exposed to criticism, but until someone proposes the ultimate democratic theory that everyone agrees on, any debate is criticisable. The worst criticism that could be levied is that there is not enough material to criticise, that the material presented does not adequately reproduce the debate that took place or that it was not fully informed.

Clearly, there are weaknesses in complicating the effort of legitimising constitutional decision-making in the way presented here. On the content side, of course, it is not inconceivable that a court succeeds in convincing only some parts of its legal and political audiences. It may fail to convince a specific audience altogether. Sometimes a particular constitutional approach or solution may convince (parts of) the political elite but not professional or academic circles, sometimes it may convince the citizens but not the politicians, sometimes it may convince an international audience but not the citizens or national political bodies. On the process side, judges might reject a deliberative discourse altogether, or, if they embrace it, it may be a constant struggle to live up to it in practice. Some argue that there are important limitations to what courts could realistically achieve anyhow.[25] Moreover, admitting that constitutional adjudication is dictated by deliberation does not entail endorsing the practice, which may be not ideal but excusable in ordinary politics, of strategic thinking or sophisticated bargaining games, and which may heavily burden the qualitative deliberation we are looking for.[26]

More generally, and relating to my opening observations, court designers seem to have two goals, which might interact in a rather paradoxical way. First, they want to keep the constitutional judge as far away from ordinary politics as possible, for otherwise the temptation to confuse constitutional possibility with political opportunity might be too great. Secondly, however, given the existence of constitutional pluralism, the judicial decision-makers should be as close to that variety as possible, because it would be contrary to the deliberative function were all reasonable perspectives not represented in the debate. Keeping constitutional judges far from legislative politics but close to the constitutional polity is a delicate balance. Perhaps reconfiguring classic terms,

---

[25] See, eg A Vermeule, *Judging under Uncertainty: An Institutional Theory of Legal Interpretation* (Cambridge, Harvard University Press, 2006).

[26] See generally, eg P Spiller and R Gely, 'Strategic Judicial Decision-Making' in K Whittington, R Kelemen and G Caldeira (eds), *The Oxford Handbook of Law and Politics* (Oxford, Oxford University Press, 2008); see also, among many others, L Epstein and T Jacobi, 'The Strategic Analysis of Judicial Decisions' (2010) *Annual Review of Law and Social Science* 341; G Vanberg, 'Legislative-Judicial Relations: A Game-Theoretic Approach to Constitutional Review' (2001) *American Journal of Political Science* 346. Sen has recently argued exactly this concerning the Supreme Court of the United States: M Sen, 'Courting Deliberation: An Essay on Deliberative Democracy in the American Judicial System' (2013) 27 *Notre Dame Journal of Law, Ethics & Public Policy* 315.

like judicial neutrality and objectivity, as the capacity to conduct a deliberative argument about constitutional meaning will help to understand what that means. Not all of the questions are answered here, however. Implying process legitimacy in the research effort entails its own methodological problems.[27] The search for an adequate methodology to assess, ideally comparatively, the legitimacy of court activity is an ongoing matter. What is beyond any doubt, however, is the great value of Mark Van Hoecke's thinking and writing about these subjects.

---

[27] On the comparative difficulties relating to determining judicial reasoning and the value of motivation of judgments see, eg M Lasser, *Judicial Deliberations: A Comparative Analysis of Judicial Transparency and Legitimacy* (Oxford, Oxford University Press, 2004).

20

Making the Case for European Comparative Legal Studies in Public Law

SUSAN MILLNS

I N THIS CHAPTER an attempt will be made to explain and justify the major benefits of comparative legal studies in Europe in the specific area of public law. This work stems from a personal interest in the protection of fundamental rights that has spanned two major legal axes: public law and comparative law. Synthesising these two orientations, this chapter makes the call for continued research into the relationship between comparative public law and European legal studies in order to better understand the requirements for the protection of fundamental rights across Europe. A degree of precision, however, is needed to clarify the hazy frontiers of this sphere of reference. The habitual classification, particularly in the continental tradition, of legal subjects into separate spheres, notably public and private, it is suggested, is not always helpful in that it creates an impediment to a more holistic consideration of rights. It is, for example, practically impossible to speak the language of human rights discourse without discussing the implications in areas, for example, of civil law, health care law, employment law, public international law and EU law. Hence, while the emphasis in this chapter is on the public law dimension of fundamental rights, this is more in recognition of the fact that such rights fall squarely within the traditional territory of constitutional law than the view that they are applicable solely in the public sphere.

There is one more clarification which needs to be made with regard to the European public law framework of the chapter: this is the evident remark that public law can no longer be confined within the frontiers of individual nation states. Public law matters, including civil liberties and fundamental rights, have to be contextualised in turn within the wider horizons of European and international law. Thus, the framework of reference of the chapter necessarily includes a supranational dimension, which seeks to address the implications of the creeping constitutionalisation of European law and the strengthening of fundamental rights protection as an essential pillar in the construction of a constitutional law for Europe.[1]

Thus, while the subject matter of fundamental rights falls broadly within the domain of public law, the approach which is advocated here is above all comparative. Like the notion of public law, however, the idea of legal comparison is far from clear-cut. By way of explanation, the following section sets out some of the implications of adopting a comparative methodology and seeks to justify a particular interpretation of comparative legal studies with regard to public law matters.

I. COMPARATIVE LAW AND LEGAL CULTURE

The comparison of laws and legal systems is a well-known method of scientific enquiry which is pursued across all continents. A special issue of the *Revue internationale de droit comparé*, published in 1999, clearly shows the worldwide interest in the activity of legal comparison comprising a global set of examples of the state of comparative legal studies in Europe (Germany, France, the UK, Italy, Spain, Belgium, Finland, Sweden, Hungary and Israel), in the Americas (the US and Brazil), and in Asia and Australasia (Hong Kong, India and New Zealand).[2] However, despite the globalisation of the activity of comparing laws, there remains a distinct lack of consensus as to the aims and the appropriate methods for effective comparison. Comparative legal studies thus covers a multitude of enterprises: a discourse on the science of comparative law[3] and the methodology of comparison,[4] an exposition of the *grands systèmes de droit*[5] and principal legal traditions,[6] a debate over the distinction between the civil law and common law traditions,[7] a technical comparison of

---

[1] The European constitutional framework may be considered with regard both to European Union law and the European Convention on Human Rights (ECHR), both of which have implications for the importation of European norms into domestic systems and have resulted in a degree of national convergence.

[2] (1999) 50 *Revue internationale de droit comparé* 747. For a summary see X Blanc-Jouvan, 'Le cinquantenaire de la revue' (1999) 50 *Revue internationale de droit comparé* 747.

[3] L-J Constantinesco, *Traité de droit comparé, tome III* (Paris, Economica, 1983).

[4] HC Gutteridge (trans R David), *Le droit comparé* (Paris, LGDJ, 1953); M Lasser, 'The Question of Understanding' in P Legrand and R Munday (eds), *Comparative Legal Studies: Traditions and Transitions* (Cambridge, Cambridge University Press, 2003) 197.

[5] R David and C Jauffret-Spinozi, *Les grands systèmes de droit contemporains*, 11th edn (Paris, Dalloz, 2002); R David and JEC Brierley, *Major Legal Systems in the World Today: An Introduction to the Comparative Study of Law*, 3rd edn (London, Stevens, 1985); JL Esquirol, 'René David: At the Head of the Legal Family' in A Riles (ed), *Rethinking the Masters of Comparative Law* (Oxford, Hart Publishing, 2001) 211; M Fromont, *Grands systèmes de droit étrangers*, 4th edn (Paris, Dalloz, 2001).

[6] HP Glenn, *Legal Traditions of the World: Sustainable Diversity in Law* (Oxford, Oxford University Press, 2000).

[7] JH Merryman, *The Loneliness of the Comparative Lawyer—and other Essays in Foreign and Comparative Law* (The Hague, Kluwer Law International, 1999). See in particular part I on the 'civil law and common law'.

national legal rules in a particular area of law,[8] a comparison of functions,[9] a study of the place of comparative law amidst the core modules of the legal curriculum[10] and, increasingly, a highly developed theoretical perspective[11] which goes well beyond legal positivism to investigate the concept of legal culture[12] and the value of an inter-disciplinary approach to comparison in law.[13] Whatever the activity denoted by the term comparative legal studies, it will be argued, in sympathy with the latter two approaches, that the work of the comparatist cannot be carried out satisfactorily without some consideration being given to the contexts in which the law is applied and particular attention being paid to the legal cultures and traditions of the countries that are the objects of enquiry.

A. The Act of Comparison: Practice and Theory

The dispute amongst comparative lawyers as to what they actually do and what (if any) sorts of methods they employ to carry out their research suggests that some thought needs to be given to the fundamental questions of what comparative legal studies is all about and, indeed, whether legal systems can be effectively compared when they are, after all, so inherently different. It is evident that the methodology of legal comparison remains relatively unadvanced[14] when viewed alongside more sophisticated comparative studies in related areas such as public administration and political science, suggesting

---

[8] K Zweigert and H Kötz, *An Introduction to Comparative Law*, 3rd edn (Oxford, Oxford University Press, 1998). This book comprises a detailed study of the law of obligations across several European jurisdictions. See also, in the area of torts, W Van Gerven, J Lever and P Larouche, *Cases, Materials and Text on National, Supranational and International Tort Law* (Oxford, Hart Publishing, 2000), particularly 1–12 and 69–74.

[9] Zweigert and Kötz, ibid, 34.

[10] G Samuel, 'Comparative Law as a Core Subject' (2001) 21 *Legal Studies* 444.

[11] P Legrand, 'Comparative Legal Studies and Commitment to Theory' (1995) 58 *Modern Law Review* 262; P Legrand, 'How to Compare Now' (1996) 16 *Legal Studies* 232; P Legrand, *Le droit comparé* (Paris, Presses Universitaires de France, 1999); P Legrand, 'The Same and the Different' in Legrand and Munday, above n 4, 240–311; A Peters and H Schwenke, 'Comparative Law beyond Post-Modernism' (2000) 49 *International and Comparative Law Quarterly* 800; G Samuel, 'Comparative Law and Jurisprudence' (1998) 47 *International and Comparative Law Quarterly* 817.

[12] J Bell, *French Legal Cultures* (London, Butterworths, 2001); HW Ehrmann, *Comparative Legal Cultures* (Englewood Cliffs, NJ, Prentice-Hall, 1976); D Nelken (ed), *Comparing Legal Cultures* (Aldershot, Dartmouth, 1997); D Nelken and J Feest (eds), *Adapting Legal Cultures* (Oxford, Hart Publishing, 2001).

[13] Legrand and Munday, above n 4; Riles, above n 5. These collections bring to the comparative study of law perspectives from anthropology, history, sociology, philosophy, politics, and literary and cultural studies. The volumes have much in common insofar as they both demonstrate that, while comparative legal studies cannot be understood without reference to its historical legacies and the work of its founding fathers, the discipline nevertheless has an important future in contributing to contemporary understandings of phenomena such as globalisation and the rise of new technologies.

[14] Zweigert and Kötz, above n 8, 33. The absence of method in comparative law is explained by the authors as resulting from the relatively late discovery of comparative law as a valid object of scientific study.

that lawyers have much to learn from these examples.[15] Such studies, in demonstrating the importance of context, show above all else that a simple textual analysis of legal norms will be insufficient to explain differences in the choice and application of particular rules of law. On the contrary, it is necessary to look more closely at both the practice and theory behind the act of legal comparison in order for a more meaningful assessment to be made.

The starting point for the present argument is the premise that comparative legal studies should be rooted in a degree of practical experience which demands that the comparatist be immersed in the legal systems of the countries which are the focus of comparison, rather than the research being a purely paper exercise aimed at a compilation of national reports outlining legal responses to a similar factual problem.[16] The importance of the exercise lies in the fact that the comparatist, as an outsider to the legal orders which he or she studies, inevitably experiences difficulties in comprehension which a period of concrete exposure to the other system can sometimes help overcome. Of course, the comparatist remains primarily attached to his or her legal system of origin and thereby necessarily views the foreign jurisdiction from this subjective position. Nevertheless, the tendency to measure other jurisdictions by one's own familiar standards can be somewhat mitigated by a better understanding of the legal culture of the other legal system(s) under investigation.

While confident, therefore, of the benefits of this type of practical experience in achieving a better understanding of the legal system of the foreign jurisdiction, the comparatist nevertheless needs to be aware of a certain colouring of her conclusions by the very subjective nature of the experience. In this respect, no comparatist can ever fully escape her own legal culture, meaning that all comparative legal studies are tainted to a greater or lesser extent by subjective judgments about the system of the other. As Pierre Legrand rightly points out: 'even if the comparatist does not make a living out of being judgmental, to compare is always to judge'.[17] It has to be admitted that the conclusions drawn throughout one's comparative are marked by the subjective nature of the activity of comparison. Being schooled, first and foremost, in

---

[15] See, eg J Ziller, 'L'accès à la fonction publique dans les Etats membres des communautés européennes: étude juridique comparative' Thesis in Law, Paris II (1986), particularly 5–12; J Ziller, *Administrations comparées: les systèmes politico-administratifs de l'Europe des douze* (Paris, Montchrestien, 1993); B Badie and G Hermet, *La politique comparée* (Paris, Armand Colin, 2001) ch 1; Y Mény and Y Surel, *Politique comparée: les démocraties: Etats-Unis, France, Grande-Bretagne, Italie RFA*, 6th edn (Paris, Montchrestien, 2001) 5–25; J Widner, 'Comparative Politics and Comparative Law' (1998) 46 *American Journal of Comparative Law* 739. With regard to sociological methods of comparison see FJM Feldbrugge, 'Sociological Research Methods and Comparative Law' in M Rotondi (ed), *Inchieste di diritto comparato* (Padova/New York, CEDAM/Oceana Publications, 1973) vol 2, 211ff.

[16] It is not denied, however, that this form of comparison may have its merits provided that the research is not simply limited to an exposition of the rules applied in a number of countries and that it contains a synthesis of conclusions.

[17] 'Même si le comparatiste ne fait pas métier de juger, comparer, c'est toujours juger': P Legrand, *Le droit comparé*, above n 11, 56.

a common law system, for example, makes it impossible to appreciate fully what French law signifies to a French lawyer. It is impossible to extricate one-self completely from a common law mentality and training, and this means that certain questions (such as the publication of dissenting opinions) appear glaringly important to a common lawyer when they are not at all so to a civil lawyer who has never been exposed to equivalent practices.

Practical experience, however, just like the purely formulaic comparison of different national legal rules, are insufficient in themselves to permit mean-ingful conclusions to be drawn from the act of comparison. To this end, it is necessary to take a more theoretical perspective in order to elaborate an appropriate conceptual framework for the comprehension of legal norms and their practical application. Such a theoretical underpinning to the act of com-parison in law pushes the comparatist to go beyond a pure examination of the legal texts themselves and to engage in a more critical scrutiny of the place of legal rules within the context of society (be it French, British or European), and in political and moral discourses. This approach is all the more impera-tive in the subject area of human rights given that this concept, in its many interpretations, is intimately linked to the historical and cultural development of Western societies, as well as to national views on key moral and ethical, life-and-death, issues.[18]

Stressing the importance of a contextual analysis to comparative law, it is acknowledged, goes against a certain amount of well-established academic writing in comparative legal studies. Some comparatists have expressed the view that any comparison of law should not go beyond the rules themselves, as to do so would leave the comparatist at risk of tainting the exercise of comparison by an analysis which is overly political or subjective.[19] As a result, this school of thought advocates that the only successful attempts at com-parative legal studies are those carried out in the area of private law, and, more narrowly still, the law of obligations.[20] Consequently, according to this

---

[18] As David Feldman accurately observes of the first order fundamental rights obligation to respect human, dignity: dignity he writes, is 'a notion which is culturally dependent and emi-nently malleable': D Feldman, 'Human Dignity as a Legal Value—Part I' [1999] *Public Law* 698.

[19] Zweigert and Kötz, above n 8, 40. Zweigert and Kötz maintain that most areas of private law are untainted by politics and are, therefore, appropriate for comparative enquiry which will normally reveal similar responses in national systems: 'if we leave aside the topics which are heavily impressed by moral views or values, mainly to be found in family law and in the law of succes-sion, and concentrate on those parts of private law which are relatively "unpolitical", we find that as a general rule developed nations answer the needs of legal business in the same or in a very similar way'. This observation leads the authors to the striking conclusion that if the comparatist, at the end of the study, finds significant divergences between the countries under investigation, this suggests that the research was not properly conducted and should be commenced afresh: 'the comparatist can rest content if his researches through all the relevant material lead to the conclu-sions that the systems he has compared reach the same or similar practical results, but if he finds that there are great differences or indeed diametrically opposite results, he should be warned and go back to check again whether the terms in which he posed his original question were indeed purely functional, and whether he has spread the net of his researches quite wide enough' (ibid).

[20] See, eg the second part of *An Introduction to Comparative Law* by Zweigert and Kötz, which contains a detailed comparative study of the law of obligations.

view, it is dangerous, if not impossible, to compare public law rules, as this branch of the legal system is too intimately linked to the state and to the moral particularities of each country to make an objective comparison viable.

Whilst it is true that many legal comparatists use private law examples to ground their research, there are some who, nevertheless, accept the necessity of a contextual (and political) dimension to the activity of comparison.[21] Moreover, beyond the realm of private law, there is an increasing awareness amongst public lawyers of the relevance and usefulness of comparative analyses to their work.[22] Following in their footsteps, the objective of this call for comparative European public law research is precisely to break away from the limited perspective that comparative methods are of use only to obligations lawyers and to insist upon their importance in the area of public law.

This insistence is justified by a number of considerations. First, it is not accepted that a clear distinction exists between public and private law giving rise to two distinct and autonomous systems of legal rules. While French legal doctrine is founded upon such a classification of norms, the tradition of the common law has never known this division. AV Dicey, in his celebrated work on the law of the English 'Constitution', observed French administrative law with fascinated horror and was quite convinced that the English wanted nothing to do with a system which ran so contrary to the rule of law.[23] For Dicey, one of the pillars of the Constitution was a strict application of the principle of equality between state and citizens. No one should be above the law, including public authorities, which should hold no discretionary or arbitrary power. Even if English lawyers speak from time to time about 'public' or 'private' law matters and the legal system has sought to introduce specialised jurisdictions, such as administrative tribunals and the Administrative Court, to deal with certain branches of law, the type of binary classification which is known on the continent has never taken hold. Hence, in institutional terms, administrative tribunals bear more resemblance to what the French call *les juridictions d'exception* (that is, jurisdictions which have competence in a particular specialised field), including, for example, employment tribunals (the

---

[21] See, eg the various works of Pierre Legrand, above n 11.

[22] In the area of Anglo-French comparative public law see, eg C Adjei, 'The Comparative Perspective and the Protection of Human Rights à la Française' (1997) 17 *Oxford Journal of Legal Studies* 281; S Boyron, 'Proportionality in English Administrative Law: A Faulty Translation?' (1992) 12 *Oxford Journal of Legal Studies* 237; E Picard, 'Les droits de l'homme et l'"activisme judiciaire"' [2000] *Pouvoirs* 113. In a similar vein, the American comparatist, Mark Tushnet, has identified three major ways ('functionalism', 'expressivism' and '*bricolage*') in which a comparison of constitutional laws can contribute to an improved understanding of the Constitution of the United States, permitting the national courts to see how the Constitution may be better interpreted following analysis of experiences elsewhere: M Tushnet, 'The Possibilities of Comparative Constitutional Law' (1999) 108 *Yale Law Journal* 1228.

[23] AV Dicey, *An Introduction to the Study of the Law of the Constitution*, 10th edn (London, MacMillan, 1959, revised 1975) 328–465. The author states that: '[i]n many continental countries, notably in France, there exists a scheme of administrative law—known to Frenchmen as *droit administratif*—which rests on ideas foreign to the fundamental asssumptions of our English common law, and especially to what we have termed the rule of law' (328–29).

equivalent of the French *conseils de prud'hommes*, which, of course, apply rules of private employment law). Moreover, the Administrative Court is part of the High Court and consists simply of a list of judges who spend part of their time on judicial review.[24] Thus, the common law system, characterised by its unified court structure and uniform application of the principle of equality before the law, demands a rejection of any attempt to establish a rigid distinction between public and private legal measures.[25] Even in France, there is an increasing *rapprochement* between the obligations held by private persons and public authorities, evident, for example, in the area of non-contractual liability for commercial and industrial services.[26] In short, the sharp division drawn by some comparatists between public and private law in order to sustain a refusal to admit the relevance of comparative legal method to public law is unsustainable when viewed from the perspective of a common lawyer.

The second reason for refusing the conclusions drawn by private law comparatists as to the exclusivity of their activities is their false assumption that private law is neutral and beyond political debate. It is necessary only to observe the way in which the law of contracts, with its requirement of good faith and provisions on unfair contractual terms, has sought to mitigate the effects of the liberal ideological assumption that all contracting parties are free to enter into a bargain and negotiate its content irrespective of their respective economic power to see that the law of obligations has distinct political overtones.[27] Likewise, torts law is replete with examples of the political choices which are made in determining liability for harm.[28] Using an example drawn from French law, there is nothing more political than the decision to award damages to a severely disabled child who asserts that he should never have been born.[29]

Finally, despite their different moral attitudes and diverse national traditions, all modern democratic states today face similar challenges raised by scientific progress, technological innovation, globalisation and the evolution

---

[24] In this respect, Dawn Oliver has noted that the Administrative Court cannot be considered an equivalent of the Conseil d'Etat, whose members are separate from the judiciary and which has its own exclusive jurisdiction, procedures and substantive law: D Oliver, 'English Law and Convention Concepts' in P Craig and R Rawlings (eds), *Law and Administration in Europe: Essays in Honour of Carol Harlow* (Oxford, Oxford University Press, 2003) 83.

[25] C Harlow, '"Public" and "Private" Law: Definition without Distinction' (1980) 43 *Modern Law Review* 241; D Oliver, 'Pourquoi n'y a-t-il pas vraiment de distinction entre droit public et droit privé en Angleterre?' (2001) *Revue international de droit comparé* 327; M Taggart, '"The Peculiarities of the English": Resisting the Public/Private Distinction' in Craig and Rawlings, ibid, 107–21.

[26] *Tribunal des conflits*, 22 January 1921, *Colonie de la Côte d'Ivoire c/ Société commerciale de l'Ouest africain*, Dalloz 1921, 3, 1, conclusions by Matter.

[27] J Wightman, *Contract: A Critical Introduction* (London, Pluto Press, 1996).

[28] J Conaghan and W Mansell, *The Wrongs of Tort*, 2nd edn (London, Pluto Press, 1999).

[29] The *Perruche* case: Cass ass plén, 17 November 2000, *Epx X c/Mutuelle d'assurance du corps sanitaire français et a.*; rapporteur P Sargos, conseiller à la Cour de cassation; conclusions by J Sainte-Rose, avocat général à la Cour de cassation; Juris-classeur périodique, 2000, II 10438, note by F Chabas.

of society, all of which may have an impact upon the fundamental rights of individuals. This commonality is recognised clearly in the steps taken to constitutionalise European law.[30] Whereas the project to elaborate a European civil code has been much contested with regard to both procedure and content, not to mention necessity,[31] this has not hindered the far smoother public law enterprise of elaborating and adopting a Charter of Fundamental Rights for the European Union.[32] Drafted following a consensual procedure characterised by its openness and transparency,[33] and given legal status in December 2009 following the adoption of the Lisbon Treaty, the Charter is testimony to a move towards the harmonisation of fundamental rights provisions in Europe and, in particular, to an agreement on their content— something which has so far been impossible to achieve in the area of civil law. Moreover, the debate over the elaboration of the Charter showed a willingness to include different voices and perspectives in a way that the discussion about the adoption of a European civil code has not done. As far as the latter is concerned, Pierre Legrand concludes that the European integration project, as exemplified by the effort to codify the law of obligations, is essentially exclusive while making a pretence of being universal.[34] For Legrand, this is because the very idea of a Civil Code is confined to

[30] See P Allot, 'The Crisis of European Constitutionalism: Reflections on the Revolution in Europe' (1997) 34 *Common Market Law Review* 439; K Armstrong, 'Legal Integration: Theorising the Legal Dimensions of European Integration' (1998) 36 *Journal of Common Market Studies* 155; G de Búrca and J Scott (eds), *Constitutional Change in the EU: From Uniformity to Flexibility?* (Oxford, Hart Publishing, 2000); I Pernice, 'Multilevel Constitutionalism and the Treaty of Amsterdam: European Constitution-Making Revisited' (1999) 36 *Common Market Law Review* 703; J Shaw, 'Constitutionalism in the European Union' (1999) 6 *Journal of European Public Policy* 579; JHH Weiler, *The Constitution of Europe: Do the New Clothes Have an Emperor? And Other Essays on European Integration* (Cambridge, Cambridge University Press, 1999); JHH Weiler, 'A Constitution for Europe? Some Hard Choices' (2002) 40/4 *Journal of Common Market Studies* 563.

[31] Communication from the Commission to the Council and the European Parliament on European contract law of 11 July 2001 [2001] OJ C255/1; G Cornu, 'Un Code civil n'est pas un instrument communautaire', *Dalloz* chron, 2002, 4, 351; S Feiden and CU Schmid (eds), 'Evolutionary Perspectives and Projects on Harmonisation of Private Law in the EU' Working Paper, Law no 99/7 (Florence, European University Institute, 1999); E Hondius, 'Towards a European Civil Code: The Debate Has Started' (1997) 5 *European Review of Private Law* 455; T Koopmans, 'Towards a European Civil Code' (1997) 5 *European Review of Private Law* 541; P Legrand, 'Against a European Civil Code' (1997) 60 *Modern Law Review* 44; Y Lequette, 'Quelques remarques à propos du projet de Code civil européen de M. von Bar' (2002) *Dalloz* chron 2202; BS Markesinis, 'Why a Code is not the Best Way to Advance the Cause of European Legal Unity' (1997) 5 *European Review of Private Law* 519.

[32] The EU's Charter of Fundamental Rights was 'solemnly proclaimed' by the institutions of the Union at the meeting of the European Council in Nice in December 2000 ([2000] OJ C364/8).

[33] The Charter was drafted by a body comprising 62 members drawn from four constituent groups: the governments of the Member States (15 members), the Commission (1), the European Parliament (16) and representatives from the national parliaments (30). Observer status was given to two representatives from the European Court of Justice and two from the Council of Europe, one of whom was drawn from the European Court of Human Rights. See further G de Búrca, 'The Drafting of the European Charter of Fundamental Rights' (2001) 26 *European Law Review* 126.

[34] P Legrand, *Le droit comparé*, above n 11, 100.

the civil law tradition and not that of the common law. Thus, a European civil code would demonstrate the 'tacit exclusion of the common law way of thinking', a way that rejects a universalistic understanding of law and has never been persuaded to mimic the continental preference for codification.[35] This reveals the paradox inherent in the codification debate:

> it does the contrary to what it says, it excludes a part of the whole [the common law] while claiming the virtues of totalising harmony . . . It is not a pluralist but a singular a way of thinking—the Romanist perspective on life in law—dissimulated under the guise of the universal.[36]

Contrary to the difficulties associated with a harmonised codification of obligations law across Europe, in the area of public law the impetus towards adopting a catalogue or charter of fundamental rights is noticeable as much at the national as at the European level. The introduction in the UK of the Human Rights Act 1998 had the effect of importing into domestic law a catalogue of rights, despite the common law underpinnings of the legal system, the resistance to codification initiatives and the lack of consensus in the past on the need for a Bill of Rights.[37] Moreover, it may well be that the possibility of convergence is stronger in the area of public law, as there exists in Europe a basic accord over the values of democracy and respect for fundamental rights.[38] This provides evidence of a commonality capable of producing an ever more harmonised pan-European approach to fundamental rights protection which is hardly as yet envisaged in the area of obligations law.

For these reasons, it is maintained that the exercise of comparison in public law pursued in a broad social and political context is fully justified. This should not, however, be taken to mean an expectation of similarity in the comparison of constitutional arrangements in different European jurisdictions. While European states are clearly committed to a similar programme of rights protection, the objective of comparative legal studies is not simply to point

---

[35] Ibid.

[36] '[I]l fait le contraire de ce qu'il dit, il exclut une partie du tout [le common law] alors qu'il clame les vertus de l'harmonie totalisante . . . [C]'est une pensée non du pluriel, mais de l'unique—la perspective romaniste de la vie dans le droit—dissimulée sous les alibis de l'universel': ibid, 101. It is in order to mount a defence of the common law that Legrand offers a practical justification for his theoretical approach to comparative legal studies (P Legrand, 'The Same and the Different', above n 11, 311).

[37] The literature on the introduction is extensive. See, eg F Klug, *Values for a Godless Age: The Story of the UK's New Bill of Rights* (London, Penguin, 2000); N Whitty, T Murphy and S Livingstone, *Civil Liberties Law: The Human Rights Act Era* (London, Butterworths, 2001).

[38] These are now cited in Art 2 of the Treaty on European Union (see below). On the degree of consensus over respect for fundamental rights in both present and future Member States see S Millns, 'Unravelling the Ties that Bind: National Constitutions in the Light of the Values, Principles and Objectives of the Constitution for Europe' in J Ziller, *The Europeanisation of Constitutional Law in the Light of the Constitutional Treaty for the Union* (Paris, L'Harmattan, 2003), 97ff.

out similarities.[39] On the contrary, it is more to uncover and explain differences which are often just as, if not more, instructive than resemblances.[40]

B. Diversity and Convergence of Legal Cultures

Rooting comparative legal studies in a contextual environment does not simply involve seeking to explain differences between legal systems in the light of historical, political and social phenomena, but implies that attention be paid also to the legal context in which norms are adopted, amended and applied. In other words, it is necessary to consider the 'legal culture' in which rules operate, for it is only with this information to hand that the particularities of national laws can be understood. The investigation of law as 'cultural fabric'[41] does, however, pose a basic problem for the comparatist. Given the evident differences between legal systems (the English–French common law–civil law traditions providing a good example of these), is it viable to attempt a comparison of national laws at all? Are not legal cultures simply too different to be the object of meaningful comparative enquiry? The case for a positive answer to this question is put forcefully by Pierre Legrand, who sees not merely difference but rather insurmountable distinctions between national systems and particularly between *les mentalités juridiques*—that is, legal mentalities, or ways of thinking about law.[42]

The diversity between systems implies that the comparatist will always find him or herself in the impossible situation of seeking to understand the 'other'. For example, on the one hand, the British comparatist, trained in the common law tradition and used to the application of the doctrine of precedent, will

---

[39] The sweeping conclusion of Zweigert and Kötz, that any comparison (in the area of obligations law) which reveals differences rather than similarities must be misguided, is, therefore, not shared, not least because it presumes a result which seems to obviate the need for, and interest of, comparative legal enquiry.

[40] In this respect, the view of Pierre Legrand that difference is not indifferent is shared ('la différence n'est pas indifférente . . . Il y a lieu, en effet, pour le comparatiste, de comprendre que le comparatisme en droit ne saurait avoir pour raison d'être que l'appréhension des différences': P Legrand, *Le droit comparé*, above n 11, 37). Legrand has gone on to celebrate the 'redemptive, empowering feature of differential thought' in an extensive rejection of the argument that difference is 'divisive and impoverishing', aiming on the contrary to assert its potential to provide 'a vital capacity for action by enabling one to resist the erosion of boundaries between subjects, by allowing one to elude misrecognition or banishment, by permitting one to avoid violent confusions' (P Legrand, 'The Same and the Different', above n 11, 241–42). For a not dissimilar critique of the emphasis in post-war American comparative law on similarity at the exclusion of difference see VG Curran, 'Cultural Immersion, Difference and Categories in US Comparative Law' (1998) 46 *American Journal of Comparative Law* 43.

[41] Legrand, 'The Same and the Different', ibid, 278.

[42] P Legrand, 'European Legal Systems Are Not Converging' (1996) 45 *International and Comparative Law Quarterly* 60. Legrand uses the expression 'the collective mental programme' to convey his sense of the concept of legal mentality (60). For a critique of the 'exaggerated stress' placed by Legrand on the study of insurmountable difference rather than similarity see D Nelken, 'Comparatists and Transferability' in Legrand and Munday, above n 4, 440–46.

never be able to appreciate fully the civil law tradition in which the judge is prohibited from creating legal rules, being merely *la bouche de la loi*, or mouthpiece of the legislator.[43] On the other hand, the French comparatist will see as profoundly odd both the British understanding of the notion of 'legal rules' and the importance attributed to 'facts' in cases. As far as rules are concerned, the pragmatism of the common law judge, which at times may seem far from requiring an application of strict principles and, thus, may permit a degree of 'invention' of legal rules, is very different from the reasoning of civilian judges, who begin with a reference to an established legal norm, which is then applied to the case in hand. As for the common law's insistence on the particular facts of cases which may ultimately determine the decision of a judge to follow or depart from an established precedent, this, too, looks odd from the perspective of lawyers trained in the civilian tradition, who are used to giving primary importance to categories of subjective rights and general legal principles. Unlike civil law, the common law appears as a 'seamless web' in which 'no legal decision can be considered independently from the facts upon which it is based'.[44]

Even the core notions of French and English law seem to have little in common. For example, an English lawyer will be trained to see in the idea of a 'contract' an exchange of promises in the sense of a bargain, while her French counterpart will be taught to view the notion of *'contrat'* as an *accord de volontés*, or meeting of minds.[45] The conclusion which must be drawn is that, in order to remain faithful to both interpretations, one has to admit the two notions have little in common both in fact and in law. Equally telling of the diversity of legal cultures is the example of delictual civil responsibility, which is founded in France upon the principle set out in Article 1382 of the Civil Code, according to which any fault which causes damage to another person must be compensated.[46] This is not at all the case in English law, where actions in tort are not the object of a general theory and are not founded

[43] Art 5 of the Civil Code makes it clear that the findings of judges in individual cases have no general application ('[i]l est défendu aux juges de prononcer par voie de disposition générale et réglementaire sur les causes qui leur sont soumises'), and Art 1351 provides that judicial decisions create no precedent, binding only the parties to the case to which they refer ('[l]'autorité de la chose jugée n'a lieu qu'à l'égard de ce qui fait l'objet du jugement'). On the general question of the specificity of the common law see P Legrand (ed), *Common Law d'un siècle l'autre* (Cowansville, Québec, Les éditions Yvon Blais Inc, 1992); on the opposite tradition of the civil law see HP Glenn, *Legal Traditions of the World: Sustainable Diversity in Law* (Oxford, Oxford University Press, 2000) ch 5.

[44] The term 'réseau sans frontière' is used by Pierre Legrand to describe the common law in which 'aucune décision judiciaire ne [peut] jamais être considérée indépendamment des faits sur lesquels elle a porté': P Legrand, 'Sens et non-sens d'un code civil européen' (1996) 48 *Revue internationale de droit comparé* 789. See also the discussion of the role of the common law in the context of the legal education of common lawyers in G Samuel and S Millns, 'L'enseignement du droit en Angleterre' (1998) *Cahiers de Méthodologie Juridique* 1527.

[45] P Legrand, 'How to Compare Now', above n 11, 234; *Le droit comparé*, above n 11, 24.

[46] Art 1382 provides that: 'Tout fait quelconque de l'homme, qui cause à autrui un dommage, oblige celui par la faute duquel il est arrivé à le réparer.'

upon a notion of general obligation, except in the area of negligence. On the contrary, each cause of action falls within a sub-category of torts law, and is governed by independent rules and principles.[47]

In the area of public law, too, the absence in the UK of principles of constitutional value in the sense in which these are recognised in France (that is, as emanating from constitutional texts) has provoked much more in the way of a 'seamless web' of case law of a broadly constitutional nature than in France.[48] In this respect, it is acknowledged that there is some evidence to support Legrand's contention that the incompatibilities between legal systems and mentalities make any exercise in comparison hazardous in the light of irreducible differences.[49] That said, the risk is more than worth running—as Legrand's work on comparisons between the common law and civilian law tradition demonstrates—if the result of the comparison is a contribution to the production of knowledge, a heightened sensitivity to the diversity of legal cultures and an awareness of the particularity of both one's own law and that of the other. Moreover, despite Legrand's scepticism about attempts to unify national legal systems at the substantive level, there is a sense in which a degree of *rapprochement* may be observed as regards French and UK legal sources in the form of a 'textualisation' of the common law (that is, an increased insistence upon rules in statutory or written form[50]) and a 'judicialisation', to borrow the terminology of Stone Sweet, of the civil law (in the sense of an increased interpretative role for the judiciary[51]). Moreover, this tendency is reinforced by initiatives aimed at a convergence on substance, particularly at the European level.[52] These initiatives include not only the obvious harmonisation measures to achieve completion of the internal market,[53] but also, as noted above, the convergence of elements of private law (notably aspects of

---

[47] See G Samuel and J Rinkes, *Law of Obligations and Legal Remedies*, 2nd edn (London, Cavendish Publishing, 2001) 21–23.

[48] See J Bell, *French Legal Cultures* (London, Butterworths, 2001) v–x and 243–57.

[49] Legrand, 'European Legal Systems Are Not Converging', above n 42, 74. According to Legrand, the 'irreducible differences' between common law and civil law traditions are the result of two distinguishing features of the English system: the inherent power of the judiciary to adjudicate and the subordination of the executive to legislative authority.

[50] As evidenced, for example, in the passage of the Human Rights Act 1998 with its incorporation of a catalogue of rights in the form of the ECHR into domestic law.

[51] A Stone Sweet, *Governing with Judges: Constitutional Politics in Europe* (Oxford, Oxford University Press, 2000). This is notable particularly in the area of the law of torts (demonstrated in exemplary fashion by the decision of the Cour de cassation to admit a claim for 'wrongful life' in the *Perruche* case, cited above n 29). It is also apparent in the area of privacy, with the absence of constitutional definition of the right to private life in France having led the judiciary to elaborate substantially upon the extent of the application of this right. See C Dupré, 'The Protection of Private Life against Freedom of Expression in French Law' (2000) 6 *European Human Rights Law Review* 627.

[52] B De Witte, 'The Convergence Debate' (1996) 3 *Maastricht Journal of European and Comparative Law* 105.

[53] These facilitate the free movement of persons, goods, services and capital throughout the European Union. See P Craig and G de Búrca, *EU Law: Text, Cases and Materials*, 5th edn (Oxford, Oxford University Press, 2011).

contract law,[54] non-contractual liability[55] and family law[56]) and public law,[57] the ensemble implying that national legal systems are not inherently incompatible on all fronts, especially when pushed to reconsider their national positions by norms enacted at the European level.

Of course, it deserves to be emphasised that legal convergence and divergence are not necessarily mutually exclusive. In this respect, it may well be that convergence can be observed in some areas of law while divergence, or, at least, respect for difference, is practised in others. This pluralistic approach is certainly evident in the sphere of respect for fundamental rights, which, although an agreed common value throughout Europe, is subjected to different interpretations amongst Member States, made possible by their often indeterminate and contingent or malleable character.

II. THE CHALLENGES OF COMPARATIVE RESEARCH

In advocating any form of comparative research, a number of challenges need to be recognised and addressed. Inevitably, comparative law, like any form of scientific enquiry, has certain pitfalls of which it is helpful for the comparatist to be aware before embarking on the exercise, and this applies particularly to the domain of public law. The difficulties associated with subjectivity and context, in the sense of the particular standpoint from which the comparatist observes the systems under investigation, have been mentioned briefly above in the context of the refusal of some comparative private lawyers to admit of the possibility of comparison in the politicised realm of public law. While not of this persuasion, Legrand nevertheless concludes that no one should embark upon comparative legal studies without taking into account the limitations of the exercise.[58] By this he means the confines of the context within which the comparison and the law is situated, as well as the history and culture of the countries being studied. Only detailed knowledge of the cultural, economic, historical, political and social context of institutions, procedures, practices and rules in effect allows recognition of similarities which go beyond name and form. The context of any particular legal system is, therefore, equally as

---

[54] C Jamin and D Mazeaud (ed), *L'harmonisation du droit des contrats en Europe* (Paris, Economica, 2001).

[55] W Van Gerven, 'Non-contractual Liability of Member States, Community Institutions and Individuals for Breaches of a Community Law with a View to a Common Law for Europe' (1994) 1 *Maastricht Journal of European and Comparative Law* 6; W Van Gerven, 'Bridging the Unbridgeable: Community and National Tort Laws after Francovich and Brasserie' (1996) 45 *International and Comparative Law Quarterly* 507.

[56] C McGlynn, 'A Family Law for the European Union' in J Shaw (ed), *Social Law and Policy in an Evolving European Union* (Oxford, Hart Publishing, 2000) 223–41.

[57] The EU's Charter of Fundamental Rights incorporated into the EU's legal order with the introduction of the Treaty of Lisbon in 2009 is producing harmonising effects upon the constitutional systems of Member States, at least insofar as the protection of fundamental rights in the implementation of EU law is concerned.

[58] P Legrand, *Le droit comparé*, above n 11, 62.

important as, if not more important than, the rules of law which are the object of comparison. Likewise, context is of primary importance if one recalls that 'the comparatist cannot escape her subjectivity or her situatedness'[59] in that she inevitably speaks from a particular location—her system and country of origin. This marks a real challenge for the comparative lawyer, who must seek to 'overcome the phenomenon of identification with the legal culture, inevitably particular, in which he [or she] has been trained as a national lawyer'.[60]

It is only in overcoming this obstacle that the comparatist can attain the 'full measure of his or her critical vocation'.[61] Of course, even practical experience in the system of the other can never completely sever the tie with the culture of origin, and its value resides, therefore, in enabling the comparatist to draw the benefits of bringing to bear an external perspective upon the foreign institution or system under investigation. A certain distance between observer and object is, after all, not a bad thing in itself. Indeed, it might be maintained that this distance ensures that the comparatist does not become lost in, or overwhelmed by, the law of the other system, and that it assists in ensuring a clearer and more measured perspective.

It should be added, finally, that the subjective light in which comparative legal studies is bathed can be extremely productive in the act of comparison itself, that is, at the final stages of analysis and conclusion. This is because comparative law, in order to produce more than a simple juxtaposition of facts concerning two or more legal systems, has to involve an analysis by the comparatist of the data gathered. It is only in carrying out this final act of comparison, which inevitably draws upon the researcher's own perspectives, experiences and legal training, that it can be hoped to offer satisfactory conclusions.

The second obstacle to effective legal comparison, and one which, unlike the issue of context and subjectivity, is often neglected, concerns the problem of language and, by implication, the translation of legal terminology. In seeking to overcome this difficulty, it seems prudent to follow the advice of other comparatists, which is quite simply to learn not to translate.[62] This is because translation, particularly if carried out literally, will result in a poor understanding of complex legal phenomena which are known only to individual systems. A good example of this would be the translation into French of the concept of the common law as '*le droit commun*' (which in French denotes the application of general rules in the absence of any more specific provision). Thus, in order to remain faithful to the subtle nuances of legal terminology, the practice has been adopted in this work to avoid translation if at all possible.

---

[59] M Lasser, above n 4, 219.

[60] '[Le comparatiste doit] surmonter le phénomène d'identification avec la culture juridique, inévitablement située, dans laquelle il s'est d'abord formé comme juriste national': P Legrand, *Le droit comparé*, above n 11, 65.

[61] Described by Legrand as 'la plénitude de sa vocation critique' (ibid).

[62] See P Legrand, *Le droit comparé*, above n 11, citing R Sacco, *Introduzione al diritto comparato*, 5th edn (Turin, UTET, 1992) 40–41.

III. THE INTEREST OF COMPARATIVE STUDY IN PUBLIC LAW

Having outlined in Section I above the broader considerations which surround comparative research, and in Section II some of the pitfalls, the purpose of Section III is to explore the reasons for comparative legal study in the area of fundamental rights. Zweigert and Kötz identify four main reasons for engaging in comparative analysis: (i) as an aid to the legislator when considering law reform; (ii) as a tool of interpretation; (iii) as a vital component of legal education; and (iv) as a contribution to the unification of law.[63] It might be added that the discipline of comparative legal studies also provides useful insights for assessing compliance with international and European norms. All of these aims are applicable to the present comparative study of rights.

The interest of a comparison of European public laws lies particularly in its constitutional dimension. This is because the twin phenomena of the modernisation and the Europeanisation of constitutional law have led to an opening of perspectives across Europe both from common law and continental systems. Despite the differences between these legal traditions, there is an increasing cross-channel dialogue that points to a coming together, if not a complete meeting, of common law and civilian legal minds, together with an increased appreciation of the merits of comparative enquiry.[64]

The value of comparing the common and civil legal, and specifically constitutional, systems lies primarily in the exploration of their traditional divergences in the light of increasing resemblances. With regard to the former, the habitual distinction made between countries practising the common law and those with a civilian tradition is often reduced to simplifications. The distinction between systems based primarily upon written law (*droit écrit*), that is, continental countries, and those with an unwritten tradition is reductionist because both written law and case law are in fact sources of legal rules in the two systems.[65] The real difference is that the legislative style (*style législatif*) used in common law countries is distinct from that of continental countries to the extent that legislation in the former is often detailed, long and precise, while in the latter it sets out guiding principles without claiming to be exhaustive.[66]

---

[63] Zweigert and Kötz, above n 8, 15ff. Of course, not all comparatists share these views. For example, some comparatists are extremely sceptical about the aim and prospects of unifying laws. For further discussion of the 'projects' which comparative law as a discipline serves see Riles, above n 5, 11–15.

[64] There is also evidence of an increased willingness on the part of the senior judiciary to engage in legal comparisons to assist their decision-making. See, eg the judgment of Lord Rodger in *Fairchild v Glenhaven Funeral Services Ltd* [2002] 3 WLR 89, which contains a comparative study of Roman, French and German law on the question of whether special rules or principles should be adopted to cope with situations in which a claimant cannot establish which of a number of wrongdoers caused his or her injury.

[65] Ibid.

[66] Ibid.

The orientation of law around fundamental principles is not part of the mentality of the common law, which has remained largely immune from the influences of Roman law.[67] Suffice to recall that the common law system is constructed around forms of action, rather than grand principles, which is profoundly at odds with the Roman legacy. Forms of action as known to the common law are not divided between *actiones in rem* or *in personam*, as in the continental tradition, so that UK law is not founded upon a scientific classification which distinguishes the law of persons from the law of things. It will be seen below that the impact of this distinction, so crucial to French legal mentality, has been profound in the construction of, for example, the concept of human dignity in France.[68] The UK experience, however, shows that a distinction between persons and things, and the rights which are associated with this division (that is, the opposition of *droits personnels* and *droit réels*), has hardly materialised, not even in cases which touch upon human dignity.[69] Moreover, until recently (particularly since the introduction of the Human Rights Act 1998), the very notion of a subjective right (or *droit subjectif* in the continental sense) played a very limited role in the common law mentality. Thus, the roots of the two legal systems and their architecture founded upon grand principles (in the continental case) and a 'seamless web' of jurisprudence (in the UK) provide a helpful framework for analysis of the evolution of the common concern to protect human rights. Both the material and personal scopes of the concept, together with its interpretation and insertion within the constitutional arrangements of each of the national systems, are instructive markers for thinking through the meanings, implications and possible uses of the concept.

There are, furthermore, two unifying factors which justify a comparative study of fundamental rights in Europe. First, the global phenomenon of technological advancement, which has revolutionised all societies, merits comparative analysis for its capacity to impact upon (that is, promote and threaten) human rights. Europe is experiencing the challenges raised by scientific progress, biotechnological developments and the information society, together with the ethical dilemmas surrounding issues such as assisted conception, animal and human cloning, gene therapy, euthanasia and assisted suicide, to which these advances give rise. Moreover, most countries are increasingly being confronted by the potential assaults upon both physical and mental integrity which may be produced by the use of new technologies. The different ways in which the European states have used legal measures to address these challenges provide important insights into the operation of their respec-

---

[67] See the discussion above of Legrand's argument that the introduction of a European civil code founded upon such general principles is exclusive of the common law way of thinking.

[68] See R Andorno, *La distinction juridique entre les personnes et les choses—à l'épreuve des procréations artificielles* (Paris, LGDJ, 1996).

[69] On the absence of a classification of real and personal rights in the common law see G Samuel, 'Existe-t-il une procédure de codification du droit anglais?' [1997] *Revue française d'administration publique* 209.

tive legal cultures, together with demonstrating the different interpretations which can be attached to the concept of rights, depending on the perspective from which it is viewed. Suffice to say at this stage, however, that the common concern to emphasise the value of fundamental rights in legal terms at this particular moment in history is not accidental. It is precisely the moment at which fundamental rights are most at risk that their status and meaning in law are most in need of clarification.

Just as the challenges of advancement are universal, so too is the obligation to respect human rights. Article 2 of the Treaty on European Union now expressly includes respect for human rights as one of the values of the EU, alongside the closely related values of respect for human dignity, liberty and equality. The commonality of the value of respect for human rights can hardly be doubted, given that it forms a key part of the constitutional arrangements of all Member States (present and future). The centrality of this value to the EU's legal order is further demonstrated by the prominence of the Charter of Fundamental Rights, now given legally binding status within the Union, and the EU's imminent accession to the European Convention on Human Rights.

For this reason, one of the ongoing key questions for research in European comparative law is the extent to which fundamental rights are protected in equal measure across Europe. Evidently, and despite the commonality of the value of fundamental rights protection across Europe, there remain important variables with regard to the standards, content, interpretation and mechanisms of protection in the different states. These often mirror national value systems.[70] How can a diversity in obligations to respect basic rights be explained if they are a characteristic common to all human beings? Are disparities to be justified as a result of differences in the legal systems or of differing interpretations of the notion itself? More precisely, from a constitutional perspective, does the absence of a written Constitution in the UK offer fewer guarantees to citizens that their rights will be respected than on the continent?

Conflicts of interpretation are inevitable and are not in themselves a bad thing. Set to intensify is a three-way tussle between the EU, the European Court of Human Rights and national systems as each seeks to establish its own (sovereign) interpretation of basic concepts such as the rights to life, to private life and to equality. Furthermore, with regard to fundamental rights themselves, conflicts are inherent in their construction, with rights claims on the part of one individual continually coming up against those made by another. Called upon to decide the balance between competing rights claims, the courts of each legal system will be required to pay close attention to developments in the others if a coherent pan-European system of human rights protection is to be established.

---

[70] N Nic Shuibhne, 'Margins of Appreciation: National Values, Fundamental Rights and EC Free Movement Law' (2009) 34 *European Law Review* 230.

In short, the legal framework of fundamental rights protection is a complex one which comprises a plurality of national and European, legislative and judicial perspectives. The impact of European law cannot be denied, however, and the common process of mainstreaming human rights in all legal systems at both national and supranational levels suggests that, while the future interpretation of human rights in Europe presents many challenges, it is a universal concern, and one which is taken most seriously by all concerned. That interpretations of rights conflict is inevitable. That all their facets should be considered is, however, vital. Constant reflection upon the capacity of existing norms to deal with the new requirements of the technologies of life and death is required in order to ensure that legal responses are appropriate, progressive, informed and sensitive to the rights and interests of the individuals concerned. The call to law, of course, will create problems in its own right: those of interpretation, legal authority and the resolution of competing rights claims have already been noted. In order to address such important and complex questions, this chapter ends with a call for a continuation of the enquiry into comparative perspectives on the consistency of human rights protection across Europe. As experience has demonstrated, the universality of fundamental rights requires a basic level of agreement. That level of agreement can be best attained through a process of comparative dialogue between European legal communities, including the judiciary, legislators, civil society activists and policy entrepreneurs.

21

Comparative Law and EU Legislation: Inspiration, Evaluation or Justification?

ROB VAN GESTEL AND HANS-W MICKLITZ

[W]e cannot take for granted that rules or institutions are transplantable. The criteria answering the question whether or how far they are, have changed since Montesquieu's day, but any attempt to use a pattern of law outside the environment of its origin continues to entail the risk of rejection. The consciousness of this risk will not, I hope, deter legislators in this or any other country from using the comparative method. All I have wanted to suggest is that its use requires a knowledge not only of the foreign law, but also of its social, and above all its political, context. The use of comparative law for practical purposes becomes an abuse only if it is informed by a legalistic spirit which ignores this context of the law.[1]

I. RESEARCH PROBLEM

USING COMPARATIVE LAW in law-making by 'looking sideways' to other legal systems is an activity that was discovered by legislators centuries ago, long before courts started to use legal borrowings.[2] Surprisingly enough, though, there is still far less known about the way in which policy-makers and legislators apply comparative law in the process of legislative drafting and about the reasons for doing this than there is with regard to the adoption of foreign law and comparative legal research by courts.[3]

---

[1] O Kahn-Freund, 'On Uses and Misuses of Comparative Law' (1974) 37 *Modern Law Review* 27.
[2] E Örücü and D Nelken, *Comparative Law. A Handbook* (Oxford, Hart Publishing 2007) 427.
[3] T Koopmans, 'Comparative Law and the Courts' (1996) 45(3) *The International and Comparative Law Quarterly* 545; K Lenaerts, 'Interlocking Legal Orders in the European Union and Comparative Law' (2003) 52(4) *International and Comparative Law Quarterly* 873; K Dzehtsiarou, 'Comparative Law in the Reasoning of the European Court of Human Rights' (2010) 10 *University College Dublin Law Review* 109.

This contribution sets out to shed light on why legislators use comparative law and what methods they apply. The focus will be on the EU legislature because, on the one hand, EU law has to accept the equality of Member States before the Treaties as well as respect their national identities,[4] while the European Parliament and the national parliaments are, on the other hand, also supposed to work together, which implies that EU law is fuelled by the laws of the Member States. Moreover, in case of shared competences, the EU legislature has to respect the subsidiarity principle,[5] and may only act if the policy aims cannot be sufficiently achieved by the Member States. This also presupposes that the European legislature knows the appropriateness of existing national legislation through comparative studies before coming up with proposals for new EU laws. After all, how else could the European legislature know when harmonisation is in order? However, some experts claim that EU institutions sometimes deliberately refuse to refer to legal concepts and doctrines applied by the Member States.[6] In that case, they might not want to provoke opposition to harmonisation of national laws by showing how European legal rules are inspired by, or borrowed from, the law of some Member State or third country because this can easily raise political objections.[7]

The use of comparative law by the EU legislature may also become politicised in a different way. A parallel can be drawn here with the introduction of impact assessments (IAs) in the EU legislative process.[8] An important official reason for the introduction of IAs was the need to consider alternatives to proposed legislation.[9] If that is really the case, it is hard to understand why comparative legal research is not a structural part of the IA process. In chapter four of the IA guidelines on gathering information and consulting stakeholders nothing can be found on comparative law methodology, while the guidelines mention that it is important to: 'look for examples of good practice in Member States, and at the experiences of third countries or international organisations'.[10] One wonders how these good practices can be recognised and incorporated in EU legislation without proper knowledge of, and paying

---

[4] Art 4(2) TEU.

[5] Art 5 TEU.

[6] G Ajani, 'Legal Change and Economic Performance: an Assessment' in A Bakardjieva Engelbrekt and J Nergelius (eds), *New Directions in Comparative law* (Cheltenham, Edward Elgar 2009) 14.

[7] Something similar applies to the autonomous interpretration doctrine of the ECJ, which has been first applied in 1964 in: ECJ, judgment of 19 March 1964, Case 75/63 *Mrs MKH Hoekstra (née Unger) v. Bestuur der Bedrijfsvereniging voor Detailhandel en Ambachten* [1964] ECR 379. In essence, the principle of autonomous interpretation means that there is only one correct interpretation of a term used in EC legislation, and that this one correct meaning must be found independently from national or other interpretations of the same term. Exceptions are only made where an EC Directive explicitly refers to national law.

[8] In-depth about this A Meuwese, *Impact Assessment in EU Lawmaking* (Alphen aan den Rijn, Kluwer Law International 2008).

[9] Communication from the Commission on impact assessment, COM(2002)276 final.

[10] IA guidelines (2009) 92 SEC 18.

explicit attention to, the methodological complexities surrounding legal transplants.

It is also interesting that several sources confirm that IAs lack objectivity and first and foremost serve to justify the proposed initiative by the Commission.[11] The 'do-nothing' option and 'non-regulatory' (eg self-regulation) options are, according to the UK House of Lords' EU committee, only superficially examined to show the superiority of the chosen regulatory option.[12] In its 2010 report on IAs, the European Court of Auditors found that most IAs are not used by the Commission to decide whether or not to go ahead with a proposal;[13] this has normally already been decided before the IA is finalised. Rather, it uses IAs to improve its proposed initiative. If this is the case with respect to the use of IAs, why would it be different for comparative legal research projects issued by the Commission to inform the legislature? Hence our research question is:

> What might be the main motives for the EU legislature, and in particular the Commission, to have the right to initiate legislation and to issue comparative legal research, and is there a risk that the methodology to compare different legal systems in order to look for possible legal transplants is affected by politics, as is apparently the case with regard to EU IAs?

This question is not only inspired by the debate on IAs. Our hypothesis is namely that the Lisbon agenda of 2000 and its successor, Europe 2020, create an academic climate in which comparative legal research may be instrumentalised to serve different needs of policy-makers and legislators.[14] With respect to the EU legislature, we believe that comparative legal research runs the risk of being reduced to delivering arguments to justify what has already been decided upon politically, as is often the case with respect to IAs.[15] To avoid any misunderstandings, we are not suggesting that every comparative legal research project that is being conducted today to underpin proposals for new

[11] The most comprehensive review of the European IA system so far was conducted by The Evaluation Partnership Limited, 'Evaluation of the Commission's Impact Assessment System' (April 2007), which showed that even members of the Evaluation Partnership and of the Council perceive IAs to be a bureaucratic requirement focused mainly on justifying the proposed initiative and thus lacking objectivity. See http://ec.europa.eu/governance/impact/key_docs/docs/tep_eias_final_report_executive_summary_en.pdf.

[12] House of Lords European Union Committee, 'Impact Assessments in the EU: Room for Improvement?', 4th Report of Session 2009–10, London, 9 March 2010, 20–21, available at http://www.publications.parliament.uk/pa/ld200910/ldselect/ldeucom/61/61.pdf.

[13] Court of Auditors, 'Impact Assessments in the EU Institutions: Do They Support Decision-Making?', Special Report 2010/3, available at http://ec.europa.eu/governance/impact/docs/coa_report_3_2010_en.pdf.

[14] The instrumentalisation, however, goes beyond this. See M Dawson, 'Three Waves of New Governance in the European Union' (2011) 36 *European Law Review* 220, who claims that the European Commission is also trying to use civil society input via new modes of governance to implement the Lisbon agenda with regard to issues where public authorities have previously failed.

[15] About this tendency in particular in the field of private law see C Von Bar, 'Comparative Law of Obligations: Methodology and Epistemology' in M Van Hoecke (ed), *Epistemology and Methodology of Comparative Law* (Oxford, Hart, 2004) 127–28.

EU policies or draft EU legislation is compromised. We do think, however, that the growing emphasis on valorisation and private funding[16] puts additional pressure on academic (comparative) legal research that is commissioned to play a role in the process of EU legislative law-making.

II. FUNCTIONS OF COMPARATIVE LEGAL RESEARCH IN EUROPEAN LAWMAKING

Most legal scholars in the field of EU law are familiar with comparative legal research by the ECJ and CFI. Although the case law offers few explicit references to comparative legal research, it is common knowledge that comparative law plays a role in the interpretation of primary and secondary EU law, as is shown in the conclusions of Advocate Generals, in the materials brought before the courts by the parties to the proceedings and by the European Commission in the preliminary reference procedure.[17] Far less is known, however, about how the Commission, the European Parliament and the Committee of Permanent Representatives make use of comparative legal research.[18] References to the different ways comparative law shapes EU legislation usually remain implicit at best because EU legislative bodies have no interest in revealing which national legal systems influenced particular provisions in EU laws.[19] In order to get an idea of how and why comparative law influences the process of legislative drafting of EU law, one therefore has to take a look behind the scenes and study, for example, impact assessments and consultation documents, green and white papers, and calls for tender by the Commission or questionnaires required by the Council to collect Member States' opinions on certain policies or proposals.[20] The publicly available documents allow for

[16] A lot of the funding of legal research by, for example, the Commission or DGs is actually not really private funding. Universities consider it as private money, or at least market-based money, because it is a matter of supply and demand and not (so much) about 'adding to the body of knowledge'.

[17] M Hilf, 'The Role of Comparative Law in the Jurisprudence of the Court of Justice of the European Communities' in A de Mestral et al (eds), *The Limitation of Human Rights in Comparative Constitutional Law* (Cowansville, Les Éditions Yvon Blais, 1986) 550 referred to the ECJ and CFI as 'laboratories of comparative law'. See also GA Bermann, 'Comparative Law in the New European Community (1998) 21 *Hastings International and Comparative Law Review* 865–869; T Koopmans, 'The Birth of European Law at the Crossroads of Legal Traditions' (1991) 39 *American Journal Comparative Law* 493; F van der Mensbrugghe, *L'utilisation de la méthode comparative en droit européen* (Namur, Presses Universitaires de Namur, 2003).

[18] At least from the Council it is plain that the reference or defence to particular national rules serve as a bargain in making a package deal—you accept my rule and I accept yours. This is one of the reasons why pieces of secondary legislation seem to get ever longer and more sophisticated.

[19] Sometimes a reference to a comparative study can be found in the preamble but without specifics regarding how the study influenced the legislative draft. See Council Resolution of 6 December 1994 on the legal protection of the financial interests of the Communities [1994] OJ C355.

[20] For an example see Council of the European Union, Note from the Council General Secretariat to all Delegations, Questionnaire on the practice and the experience of the national authorities when dealing with cases regarding transfer of criminal proceedings between Member

an initiation assessment at least with regard to the role and function of the European Commission.

Although there are no official overviews of the different applications of comparative law research in the process of EU law-making, we assume that comparative law serves at least three main functions for the EU legislature: (i) as a source of inspiration in the drafting process; (ii) as a (legal) method of evaluation in the consideration of regulatory alternatives; and (iii) as a political tool for the justification of policy choices. In practice, these categories overlap, but for analytical purposes it is important to keep them apart because they represent different motives behind the use of comparative law by the EU legislature.

During the early days of the European Community, comparative law was a rich source of inspiration for the harmonisation of the laws of the Member States. Comparative research was often undertaken to look for common ground in the laws of the Member States and to find general principles of European law to inform the legislature.[21] This had to do with the way in which the research was organised. The different units within the directorates—more concretely, the competent public officials in charge—had a personal budget which enabled them to mandate individual academics or institutions with research projects up to 15,000 ECU (nearly equivalent to the euro). Beyond that benchmark, the project had to be tendered. This means the officials de facto had the power to decide that a particular project was to be executed by a particular person/institution which they trusted to do a good job. After the introduction of the Lisbon agenda in 2000, this informal practice changed.

The philosophy of the EU legislature came to define Europe's path towards a new knowledge-based and competitive economy.[22] An important conclusion of the Lisbon Council on 23–24 March 2000 was that:

> The Union has today set itself a new strategic goal for the next decade: to become the most competitive and dynamic knowledge-based economy in the world capable of sustainable economic growth with more and better jobs and greater social cohesion.[23]

A new trend in the research issued by the Commission became looking for 'what works' in light of the goals set by the Lisbon agenda. The already mentioned IA system fits in this picture, as does the tendering of legal research. This has diminished the discretion to mandate projects to independent experts who are not necessarily interested in offering the most research for the lowest price. Comparative research had to cover more and more Member States,

States, 7486/09, COPEN 48, 11 March 2009, available at http://register.consilium.europa.eu/pdf/en/09/st07/st07486.en09.pdf.

[21] A good example is the elaboration of the Directive 92/59 on product safety, to be discussed later.

[22] MJ Rodriguez (ed), *Europe, Globalization and the Lisbon Agenda* (Cheltenham, Edward Elgar, 2009) 1.

[23] See http://www.europarl.europa.eu/summits/lis1_en.htm.

including, after the 2004 enlargement, countries from the former Eastern Bloc. This is where the 'comparative law by numbers' finds its origin.[24] The second major consequence was the institutional shift from comparative research undertaken by universities and independent research institutes to consultancy firms, which are more likely to act as 'hired guns' (read: organisations proficient in obtaining power for others). In many cases, consultancy agencies took over the administrative part of the research projects, hiring academics or other experts to execute the research, while remaining in charge of the acquisition, the project management and reporting.

This remains pretty much the situation today, and there are few signs of change for the near future. On the contrary, the Europe 2020 agenda,[25] which has been translated into a supporting funding programme for academic research of no less than €80 billion—Horizon 2020—continues the policy started by the Lisbon agenda with no visible attempt to critically review the EU's research policy so far. The policy goals in Horizon 2020, such as healthy ageing, climate change and food safety, have also been transferred to the European Research Area as research targets. Or, as the website of the EU Framework Programme for Research and Innovation puts it:

> Horizon 2020 will tackle societal challenges by helping to bridge the gap between research and the market by, for example, helping innovative enterprise to develop their technological breakthroughs into viable products with real commercial potential. This market-driven approach will include creating partnerships with the private sector and Member States to bring together the resources needed.[26]

The whole undertone in Horizon 2020 is that academic research is supposed to deliver outcomes that help to further economic growth and technological and social innovation.[27] Of course, this is not necessarily a bad thing. As far as legal research is concerned,[28] valorisation can stimulate a 'law in context' approach, in which researchers are pushed to look beyond the law in books in order to study the law in action. This may very well benefit the development of multidisciplinary legal research methods and spur cooperation between comparative lawyers and social scientists, as is evident from the legal origins debate in which comparative law and economic approaches are merged to study the extent to which economic welfare is influenced by the legal infrastructure of

---

[24] M Siems, 'Numerical Comparative Law—Do We Need Statistical Evidence in Law in Order to Reduce Complexity' (2005) 13 *Cardozo Journal of International and Comparative Law* 521; R Michaels, 'Comparative Law by Numbers? Legal Origins Thesis, Doing Business Reports, and the Silence of Traditional Comparative Law' (2009) 57 *American Journal of Comparative Law* 765.

[25] See the Communication from the Commission, 'EUROPE 2020: A Strategy for Smart, Sustainable and Inclusive Growth', COM(2010) 2020 final.

[26] http://ec.europa.eu/research/horizon2020/index_en.cfm?pg=h2020.

[27] See, eg http://ec.europa.eu/europe2020/making-it-happen/key-areas/index_en.htm.

[28] Taking a closer look at the 'grand challenges' of Horizon 2020 teaches that the room for traditional legal research, such as private law, constitutional and administrative law, is probably limited, whereas 'law and ...' research, such as law and economics and law and technology, stands a better chance of getting funded.

different jurisdictions.[29] On the other hand, putting more emphasis on 'bridging the gap between research and the market', in combination with budget cuts for scholarly legal research in national universities, may stimulate 'advocacy scholarship'. This is research focused on 'desired' outcomes and defending the position of one's 'client' (read: the contractor). According to scholars such as Robert Spitzer, this is already a weak spot in traditional legal research because most lawyers are not trained in research methodology, while the law school curriculum is heavily focused on rhetoric and the art of persuasion.[30]

In order to illustrate the potential problems this may cause for comparative legal research, we will discuss some examples in the next paragraph. We will use examples largely from existing research, partly based on our own experience.

III. INSPIRATION

'We need to do something, but we do not know what and how.' This is the formula that describes a research policy of the European Commission that seeks for inspiration from different legal systems. The first example derives from the field of advertising and sales promotion. As early as 1984, the EEC adopted Directive 84/450EEC on Misleading Advertising. The European Commission originally favoured a piece of Union law that should cover not only misleading but also unfair advertising. However, the UK resisted putting advertising under a general verdict of unfairness. Nearly 20 years later, in 2005, the EU adopted the Directive on Unfair Commercial Practices 2005/29/EC. Contrary to what one might have expected, the debate was no longer about the extension to unfairness but about the scope of application. Whereas a number of Member States, in particular Austria and Germany, were advocating in the legislative process for a holistic approach to b2b (business-to-business) and b2c (business-to-consumer), DG Sanco was advocating for a separation of the two areas. The reason might very well have been a power game within the Commission. A broader scope would have made it necessary for DG Sanco to negotiate with DG Market on the design of the Directive. Once the inner conflict was solved, DG Sanco was free to seek guidance on how to draft the European law on unfair advertising. The study preparing the Directive was conducted in 1999.[31] The applicant had to write a draft on the scope of the research, the countries to be covered and the method applied, which allowed

---

[29] For an example see S Deakin and K Pistor (eds), *Legal Origin Theory* (Cheltenham, Edward Elgar, 2012).

[30] RJ Spitzer, *Saving the Constitution from Lawyers. How Legal Training and Law Reviews Distort Constitutional Meaning* (Cambridge, Cambridge University Press 2008) 23–25.

[31] Study on the Feasibility of a General Legislative Framework on Fair Trading by VIEW Institut für Europäisches Wirtschafts- und Verbraucherrecht (responsible since its foundation in 1994 H-W Micklitz); it is available together with others studies on the following website of the European Commission: http://ec.europa.eu/dgs/health_consumer/library/surveys/sur21_vol2_en.pdf.

the official in charge to negotiate about the design of the research on the basis of several research proposals. It was agreed that the study should cover desk research of the existing EU law, reports on a selected number of Member States, a comparative analysis[32] and an EU proposal for a directive. At the time, the European Commission did not influence the content of the proposal in any way. The main drafting was done by Jürgen Keßler and Hans-W Micklitz. There was an implicit expectation from the European Commission— specifically, from the public official in charge—that the scope of application of the Directive 84/450/EEC on misleading advertising should be enlarged and a general fairness test integrated.

In 2013 the European Commission published a report[33] in which it indicated its considerations to elaborate a directive on unfair trading practices in the b2b supply chain—this refers to a particular field of unfair commercial practices— and to seek advice on the feasibility of such a project. It therefore launched a tender,[34] which was eventually won by the College of Europe. The deadline for the delivery of the study was end of September 2013. The tender clearly indicates what the European Commission expects on the explicit assumption that there is a misuse of power in supply chains:[35]

> The third objective of the study is to assess and classify the different approaches identified, be they regulatory or non-regulatory as well as the enforcement mechanisms in terms of their efficiency and suitability in addressing the problem of business-to-business unfair commercial practices in the retail supply chain. The study should also provide options on how to possibly address the problem of the fragmentation of the Internal Market resulting from diverging rules on business-to-business unfair commercial practices in the retail supply chain.

What matters even more is the methodology. National reporters were consulted on the design by the College of Europe by way of a long list of pre-defined highly sophisticated research questions. The questions and the feedback from the national reporters were then debated in order to come up with an agreement with the European Commission. However, how can 28 opinions on research design be safely merged to the satisfaction of all national reporters, in particular if the European Commission seems also to have had a strong say?

One thing, however, is certain: the project has embarked on new territory, where little is known and little case law is available. What should have been necessary was to answer the questions on the basis of empirical research—for which time and money was lacking, however. The simple reliance on case law and legislation certainly does not provide for a full picture. It is well known

---

[32] H-W Micklitz and J Keßler (eds), 'Marketing Practices Regulation and Consumer Protection in the EC Member States and the US' (2002) 10 *VIEW Schriftenreihe*.

[33] Green Paper on Unfair Trading Practices in the Business-to-Business Food and Non-Food Supply Chain in Europe, COM (2013) 37 final.

[34] See under Market 2012/049 E T, available at http://ec.europa.eu/dgs/internal_market/calls/archive/2012_en.htmhe (the tender comprises 57 pages, out of which only a few deal with the content).

[35] Ibid, 20.

that the partners of a supply chain prefer to resolve possible conflicts outside of the courts.[36] Methodologically, the research questions served a twofold purpose: first, as guidance for the national reports, which had to be prepared for all 28 Member States (including Croatia) and secondly, as a blueprint for a table in which the core findings of the national reports had to be inserted. The same approach applies to the comparative analysis. There will be a written report, but the essence and substance of the comparative analysis needs to be summarised in the table. This is rather dubious because not only will the nuances need to be left out, but those responsible for the comparative analysis will have at least the national reports in the back of their mind, whereas the European Commission, the Parliament and the Member States in the Council will probably first and foremost study the table and examine whether their national legal order is correctly presented. Last but not least, the College of Europe will have to present an impact assessment. This is part of the tender: it will provide a comparative assessment of the existing instruments and mechanisms, and cluster the 28 countries according to the approach taken, as well as assess the impact of the existing approaches on the internal market. This all forms part of the original budget that the College of Bruges had asked for.

IV. EVALUATION

'*We are not sure whether we need to do something—please provide us with arguments for the pros and cons.*' This is the formula where comparative legal research serves a similar function as an IA or is conducted as part of an IA. Although comparative legal analysis cannot be used to discover whether a certain EU policy or EU legislative draft is going to work as planned because it has not been adopted yet, there is a potential falsification element involved in the sense that what can be investigated is whether the policy assumptions underlying a legislative draft are based on solid information, for example, with respect to the legal regimes and institutions of the Member States. If this is not the case, it is likely that the draft is probably not going to work as intended.[37]

---

[36] There is a wealth of studies on long-term contracts available, eg S Macaulay, 'Non-Contractual Relations in Business—a Preliminary Study' (1963) 28 *American Sociological Review* 55.

[37] Of course comparative law may also play a role in the context of *ex post* evaluations, but in that case the comparison usually concerns the implementation process. Moreover, three qualifications are in order there: (i) *ex post* evaluations of EU legislation are still relatively rare, especially compared to the evaluation of expenditure programmes; (ii) most *ex post* evaluations do not measure the effectiveness of EU laws *stricto sensu* because it is extremely difficult to measure whether policy changes have occurred as a consequence of a certain piece of legislation (and not because of exogenous circumstances), especially in a multilevel legal order, where EU laws either need to be implemented via national laws (eg directives) or otherwise depend for execution and enforcement on the implementation structures of the Member States (eg regulations); and (iii) comparative legal research is normally not a suitable method to test the effectiveness or efficiency of EU laws because this requires empirical research.

The latter being said, a good example of a comparative project with a focus on (*ex ante*) evaluation conducted around the turn of the millennium was a study concerning legislation with regard to private security companies in the EU, drawn up in the context of the third European Conference on Private Security, which was held in Brussels in December 2001.[38] The study was in a certain sense a follow up of a previous study by Brion, Kaminski, Carteret and Smulders, which showed that, as a consequence of the freedom of movement and establishment, there were no longer any legislative barriers against private security companies offering services across countries. This made it increasingly difficult for Member States to exercise control over the quality and professionalism of these companies, the protection of workers in this industry[39] and the respect for public order as a result of the foreign private security companies entering the market avoiding the legislation of the host state.[40]

The study argues that the private security sector has been growing significantly in the EU and is increasingly taking on roles previously provided in-house by private or public sector undertakings, although the standards with respect to licensing, training, use of force and working conditions differ quite substantially. The research therefore argues that a common set of (minimum) rules should apply in relation to private security companies responsible for checking the criminal record of any individual applying for employment in the sector, not only facilitating staff mobility and recognition of authorisations across Member States, but also guaranteeing professional and moral conduct. Two very different problems were highlighted in the study: (i) the rules applying to the use of dogs and weapons on duty, which differ quite heavily throughout the Member States; and (ii) services by private security companies tendered on the basis of the lowest price bid, thus running the risk of a race to the bottom in terms of labour standards.

Although we do not want to suggest that the outcome of the research is wrong content-wise, a few things are disturbing. First of all, the research project has as overarching aim: informing social partners, who signed a joined declaration on the European harmonisation of legislation governing the private security sector, but without a specific research question or an assessment framework with criteria to evaluate when and where harmonisation might be

---

[38] T Weber, 'A Comparative Overview of Legislation Governing the Private Security Industry in the European Union', Final Report of a project for CoESS/UNI Europa (ECOTEC Research and Consulting Ltd, Birmingham, 2002).

[39] See ECJ Case C-54/07 *Feryn* [2008] ECR I-5187, 16, in which a private security company advertised a job vacancy but excluding Moroccans: 'I must comply with my customers' requirements. If you say "I want that particular product or I want it like this and like that", and I say "I'm not doing it, I'll send those people", then you say "I don't need that door". Then I'm putting myself out of business. We must meet the customers' requirements. This isn't my problem. I didn't create this problem in Belgium. I want the firm to do well and I want us to achieve our turnover at the end of the year, and how do I do that?—I must do it the way the customer wants it done!'

[40] F Brion, D Kaminski, M Carteret and P Smulders, 'Etude de droit comparé sur la réglementation du secteur de la sécurité privée', Rapport final (Université Chatolique de Louvain, November 2001).

appropriate. This leaves the impression that the outcome of the research is predetermined, especially because there is no inquiry as to possible alternatives to intervention by the European legislature.

Secondly, one wonders why this research was granted to a private consultancy agency and conducted by a researcher who was apparently not a specialist in private security issues, instead of to one or more experts in the field of criminology or private security.[41] This is all the more strange since there (i) was a lively debate going on in the field of criminology at the time on private security companies in Europe while (ii) the topic is highly sensitive because it concerns transboundary security services in a domain full of 'old boys' networks' between public and private policing.[42]

Thirdly, the study is also a good example of the summarising in 'tables' of the comparative information, mentioned in the previous paragraph, while the 'methodology paragraph' (four sentences) refers to a questionnaire (not enclosed in the report), a literature review (references to only four sources) and interviews 'where appropriate' (no list of interviewees is included). Last but not least, the report does not clearly discern between conclusions and recommendations to the legislature, for example where it is suggested that:

> in the interest of the professionalisation of the sector, the setting of an obligatory minimum standard of training appears desirable and the work of CoESS and Uni-Europa [the social partners responsible for commissioning the research] in developing basic training for guards can contribute to this process.

Although setting minimum criteria for training would probably not hurt, it is uncertain to what extent that is the best solution to the discovered problems.

Another example where comparative research was conducted lies in the field of family law, and more particularly in the field of adoption. Here the Commission tendered a comparative study on adoption procedures in the Member States of the European Union on 8 August 2007.[43] The tender is a 37-page-long specification of what is expected from the researchers. The purpose of the study, according to the tender, is twofold:

> 1) to produce a comparative analysis of the situation in the 27 Member States as regards legislation, organisational arrangements, procedures and practices relating to intercountry adoption and in particular adoption between the Member States of the European Union, and 2) to identify practical difficulties and problems encountered in this area by European citizens, in particular those which prevent or hinder their exercising parental responsibility, and to identify possible solutions to these problems, including the possibility of setting up a European adoption procedure between Member States.

---

[41] The information about the author of the research project has been derived from http://www.ghkint.com/Services/PublicPolicy/SocialDialogue/TinaWeber.aspx.

[42] See, eg the special issue (1999) 7(2) *European Journal on Criminal Policy and Research*.

[43] JLS/C/4/FFM/jd/D(2007)10782.

What is remarkable, because of the limited competence of the EU in family law matters and the specific exclusion of adoption from the scope of Council Regulation 2201/2003 concerning jurisdiction and the recognition and enforcement of judgments in matrimonial matters and matters of parental responsibility,[44] is that in the tender document the Commission seems to steer the direction in which the conclusions of the research project should go, namely:

> Closer cooperation on adoption between the Member States might be regarded as one of the *inevitable* consequences of the free movement of citizens and the gradual emergence of a European judicial culture built on the diversity of the legal systems, the promotion of citizens' rights and unity through European law.[45]

In addition, the tender refers to a recent Eurobarometer showing strong support from citizens for EU action in this area. Whether Article 81 TFEU provides a proper legal basis for harmonisation and to what extent the subsidiarity principle might put EU legislative action at risk is, however, not included as a research question in the tender.[46] What is required in the tender is that the researchers not only analyse the adoption rules and procedures of all 27 Member States and somehow find solutions for the problems found in the different jurisdictions, but also collect statistical data on a number of specified issues, conduct a survey and do at least 500 interviews—and all this within 12 months from signing the contract.

Studying the 499-page-long final report teaches that the 'comparative' legal research methodology is based on country reports drafted by national experts on the basis of a list of criteria delivered by the contracting party.[47] The 'synthesis' of the comparative findings in the report contains not much more than an overview in tables of similarities and differences. For instance, in the majority of the Member States (17) the legal instruments for national and inter-country adoption are the same. On the other hand, most Member States have completely different provisions with regard to the prospective adoptive parents as to their age and civil status (single, married, heterosexual couple or same sex couple). No analysis can be found as to the reasons behind these differences or why certain countries have developed different practices with respect to dealing with practical problems in border-crossing adoptions, while there is a vast set of national 'solutions'. Apart from that, no information is given as to how the researchers have made the jump from the country reports to the policy recommendations, which largely consist of EU-focused options,

---

[44] Art 1(3).

[45] JLS/C/4/FFM/jd/D(2007)10782, 6–7 (emphasis added).

[46] It is not only with regard to transboundary family law issues that there seems to be a desire for further harmonization: the same can be said for domestic family law issues. See DG Internal Policies, Citizens' Rights and Constitutional Affairs, 'Which Legal Basis for Family Law? The Way Forward 2012', available at http://www.europarl.europa.eu/document/activities/cont/201212/20121219ATT58314/20121219ATT58314EN.pdf.

[47] See http://ec.europa.eu/civiljustice/news/docs/study_adoption_legal_analysis_en.pdf.

varying from the creation of a European adoption agency to harmonisation of national legislation on the basis of existing international conventions.

All in all, we can conclude that the comparative legal research in this project is very thin as far the methodology is concerned. The report mainly provides a list of facts and problems in the different Member States in order to provide an overview of the legal rules and procedures with respect to inter-country adoption to supplement the empirical part of the research,[48] which seems to be set up to show how big the problem actually is and not really to find out what the Member States might learn from each other or how the EU legislature could learn from the different state practices. More than being a true evaluation of transboundary adoption in the sense of looking for both worst and best practices, the research is mainly oriented towards looking for problems, leaving aside why these problems have occurred in the Member States, what has been done before to tackle them, and whether or not EU legislation is the best option to solve the problems.

V. JUSTIFICATION

'*We know what we want to do—please provide us with arguments.*' This is the formula where comparative research serves legitimacy purposes only. We will use the history of the pending draft Regulation on a Common European Sales Law as a blueprint.[49] For our purpose we will condense a story which stretches over the last decade and focus on two aspects: the role and function of comparative research in the 'academic' Draft Common Frame of Reference and the role and function of comparative research in the 'political' Common Frame of References, which might eventually lead to the adoption of the said Common European Sales Law.

The starting point for the 'academic' Draft Common Frame of Reference (DCFR) goes back to the year 2001, when the European Commission published its Communication on European Contract Law.[50] The paper offered four options; one of them was the development of a European civil code. Obviously the European Commission had no resources to do the investigation itself. In launched a tender, but it was a semi-open tender, as it was pretty clear that the two established working groups—the Study Group and the Acquis Group[51]— were the ones who should get the contract which lasted for a couple of years.

---

[48] It is interesting that the team leader of the Civil Justice Unit who guided the research project made it clear that the Commission was not really statisfied with the outcome of the study and stressed that the Commission had no means of verifying the appropriateness or accuracy of the data. See http://www.coe.int/t/dghl/standardsetting/family/adoption%20conference/Presentation%20DE%20LUCA.pdf (document also on file with the authors).

[49] Well presented on the home page of DG Justice, http://ec.europa.eu/justice/contract/dates/index_en.htm.

[50] COM(2001) 398 final.

[51] For details of their websites see http://www.sgecc.net/he (The Study Group) and http://www.acquis-group.org/ (Acquis Group).

There was no true alternative. The Study Group has existed since 1980, when it was called the Lando-Group,[52] and gained a high reputation over time on solid comparative research in the field of contract law. The Acquis Group was founded in 2002, one year before the call for tender. It was less well established, but had already sought contact with the Study Group in order to join forces in the elaboration of what later became the 'Common Frame of Reference'. It is not known whether, or to what extent, the European Commission influenced the design of the project and the chosen methodology. However, the Study Group had an established reputation in the use of comparative research methods to examine the principles of European contract law.[53] It is a matter of fact that the European Commission was quite critical, in the 2001 Communication, of the Code being the appropriate solution. The European Parliament adopted two strong resolutions,[54] before the European Commission finally came up with the rather cautiously worded 2001 Communication. It seems, however, as if the European Commission left the two groups with much leeway on which one of four options they would choose. In making and accepting the Study Group, one of the two pillars of the group that had to develop the Common Frame of Reference, the European Commission accepted the comparison of different private legal orders as the key building block of the project. The Acquis Group, as its name indicates, had set itself the task of analysing the existing European Private Law rules, enshrined in Regulations and Directives. Here no comparative research is involved.

The Study Group undertook extensive analysis of the different private legal orders, but it never intended to study all 27 legal orders in full. The findings of the Study Group had to be merged with those of the Acquis Group. This was the mandate given to the two groups in their study contract once they had won the tender. The research outcome is impressive: the Acquis Group published the Acquis Principles, and the Study and Acquis Group jointly published the online edition of the DCFR as well as the full version,[55] which comprises six volumes, with extensive comparative comments on each and every article of what very much looks like a European civil code. In sum, comparative legal analysis played a crucial role in the preparatory process. This was very much traditional doctrinal analysis in the meaning of the functional method developed by Zweigert and Kötz in their *Introduction to Comparative Law*.[56] None of the new rhetoric introduced in Lisbon was brought forward by the Commission. There was no pressure

---

[52] http://de.wikipedia.org/wiki/Lando-Kommission.

[53] C Von Bar and R Zimmermann, *The Principles of European Contract Law* (2002).

[54] On 26 June 1989 ([1989] OJ C158/400) and 25 July 1994 ([1994] OJ C205/518).

[55] We refrain from quoting the six books and instead refer the reader to the webpage of the publisher, http://www.sellier.de/pages/de/buecher_s_elp/europarecht/643.draft_common_frame_of_reference_dcfr_full_edition.htm.

[56] K Zweigert and H Kötz, *An Introduction to Comparative Law*, 3rd edn (Oxford, Oxford University Press, 1998).

on stock taking, there was no empirical analysis and there was no impact assessment, at least not at that stage. That is why the drafters of the DCFR could term their findings an 'academic' draft, although this is partly wrong as the two groups were working under a mandate from the Commission and received a considerable amount of research money. This means they had become an integral part of the European Commission's legislative machinery. In order to avoid misunderstandings, at that stage the European Commission did not exert any influence on the outcome. However, the project would never have come to end in 2008 if various national funding organisations had not been willing to provide substantial resources. One possible reason might have been that the European Commission did not provide enough funds to finance the whole project. National funding organisations, from the Netherlands and from Germany, but also indirectly the universities to whom the members of the group belonged, contributed heavily. These outside subsidisers were obviously willing to accept the overall design as agreed upon by the troika of the Study Group, the Acquis Group and the European Commission. We do not know what the motives behind this were. It might well be that the leading figures in the two groups were strong enough to gain support from their national funding organisations. This, however, implied the need to present the exercise as an academic project. Member States would certainly not be ready to fund legislative initiatives of the European Commission.

The political phase started when Commissioner Reding took office in the DG Justice in 2009. She brought the overall project of a potential European contract law to life. The European Commission gave the impression that it did not really know what to do with the academic Draft Common Frame of Reference, which was first published in 2008. The pressure from Parliament was high, but the European Commission was aware of the political reluctance in at least a number of Member States. Commissioner Reding's first step constituted the nomination of an expert group, which brought together the vast majority of members from the Study Group and the Acquis Group.[57] Under the auspices of the European Commission, the expert group was given the mandate to transform the 'academic' Draft Common Frame of Reference into a 'political' draft. This is not the place to comment on the content, on how the European Commission reduced what was in fact a draft European civil code to a draft European sales law with emphasis on transborder sales.

For the purposes of this chapter, there were two relevant issues. For the first time, the European Commission accepted full—and not half-hearted[58]—political responsibility for the potential outcome and therewith for the methods and the procedure, which should be applied to reach the politically desired result. Secondly, Commissioner Reding gave clear instructions on the

---

[57] Commission Decision 2010/233/EU of 26 April 2010 [2010] OJ 105/109.
[58] The European Commission was pushed into action by the European Parliament and hesitated for years before it came up with the 2001 Communication.

'desired' outcome of the project. The politically 'acceptable' outcome was not a fully fledged European civil code, but a European sales law for transborder transactions. These guidelines determined the mandate of the expert group—what could be termed the 'political' Draft Common Frame of Reference—and later elaborated the transformation of the political DCFR into the proposal for a Regulation on the Common European Sales Law.[59] The expert group was put under pressure to use the 'academic' Common Frame of Reference as a toolbox.[60] The articles and rules were jiggled around and made compatible to political acceptable requirements. This was not research, but technical drafting in an extremely dense form. The findings of the expert group, the political Draft Common Frame of Reference, had to undergo the impact assessment procedure.[61] The results were easily predictable.[62] The European Commission got what it wanted: a slimmed-down version of the academic DCFR and the green light via the impact assessment.

VI. CONCLUSION

In this chapter we have argued that, of the three main motives for issuing comparative legal research by the EU legislature, the function of comparative law as a source of inspiration and evaluation has become less important, whereas its potential for justifying predetermined policy goals and plans for new legislation has grown. Our hypothesis, which needs to be further researched by studying a much larger sample of comparative studies, is that comparative legal research is increasingly being used by policy-makers and politicians in order to legitimise existing plans for law reform in a similar way to how IAs have been transformed from a potential tool to stimulate evidence-based policy making into an instrument that sometimes comes closer to policy-based evidence making.

Of course, we do not claim that every comparative legal research project that is issued to serve law reform purposes at the EU level is compromised;

---

[59] COM(2011) 635 final.

[60] Personal communication from a member of the group to the authors. However, the Commission had already provided clear guidance in the Commission Decision 201/233/EU: the group should assist the Commission in preparing a proposal for a Common Frame of Reference in the area of European contract law, including consumer and business contract law, using the Draft Common Frame of Reference as a starting point and taking into consideration other research work conducted in this area as well as the Union acquis. The group should, in particular, help the Commission select those parts of the Draft Common Frame of Reference which are of direct or indirect relevance for contract law, and restructure, revise and supplement the selected contents.

[61] COM(2011) SEC 1165, Working Staff Document, available at http://eur-lex.europa.eu/LexUriServ/LexUriServ.do?uri=SEC:2011:1165:FIN:EN:PDF.

[62] For a reconstruction of the events between the publication of the Feasibility Study of the Expert Group and the publication of the Proposal for CESL see H-W Micklitz, 'A "Certain" Future for the Optional Instrument' in R Schulze and J Stuyck (eds), *Towards a European Contract Law* (Munich, Sellier Publishing, 2011) 181–94.

we do, however, claim that the 2000 Lisbon agenda was the start of a wider trend towards instrumentalisation of scholarly legal research to serve economic and political purposes. This trend becomes clear on the macrolevel by looking at research funding programmes such as Horizon 2020, which first and foremost treat academic research as an instrument to foster innovation, and on the microlevel by looking at tenders for comparative legal research projects that sometimes leave very little room for investigation of regulatory alternatives and falsification of proposed policy plans. What is worrisome from an academic perspective is the lack of attention for methodological issues in comparative legal research projects initiated by the Commission or one of the Directorate Generals. Some of the studies we have looked into seem to be impossible missions from an academic perspective, such as the assignment to study the legal regime of all EU Member States on certain issues within the time-frame of one year to look for best practices, while the study is supposed to include (time-consuming) empirical legal research (large-scale questionnaires and hundreds of interviews).

What we find remarkable is the lack of attention from the academic legal community in general, and the fora for comparative scholarly legal research in particular, for legal transplanting by the legislature. Where the ECJ and CFI seem to have taken a step back with regard to the application of comparative law,[63] legal transplants initiated either by the legislature or by the executive seem to have become increasingly popular lately. This makes it even more peculiar that legislative use of comparative law faces less scrutiny by legal scholars, whereas legislators are probably more liable than judges to misuse comparative law due to economic and political compulsion.[64] What comparative lawyers should realise is that an ongoing instrumentalisation of comparative legal research can easily undermine the public trust in legal scholars in general and comparative lawyers in particular. Therefore, we challenge them to falsify our instrumentalisation hypothesis by studying a larger sample of comparative legal research projects from before and after 2000 in order to find out the extent to which comparative legal research projects actually serve to justify predetermined policy plans and proposals for new EU legislation. Taking this challenge up might also teach a lot about how legal transplanting works in the daily practice of the EU.

---

[63] A Bakardjieva Engelbrekt, 'Comparative Law and European Law: The End of an Era, a New Beginning, or Time to Face the Methodological Challenges?' in M Derlén and J Lindholm (eds), *Festskrift till Pär Hallström* (Uppsala, Iustus Förlag, 2012) 39.

[64] D Barak-Erez, 'The Institutional Aspects of Comparative Law' (2009) 15 *Columbia Journal of European Law* 492.

Author Index

Subject Index